Educating the Learning Disabled

Educating the Learning Disabled

Ernest Siegel
Ruth F. Gold

Adelphi University

With Contributions by
David Levinsky
Joan Lange Bildman

Macmillan Publishing Co., Inc.
New York

Collier Macmillan Publishers
London

Copyright © 1982, Macmillan Publishing Co., Inc.

Printed in the United States of America

Macmillan Publishing Co., Inc.
866 Third Avenue, New York, New York 10022

Collier Macmillan Canada, Inc.

Library of Congress Cataloging in Publication Data
Siegel, Ernest.
    Educating the learning disabled.

    Bibliography: p.
    Includes index.
    1. Learning disabilities.   I. Gold, Ruth.
II. Levinsky, David.   III. Bildman, Joan Lange.
IV. Title.
LC4704.S5   1982   371.9   81-7284
ISBN 0-02-410400-0   AACR2

Printing: 1 2 3 4 5 6 7 8   Year: 2 3 4 5 6 7 8 9

Foreword

The roots of LD can readily be traced to the turn of the century and earlier. But as an organized social movement, LD has been known as such for less than two decades. Though brief, this period is sufficiently long to foster clearly discernable stages of development. The initial strands of concern and knowledge which were to become LD have substantially lost their identity: Some are in danger of losing their impact entirely.

History is particularly important in areas where development is rapid, for quick growth without historical roots can be short-lived. Drawing on other fields—quite directly from some and barely perceptively from others—LD secured for itself a pivotal role in our understanding and treatment of children. Little of this potential influence has been actualized, in large part due to the incomplete process of solidification of LD's position as part of the special education community and adjustment of the other disciplines to adjunct roles. Realization of this potential will require new interdisciplinary alliances requiring understanding and respect.

A crucial period for a field is encountered when a particular segment of the intellectual community gains control of the field's name and direction. Education—not medicine, psychology or any other of the contributing fields of thought and human service—produces "learning disability" specialists! Hence, the field is increasingly populated by education-trained personnel, yearly eroding its multidisciplinary core. Today's perspective can readily fall prey to exclusiveness. Burgeoning growth is easily curtailed by both ambient economic forces and opposition from disenfranchised associates. LD presently faces both challenges.

In a time when legislatures reconsider whether LD should be a handicap, the learning disabled have a strong ally in authors who recognize strength in diversity. Siegel and Gold implicitly know that no field stands alone—not LD, not even Education. There is no sociological theorizing necessary to lead them to this conclusion:

v

They need only the purpose of understanding and helping children. Why does multidisciplinary intervention occupy the book's major chapters rather than minute diagnostic prescriptions? Because the authors implicity know that LD children need the best thinking of all professions. Why is so much space devoted to discussion of issues rather than simple factual exposition? Because the authors know their readers are entering a *process* of learning and service. They require the reader to consider many ideas, many options. They rightfully know there is no single correct prescription and that truly competent professionals must draw upon the thinking of many fields.

A field's survival is based on its personnel, specifically on their ability to produce the results they advertise. Recognizing the range of knowledge necessary, the authors make the reader both knowledgeable and humble. What one needs to know may be found in another discipline so one had better know, at the very least, what one doesn't know! Both for the individual reader—and for the vitality of the field— experiencing this book's open-mindedness is most constructive. It reminds us of how dependent the lives of children are on the knowledge of adults—and on their willingness to share that knowledge despite varying allegiances.

Gerald M. Senf, Ph.D.
Editor-in-Chief
Journal of Learning Disabilities

Preface

Because the learning disabled are so inconsistent, erratic, easily misunderstood, and, in many ways, enigmatic; because the very mildness of their condition generates unique problems; and because such a wide range of individual differences exists within this population, issues and controversies not surprisingly abound. These are presented throughout this book, beginning with the first chapter, *History and Definition*—in which at least a dozen issues emerge—and through to the last chapter, *Issues, Trends, and Prognosis.* We attempt to present both sides to every question, to reconcile opposing viewpoints when warranted, and to also state our own opinions. This proliferation of controversies should not be regarded with dismay, but rather as a challenge—a challenge to sort out personal beliefs, to refine diagnostic and remedial instruments, to make ongoing evaluations of programs, to encourage and participate in appropriate research, and to identify new targets of concern. We should emerge more critical, yet more humble, openminded, receptive to new ideas, and inspired to renew our commitment to the learning disabled.

This text serves introductory learning disabilities courses for preservice and inservice teachers and as a reference for the other professionals who will work with this population. It is divided into four sections. The first, "Orientation," includes chapters on history and definition, neurological aspects of learning disabilities, characteristics, etiology, and diagnosis. This section provides the background and theoretical underpinnings leading to an understanding of the interdisciplinary interventions described in Section Two (consisting of biochemical, psychotherapeutic, behavioral, and perceptual theories) and the various educational approaches included in the third section. This base is important since the instructional framework presented, though eclectic, leads to a unified approach stressing the unique qualities of each learning disabled (LD) person. It requires those working in the field to match the methods and tasks with the individual needs of the student, regardless of age, degree of handicap, and learning strength–weakness profile.

Besides discussing general teaching principles in Chapters 10 and 11, additional chapters contain specific suggestions for choosing and implementing strategies in all areas of the curriculum: language arts (including reading), mathematics, social studies, science, physical education, the arts, and in the extended life skills curriculum of career education, sex education, social awareness, and so on. The last section, "Issues, Trends, and Prognosis," highlights some of the recent controversies in the field and points to the directions the learning-disabled population as well as the practioners appear to be heading.

Effective teamwork can only exist when those in the field are knowledgeable in both theory and practice, and above all, understand and respect the individual child or adult with whom they work. We hope that this text will help them reach this goal.

Acknowledgments

We are genuinely grateful for all the support and encouragement we received along the way. The library staffs at Adelphi University, Garden City, N.Y. and Queens Associations for Neurologically Impaired Brain-Injured Children were extremely cooperative in helping us locate source materials. We are most appreciative of those individuals who took the time to share their information, views and materials with us. These include: Winifred D. Kirk, University of Arizona, Abraham S. Tannenbaum, Teachers College, Columbia University, Larry Faas, Arizona State University, Lila Blum, Executive Director, Nassau County ACLD, Arlene Spiller, Editor of the Newsletter, *Perceptions*, Millburn, N.J., William M. Cruickshank, Director of the Institute for the Study of Mental Retardation and Related Disabilities at the University of Michigan, John F. Cawley, University of Connecticut, Gerald M. Senf, Editor-in-Chief of the Journal of Learning Disabilities, Dorothy Otnow Lewis, Yale University, Sister Lucina Hayes, College of St. Rose, New York, Thomas G. Gregory, Director of Research, Boys Town, Nebraska, Gerald G. Glass, Adelphi University, Laura L. Rogan, Clinical Director of the Cove School, Evanston, Illinois, John Preston, of Academic Therapy and Paul Irvine, Yorktown Heights, Board of Cooperative Educative Service (BOCES).

For their review of portions of the manuscript, we thank our spouses, Rita L. Siegel and Bernard Gold, and for his analysis of chapter two, Neurological Aspects of Learning Disabilities, Warren C. Eickelberg, Biology Department, Adelphi University.

We were fortunate to have received the capable and concerned assistance of the typists: Debbie Pompi, Debbie Gordon, Peter Siegel, and Beverly Rappaport.

We also wish to acknowledge the encouragement we received from our colleagues and staff of the Education Department at Adelphi University and to thank the students in our courses for sharing their opinions and for raising questions which helped us to crystalize our thinking.

In addition to all the above, this book could not have been completed without the support, encouragement, and understanding of our families.

Ruth F. Gold
Ernest Siegel

Throughout the book, the teacher is referred to as "she." This arbitrary choice was made to alleviate the awkwardness of continuously using "he or she." Similarly throughout the text, the child is called "he" for simplicity's sake.

Contents

Orientation

Interdisciplinary Intervention

Educational Interventions

part Three

Perspectives

part Four

Orientation

part One

History and Definition

1

HISTORY

General Background

The term *learning disabilities* has gradually replaced the earlier terms of brain injury, minimal brain dysfunction, central nervous system (CNS) disorder, neurologically handicapped, perceptually impaired and others—and for many reasons. In 1968, Siegel wrote:

> Recent years have witnessed a growing practice among some educators of classifying certain children as "learning disabled." This practice undoubtedly came about as a reaction to the many weaknesses inherent in the traditional medical/psychological basis for classification of exceptional children (e.g., "mentally retarded," "brain injured," "emotionally disturbed," etc.). It may also have evolved, in part, because of its implication to positive action (i.e., What do you do for a child suffering from specific learning disabilities? Why, you *teach* him, of course!). It may even be a result of the unconscious desire of educators to demonstrate the importance of their discipline to the psychological and medical professions (p. 433).

Learning disabilities is an educational term, but it has its origins in diverse disciplines, including: neurology, psychology, speech pathology, opthamology, and remedial reading (Kirk & Gallagher, 1979, p. 285). Wiederholt (1974) has conceptualized a two-dimensional model for viewing the learning disabilities entity. One dimension consists of three separate disorders overlapping in time, each leading to the present classification of learning disabilities: (1) disorders of spoken language; (2) disorders of written language; and (3) disorders of perceptual-motor processes. The other dimension is that of chronology. It is divided into three phases: (1) the Foundation Phase (about 1800–1930), composed largely of neurologists (e.g.,

Broca, Orton, Goldstein, Strauss) and opthamologists (e.g., Hinshelwood); (2) the Transition Phase (about 1930-1963)—this last date can be pinpointed since the National Association for Children with Learning Disabilities (ACLD) was formed in 1963; and (3) the Integration Phase (1963-present). These latter two phases are multidisciplinary in nature, representing such diverse fields as: optometry (e.g., Getman), psychology (e.g., Kirk, Frostig, Cruickshank), speech pathology (e.g., Eisenson, Myklebust, McGinnis) and special education (e.g., Fernald, Lehtinen). There is a rationale for—as well as a modus operandi of—this team approach: "As with many other areas of special education, the medical profession identifies the severe problems but is unable, in many instances, to cure the disability. Psychologists enter the field to study the behavioral characteristics that need intervention. Educators are then recruited to provide the intervention" (Kirk & Gallagher, 1979, p. 285).

According to Wiederholt (1978, pp. 11-29), the Foundation Phase focused upon individuals who had acquired brain injuries in adulthood (e.g., wounded war veterans, stroke victims) and who had subsequently demonstrated loss of previously acquired skills. The Transitional Phase was marked by an attempt to translate the basic theory of the initial stage (namely, that insult to the brain results in perceptual, learning, and/or behavioral deficits) into diagnostic and remedial practices. The Integration Phase "put it all together" under the banner of learning disabilities. It was marked by a mushrooming of publications and educational programs specifically for the learning disabled, a surge of organizational growth, and the emergence of pressure groups resulting in pertinent legislation. Relatively recently, top priority has been given to the learning disabled adolescent and young adult (Wiederholt, 1978, p. 17).

Three major differences exist between the first phase depicted by Wiederholt and those following:

1. The Foundation Phase concentrated on adults whereas the subsequent ones deal primarily with children.
2. Initially the stipulation was for *demonstrable* brain injury, but later phases were characterized by the acceptance of the concept of *presumed* brain injury.
3. The first stage dealt entirely with patients who had *acquired* brain injury, and hence had, at one time, exhibited intact neurological and perceptual functioning. The Transition and the Integration Phases, on the other hand, emphasize individuals who manifest *developmental* disabilities—that is, they have *never* functioned normally in their impaired areas (Wiederholt, 1978, p. 12).

The Contributions of Alfred A. Strauss*

A distinct relationship exists between the concepts of brain injury and learning disabilities. In fact, they are often considered synonymous. Peters, Davis, Goolsby,

---

* We have taken the unusual position of devoting considerable space to one individual, fully cognizant that there have been many professionals since Strauss who likewise have made monumental contributions in the field of learning disabilities. Also, like any pioneer, Strauss had his precursors and contemporaries who were indispensable in adding to the body of literature and who profoundly influenced his beliefs. In fact, William Cruickshank (*The Education*

Clements and Hicks (1973) state unequivocally that *minimal brain dysfunction* is the medical counterpart for the educational term, *specific learning disabilities.* Hence, any historical review of the term learning disabilities must necessarily begin with the earlier designation of brain injury.

Theories. Alfred A. Strauss, a neuropsychiatrist, and Heinz Werner, a psychologist, who emigrated from Germany prior to 1937 to escape Hitler, became staff members of the Wayne County Training School in Michigan. Afterwards, they created the Cove Schools in Michigan (in 1947) and Illinois (in 1950) for brain-injured children. Some of Strauss's theories which influenced the direction of the brain-injury/learning disabilities field follow:

1. The individual should be viewed as an organism. (Strauss was greatly influenced by the work of Kurt Goldstein (1939), a Germany physician who observed—and treated—World War I veterans presenting observable brain injury and formulated the concept of each individual being, in reality, an organism. ". . . the organism operates as a whole, and . . . we must give increasing attention to the [resultant] disturbances . . . of the total functioning of the organism rather than concentrate our attention solely upon the part . . . in which the accident occurred" (Strauss & Kephart, 1955, p. 1). Moreover, the child should be regarded as a *growing* and *changing* organism. Besides considering all the possible manifestations of brain injury to the total organism, as in the case of adults, one must additionally focus upon the effect of the brain damage upon functions still in the process of development and upon the deleterious effects that must eventually ensue (Strauss & Kephart, 1955, p. 1). With respect to this point, Mink (1964, p. 325) refers to Montessori's theory of sensitive periods for learning: "If this sensitive period is missed—if the function is not developed—then the opportunity for *optimum* [emphasis added] development is lost. For example, when the very young child is in the 'sensitive period' for the development of language, he does so without lessons or conscious effort. If he is in an environment where several languages are spoken, he will learn all of them. Contrast this with the effort expended by an adult in learning a new language."

2. All localized lesions, *regardless of their geography* (and irrespective of specific concomitants—e.g., occipital lobe damage will result in visual loss; parietal damage causes deficit in tactile functioning) "are followed by a similar kind of disordered behavior" (Strauss & Lehtinen, 1947, p. 20)—namely, the typical traits of brain-injured children: distractibility, hyperactivity, impulsivity, irritability, and so on. This theory states, in effect, that all categories of brain injury, such as cerebral palsy, epilepsy, aphasia, exogenous mental retardation (and, in fact, Strauss worked with many such children in his training schools—Strauss & Lehtinen, 1947, pp. 2-5;

---

of Exceptional Children in Youth, *Third Edition*, Englewood Cliffs, New Jersey: Prentice-Hall, 1975) makes a cogent point contending that the term "Strauss Syndrome"—sometimes used in lieu of "brain injured," or "learning disabled," etc.—is not an apt one inasmuch as "it does not acknowledge the contribution of Dr. Heinz Werner, a coworker of Strauss, who made at least an equal contribution to the field" (p. 243). Our position is that to have given equal emphasis to all of the leaders in the LD field would somehow have trivialized the unique impact of Strauss. In focusing upon him, our intention has not been to detract from the role played by others, but rather to reset, in perspective, the stage—as recalled by most parents, and probably by most professionals, too—upon which the LD movement first marched. The readers, of course, are urged to exercise their own judgment regarding the efficacy of this approach.

Strauss & Kephart, 1955, pp. 224–37) will exhibit, in addition to their basic deficit, this same kind of "disordered behavior."

3. The brain injury can be diffused instead of existing in a circumscribed site and/or so slight that it escapes detection by the customary diagnostic instruments (history taking, neurological examination, electroencephalogram (EEG), and so on. (Strauss & Kephart, 1955, p. 42; Strauss & Lehtinen, 1947, p. 112). Significantly, Strauss's theories had strong underpinnings of cause-effect relationships. He had observed—and demonstrated—that (1) brain injury in adulthood causes a behavioral pattern typified by "shell shocked" veterans, and that (2) brain injury in childhood (e.g., post-encephalitic children) results in the identical behavioral syndrome. Strauss may have downgraded the value of medical evidence of brain injury in those cases where the only definitive clue lay in behavioral symptoms, but more importantly he was convinced that the diagnostic instruments of the neurologist were too crude, in many instances, to detect *minimal* brain damage, and he did not wish children presenting this characteristic—in his opinion, *unmistakable*—behavior of brain injury to lose out on special educational services and programs by default. Hence, in the absence of positive EEG, positive neurological findings, uneventful historical data, and so forth, he was still willing to concede organicity in select cases. This procedure of diagnosing brain injury without medically-substantiated evidence, and on the sole basis of clinical observation of the child's behavior is obviously a controversial one. But Strauss was not alone in his belief. For example, Gesell & Amatruda (1947, p. 240) wrote

> . . . an entirely negative birth history and an uneventful neonatal period may nevertheless demand a diagnosis of minimal injury because of persisting or gradually diminishing behavior signs. In obscure or doubtful cases the following is a safe rule: Do not assume that there has certainly been a cerebral injury, *but assume that every child who is born alive has run the universal risk of such injury* [emphasis added].

4. An individual may suffer from brain injury, yet need not necessarily be mentally retarded. Strauss, particularly in his later years, turned his attention to the brain-injured child of normal or higher intelligence.* This had the effect of (1) giving parents more hope, (2) justifying legislative and financial support (since the client would be expected to make some substantial repayments to society), and (3) sparking the development of suitable programs from preschool through college.

5. Brain injury is the result of exogenous (outside of the genes, hence accidental) etiologies. By highlighting this factor of exogeneity, Strauss certainly was instrumental in encouraging the medical profession (particularly obstetricians, gynecologists and anesthetists) and the pharmacologists to conduct research and monitor their own procedures in an attempt to seek preventative measures. Also, as Farnham-Diggory (1978, p. 9) observes: "Until the concept of brain injury was introduced, children who behaved badly and failed in school were considered to be somebody's fault. But an accident to the brain was nobody's fault: one could stop feeling guilty and set about seeking help."

---

* Since then other authors have addressed themselves to this point. In fact, Thompson (1971), in an article entitled, "Language Disabilities in Men of Eminence," hypothesized that such individuals as Thomas Edison, Albert Einstein, Woodrow Wilson and August Rodin suffered from minimal brain dysfunction.

6. Strauss believed that the effects of brain injury (with respect to perception, learning, and behavior) can be assessed, and appropriate remediation techniques are available. The specialized programs, methodologies, and services embodied in his training schools were rooted in this belief.

7. The prognosis is generally a favorable one. (Here, obviously, Strauss is focusing upon the *minimally** brain injured only—not those with overlapping conditions of mental retardation, cerebral palsy, and/or aphasia). Strauss was influenced by the work of Lashley (1929) who proposed the "law of mass action" (p. 25): As a result of experiments in which he (Lashley) removed one portion of the cerebrum from one rat, another portion from another rat, still another from a third, and so on, (much like removing one sector each from a group of oranges until the composite of the removed sectors equals one whole orange), he concluded that the brain acted as a mass, since regardless which sector was excised, each rat could still learn various maze tasks. According to Gallagher (1960, p. 19), "Lashley concluded that while there are certain parts of the brain responsible for special functions, mainly the sensory and motor areas, that *other parts of the brain are interchangeable. Under special circumstances healthy and unaffected areas of the cortex may take over the function of damaged portions*" [emphasis added].

Impact. Strauss, more than any other single individual, had tremendous impact upon the emerging fields of brain injury/learning disability. His books, *Psychopathology and Education of the Brain-Injured Child*, *Volume I*, coauthored with Laura Lehtinen in 1947, and *Volume II*, coauthored with Newell Kephart in 1955 (both published by Grune & Stratton in New York) quickly became landmarks. These highly technical books were pounced upon by both teachers and administrators, who used them as guidelines in their efforts to provide services for this hitherto neglected population of exceptional children, and by sophisticated parents who, striving desperately to understand and to help their children, exerted legislative pressure and rendered support and encouragement to educators and other professionals needed in the movement. These two volumes plus the text written expressly for parents and laypeople, *The Other Child*, authored by Richard Lewis (a professional writer) with Strauss and Lehtinen (Grune & Stratton in 1951, revised in 1960) served as a banner around which parents of all brain-injured children could rally. Parents could finally go to educators and school administrators and say, in effect, "Look. I have a child like this. He has good potential. His needs are not being met in the public schools and there are no private schools for him. He requires the kind of program described in these books." And many professionals heeded this cry. Classes for brain-injured children—in public schools as well as private schools, day schools as well as residential—began to appear, all of them seeking to serve the population described by Strauss and utilizing his principles regarding methods, materials, curriculum, and program.

The literature abounds with testimony to Strauss (and his colleagues) as the forerunner of the brain injury/learning disability movement. Tarnopol (1971, p. 8) writes: "Strauss and Lehtinen . . . made the first comprehensive presentation of the

---

* A summary point made by Lashley (1929) is: "The amount of reduction in efficiency of performance is proportional to the *extent of injury* [emphasis added] and is independent of locus" (p. 175). Clearly, Lashley, as well as Strauss, differentiated between *major* brain lesions (which produce significant negative manifestations) and *minimal* brain injury (in which the prognosis is relatively favorable).

learning problems of brain-injured children." Johnson and Morasky (1977, p. 10) state: "It was not long before the work of Strauss and Werner became the standard for most of those working in [this] behavioral area." Bryan and Bryan (1978, pp. 17–18) point out: "By focusing upon children rather than adults, upon the intellectually incompetent rather than the competent, they brought about a courtship, if not a marriage, of the fields of neurology and education. . . . The views of Strauss and Werner, and later collaborators Laura Lehtinen and Newell Kephart, all under the influence of Kurt Goldstein, were to be widely disseminated in two volumes, both entitled *Psychopathology and Education of the Brain-Injured Child* . . . these [are] probably the most influential books written in the fields of learning disabilities. . . ." In the opinion of Lerner (1976, p. 15), "Learning disabilities as a comprehensive field of study . . . is generally considered to have begun in 1947, with the appearance of *Psychopathology and Education of the Brain-Injured Child*, by Alfred A. Strauss and Laura E. Lehtinen." She (1981) also credits Strauss and his coworkers with "[1] perceiving a homogeneity in a diverse group of children who had been misdiagnosed by specialists, misunderstood by parents, and often discarded by society, and . . . [2] alerting many professions to the existence of a new category of exceptional children." (p. 33) Other authors who attest to the widespread effects of Strauss's works include: McCarthy and McCarthy (1969, p. 2); Farnham-Diggory (1978, p. 9); Benton (1974, p. 49).

The Cove School for Brain-Injured Children (which Strauss and Werner founded) served as a reference point, a model, a home base. The school lent credibility to his writings, and vice-versa. It facilitated the field testing of his theories. It afforded other professionals the opportunity to work side-by-side with Strauss, among whom were Laura Lehtinen, Newell Kephart, Ray Barsch, and Elizabeth Freidus. (This working relationship had a rippling effect since these professionals made further contributions: publications, leadership and advisory roles in ACLD chapters and in various task forces, teacher preparation, etc.). As other schools and classes for brain-injured children began to spring up, they virtually all reflected Strauss's guidelines, beginning with his definition of brain injury (see pages 5–17, 12) which helped formulate criteria for admission, and reflected (if not replicated) his concepts of small class size, structured environment, emphasis upon remediating perceptual process impairment, and so forth.

Undoubtedly Strauss was on the scene at the right time. He did not create brain-injured children. They existed all along, but had been misdiagnosed as mentally retarded or emotionally disturbed, and, in many cases, were undiagnosed, struggling to keep up with the nonhandicapped. With the onset of Strauss's writing and with the founding of his schools, parents and dedicated professionals could now force the issue of appropriate intervention. The "accidental" factor inherent in the concept of exogeneity and the favorable prognosis Strauss espoused for the brain-injured population were strong drawing cards. Finally, the fact that he was a *physician* was significant. In our achievement-oriented culture, physicians are accorded a high spot on our sociological totem pole: a medical authority can make recommendations to the educational discipline, but the reverse is not true.

From Brain Injury to Learning Disability

In 1955 the New York City Board of Education had one class for brain-injured children; today there are over 600. This unprecedented spiralling of facilities for brain-injured (that is, learning disabled) children, which occurred between the mid-fifties and today, is not indigenous to New York City, but rather is symbolic of the concern for the welfare of these children nationally as well as internationally. Some regions started early, some later, but today programs for the learning disabled constitute a sizable—if not the chief—segment of the total special education services offered by school systems across the nation.

When the New York Association for Brain-Injured Children (NYABIC)—now known as the New York Association for the Learning Disabled (NYALD)—was formed in the mid-fifties, other groups were being started elsewhere. They frequently had their own nomenclature: Evanston Fund for Perceptually Handicapped Children; California Association for the Neurologically Handicapped Children, etcetera. On April 6, 1963, a meeting was held in Chicago, sponsored by the Fund for Perceptually Handicapped Children and by the National Orthopsychiatric Association. Its primary goal was to weld a national parent group. Samuel Kirk proposed the term "learning disabilities," since inability to learn readily seemed to be the one characteristic common to all the groups of children represented by the various parent group members. (Kirk had been interested in this group of children for some time and had previously written about learning disabilities, expressing concern for children who manifest learning problems despite the absence of mental retardation (1962).) As a result of this meeting, the Association for Children with Learning Disabilities (ACLD) was formed at the national level. Members included parents as well as professionals. Other original groups soon expanded and many—but not all—of the existing chapters changed their names to ACLD. Almost overnight new chapters at the national, regional, state, and local levels formed. The loud voices of parents—now organized into effective, sophisticated ACLD chapters—were instrumental in making the learning-disabled population highly visible and in catapulting it upon the education scene. The manifestations were myriad. Among them were:

1. The rapid growth of many private schools (residential as well as day schools) and summer programs specifically for the learning-disabled population.

2. The publication of new professional journals in the field of learning disabilities, such as the *Journal of Learning Disabilities* in 1968 and *Academic Therapy* in 1965. Also, many existing journals began focusing more and more upon the learning disabled. *Exceptional Children* (1964) devoted its entire December issue to learning disabilities. *Rehabilitation Literature*, published by National Society for Crippled Children and Adults, printed a special issue consisting of a selection of *Review Digest Abstracts* of books and articles dealing solely with brain injury between January 1960 and March 1962.

3. The founding and/or expansion of companies manufacturing teaching and/or testing materials for the learning disabled. A notable example of this is *Developmental Learning Materials* (DLM), Niles, Illinois.

4. The publication of three federally funded task force reports: *Minimal Brain Dysfunction in Children: Terminology and Identification* by Sam Clements (1966); *Minimal Brain Dysfunction: Educational, Medical and Health Related Services* by Norris G. Haring and C. A. Miller, eds. (1969); and *Central Processing Dysfunction in Children* by J. C. Chalfant and M. A. Scheffelin (1969). These reports constituted position papers as well as reviews of research and therefore served as reference points for professionals, legislators, and parent group leaders.

5. The founding of the Division for Children with Learning Disabilities

(DCLD), a division within the council for exceptional children (CEC) in 1968. Despite the fact that it is the most recent division of CEC, it has one of the largest memberships. In 1978 it began publishing its own journal, *Learning Disability Quarterly.*

6. The expansion of college programs for training teachers of the learning disabled and the recognition and financial support by the federal government and by state departments of education of the learning disabled as a significant segment of the exceptional population. (The federal government did not recognize learning disability as a distinct category of exceptionality until the late seventies.)

7. The increased dissemination of information regarding learning disabilities via newspaper and magazine articles, training films, and radio and television coverage (including public broadcasting as well as major network productions).

8. The promulgation of pertinent legislation. For example:

• Public Law 91-230 (entitled "The Education of the Handicapped Act of 1967"), added as Part G to its Title VI, authorization to the Office of Education to set up programs specifically for the learning disabled.

• In 1971 The Bureau for the Education of the Handicapped (BEH) of The United States Office of Education initiated a nationwide program for funding Child Service Demonstration Projects (CSDP). These exemplary programs, once established, served as models as well as challenges to the various states to establish sufficient and appropriate services for the learning disabled. By 1977 forty-four states had established centers funded by BEH (Wiederholt, 1978, p. 16). The BEH also funded Leadership Training Institutes (LTI) for Learning Disabilities between 1971 and 1975. The function of the LTIs included serving as technical advisors for the CDSPs and to survey and to analyze data relating to current school practices for the learning disabled (Myers & Hammill, 1976, p. 41).

• Public Law 94-142 (known as "The Education for All Handicapped Act of 1975") makes specific reference to children with learning disabilities. It mandates that school districts provide free and appropriate education to all handicapped children *including the learning disabled*—and it funds excess costs thereof. (This is a far cry from the early days when parents of recently diagnosed brain-injured children found themselves in limbo. Gordon (N.D., but probably in the late fifties) wrote: "It is particularly confusing to parents that professional workers are often unable to agree on a diagnosis, let alone a course of treatment. Articles appear, calling attention to the 'myth' of brain injury. Often, parents of brain-injured children find themselves in the ludicrous position of having to explain the idea of 'brain injury' to physicians, psychologists, and teachers. . . ." (p. 4).)

The field of learning disabilities is, however, still in its infancy. In the short period of time since it has catapulted upon the educational scene, it has expanded in geometric proportions and has generated a myriad of educational controversies (Wiederholt, 1974). Despite the lack of concensus, the overall direction has been a forward one. There has been increased knowledge regarding instructional intervention, educational services, and about the teaching-learning process itself—gains that not only improve the fate of the learning disabled, but redound to the benefit of all categories of children, including the nonhandicapped as well.

DEFINITION

Definitions of Learning Disabilities: Some Major Examples

Definitions of categories within the exceptional population invariably have far-reaching effects. They dictate the groups' prevalence and characteristics. They determine the means of identifying and assessing as well as the vehicles for intervention. They enunciate a priority order for the roles of the various professional disciplines. They even act as a trend-setter for terminology. The following are some of the principle definitions that have greatly influenced not only the field of learning disabilities, but all of education. They are listed in matrix form in order to accommodate their comparison to four fundamental points, which today constitute the definitional criteria for learning disabilities: (1) underachievement in academic areas, (2) impairment in some broad developmental process (e.g., perception, language), (3) presence of brain injury (or at least presumed brain injury), and (4) the exclusion of other categories. We begin with Strauss's definition of brain injury since all others evolved from it.

Definitional Criteria for Learning Disabilities

An analysis of the table of definitions on pages 12–14 reveals considerable consensus (albeit a lack of unanimity) regarding four basic definitional aspects of learning disabilities.

Underachieving. As far as educators are concerned, this remains the chief criterion for learning disabilities. It is tangible: either the child is living up to his mental age or he is not. This criterion is clearly within the teacher's sphere of influence. Teachers feel that they can do little with organicity or with underlying process deficit, but they can take steps to bring academic achievement in line with potential. Nevertheless, there are problems inherent in defining learning disabilities in terms of underachievement:

1. It can become a political and economic ploy. If there are insufficient funds to accommodate the learning disabled population, the degree of required disparity can be "upped," thus lowering the incidence.* The opposite, of course, is also true. In fact, this is precisely what happens with the current federal regulations: "The Commissioner may not count . . . children with specific learning disabilities to the extent that the number of those children is greater than two percent of the number of all children aged five through 17 in the State."

The official definition of *Specific Learning Disabilities* adopted by New York State in 1977 followed that federal guideline, addressing itself to the degree of underachievement rather than to the incidence, but accomplishing the same results: "A child who exhibits a discrepancy of 50 percent or more between expected achievement based on his intellectual ability and actual achievement, determined on an *individual basis*, shall be deemed to have a specific learning disability." In July, 1980, a Federal District Court ruled that this identification procedure was in

---

* A survey of 42 state education departments concerning their respective definitions of learning disabilities was made in 1976 (Mercer, Forgnone & Wolking). Though few states reported the inclusion of a discrepancy clause, the authors suggest that there may be wider use of this within school districts.

Table 1-1. Comparison of Definitions

Definition	Underachievement
A brain-injured child is a child who before, during, or after birth has received an injury to or suffered an infection of the brain. As a result of such organic impairment, defects of the neuromotor system may be present or absent; however, such a child may show disturbances in perception, thinking, and emotional behavior, either separately or in combination. These disturbances can be demonstrated by specific tests. These disturbances prevent or impede a normal learning process. Special educational methods have been devised to remedy these specific handicaps. *STRAUSS* (Strauss & Lehtinen, 1947, p. 4).	Yes ("These disorders prevent or impede a normal learning process.")
A learning disability refers to a retardation, disorder, or delayed development in one or more of the processes of speech, language, reading, spelling, writing, or arithmetic resulting from a possible *cerebral dysfunction* and/or *emotional or behavioral disturbance* and not from mental retardation, sensory deprivation, or cultural or instructional factors. *KIRK* (1962, p. 263). This later became the definition used by the National Association for Children with Learning Disabilities at its inception in 1963.	Yes (... retardation, disorder, or delayed development in ... reading, spelling, writing, or arithmetic ...")
... manifest an educationally significant discrepancy between their estimated intellectual potential and actual level of performance related to basic disorders in the learning processes, which may or may not be accompanied by demonstrable central nervous system dysfunction, and which are not secondary to generalized mental retardation, educational or cultural deprivation, severe emotional disturbance, or sensory loss. *BATEMAN* (1965, p. 220).	Yes ("manifest an educationally significant discrepancy between their estimated intellectual potential and actual level of performance....")
The term "minimal brain dysfunction syndrome" refers ... to children of near average, average, or above average general intelligence with certain learning or behavioral disabilities ranging from mild to severe, which are associated with deviations to function of the central nervous system. These deviations may manifest themselves by various combinations of impairment in perception, conceptualization, language, memory, and control of attention, impulse, or motor function. Similar symptoms may or may not complicate the problems of children with cerebral palsy, epilepsy, mental retardation, blindness, or deafness. These aberrations may arise from genetic variations, biochemical irregularities, perinatal brain insults or other illnesses or injuries ... severe sensory deprivation could result in central nervous system alterations. ... During the school years, a variety of learning disabilities is the most prominent manifestation of the condition which can be designated by this term. *HEW–PHASE I* (CLEMENTS, 1966).	Yes ("During the school years, a variety of learning disabilities is the most prominent manifestation. ...")
Children with special learning disabilities exhibit a disorder in one or more of the basic psychological processes involved in understanding or using spoken or written languages. These may be manifested in disorders of listening, thinking, talking, reading, writing, spelling or arithmetic. They include conditions which have been referred to as perceptual handicaps, brain injury, minimal brain dysfunction, dyslexia, developmental aphasia, etc. They do not include learning problems which are due primarily to visual, hearing, or motor handicaps, to mental retardation, emotional disturbance, or to environmental disadvantage. *NATIONAL ADVISORY COMMITTEE ON HANDICAPPED CHILDREN* (U.S. Office of Education, 1968).	Yes. ("These may be manifested in disorders of ... reading, writing, spelling or arithmetic.")

Neurological Basis	Process Deficit	Exclusionary Factor
Yes. He stipulates that there must be provable brain injury or at least presumed injury ("...defects of the neuromotor system may be present or absent ...")	Yes. ("...a child may show disturbances in perception ...")	None. In fact, his theory states that *all* instances of brain injury, whether they result in cerebral palsy, aphasia, mental retardation, etc., will *invariably* be accompanied by the behavioral and learning problems of the *minimal* brain-injured.
Maybe. ("...results from a *possible* cerebral dysfunction"). This definition denotes two possible causes: brain injury *or* emotional disturbance.	Yes	Yes. Kirk includes the emotionally disturbed (and of course, cerebral dysfunction), but excludes "mental retardation, sensory deprivation, or cultural or instructional factors."
Maybe. ("...which may or may not be accompanied by demonstrable central nervous system dysfunction").	Yes	Yes. Bateman excludes all the categories excluded by Kirk. In addition, she removes the emotionally disturbed.
Yes	Yes	Yes. The mentally retarded are specifically excluded. Like Strauss, Clements states that more severe categories of brain injury (cerebral palsy, epilepsy, mentally retarded, nonperipheral blindness or deafness) could be accompanied by the MBD Syndrome. Also he states that sensory deprivation could lead to Central Nervous System alterations, and hence, to the MBD Syndrome. The emotionally disturbed are not mentioned.
Yes. ("They include conditions which have been referred to as perceptual handicaps, brain injury, minimal brain dysfunction, dyslexia, developmental asphasia, etc.")	Yes	Yes. All categories other than brain injury are excluded. ("They do not include ... visual, hearing, or motor handicaps ... mental retardation ... *emotional disturbance* [emphasis added] or ... environmental disadvantage.")

Table 1-1.   (Continued)

Definition	Underachievement
. . . in those having a psychoneurological learning disability, it is the fact of adequate motor ability, average to high intelligence, adequate hearing and vision, and adequate emotional adjustment together with a deficiency in learning that constitutes the basis for homogeneity. This group of children is homogeneous in that they have integrity emotionally, motorically, sensorially, and intellectually, but, despite these integrities, they cannot learn in the usual or normal manner.	Yes. ("it is the fact of . . . average to high intelligence . . . together with a deficiency in learning which constitutes the basis for homogeneity"; "despite these integrities, they cannot learn in the usual or normal manner.")
. . . psychoneurological learning disability . . . means that behavior has been disturbed as a result of a dysfunction in the brain and that the problem is one of altered processes, not of a generalized incapacity to learn. *JOHNSON & MYKLEBUST* (1967, pp. 8, 9).	
A child with learning disabilities is one with adequate mental ability (i.e., intelligence), sensory process, and emotional stability but evidences specific deficits in perceptual, integrative, or expressive processes. The output is, therefore, a child who suffers from severely impaired learning efficiency. *COUNCIL FOR EXCEPTIONAL CHILDREN* (1971).	Yes. ("A child with learning disabilities is one with adequate mental ability . . . who suffers from severely impaired learning efficiency.")
". . . a disorder in one or more of the basic psychological processes involved in understanding or in using language, spoken or written, which may manifest itself in an imperfect ability to listen, think, speak, read, write, spell or do mathematical calculations. The term includes such conditions as perceptual handicaps, brain injury, minimal brain dysfunction, dyslexia, and developmental aphasia. The term does not include children who have learning problems which are primarily the result of visual, hearing, or motor handicaps, of mental retardation, or of environmental, cultural, or economic disadvantage." *FEDERAL REGISTER* (August 23, 1977).	Yes. (". . . a disorder which may manifest itself in an imperfect ability to . . . read, write, spell, or to do mathematical calculations.")
Learning disability is a generic term that refers to a heterogeneous group of disorders manifested by significant difficulties in the acquisition and use of thinking, listening, speaking, reading, writing or mathematical abilities. Such disorders are presumed to be due to central nervous system dysfunction which can result from such factors as anatomical differences, genetic factors, neuromaturational delay, neurochemical metabolic imbalance, severe nutritional deficiency or trauma. Even though a learning disability may occur concomitantly with other handicapping conditions (e.g., sensory impairment, mental retardation, social and emotional disturbance) or environmental influences (e.g., cultural differences, insufficient-inappropriate instruction, psychogenic factors), it is not the direct result of those conditions or influences. (HAMMILL, D. D., 1981. Recommendation to the Division for Children with Learning Disabilities (CEC) Board of Trustees Meeting, Oct. 31, 1980.)	Yes. (". . . significant difficulties in the acquisition and use of thinking, listening, speaking, reading, writing or mathematical abilities.")

violation of federal law, a major contention being that it results in serious under-counting of learning disabled children. Later, this was reversed.

    2. Because of the current imperfect state of the art with respect to measuring the functioning levels of listening, speaking, reading, writing, and computing, verifying a mandated discrepancy figure may be unachievable at this time. Ohlson (1978) notes that "applying achievement expectancy formulas to school populations in-

Neurological Basis	Process Deficit	Exclusionary Factor
Yes. (". . . behavior has been disturbed as a result of a dysfunction in the brain . . .")	Yes. (". . . the problem is one of altered processes, and not of a generalized incapacity to learn.")	Yes
No	Yes	Yes
Yes. ("The term includes such conditions as perceptual handicaps, brain injury, minimal brain dysfunction, dyslexia and developmental aphasia.")	Yes	Yes. All categories other than brain injured are excluded. No mention is made of the emotionally disturbed.
Yes. ("such disorders are presumed to be due to central nervous system dysfunction . . .")	No	Yes. Similar to Bateman and National Advisory Committee on Handicapped Children, except that this definition explicitly states that LD can exist concomitantly with other handicapping conditions.

creases the likelihood of identifying as poor achievers many children who actually represent errors in measurement" (p. 11).

3. If we focus completely upon underachievement in school subjects only (reading, writing, arithmetic, and so on), and mandate a designated degree of underachievement (in terms of years "behind"), then learning-disabled children in kindergarten and in first grade will never be identified.

4. By emphasizing underachievement in academic functioning and developmental process deficits, such major considerations as social immaturity and problems in adaptive behavior are downgraded.

5. It is possible to focus upon the criterion of underachievement to such a degree, that other equally important definitional aspects (e.g., central nervous system dysfunction, underlying process impairment in broad developmental areas such as language and perception) become trivialized. Although teachers, by and large, welcome the stress upon educational aspects, there is a concern less underachievement, per se, become equated with learning disabilities.

Underlying Process Deficit. Although this is the most esoteric of the definitional criteria for learning disabilities, there is a compelling rationale for its inclusion. Without it, we are pushed substantially towards an all encompassing, *literal* interpretation of the term learning disabled. Classes for *LD* children would soon become a dumping ground for all learning and behavioral problems. The concept of process deficit allows us to discriminate between the careless reader and the one who fails at the symbolic level (i.e., the dyslexic); between the child whose penmanship is untidy (perhaps he writes too hurriedly) and the one who makes gross errors in formation and orientation (i.e., the dysgraphic); between the child who forgets some of the arithmetic facts and the one who is deficient in spatial and quantitative relationships (the dyscalculic); between the hostile, negative child who is *willfully* disruptive and the child who is disinhibited, impulsive, and irritable owing to faulty interplay between the reticular (that part of the brain which is the seat of emotional functioning) and the cerebrum (which governs the emotions).

Another advantage of this concern for process deficit is that it enhances the likelihood of early identification. Denhoff, Hainsworth and Hainsworth (1971, p. 111) laud the CEC definition of learning disabilities which projects process deficits rather than academic lags. After all, they point out, if we stipulate that a child must demonstrate a two-year lag in academic skills before he can be classified as learning disabled, he cannot be helped until he has first experienced several years as a school failure; however, the stress upon process deficits manifoldly increases the odds that he will be identified prior to school enrollment.

Yet the concept of underlying process deficit remains an elusive one. Many researchers have stated that process training has not proven to be an effective means of increasing academic performance (Cohen, 1969; Newcomer & Hammill, 1975; Hammill & Larsen, 1974). In fact, Hammill (1972) analyzed 25 experimental studies, each of which was designed to deal with the relationship between visual perceptual training and improvement in reading. He has concluded that little evidence exists that training in visual perception has any effect upon visual perception, let alone upon reading. On the other hand, one hesitates to dismiss the collective works and theories of such giants as Strauss, Kephart, Wepman, Frostig, Kirk, Myklebust, and so on. Until we have more definitive research findings, teachers should proceed with caution. Generally, it is a good idea to (1) employ process training sparingly; (2) to use it only with those learning disabled children demonstrating a specific process deficit; (3) to utilize it to a larger extent with those students who are in the readiness stage and are not yet prepared to acquire academics and; (4) to make frequent observations, assessments, and modifications. A viable overall approach would be to combine the *format of process training* (e.g., tachisto-scopic exposure of visual stimuli, tracing outlines with a flashlight beam, scanning) with the *substance—that is, content—of task training* (e.g., letters, words, and num-bers instead of geometric shapes). Above all, we should remember that perceptual training was never meant to replace instruction in the academics, but to augment it.

Neurological Basis for Learning Disabilities. Perhaps those who are tempted to say that learning disabilities do not—or need not—imply brain injury, are really reflecting their dissatisfaction with the concept of *presumed* brain injury. They might willingly agree with the organic criterion if one spoke in terms of *provable* brain injury, *demonstrable* lesions, or *positive* neurological findings, but they deem it somewhat unscientific to accept a diagnosis of brain injury on the sole basis of clinical observation of behavior. This controversy has permeated the field since its inception. As early as 1947, Strauss had to face critics who frowned disapprovingly at his willingness in some instances, to concede brain injury simply by virtue of the impact that some children's behavior made upon him even though medical findings were totally negative (see page 6). Clements' (1966) concept of *minimal brain dys-function* was a step toward reconciling these conflicting views. Somehow it was felt that, in these questionable instances, it would be more palatable to accept a verdict of brain *dysfunction* rather than brain *injury*. In addition, although many parents and teachers welcomed the term learning disabilities because of its implied acci-dental etiology (see page 6), a sizable number did not.

Despite the fact that many professionals in the field of learning disabilities continue to express dismay at the notion that brain injury is the cornerstone of learning disabilities, interestingly almost every major definition includes this crite-rion (either as an outright affirmative or at least as a "maybe"). In a response to John Elkins' review of his book *Learning Disabilities in Home, School and Com-munity*, Cruickshank (1978) stresses the relationship between learning disabilities and neurological deficits: "There is no confusion in my mind regarding the neuro-logical base of brain injury and learning disabilities. . . ." In his view, failure to dif-ferentiate between learning disabilities and environmentally-produced problems will continue to cause confusion. Learning disabilities "are academic or adjustment deficiencies, the result of perceptual processing deficits which in turn are the result of *a diagnosed or (often in the present state of knowledge) an inferred neuro-physiological dysfunction*" [emphasis added] (p. 328).

The Exclusionary Factor. Various categories have necessarily been excluded from the definition of learning disabilities since (1) all learning disabled do not have the same characteristics, and (2), even more importantly, many of the typical traits of the learning disabled are frequently found among other categories of exceptionality.

The Mentally Retarded. Granted, it seems particularly ironic that the mentally retarded are excluded from the definition of learning disabilities in view of the fact that the very term mentally retarded is the *only* category (prior to the emergence of the learning disabilities entity) to denote inability to learn adequately and/or readily. We must also remember that much of what we now know about the learn-ing disabled and methods for working with them come directly from research related to the brain-injured retarded (that is, Strauss's exogenous retardates). Understandably many authors decry the omission of mental retardation. Lewis (1977) considers it to be an ambiguity that is symptomatic "of the chaos that pervades the field." He argues, "I have yet to hear a scientific definition that will convince me that a retarded child is one thing and a learning-disabled child another" (p. 255). Indeed, the policy of some school administrators to place learning disabled and educable mentally retarded within one special education classroom can be considered an expression of this viewpoint.*

Cruickshank (1977), in a similar vein protested that "perceptual processing deficits are to be found in children of every intellectual range" (p. 54). Earlier, he and a coauthor (Hallahan & Cruickshank, 1973) contended that, by exclusion of the MR, the opportunity to diversify the education of the exogenous retardates—since their deficits are clinically different from the familial ones—was lost.

Upon reflection, this does not necessarily follow: It is quite possible that master teachers of MR classes, even before the advent of Strauss, surmised that within their classroom were children with two distinctly different behavior and learning patterns—those with erratic, unpredictable, explosive behavior, presenting a scatter of high and low performance scores, contrasted with children who evidenced predictable, orderly behavior, less scatter, but low performance in all areas. (The former was later called exogenous, the Strauss Child, etc., while the latter was of the endogenous variety.) With the publication of the Strauss books and works by Cruickshank and other researchers, these teachers were able to provide even more effective intervention without the necessity—indeed the burden—of integrating an unwieldly large IQ range in the same classroom.

Also, even if optimal intervention occurs, the mentally retarded will still function below normal academically (assuming, of course, that the original IQ is valid). Parents of the learning disabled were brought together by the realization that their children were encountering problems in learning despite normal to above-average intelligence. Because they were not retarded, it was felt these children should not be assigned to classes for the educable mentally retarded (EMR) given the substantial differences between these two groups with respect to syllabus, long-range goals (that is, expectations), inate abilities, and prognosis. Nevertheless, Myers and Hammill (1976, p. 6) suggest that teachers of EMR be aware that some of the children in their classes meet the definitional criteria for the learning disabled (except for the exclusionary clause) and therefore need suitable supportive services.

An easy way to separate the two conceptually does exist. Although it amounts to "stacking the deck," it may still help us to decide whether or not there is a justifiable reason for the exclusion: Don't compare a brain-injured, perceptually-handicapped, underachieving EMR, IQ 74, with a correctly classified learning-disabled child having an IQ of 80, and defiantly challenge the diagnosticians to point toward any substantial differences. Instead, contrast a low functioning EMR

---

* Smith et al. (1977) report that of 200 children labeled learning disabled and enrolled in classes for the learning disabled, ". . . 37% were found not to have the prerequisite of normal intellectual ability as determined by the criterion of a full scale IQ of at least 76 and either a Verbal or Performance IQ of at least 90." Hopefully, in most cases, the motivation for such practices reflect a genuine concern for the children's needs and do not stem from budgetary considerations.

(IQ 60) with a high functioning learning-disabled child (IQ 130). The differences are staggering, and it is precisely these differences which served as impetus to the learning disabilities movement.

The Emotionally Disturbed.[*] Some definitions (the earlier ones) included the emotionally disturbed, others specifically excluded them, still others simply avoided mentioning them. Parents of learning-disabled children generally prefer to exclude the emotionally disturbed. First of all, there is a widespread belief among laypeople as well as some professionals (by and large, a misconception) that parents are at the root of their children's emotional problems. The learning disabilities classification supports no such etiological accusation. Besides, prior to the formation of learning-disabled classes, these children, misdiagnosed and/or misplaced were often assigned to classes for the emotionally disturbed (and EMR), where their parents perceived that their needs were not properly met. They felt, as did Johnson and Myklebust (1967, p. 9) that their children were intact emotionally, intellectually, motorically, and sensorially, "but despite these integrities, they cannot learn in the usual or normal manner." Granted, it is not always easy to differentiate between emotionally disturbed and learning-disabled children for a variety of reasons: (1) Many, if not all, learning disabled have what is commonly called "overlays of emotional disturbance." (2) Many emotionally disturbed have problems in learning, and conversely, the learning disabled, having experienced repeated failure, rejection, mismanagement, and inadequate support, are at high risk to develop, especially in adolescence and young adulthood, emotional illness of far greater magnitude than the "overlays" level. (3) Many emotionally disturbed children exhibit some of the typical traits of the learning disabled. For example, they both may be distractable, owing to the learning-disabled child's inability to filter out extraneous sensory data and to the emotionally-disturbed child's preoccupation with himself. They both may be destructive, a reflection of spatial disorientation, kinesthetic imperception, and motor disinhibition in the case of the learning disabled and to negativism in the emotionally-disturbed child. They both may repeat actions and words aimlessly, called *perseveration* when it applies to the learning disabled and *obsessive compulsion* when speaking of the emotionally disturbed. (4) Like the learning disabled, the emotionally disturbed frequently exhibit perceptual problems (e.g., low self-esteem can lead to distorted body image causing them to perceive themselves as smaller—that is, less significant—than they really are). (5) Brain injury (caused by exogenous factors) and MBD (genetic) can be expected to occur in the emotionally-disturbed population with the same prevalence as in the nonhandicapped.

Despite this overlap, authors have advanced some cogent reasons why we should seek to differentiate these two populations. Grouping both the brain injured and the emotionally disturbed in the same classroom under the rubric of learning

[*] Throughout this text, we have tended to use the term *emotionally disturbed* instead of *behaviorally disordered*. Technically, there are differences, the chief one being that behavior disorders are observable, whereas emotional disturbances cannot be seen, only inferred. Nevertheless, it is common practice among authors (James M. Kauffman, *Characteristics of Children's Behavior Disorders*, Second Edition, Columbus, Ohio: Charles E. Merrill, 1981; Frank M. Hewett and Frank D. Taylor, *The Emotionally Disturbed Child in the Classroom*, Second Edition, Boston: Allyn & Bacon, 1980) to use these terms interchangeably.

disabilities,* a practice which naturally evolved from the original definition in 1962 (see table, page 6), has been challenged. Messinger (1965) points out that: (a) emotionally-disturbed children, unlike brain-injured children, often show highly developed defenses against learning and are intensely hostile toward teachers and other adults; (b) emotionally-disturbed children often perceive themselves as different from brain-injured children in their class, and this perceived deviancy then leads them to work against the efforts of the teacher and the class; and (c) structured environment is often advantageous to the brain-injured child whereas frequent deviation from curriculum and flexibility are apt to be effective approaches when teaching emotionally-disturbed children.

The similarities between the two groups need not blind us to the differences. Some in-roads have been made in differential diagnosis with respect to these two populations. A neuropsychiatrist, Whieldon (1962, p. 24), in contrasting children whose problems were psychogenic with those whose deficits in learning and behavior stemmed from brain injury, found: (1) motor hyperactivity manifests itself at birth in the case of the organic, whereas it frequently makes its initial appearance at age 10 or 12 in the psychogenic; (2) the brain-injured children "seem to get over their moods quickly," but the psychogenic evidence a sullen and withdrawn attitude for significantly longer time periods, and (3) the brain-injured child is basically *emotionally labile* (that is, given to mood swings) whereas the psychogenic are truly *emotionally disturbed.*

Morris and Dozier (1961) add that not only do brain-injured children manifest driven behavior since birth (as compared with the later age of onset in the emotionally disturbed) but with more consistency and persistence; emotionally-disturbed children's behavior inadequacies fluctuate and are more variable. Morris and Dozier also contend that the brain-injured child is likely to behave in the examining room (or elsewhere) in consonance with the parents' previous description of him; the emotionally disturbed, on the other hand, though reported to be "holy terrors" at home, may evidence conformity and cooperation during the office visit (particularly the initial visit). Furthermore, Morris and Dozier state that many brain-injured children frequently make positive first impressions, only to "wear out their welcome" shortly thereafter. No such pattern is evidenced in the case of the emotionally disturbed; the types of relationships they have with others fluctuate. Finally, these researchers report that much of the explosive behavior of brain-injured subjects is likely to be impersonal in nature: For example, excessive roughness in handling objects can occur even when the child is alone (and doesn't realize that he is being observed). "Hyperactive-aggressive behavior may be present on awakening and before at least overt personal conflicts have developed . . . [and] in a new relationship with another child before the usual difficulties have a chance to develop" (p. 235). This is not the general pattern for emotionally-disturbed children.

The Disadvantaged. In the early years of the brain-injured movement, cynical professionals were frequently heard to say, "if it happens in Harlem, we call it 'mentally retarded,' but in Scarsdale [an affluent suburb of New York City], its called

---

* Instead of differentiating between these two categories, some states use the term *Educationally Handicapped* to encompass both the LD and the emotionally disturbed.

'brain injury.' " This complaint held some truth and the trend was to continue for many years. As recently as the 70s, Franks (1971) assessed ethnic and social-status characteristics in children enrolled in EMR classes and in learning-disabled classes (grades 1-8) in the state of Missouri. He found that blacks constituted 34 percent of the EMR class enrollment but only 3 percent of the learning-disabilities classes. There are many reasons for this. It might be that the unfortunate plight of the lower socioeconomic families makes it difficult for them to seek attention for "minimal" problems. And hence, many poor, learning disabled were "passing"— that is, they went along undiagnosed, blending in with the community at large, albeit with spasmodic adjustment problems. Also the socioeconomically disadvantaged status frequently masks mild handicaps such as learning disabilities (Meyen & Moran, 1979, p. 529). In other words, school administrators were prone to attribute any shortcomings of lower class learning-disabled students to membership in the disadvantaged and minority population, rather than to suspect underlying neurological deficit. Also, a significant number of the disadvantaged may fail intelligence tests because of cultural bias of the items. At any rate, brain injury (and learning disabilities) have frequently been referred to as a "middle-class disease" despite the fact that many of the known causes of brain damage are strongly linked to poverty (poor prenatal care, inadequate obstetric and pediatric services, malnutrition, etc.). Only recently are more members of the poor, minority, and disadvantaged communities enrolled in classes for the learning disabled.

The disadvantaged were never excluded *in toto* from the principle definitions of learning disabilities; rather, the exclusion applied to a distinct subgroup of this population. However, considerable confusion regarding this point has always existed and some authorities erroneously concluded that *all* disadvantaged are excluded. For example, Coles (1978, p. 314) writes ". . . by excluding environmental disadvantage . . . [the definition] limits attention to middle- and upper-class children." The key word in this definition is the qualifier "primarily." That is, a differentiation is made between those disadvantaged who evidence learning problems as a direct consequence of environmental deprivation (in other words, *primarily* because of paucity of sensorial stimulation, limited socialization opportunities, nominal language experience, lack of opportunity, and so forth), but who are neurologically intact, and those who have central nervous system (CNS) impairment-based learning deficiencies. Myers and Hammill (1976, p. 7) point out that "a child or an adult who is a nonreader because of inadequate opportunity to learn to read or poor instruction is not necessarily learning disabled . . . [They] suffer from a lack of information and not from an inability to process information proficiently." The responsibility for their educational needs rests more squarely within the province of general educators, many (but alas, not enough) of whom are rising to meet the challenge.

Sensorially Impaired. These were excluded from the principle definition of learning disabilities for two reasons. First, the learning-disabled child's problems are theorized to emanate from the perceptual rather than from the sensory level. Also, the severely sensorially impaired (that is, the blind and the deaf) require a highly specialized approach—Braille, signing, etc.—which are not part of the methodology typically advocated for the learning disabled.

Motorically Impaired. The cerebral palsied, according to Strauss's theories, would evidence not only motor impairment but also the behavioral/learning syndrome of the learning disabled. In fact, in the late 50s, New York Association for Brain-Injured Children and United Cerebral Palsy of New York merged. Since both groups represented children who, by definition, suffered from brain injury, it was reasoned that they had many common goals which could best be reached by pooling their respective resources. This merger was dissolved after a year owing largely to the different thrusts of concern. Namely, the cerebral palsied had many specific needs, for example, prosthesis, occupational therapy, physical therapy, speech therapy (with a large emphasis upon articulation), not indigenous to the minimally brain injured. In reality, the most propitious way to regard the cerebral palsied—or for that matter, the blind and/or deaf learning-disabled child—is to consider them multihandicapped.

Instructional Factors. The exclusion of this factor by Kirk (1962—see Table 1-1, page 12) states, in effect, that inferior instruction can cause learning *problems*, but that this should not be confused with learning *disabilities*. Parents, and some professionals, however, perhaps in an effort to goad educators on to greater and more effective endeavors and/or perhaps to take the onus away from the child, have at times deemed the problem one of *"teaching* disorders." They proclaim, "there's nothing wrong with the child; he could learn if only the teacher could teach." Upon reflection, this argument is of limited value at best. It smacks of name-calling, no matter who is calling whom names. Also, it does not account for the many learning-disabled children who still evidence considerable learning disorders despite the intervention of talented and dedicated teachers and, conversely, the multitude of nonhandicapped children who seem to learn incidentally, tangentially, independently, almost irrespective of the quality of instruction.

Brain Injury Without Learning Disabilities

It is interesting to observe that none of the definitions of "brain injury," "minimal brain dysfunction," or "learning disabilities" address themselves to CNS-impaired children who do *not* manifest learning difficulties. It has been established that 25–30% of the cerebral palsied population (no question here about brain injury) are not mentally retarded. In fact, many are highly intelligent—*and good learners.* Among these are: Earl Carlson, surgeon, and author of *Born That Way* (John Day, 1941); Frances Berko, university professor at Cornell and a researcher of renown; Gwen Frostig, artist, author, and publisher; and Christy Brown, a poet and author of the bestseller, *Down All the Days* (Stein & Day, 1970), so physically handicapped that he had to use his toes to negotiate an electric typewriter.

If a cerebral-palsied individual need not evidence learning deficiencies, it should be patently clear that there are some *minimally* brain injured who likewise are facile learners. For example, one brain-injured pupil enrolled in a regular ninth-grade class made the following scores on the nationally administered Iowa Tests for Educational Development (SRA) (Fig. 1-1).

According to the test results, this pupil—incidentally, *the diagnosis of his brain injury was corroborated by positive neurological findings*—surpassed ninety-nine out of one hundred of any randomly selected ninth-grade pupils in four of the sub-

	GRADE	1 BACKGR'D SOC.STUD.		2 BACKGR'D NAT.SCI.		3 CORR. OF EXPRES'N		4 QUANT'VE THINKING		5 READING SOC.STUD.		6 READING NAT.SCI.		7 READING LIT.		8 GENERAL VOCAB.		1–8 COM- POSITE		9 USE OF SOURCES	
IOWA TEST	09	26	99	27	99	14	68	32	99	24	97	20	92	19	89	21	94	24	98	26	99
		STD	%ILE	STD	%ILE	STD	%ILE	STD	%ILE	STD	%ILE	STD	%ILE	STD	%ILE	STD	%ILE	STD	%ILE	STD	%ILE
	IOWA TESTS OF EDUCATIONAL DEVELOPMENT – SRA PRESSCORE®																				

Figure 1-1. Iowa Test scores of a minimally brain-injured student.

ject categories, and scored above ninety-eight of the students in tests 1–7 compositely! Many brain-injured children (now called learning disabled) go on to college and to graduate school. Many of them, of course, experience difficulties along the way and must learn to compensate for their learning disabilities, but a significant number learn readily and have always done so. Undoubtedly, some of these instances can be explained in terms of a high IQ masking underachievement (e.g., a learning-disabled pupil with 140 IQ performing 20 points lower—the lowered base still being sufficiently high to insure school success). Nevertheless, in the absence of any research to the contrary, it is safe to assume that there are many brain injured who are adequate learners and who do not underachieve.

Thus a scathing criticism of the definition of learning disabilities, which was voiced the time of its inception (Siegel, 1968), remains unresolved to this date: The definition makes no allowance for the brain-injured child who does not have any disorder in learning. Stated differently, a semantic enigma emerges: *a learning disabled child (read, "brain-injured child") need not have any learning disability*.

Nomenclature

From the late 1940s and early 50s, when the term brain injured exploded upon the scene, to the present, numerous designations for the child we now called *learning disabled* have appeared. Factors that affect the choice of terminology include: (1) the emotional impact of the given term (i.e., one designation may have more of a negative connotation than another); (2) degree of input from the various disciplines (i.e., the earlier designations were medical in nature: brain injured, brain damaged, CNS impaired, neurologically impaired, etc.; later ones had medical/ psychological implications: e.g., perceptually handicapped; then came the behavioral terms, e.g., Hyperkinetic Impulse Disorder, Attentional Deficit Disorder,* The Clumsy Child Syndrome; and finally, educational nomenclature evolved; e.g., dyslexia, specific language disabilities, learning disorders, and of course, *learning disabilities*); and (3) whether or not it has pragmatic value (i.e., does it point toward a course of educational intervention?).

The following discussion will deal with only three of the terms. Many of the arguments (both pro and con) amplified here would hold in a number of other

---

* Lerner (1981) points out that even the medical discipline has veered towards behavioral nomenclature as can be seen by the recent recommendations of the Journal of Pediatrics (1979) and the Diagnostic and Statistical Manual (1980) that the term Attentional Deficit Disorder (ADD) be applied to individuals suffering from learning disabilities. She believes that "the focus on attentional problems appears to be of common interest to both the medical and educational fields and, hence, an area of possible coordination between them" (p. 52).

instances as well: for example, the charge that "brain injury" is medical vocabulary and hence useless to educators would also apply to "CNS impaired," "neurologically handicapped," "minimal cerebral dysfunction," and so forth. The complaint that not all children classified as "learning disabled" have all the characteristics generally attributed to this group would be equally pertinent to all the other designations.

Brain-Injured. This was the first term used that impacted on the educational community. Earlier medical appelations existed—e.g., Brain-Stem Syndrome (Kahn & Cohen, 1934), Post-Encephalitic Behavior Disorders (Bender, 1942), but these were not adapted by education administrators—that is, they did not lead to the formation of special education classes bearing these designations. Parents embraced "brain injured" for two specific reasons; first, the causes were attributed to accidental factors and not to parental mismanagement or to genetic factors. (Today, of course, it is known that some instances of brain injury—or learning disabilities—are endogenous). Secondly, a child could be brain injured, and yet not mentally retarded. The earlier medical nomenclatures did not differentiate the two—hence less stigma and a better prognosis. (Still another advantage is that, because brain injury is a medical term, it facilitates funding. Some years ago, Gordon (1968) in an editorial column called "on not abandoning the concept of 'brain injury,'" stated:

> Parents of brain-injured children have done such a good job of educating professionals that professionals are now ready to take over. But please, parents, don't let them. Terrible things happen when "they" take over. First, they change names. Suddenly, brain injury is a learning or a perceptual disability; and lo and behold, almost everybody has one. Then the witch doctors move in with one-shot "solutions" followed by the pushers (publishers of educational material). Then an enormous wave of optimism begins to obscure the essential dilemma.

A frequently cited objection to "brain injury" is that it is essentially a medical term and, notwithstanding that fact that it lends itself to funding and legislation, does not point to any direction for the educator* (Stevens & Birch, 1957; Kirk, 1963). Another objection is its lack of precision: that is, in a generic sense, brain injury means *any* injury to the brain, and hence would encompass a variety of conditions such as cerebral palsy, epilepsy, aphasia, mental retardation, and some varieties of schizophrenia. Still another objection stems from the willingness of some physicians, at times, to diagnose brain injury on the basis of behavior even in the absence of medical corroboration (Birch, 1956; Sarason, 1959; Benoit, 1962).

Minimal Brain Dysfunction. This term was introduced by Clements (1966). It was a step toward rectifying some of the weaknesses of its predecessor, *brain injury*.

---

* Strauss and his followers, of course, would take issue with this, pointing out their belief that brain injury *invariably* leads to a breakdown in ordered behavior coupled with perceptual impairment. These, in turn, call for structured environment and specialized training which involves strengthening the weak modalities as well as working around them through the intact channels.

The word *dysfunction* seems to demand less rigorous proof than does the word *injury:* that is, when a child exhibits hyperactivity, distractibility, impulsivity, emotional lability, incoordination, etcetera, then, ipso facto, whether or not an injury can be demonstrated, one can say, at the very least, that the brain stem (old brain) and cortex (new brain) are not *functioning* together properly. (Of course, more conservative writers could demand verification of the *dysfunction* just as readily.)

The word *minimal* clearly stipulates that only the mildest of the brain-injured population receive the focus of our attention, thus reinforcing the exclusionary clause found in most definitions of the term learning disabled. The designation *minimal* seems appropriate in that (1) it is in consonance with the "continuum theory" (Knoblock & Pasamanick, 1962) which states that there is a continuum of brain damage ranging from minimal to severe with a corresponding degree of symptomatology, and (2) it calls attention to the relative mildness of this population's behavioral deficits: the MBD child has motor impairment, but if it were more than mild, we would call it cerebral palsy; he has deficits in attention and impulse control, but if it were more severe, it would be known as autism or psychosis (Clements, 1966). (See Table 1-2.)

Gardner (1973) is another author who prefers the term minimal brain dysfunction. He voices dissatisfaction concerning brain injury, "with its implication of the rarely applicable traumatic causative factor" (p. 7) and with *learning disabilities*, which is too unbounded, suggesting to him "the whole gamut of learning disorders, both psychogenic and organic in etiology" (p. 7).

Millon (1964, p. 534), however, objects to the term *minimal*, pointing out that it might be incorrectly interpreted as an *across-the-board*, albeit mild, depression of intellectual functioning. He prefers the adjective "circumscribed" instead. Also, Cohn (1964), contradicting the continuum theory of brain injury, points out "it has not been demonstrated neuropathically that minimum clinical signs are in fact related to minimal brain damage. . . . Minimal signs may be concomitant with remarkable lesions of the brain" [and vice-versa] (p. 180). Finally, much to their dismay, parents have been discovering that the term "minimal" is, at times, erro-

Table 1-2.   Classification Guide, Brain Dysfunction Syndromes

Minimal (minor; mild)	*Major (severe)*
1. Impairment of fine movement or coordination.	1. Cerebral palsies.
2. Electroencephalographic abnormalities without actual seizures, or possibly subclinical seizures which may be associated with fluctuations in behavior or intellectual function.	2. Epilepsies.
3. Deviations in attention, activity level, impulse control, and affect.	3. Autism and other gross disorders of mentation and behavior.
4. Specific and circumscribed perceptual, intellectual, and memory deficits.	4. Mental subnormalities.
5. Nonperipheral impairments of vision, hearing, haptics, and speech.	5. Blindness, deafness, and severe aphasias.

From Sam D. Clements, *Minimal Brain Dysfunction in Children.* Wash., D.C.; Dept. of Public Health Services, Publication No. 1415, 1966, p. 10.

neously equated with "trivial," thus supplying some educators, administrators, rehabilitation workers, and legislators with a convenient rationale for denying services and programs to this population.

Learning Disabilities. This term was created to weld a national organization for the variously designated parent groups scattered across the country. It had a unifying effect and was a clarion call to action: (One can take steps to help a handicapped learner improve.) Parents no longer had to deal with implications of defective genetics or irreversible medical conditions (brain damage is essentially incurable), and one could easily invest the term with an aspect of temporariness. Teachers welcomed it because, for the first time, the trump card was placed squarely in their hand. They no longer had to take a back seat in acquiescence to the medical and psychological professions. Because causative factors were played down, one could deal directly with behaviors (i.e., learning deficits). Observable behaviorable objectives could be articulated, appropriate material and instructional methods could be formulated, and the degree of interventional efficacy measured.

What then are the objections to this term? Just as the adjective brain injured has a generic connotation from a medical point of view and thereby lends itself to semantic imprecision regarding population composition, now "learning disabilities" exudes a generic connotation in the educational realm, opening up, as Hallahan and Cruickshank (1973, pp. 6-7) put it, a Pandora's Box: classes for learning disabilities often became dumping grounds for children who manifested sensory handicaps, delinquent behaviors, reading deficits, speech impairment, intellectual disorders, and so forth. Although broadly speaking, children in each of these areas do indeed have a disability in learning, grouping them together on the sole basis of this generalized display of learning deficit while ignoring the more basic medical-psychological entity and sympomatology is not what the founders of the ACLD movement had in mind. When heterogeneity within a class becomes so extreme, it renders the teacher virtually incapable of accommodating individual differences in a manner that even approaches the goals of positive intervention (Hallahan & Cruickshank, 1973, p. 9). Others have voiced similar objections toward the practice of mixing LD and ED (Messinger, 1965; Kronick, 1977). (See pages 19-20.)

Still another argument against the concept of learning disabilities is that it tends to ignore behavioral deficits per se. The LD designation insists on underachievement as a definitional criterion but does not mandate the manifestation of any of the Strauss Syndrome traits. Hence, it leaves in limbo those brain-injured individuals who, despite evidencing hyperactivity, distractibility, impulsivity, and the like, remain intact learners. This is ironic in view of the fact that the original "brain injured" category—by not stressing academic underachievement—was able to accommodate this segment of the exceptional population. Now, despite the fact that a sizeable number of their parents were founders of the BI and LD movements, many BI young adults who are not handicapped learners are denied servies (specialized psychological services, OVR resources, etc.) which they desperately need.

It might be fruitful to recognize that the term "learning disabilities" has the impetus of an early start. (True, "brain injured" came first, but "learning disabilities" has been around since 1963 and has consistently lead all the contending nomenclatures by an ever-increasing margin.) Professionals might be well-advised to accept the term—recognizing its limitations as well as its strengths, its implications, and above all, the intent of its originators—and get on with the task of helping children. Efforts devoted toward endeavoring to create the perfect label are doomed to failure.

> Without systems and patterns, we have no order, only chaos. If man never learned to generalize, each situation would be unique, and one would never profit from experience. In any categorizing model, we conscientiously seek similarities, while deemphasizing individual differences, hence losing some information. *It is possible, then, that any classification system will necessarily possess some limitations* [emphasis added] (Siegel, 1968, p. 433).

Definitions of Learning Disabilities: Some Final Guidelines

There are inherent pitfalls in the process of defining categories of children. The very act of classifying populations of children emphasizes *intergroup* variability (e.g., what are the essential differences between learning disabilities, emotional disturbance and EMR?). Yet the factor of *intragroup* variability (differences within a single group) is crucial lest we fall into the trap of overgeneralizing and fail to see each child, regardless of his classification, as first and foremost a human being. Gallagher (1964, p. 165) goes a step further and points out that ". . . differences in the level of developmental skills *within* the individual child . . . [are] sometimes . . . more important for educational planning than perceived differences *between* children."

Thus, the definition, the concept, the term learning disabilities, despite having served as a catalyst, providing both the rationale and the impetus for increased interest in—and services for—a group of children who have hitherto been misunderstood, is not without its flaws. Yet, it may be possible to help them despite the current imperfection of definitions. The key is to concentrate on *children*, not *words*. Instead of taking inordinate periods of time trying to formulate the ultimate definition, we might better devote our energies toward observing learning-disabled children, interacting with them, delivering services to them, in short "getting to know them." Despite the fact that definitions come and go, that the cry for a noncategorizational approach (which, in reality, is a classification system of its own) waxes and wanes, that the "anti-labelers" incessantly bring their message to the forefront, *practitioners* go on providing relevant services to the learning disabled, continuing to believe that "we can know them best by the impact they make upon us." (See pages 321–23.) There is no substitute for experience. In a *Journal of Learning Disabilities Questionnaire* (Kirk, Berry & Senf, 1979) in which respondents must tell whether they agree or disagree with a series of statements, it is probably no accident that the first item reads, "I know an LD child when I see one, but defining the term is nearly impossible" (p. 239). It was found that 27.2% agreed with this statement and 5.2% strongly agreed. Gerald Senf (personal communication, 8/15/80), theorizing that this figure would have been even larger were it not for the second part of the question, writes: "While I think that people [i.e., educators and other professionals] would typically agree with the notion that 'I know an LD child when I see one,' they were unwilling to agree that the definition was impossible."

REFERENCES

Bateman, B. An educational view of a diagnostic approach to learning disorders. In Jerome Hellmuth (Ed.), *Learning Disorders Vol. I.* Seattle: Special Child Publications, 1965.

Bender, L. Post-encephalitic behavior disorders in children. In J. Neal (Ed.), *Encephalitis: a clinical study.* New York: Grune & Stratton, 1942.

Benoit, E. A functional theory of mental retardation. *The A.A.M.D. Education Reporter*, April, 1962, *2*, 4–6.

Benton, A. L. Clinical neuropsychology of childhood: An overview. In Ralph M. Reitman and Leslie Dawson (Eds.), *Clinical neuropsychology: Current status and application.* Washington, D.C.: V. H. Winston & Sons, 1974.

Birch, H. G. Theoretical aspects of psychological behavior in the brain damaged. In Morton Goldstein (Prepared by), *Psychological services for the cerebral palsied.* New York: United Cerebral Palsy Association of New York State, Inc., 1956, pp. 48–61.

Bryan, T. H. and Bryan, J. H. *Understanding learning disabilities, 2nd. Ed.* Sherman Oaks, Ca: Alfred Publ. Co., 1978.

Chalfant, J. C. and Scheffelin, M. A. *Central processing in children: A review of research*, Phase III, (NINDB Monograph No. 9.) Bethesda, Md: National Institute of Neurological Disease and Stroke, 1969.

Clements, S. D. *Minimal brain dysfunction in children: terminology and identification—Phase I* (NINDB Monograph No. 3). Washington, D.C.: U.S. Department of Health, Education, and Welfare, 1966.

Cohen, S. A. Studies in visual perception and reading in disadvantaged children. *Journal of Learning Disabilities*, 1969, *2*, 498–507.

Cohn, R. The neurological study of children with learning disabilities. *Exceptional Children*, December 1964, *31*(4), 179–185.

Coles, G. S. The learning-disabilities test battery: empirical and social issues. *Harvard Educational Review*, August, 1978, *48*(3), 313–340.

Council for Exceptional Children. Annual convention papers. Arlington, Va., 1971.

Cruickshank, W. (book review rebuttal) *Journal of Learning Disabilities*, May, 1978, *11*(5), 328–329.

————. Myths and realities in learning disabilities. *Journal of Learning Disabilities*, January, 1977, *10*(1), 51–58.

Denhoff, E., Hainsworth, P. and Hainsworth, M. Learning disabilities and early childhood education: An information-processing approach. In Helmer R. Myklebust (Ed.), *Progress in learning disabilities, vol. II.* New York: Grune & Stratton, 1971.

Diagnostic and Statistical Manual (DSM III), American Psychiatric Association, 1980.

Farnham-Diggory, S. *Learning disabilities.* Cambridge, Mass.: Harvard University Press, 1978.

Federal Register. August 23, 1977.

Franks, D. J. Ethnic and social status characteristics of children in EMR and LD classes. *Exceptional Children*, March, 1971, *37*(7), 537–538.

Gallagher, J. J. *The tutoring of brain-injured mentally retarded children.* Springfield, Ill.: Charles C. Thomas, 1960.

_____. Learning Disabilities: An Introduction to Selected Papers. *Exceptional Children. 31*(4), 8–9, Dec., 1964.

Gardner, R. A. *MBD: The family book about minimal brain dysfunction.* New York: Jason Aronson, 1973.

Gesell, A. L. and Amatruda, C. S. *Developmental diagnosis, normal and abnormal child development,* 2nd ed. New York: P. B. Hoeber, 1947.

Goldstein, K. *The Organism.* New York: American Book, 1939.

Gordon, S. *The brain-injured adolescent* (pamphlet). New York: New York Association for Brain-Injured Children (N.D.).

_____. *On not abandoning the concept of "brain-injury,"* Vol. III (1), (editorial), Houston: Texas Association for Children with Learning Disabilities, January, 1968.

Hallahan, D. P. and Cruickshank, W. M. *Psycho-educational foundations of learning disabilities.* Englewood Cliffs, New Jersey: Prentice-Hall, 1973.

Hammill, D. Training visual perceptual processes. *Journal of Learning Disabilities,* November, 1972, *5*(9), 552–559.

Hammill, D., and Larsen, S. C. The relationship of selected auditory perceptual skills and reading ability, *Journal of Learning Disabilities,* 1974, 7, 429–436.

Hammill, D. Recommendation to the DCLD (CEC) Board of Trustees Meeting Oct. 31, 1980. Reported in DCLD *Newsletter* Vol. 6 No. 4, Spring, 1981.

Haring, N. G., and Miller, C. A. *Minimal Brain Dysfunction: Educational, Medical, and Health Related Services.* (Phase II, N & SDCP Monograph, Public Health Publication No. 2015.) Washington, D.C.: U.S. Department of Health, Education and Welfare, 1969.

Johnson, D. and Myklebust, H. *Learning disabilities: educational principles and practices.* New York: Grune & Stratton, 1967.

Johnson, S. W. and Morasky, R. L. *Learning disabilities.* Boston: Allyn & Bacon, 1977.

Journal of Pediatrics. 95(5):734–735. November, 1979.

Kahn, E. and Cohen, L. Organic driveness: A brain stem syndrome and an experience, *New England Journal of Medicine,* April, 1934, *210*, 748–756.

Kirk, S. A. Behavioral diagnosis and remediation of learning disabilities. Proceedings of the Conference on Exploration into the Problems of the Perceptually-Handicapped Child, First Annual Meeting, Vol. 1, Chicago, April 6, 1963.

_____. *Educating exceptional children.* (1st ed.). Boston: Houghton Mifflin, 1962.

Kirk, S. A., Berry, P. B., and Senf, G. M. A survey of attitudes concerning learning disabilities. *Journal of Learning Disabilities,* April, 1979, *12*(4), 239–245.

Kirk, S. A. and Gallagher, J. J. *Educating exceptional children, 3rd ed.* Boston: Houghton Mifflin, 1979.

Knoblock, H., and Pasamanick, B. The developmental behavioral approach to the neurologic examination in infancy, *Child Development,* 1962, *33*, 181–198.

Kronick, D. The pros and cons of labeling, *Academic Therapy,* September, 1977, *13*(1), 101–104.

Lashley, K. S. *Brain mechanism and intelligence: A quantitative study of injuries to the brain.* Chicago: Univeristy of Chicago Press, 1929.

Lerner, J. *Learning Disabilities: Theory, Diagnosis, and Teaching Strategies.* 3rd ed. Boston: Houghton Mifflin, 1981.

_____. *Children with learning disabilities, 2nd ed.* Boston: Houghton Mifflin, 1976.

Lewis, R. S. *The other child grows up.* New York: Times Books, 1977.

Lewis, R. S., Strauss, A., and Lehtinen, L. *The other child, 2nd ed.* New York: Grune & Stratton, 1960.

Lewis, R. S. (with Strauss, A. and Lehtinen, L.). *The other child, 1st ed.* New York: Grune & Stratton, 1951.

McCarthy, J. and McCarthy, J. *Learning disabilities.* Boston: Allyn & Bacon, 1969.

Mercer, C. D., Forgnone, C., and Wolking, W. D. Definitions of learning disabilities used in the United States, *Journal of Learning Disabilities*, July, 1976, *9*(6), 376–386.

Messinger, J. F. Forum: Emotionally disturbed and brain-damaged children—should we mix them? *Exceptional Children*, 1965, *32*, 237–238.

Meyen, E. L., and Moran, M. R. A perspective on the unserved mildly handicapped, *Exceptional Children*, April, 1979, *45*(7), 526–530.

Millon, T. *Modern psychopathology: A biosocial approach to maladaptive learning and functioning.* Philadelphia: W. B. Saunders, 1969.

Mink, L. Adaptation of the Montessori method in developing visual perception in the special child. In Jerome Hellmuth (Ed.), *The special child in century 21.* Seattle: Special Child Publications, 1964.

Morris, D. P., and Dozier, E. Childhood behavior disorders: subtler organic factors, *Texas State Journal of Medicine*, March, 1961, *57*(3), 134–138.

Myers, P., and Hammill, D. *Methods for learning disorders, 2nd ed.* New York: Wiley, 1976.

National Advisory Committee on Handicapped Children. *Special Education for Handicapped Children (First Annual Report).* Washington, D.C.: U.S. Department of Health, Education and Welfare, January 31, 1968.

Newcomer, P., and Hammill, D. *Psycholinguistics in the schools.* Columbus, Ohio: Charles E. Merrill, 1975.

Ohlson, E. *Identification of specific learning disabilities.* Champaign, Illinois: Research Press, 1978.

Peters, J. E., Davis, J. S., Goolsby, C. M., Clements, S. D. and Hicks, T. J. *Physician's Handbook: Screening for MBD.* CIBA Medical Horizons, 1973.

Sarason, S. B. *Psychological problems in mental deficiency.* New York: Harper and Brothers, 1959.

Siegel, E. Forum: Learning disabilities: Substance or shadow, *Exceptional Children*, Feb., 1968, *34*(6), 433–438.

Smith, M. D., Coleman, J. M., Dokecki, P. R., and Davis, E. E., "Intellectual characteristics of school labeled learning disabled children, *Exceptional Children*, March, 1977, *43*(6), 352–357.

Stevens, G. D., and Birch, J. W., A proposal for clarification of the terminology used to describe brain-injured children. *Exceptional Children*, May, 1957, *23*, 346–349.

Strauss, A. A., and Kephart, N., *Psychopathology and education of the brain-injured child, volume II.* New York: Grune & Stratton, 1955.

Strauss, A. A., and Lehtinen, L. E., *Psychopathology and education of the brain-injured child, volume I.* New York: Grune & Stratton, 1947.

Tarnopol, L. Introduction to neurogenic learning disorders. In Lester Tarnopol (Ed.), *Learning disorders in children.* Boston: Little, Brown, 1971.

Thompson, L. J. Language disorders in men of eminence, *Journal of Learning Disabilities*, January, 1971, *4*, 34–45.

Whieldon, J. A. Medical implications. In Edward C. Grover and Amy A. Allen (Eds.), *A demonstration project for brain damaged children in Ohio.* Columbus, Ohio: Department of Education, 1962.

Wiederholt, J. L. Historical perspectives on the education of the learning disabled. In Lester Mann and D. A. Sabatino (Eds.), *The second review of special education.* Philadelphia: JSE Press, (Also New York: Grune & Stratton) 1974.

————. Adolescents with learning disabilities: The problem in perspective. In Lester Mann, Libby Goodman, and J. Lee Wiederholt (Eds.), *Teaching the learning-disabled adolescent.* Boston: Houghton Mifflin, 1978.

Neurological Aspects of Learning Disabilities

2

A review of the literature indicates a strong link between neurological function and learning disabilities. To gain insight into the way LD children perform, to comprehend the implications of the neurological viewpoint, to evaluate new research, to understand and apply the diagnostic process, and to plan appropriate interventions, one needs a basic knowledge of the central nervous system (CNS) as it relates to learning disabilities.

ANATOMY OF THE BRAIN

The CNS includes the spinal cord and the brain, and is composed of nerve cells and nonneural cells (glia). The spinal cord carries ascending and descending fibers which convey sensory information to the brain and autonomic and motor messages from the brain. The spinal cord is an important center for the integration of motor activities.

The brain, a complex organ containing billions of complexly interconnected cells, is composed of the brain stem, the cerebellum, and the cerebrum or cerebral cortex. All parts of the brain are involved in learning. The brain stem and cerebellum are considered phylogenetically "old" structures, whereas the cerebrum or "new" brain is considered a recent development in evolution, and is a highly developed organ only in higher mammals, especially humans. Many researchers feel that a recapitulation of the stages of evolution through developmental levels in a child's growth from embryo to fetus occurs—and some similar embryological events occur in all vertebrates (Strauss & Lehtinen, 1947).

The *midbrain* houses the *reticular formation* which extends from the spinal cord to the thalamus. The reticular formation is believed to activate or "arouse" electrical activity in the cerebral cortex and play a role in the regulation of sleep and waking and in the arousal of behavior (Thompson, 1975). The reticular-activating system appears to be the brain's filtering mechanism which reduces irrelevant stimuli. If the system is defective and overstimulation occurs, attention-control problems can arise (see p. 42).

The *cerebellum* is involved in the control and coordination of the motor system, especially muscle effectors. It receives connections from the vestibular system, spinal sensory fibers, auditory and visual systems, the reticular formation, and the cerebral cortex. It communicates to the rest of the brain through the brain stem and sends fibers to the thalamus, reticular formation, and other brain stem structures (Thompson, 1975, p. 103). Damage to the cortex of the cerebellum can effect motor performance, for example, rate, direction, and steadiness.

The *cerebrum* is divided into two hemispheres, the right and left, which are connected by a bundle of fibers called the corpus callosum, allowing for instantaneous communication between both hemispheres. The surface contains many convolutions, that is, ridges (gyri), valleys (sulci), and fissures (deep sulci), which increase the surface area. The hemispheres are not symmetrical but complementary. The dynamic relationship between the subsystems of the brain is seen in the inter-

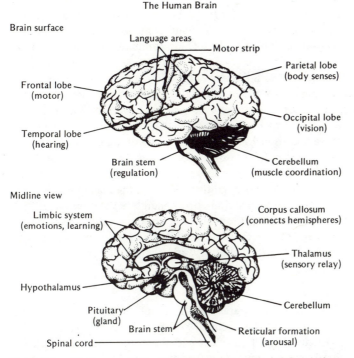

Figure 2-1. The human brain. Top: the surface of the left hemisphere of the human brain, with major areas and their functions labelled. Bottom: a midline view of the right hemisphere with the major areas/ structures and their functions labeled. (Adapted from Timothy J. Teyler. "The Brain Sciences," in Jeanne S. Chall and Allan F. Mirsky, eds. *Education and the Brain*, Chicago, Ill.: The University of Chicago Press, 1978, p. 10.

dependent functions. Some functions are governed by both hemispheres and others are controlled largely by only one.

Motor activities are controlled by the motor strip (precentral gyrus) in the opposite hemisphere; that is, movements of the left hand are controlled by the motor strip in the right hemisphere. Visual and auditory functions on both the left and right sides are controlled by both hemispheres. The left hemisphere is dominant for language skills in most people whether right- or left-handed, although a small percentage of right-handed and a larger percentage of left-handed individuals appear to have speech located in the right hemisphere (Herron, 1976; Geschwind, 1968; Rossi and Rosadini, 1967).

Much of our understanding of the functioning of each cerebral hemisphere has been gained from studies of patients who have had the corpus callosum severed in order to eliminate severe, possibly fatal, seizures. Investigators have used apparatus and procedures that can test sensory and motor functions of each side independently or together (Gazzaniga et al., 1965; Sperry & Gazzaniga, 1967; Milner, 1967; 1972; Ornstein, 1978). Most researchers have found that verbal expression (both written and spoken) is processed in the left hemisphere. The right hemisphere perceives, learns, and remembers visual stimuli but cannot originate speech or writing about them.

According to Ornstein (1977), the left hemisphere is considered to operate in a concrete, rational manner. It controls language, rational cognition, and a sense of time. The right hemisphere operates intuitively and controls spatial relationships, creative behavior, and intuitive thinking. The left interprets verbal information; the right, visual.

Each hemisphere is divided into four lobes (see Figure 2-1): frontal, temporal, parietal, and occipital, so named for the bones of the skull covering them. The function of each lobe differs. Sensory, motor, and associational zones are located within them. The sensory zones control bodily sensation and the motor zones control movement. Some of the associational areas are involved with understanding of language and the perception of complex sensory information. The precise function of other areas of the associational zones have not yet been clearly demonstrated but are assumed to be involved in complex cognitive tasks. (As the mammalian scale of evolution ascends, the amount of association cortex increases (Thompson, 1975).) An important function of the association areas is communication between the modalities. The development of speech requires the ability to form stable intermodal relationships, particularly visual-auditory and tactile-auditory (Geschwind, 1965).

Frontal Lobe

The *frontal* lobe is a relatively large area of the brain. It plays an important part in regulating cortical arousal (Thompson, 1975, p. 447). A reciprocal arrangement between the reticular activating system and the frontal cortex appears to exist. Activation of the reticular formation causes the frontal lobes to act, which, in turn, signals the reticular activating system to decrease the activity. Researchers believe that destruction of frontal cortex can lead to hyperactive behavior.

The anterior section of the frontal lobe is connected to the brain stem and other parts of the brain and is believed to control abstract thinking, judgment, and tactfulness. Damage leads to deficits in short-term memory, the learning of new tasks, and hyperactivity (Thompson, 1975, p. 446-448). Spatial and temporal memory are affected by right frontal lobe damage, while verbal memory is affected by lesions in the left side (Thompson, pp. 548-549).

Control of basic motor movements from wiggling a toe to swallowing is organized in an orderly way along the motor strip. The *premotor strip*, which is anterior to the motor strip, is responsible for more complex motor movements.

Broca's area is located directly below the motor strip generally in the left hemisphere, adjacent to the region that controls muscle movements related to speech. The coordination of these muscles is believed to be controlled in Broca's area. Damage in this area leads to motor aphasia, with slow, labored speech without loss of content.* Broca's area is connected by pathways to *Wernicke's area*, found in the left posterior association cortex and part of the auditory association area. Wernicke's area is the region for language production and concept formation, and controls comprehension of all forms of oral and written language. Pathways extend from Wernicke's area to and from visual and auditory cortex in both hemispheres. Depending upon the locus of damage, different types of language disorders can occur.

Temporal Lobe

The primary auditory cortex, found in the *temporal lobe*, controls reception, comprehension, and interpretation of sound. A lesion in this area causes receptive aphasia, an inability to comprehend spoken language. The individual can hear but cannot understand what is said.

The specific functions of the rest of the temporal lobe are not well known. Stimulation of the temporal lobe reportedly causes auditory noises, vestibular disorders (dizziness), auditory or visual hallucinations, complex emotional behavior, fear, confusion, and memory deficits (Penfield & Roberts, 1959). Individuals who have had bilateral temporal lobectomies become impaired in the ability to form new associations and remember recent events, although they can still recall the distant past. Similarly, although verbal awareness memory is damaged, motor skill learning remains intact (Milner, 1967; 1972).

Parietal Lobe

The *parietal lobe* is the primary receptor cortex for impulses from the sensory receptors in the skin. These receptors enable us to be aware of body position and movements and to make tactile discriminations relative to size, shape, temperature, texture, and so on. The parietal lobe is also the primary receptive cortex for the integration of language, reading, and writing processes. In addition, Geschwind (1965) believes that the parietal association area is important in the development of language since object memory depends on association between other modalities and audition.

---

* Aphasia is a loss or impairment of speech. There are some disagreements in the definition of aphasia in regard to children. Some theorists differentiate between acquired aphasia, the loss of established language skills, and developmental aphasia, a failure to develop language skills. Others, such as Eisenson, believe that childhood aphasia is the result of CNS dysfunction with language disorders occurring in association with such behavioral deficits as perseveration, hyperactivity, and emotional lability (Bloom & Lahey, 1978).

Occipital Lobe

The primary visual area, the *striate cortex*, is located in the occipital lobe in the posterior region of each hemisphere. Blindness results when there is belated destruction of the occipital cortex. Damage in specific areas leads to specific visual deficits such as loss of peripheral vision or blindness in part of the visual field.

Cells of the Brain

Although just a few millimeters thick, the cortex contains several distinct layers composed of cells differing in type, size, and number. In general, the layers contain the termination of axons, output neurons, local processing neurons, and glia (non-neural) cells.

Two major types of cells found in the brain are the *neuron* and *glia*. There are approximately 12 billion neurons and 120 billion glia cells in the brain. The function of the glia cells is not certain. Some researchers presumed that their main function was to provide support for the neurons, but they may also have other functions, for example, exchange of nutrients and removal of wastes (Thompson, 1975, p. 91). Glia are believed to affect the excitability of neurons, and they have also been found to change during motor learning. Frostig and Maslow (1979) suggest that since they do regenerate they may help re-establish lost functions caused by brain damage.

The total number of neurons (between 20 and 200 billion at birth) never increase. Indeed, thousands are lost daily never to be replaced (Teyler, 1978). The immature neurons, which in general are spheroidal and lacking processes, change their shape rapidly as development takes place and the cells put out axons and dendrites. Pysh and Weiss (1979) report that mice raised in an environment that encouraged physical activity, in contrast to littermates raised in an environment where movement was severely restricted, developed heavier brains and motor neurons with larger dendritic branches and more dendritic spines. These results suggest that the development of motor neurons can be modified by experience.

Although there are different types of neurons found in different parts of the brain, all have certain features in common: short, branching processes, *dendrites*, which extend from the cell body; a cell body containing the nucleus; and the *axon*, a long process (sometimes extending to three feet) frequently covered by a myelin sheath.

Myelin protects and insulates the axon, and speeds neural transmission. Speed of transmission of neural impulse along the axon is determined by the diameter of the fiber and the degree of myelinization. The myelin sheath allows the axon to conduct impulses at a more rapid rate. There are gaps in the myelin sheath called nodes of Ranvier. Saltatory* impulse transmission can occur between adjacent nodes, speeding the conduction rate. The myelinization process is not complete at birth and continues in some regions until puberty. Myelinization proceeds according to phylogenetic development from the sensory-motor and limbic areas of the brain to the association areas.

Areas that myelinate last are more vulnerable to injury and a developmental

---

* That is, the transmission leaps across the axons and need not travel the length of the fiber.

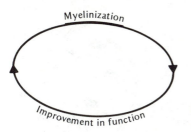

Figure 2-2. The relationship between myelinization and function.

delay in the myelinization sequence can also cause problems in motor development, sensory processing, and/or cross-modal integration.

The absence of a given brain function (that is, the child may not as yet have reached a particular developmental level) does not prevent myelinization. However, it has been found that myelin development is stimulated and accelerated by function (Figure 2-2). Improvement in speed, steadiness, and strength coincides with myelin development. The degree to which myelinization is completed enables us to assess the degree of maturation of the CNS.

The *synapse* is the space between two neurons or a neuron and a muscle. Synapses are found mainly at the cell body and the dendrites. "A typical neuron in the brain has thousands of synaptic terminals from other neurons forming synapses on it, and it in turn may form synapses on many other neurons" (Thompson, 1975, p. 95). Information (input) is received through the dendrites and is processed. The result of the processing (output) leaves the cell via the axon. When the message reaches the axon terminal (bouton), a neurotransmitter (chemical) is released which diffuses across the synaptic gap, attaches to receptor sites in the dendrite of the next neuron, and either excites or inhibits that neuron. The neurotransmitter is stored inside the axon terminal and is released only when the neuron is active.

Neurons conduct in an all-or-none-manner. When action potential is produced, that is, the discharge threshold is reached, the impulse will travel through the neuron (see Figure 2-3). The size of the nerve cell discharge is constant. The amplitude and velocity of the discharge are determined by the nature of the axon, that is, its size and the presence or absence of myelin (Thompson, 1975, p. 130). The ability of a synapse to produce an action potential depends on several factors: the type of neurotransmitter, the transmembrane charge; the amount of neurotransmitter released; the distance of the synapse from the "trigger zone" on the axon (axon hillock); the activities of other synapses on the recipient cell; and the past history of the synapse—some synapses are changed by prior "experience," (Teyler, 1978, p. 8).

Neurotransmitters

Communication in the brain depends on chemical neurotransmitters. These transmitters, which are stored in synaptic terminals, are released by electrical impulses and flow to the dendrites or cell body of another neuron. Some of the neurotransmitters which have been identified are: acetylcholine, norepinephrine, dopamine, and serotonin. Each neuron appears to be capable of secreting chemicals which in turn stimulate or inhibit other neurons. Neurons have many thousands of receptors which can react to the neurotransmitter. The transmitters are localized in specific

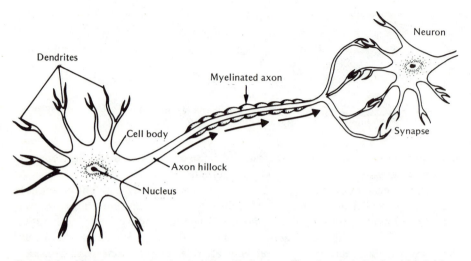

Figure 2-3. Model neuron showing impulse conduction. The electrical signals which initiate the interaction between nerve cells are propogated along the outer membrane of the axons.

neuron clusters whose axons are linked to specific brain regions (Iversen, 1979). The relationship between the presence of specific neurotransmitters and behavior is being investigated by many researchers. Many drugs that affect the moods and emotions appear to alter the levels of neurotransmitters (Schildkraut & Kety, 1967). Sedative drugs decrease the level while mood elevators increase them. The effect of drugs in the treatment of the learning disabled is discussed in Chapter 6.

DOMINANCE AND LATERALITY CONTROVERSIES

Failure to establish cerebral dominance in the left hemisphere was considered by Orton (1937) to be the cause of developmental *alexia*, a severe reading disorder which included among its symptoms the reversal of letters and words (*Strephosymbolia*). He believed that there are exact sensory records in the brain, *engrams*, which could be retrieved when required. According to Orton, these engrams exist in both hemispheres in opposite orientation and, if hemispheric dominance has not been established, at times the incorrect, mirrored stimulus will be retrieved. He reasoned that, since the language center is in the left hemisphere and the left hemisphere also controls movement of the right side of the body, right-handed and right-sided activities should be encouraged, thereby strengthening the use of the left hemisphere for language development as well.

Although today Orton's theory appears to carry little weight, "The notion that learning disabilities are somehow related to faulty cerebral dominance is an old notion that still is very much alive today" (Kinsbourne & Hiscock, 1978, p. 171).

Laterality is frequently judged by preferred hand use. However, measures of eye and ear preference are also included. Inconsistency of sidedness is called crossed, or mixed, dominance. When all three measures indicate same side preference (RRR or LLL), laterality is considered to be established.

The determination of handedness can be difficult to ascertain. There are people who use 1) both hands with equal skill, 2) both hands, but are hand-specific for different activities, and 3) both hands hesitantly for any activity; their performance is poor, uncoordinated, and awkward.

Some studies indicate that the incidence of left-handers and those with mixed dominance is greater among the handicapped than in the general population. Several researchers, however, dispute these findings (Yule & Rutter, 1976; Kinsbourne & Hiscock, 1978). As Kinsbourne and Hiscock note, many normal children have mixed eye/hand dominance and many LD do not. Orton (1937) considered the child who showed mixed dominance to be at risk, whether left-handed and right-eyed, or right-handed and left-eyed. Denckla (1978) finds nonright-preferring children to be at risk for LD. Research has suggested that brain damage early in life can cause a shift in function from the injured hemisphere to the other (Penfield & Roberts, 1959; Heilman, 1978). This may account for many of the cases of mixed dominance.

Based on the data available, consistency, rather than handedness or mixed dominance, seems to be a critical factor, with children who use both hands with hesitancy at greatest risk. A relationship, however, does not imply causality; the lack of established handedness does not appear to cause LD. An unknown "factor," which either delays or prevents the establishment of laterality while also affecting the ability to develop skills needed for satisfactory academic performance, may exist. To date, training right-sided motor development has not improved either reading or language performance.

SPEECH AND LANGUAGE

The language functions of most people originate in the left hemisphere. Early damage in either hemisphere, before the age of five, inteferes with normal language development. By the fifth year of age, language lateralization is complete (Krashen, 1973).

If there is major damage to the left hemisphere, the right hemisphere can help develop language, although some aspects of it may be deficient: for example, slower processing and retrieval, weak syntactic, grammatic, and sequencing ability, and impaired short-term memory. The possibility of the nondamaged hemisphere taking over speech functions is more likely before and during maturation than after (Rudel, 1978; Heilman, 1978; Geschwind, 1968). Delayed effects may arise if the damaged portion has not yet matured and is not yet being utilized, for example, damage to areas related to reading would not be observed for many years.

Heilman (1978) suggests that there are fibers in the corpus callosum which go to similar areas in both hemispheres. When the left hemisphere language area is operating well, the left hemisphere inhibits the right hemisphere from acquiring language via fibers from the corpus callosum to the right hemisphere. If either the left hemisphere or the corpus callosum function improperly, inhibition does not take place and the right hemisphere develops language function. The inhibition linkages grow stronger with maturity. In addition, the right hemisphere may become so committed to visio-spatial skills that, in the adult, it may be unable to acquire language even after left hemisphere damage or severing of the corpus callosum. Rudel (1978) believes that with early damage in the left hemisphere there is a release of language potential (rather than a shift of function) in the right hemisphere. This viewpoint is similar to Heilman's theory of inhibition fibers.

Development consists in part of changing strategies. Before ten years of age, spatial tasks rely on language; thereafter, nonverbal strategies come into play. Better performance can be caused by new strategies rather than neural reorganization for compensation. The corpus callosum completes myelinization at about ten years of age. This structural change can also cause improved performance. In general, given the varied possibilities, the earlier the damage occurs, the greater the likelihood of recovery (Rudel, 1978).

REFERENCES

Benson, F. B., and Geschwind, N. Developmental gerstmann syndrome, *Neurology*, 1970, *20*, 293–298.

Bloom, L., and Lahey, M. *Language development and language disorders*. New York: Wiley, 1978.

Denckla, M. B. Minimal Brain Dysfunction. In Jeanne S. Chall and Allan F. Mirsky (Eds.), *Education and the brain*. Chicago: University of Chicago Press, 1978.

Frostig, M. and Maslow, P. Neuropsychological contributions to education. *Journal of Learning Disabilities*. 12(8), 538–552. October, 1979.

Gazzaniga, M. S., Bogen, J. E., and Sperry, R. W. Observations on visual perception after disconnection of the cerebral hemisphere in man, *Brain*, 1965, *88*, 221–236.

Geschwind, N. Disconnexion syndromes in animals and man, *Brain*, 1965, *88*, 237–294.

————. Neurological foundations of language. In Helmer Myklebust (Ed.), *Progress in learning disabilities, vol. 1*. New York: Grune & Stratton, 1968.

Heilman, K. M. Language and the brain: Relationship of localization of language function to the acquisition and loss of various aspects of language. In Jeanne S. Chall and Allan F. Mirsky (Eds.), *Education and the brain: The Seventy-seventh Yearbook of the National Society for the Study of Education, part II*. Chicago: University of Chicago Press, 1978.

Herron, J. Southpaws: How different are they? *Psychology Today*, March, 1976, 50–56.

Iversen, L. L. The chemistry of the brain, *Scientific American*, September, 1979, *241*:(3) 134–149.

Kinsbourne, M., and Hiscock, M. Cerebral lateralization and cognitive development. In Jeanne S. Chall and Allan F. Mirsky (Eds.), *Education and the brain*. Chicago: University of Chicago Press, 1978.

Krashen, S. D. Lateralization, language learning and the critical period: some new evidence, *Language Learning*, 1973, *23*, 63–74.

Milner, B. Brain mechanisms suggested by studies of temporal lobes. In Clark H. Millikan and Frederic L. Darley (Eds.), *Brain mechanisms underlying speech and language: Conference proceedings*. New York: Grune & Stratton, 1967.

————. Disorders of learning after temporal lobe lesions in man, *Clinical Neurosurgery*, 1972, *19*:421–446.

Ornstein, R. The duality of the mind: a symposium in print, *Instructor*, January, 1977.

———. The split and the whole brain, *Human Nature*, 1, May, 1978, 76–83.

Orton, S. T. *Reading, writing and speech problems in children.* New York: W. W. Norton, 1937.

Penfield, W., and Roberts, L. *Speech and brain-mechanisms.* Princeton, New Jersey: Princeton University Press, 1959.

Pysh, J. J., and Weiss, G. M. Exercise during development induces an increase in Purkinje cell dendritic tree size, *Science*, Oct. 12, 1979, 230–232.

Rossi, G. F., and Rosadini, G. Experimental analysis of cerebral dominance in men. In M. C. Millikan and F. L. Darley (Eds.), *Brain mechanisms underlying speech and language*, New York: Grune & Stratton, 1967.

Rudel, R. G. Neuroplasticity: implications for development and education. In Jeanne S. Chall and Allan F. Mirsky (Eds.), *Education and the brain*. Chicago: The University of Chicago Press, 1978.

Schildkraut, J., and Kety, S. Biogenic amines and emotion, *Science*, 1967, *156*, 21–30.

Schwartz, J. H. The transport of substances in nerve cells, *Scientific American*, April, 1980, 152–171.

Sperry, R. W., and Gazzaniga, M. S. Language following surgical disconnection of the hemispheres. In M. C. Millikan and F. L. Darley (Eds.), *Brain mechanisms underlying speech and language*, New York: Grune & Stratton, 1967.

Strauss, A. A., and Lehtinen, L. E. *Psychopathology and education of the brain-injured child.* New York: Grune & Stratton, 1947.

Teyler, T. J. The brain sciences: an introduction. In Jeanne S. Chall and Allan F. Mirsky (Eds.), *Education and the brain: The Seventy-seventh Yearbook of the National Society for the Study of Education, part II.* Chicago, Ill.: The University of Chicago Press, 1978.

Thompson, R. F. *Introduction to physiological psychology.* New York: Harper & Row, 1975.

Yule, W., and Rutter, M. Epidemiology and social implications of specific reading retardation. In R. M. Knights and D. J. Kakkir (Eds.), *The neuropsychology of learning disorders*. Baltimore: University Park Press, 1976.

Characteristics

3

BASIS FOR CHARACTERISTICS OF LEARNING-DISABLED CHILDREN

The characteristics of LD children flow from two basic sources. The first is the definitionally stipulated brain injury (or MBD) which results directly in "process impairment" in such basic areas as: coordination, perception, memory, language, and cognition. The overall neurological impairment can be conceptualized as diminished functioning of several brain mechanisms. One is the *filtering mechanism*, in which the "old brain" (reticular) does not adequately filter out extraneous sensory data, but instead sends *all* stimuli to the projection areas of the "new brain" (cerebrum)—hence the expression, "stimulus-bound" to describe brain-injured children (Strauss & Kephart, 1955) (see pages 32-33). Gibson viewed perceptual learning, itself, as a filtering process, "an increase in the ability to extract information from the environment as a result of experience and practice with stimulation coming from it" (1969, p. 63). Another is the *checking mechanism* whereby the new brain fails to control, govern, or "*check*" emotional impulses emanating from the old brain (see pages 32-33, 34).

The second major source of the LD child's behavioral syndrome consists of secondary psychological factors. That is, given a child who, because of organicity, is unable to negotiate smoothly with his sensory-perceptual world, it is only natural for a certain degree of stress to build up. Repeated frustration and failure lead to rejection which, in turn, generates such traits as anxiety, depression, irritability, hostility, and poor self-concept. Although the emotional factors are secondary to the neurological, they are frequently considered to be of graver consequence. Kranes (1980, p. 214) feels that "the psychological blows society heaps upon them," rather than the brain injury, per se, are at the root of the LD behavioral syndrome.

COMMON CHARACTERISTICS OF THE
LD POPULATION

Because the traits of LD are so numerous, researchers have frequently grouped them in categories. For example, Cartwright, Cartwright, and Ward (1981) subsume the array of LD characteristics under four major domains: cognitive, language, motor, and social. Myers and Hammill (1976) list six overall areas of disorder: (1) motor activity, (2) emotionality, (3) perception, (4) symbolization, (5) attention, and (6) memory. Clements (1966) utilized 15 distinct categories of symptomatology for identifying LD children, including: physical characteristics, sleep characteristics, social-relationship capacities, characteristics of social behavior, and characteristics of behavior. Krupp and Schwartzberg (1960, p. 65) believe that the brain-injured child's behavioral traits can be summarized into four areas of deficit: (1) faulty powers of inhibition, (2) impaired perception, (3) predisposition to anxiety, and (4) erratic behavior induced by secondary psychological defense mechanisms. We prefer to list and to treat traits singly rather than in groups because categorizing traits is an arbitrary process. For example, Clements (1966) lists perseveration as a disorder of attention, whereas Myers and Hammill (1976) place it under disorders of emotionality. Cartwright, Cartwright, and Ward (1981, p. 108) find that some sources place hyperactivity in the social domain but other list it in the motor category.

The following traits we have chosen to elaborate upon meet at least one of these criteria: (1) authors continue to refer to them (many of them were listed in surveys by Beck (1961) and Clements (1966) in which a number of authors were polled regarding their opinions of characteristics that typify brain-injured and MBD children);(2) they have frequently appeared in our own observations (formal as well as informal) of LD children and young adults over the past 20 years; and (3) where they exist, they constitute a significant handicap in the LD child's adjustment. (The order in which we discuss them is arbitrary.)

Perceptual Deficits. LD children are generally thought to be defective in the area of perception. In fact, both terms—learning disabled and perceptually handicapped—are often interchanged.

In the simplest depiction of perceptual functioning, a hierarchy is postulated: sensation (immediate arousal by the stimulation of a sensory organ, but devoid of meaning) precedes perception (the process of organizing and giving initial meaning to the raw sensory data), and leads to conceptualization (abstraction, or generalization of ideas based upon the newly formed percepts).

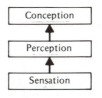

Although this basic model is convenient as an introduction to the subject, it is not totally accurate. In reality the sensation-perception-conception triad is far more complex (Forgus & Melamud, 1976; Gibson, 1969). Even the lowest level, sensa-

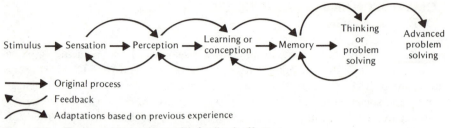

Original process

Feedback

Adaptations based on previous experience

Figure 3-1. The perceptual process with feedback effect.

tion, is not a simple stimulus-response mechanism since the interaction with the environment (experience) affects the choice of stimuli to which we respond. A "city person" walking in the woods with a naturalist may be aware of plants and trees in general, while the naturalist would be able to differentiate among them and even pick out the tracks of the animals inhabiting the woods.

Feedback learning, (i.e., the ability to store and utilize information acquired through experience and memory) modifies the selection and interpretation of stimuli. This holds even when the original stimulus is no longer available.* As new learning occurs, the perception of stimuli is changed. The stored data now are the models by which new sensations and perceptions are judged and are also used in problem-solving of all types, that is, thinking. Perceptions become more complex and modified by experience, and the individual is able to engage in more advanced abstract thinking and problem-solving. (See Figure 3-1.)

Several areas of perception have been identified: sensory input modalities (e.g., visual, auditory, tactile); whole and part perception; form perception; directional perception and social perception. In addition cross-modal integration and modality preference are related areas which have been studied with respect to the performance of learning-disabled children.

In order to perceive (used in the broadest sense), one must be able to: a) discriminate, that is recognize similarities and differences in stimuli along various dimensions; b) tell the figure from the ground; c) associate the stimuli with previous experience, that is, generalize; d) store the impression for the future (learn); and e) retrieve or remember an individual stimulus or a sequence of stimuli (memory or imagery).

Auditory Perception. Auditory skills are subsumed under three main headings: acuity, perception, and comprehension. Auditory acuity is discussed in Chapter 5; listening and comprehension skills are included in Chapter 12 under Language Arts Skills.

Auditory perception problems appear to be the result of processing problems. Chalfant and Scheffelin (1969) identify seven steps in auditory processing:

1. attention to stimuli
2. sound versus no sound
3. sound localization (source)
4. discriminating sounds varying on one dimension
5. discriminating sounds on more than one dimension

* What is retrieved is sometimes referred to as mental imagery if it represents a particular object or even a melody. There are several dimensions to memory: short and long term, meaningful and nonmeaningful, sequential and nonsequential, spatial, and temporal. The many combinations of these dimensions impact upon learning.

6. sound preselected as figure versus sound preselected as ground

7. identifying the sound source

Deficits in any of these steps can cause poor performance in identifying sounds, discriminating among sounds, reproducing pitch, rhythm, and melody, selecting the significant sounds from others, combining speech sounds into words and sentences, and understanding environmental sounds. These problems are not the result of deficits in acuity.

Visual Perception. Problems in visual processing have been identified as difficulty in examining details, identifying dominant cues, integrating stimuli to obtain meaning, classifying objects, and comparing the visual hypothesis with the actual object (taking a second look, so to speak) (Chalfant & Scheffelin, 1969).

Two main classes of visual processing tasks have been noted by Chalfant and Scheffelin: ocular-motor and cognitive. The ocular-motor tasks include distinguishing light from no light, seeing fine detail (acuity), binocular vision (overlapping of the vision from both eyes into one image), convergence (coordinated movement of the eyes), and scanning. Three types of scanning have been identified: 1) natural zig-zag movement that occurs when one looks around a room; 2) pursuit or tracking of a moving object, and 3) learned systematic movement used for reading.

Cognitive processing includes visual analysis (being aware of the component parts of the stimulus), visual integration (coordination of mental processes), and visual synthesis (combining the parts into a recognizable entity). Among the associated cognitive tasks are: 1) *spatial relationships*, 2) *visual discrimination* including *visual closure* (the recognition of an object though there is a lack of continuity or parts of the object are missing) and *figure-ground distinction*, and 3) *object recognition.*

Haptic Perception. Haptic perception refers to the integration and understanding of stimuli that are experienced through the tactile and kinesthetic systems. Tactile perception refers to the sense of touch and includes the feeling of pressure, temperature, pain, localization of stimuli, encompassing such variables as shape, size, texture, and consistency (hard, soft, viscous, etc.). The movement and stimulation of joints and deeper tissue as well as dynamic muscular exertion provide kinesthetic feedback stemming from a variety of data: posture, weight, balance, position in space, dynamic body movements, and so forth.

Haptic perception has received less direct emphasis despite the fact that "the development of the spatial world proceeds outward from the body, those areas open to manipulation and handling being structured first" (Strauss & Kephart, 1955, p. 75). The kinesthetic modality plays an important part in all of the perceptual-motor theories, however, since it is fundamental to the development of a reliable body image. Many components of the theories of Kephart, Barsch, Getman, and others—balance, posture, laterality and directionality,* midline crossing,** etc.— are all functions of the kinesthetic process.

---

* Laterality refers to sidedness—that is, the preference for using either the right side of the body (hand, eye, foot) or the left side, whereas directionality is the ability to extend this body image awareness of left–right, up–down, front–back into spatial events.

** Roach and Kephart (1966) state that "growth and motor development proceed from the axis of the body (midline) outward to the periphery" (p. 5). Many visual-motor tasks require midline crossing—the hand and/or the eye must move from one side of the body, approach the midline, cross it, and go over to the other side. Neurologically-handicapped children often encounter difficulty in this process. For example, they may "walk" the chalk across the board, thereby avoiding midline crossing (p. 54).

Since perception is such a basic, all-encompassing process, it stands to reason that impairment in this area can take its toll in a variety of ways. Auditory distortion can result in faulty speech patterns. Inadequate abilities in memory, discrimination, or sequencing—whether auditory or visual—can contribute to poor spelling, difficulty in recalling arithmetic facts, clerical errors, and so forth. Poor closure skills often lead to learning difficulties, in general, in that it becomes necessary for the learner to receive more than the average number of stimulus cues in order to comprehend. Kinesthetic imperception results in clumsiness, affecting such areas as penmanship, self-care skills, mechanical tasks, athletics, and driving a car. Tactile impairment also will have an adverse effect upon manual dexterity (Haeussermann, 1958); in addition, it can be associated with attention deficits (Eisenberg, 1964).

Ayres (1964) postulated that in normal individuals, the protective cutaneous afferent system (which responds to tactual stimuli with arousal, alertness, and movement) balances with the discriminative cutaneous afferent system (which enables us cognitively to interpret the tactual stimuli), while in brain-injured individuals, the protective system predominates, resulting in excitability and hyperactivity. Temporal distortion can feed into perservation. (That is, the LD child may experience difficulty in judging *when* to stop.)

However, perceptual impairment need not be regarded as irreversible, amelioration being a function of both experience and specialized instruction. Experience increases the ability to improve discrimination and filtering, enabling the individual to perceive with greater specificity and make finer distinctions more quickly (Forgus & Melamud, 1976). Piaget (1966) believes that perceptual activities are directed by active intelligence since perception depends on the individual's structuring of sensory information.

*Hyperactivity.** Psychoeducational reports of LD children frequently mention this trait, and, with the exception of marked underachievement, it is probably teachers' leading complaint regarding the behavior pattern of LD children (Myers & Hammill, 1976, p. 27). Smith (1979, p. 18) refers to it as "uncoordinated, random, unthinking, unfocused, restless, excessive movement stemming from an immature brain." Lynn (1979, p. 5) believes that hyperactivity associated with the LD child denotes "general motor restlessness, inability to sit still, to sleep at night, and often also an incapacity to restrain impulses." It is generally conceded that the typical LD hyperactive child is not really overactive on a consistent basis. His behavior should instead be viewed as *disorganized activity* (Peters, Davis, Goolsby, Clements, and Hicks, 1973, p. 6). The hyperactivity is not "across-the-board." It may very well be that his total energy level is neither more nor less than that of normal children but, because he "misses the point" so frequently, he may be active when we expect him to be quiet, and quiet when activity is warranted. Obviously his deviant active behavior is noted more frequently than his inappropriate inactive moments. The hyperactive LD child is not "a motor machine run amok" since this trait is not

---

* The term hyperkinesis is often used interchangeably with hyperactivity. However, some authors contend that they are not the same. Lerner (1971, p. 54) points out that hyperkinesis represents extreme hyperactivity and is regarded by neurologists as one of the soft signs of brain injury. Davids (1971) lists hyperactivity as one of seven subtraits of hyperkinesis. The others are short attention span, variability (unpredictable behavior and wide fluctuations in performance), impulsivity, irritability, explosiveness, and poor school work.

manifested during unstructured times; rather it comes to the forefront in task-oriented situations—especially when the task is not chosen by the child himself, but is imposed upon him by others (Bryan & Bryan, 1978, p. 136). Zentall (1975) contends that hyperactive behavior may prove utilitarian in the case of LD children, functioning as a self-regulation control.

> The increase in activity typically associated with the hyperactive child may well be an attempt to increase insufficient stimulation, rather than being a consequence of overwhelming stimulation. Using this model, activity can be seen as a regulator which maintains optimal stimulation for the child (p. 552).

Hyperactivity in brain-injured children, according to Bender (1949), can be regarded "as an effort continually to contact the physical and social environment, to reexperience and integrate the perceptual experiences in a continual effort to gain some orientation in the world" (p. 410).

Distractibility. Strauss and Lehtinen (1947, pp. 25-26) point out two overall aspects of distractibility. First is the "forced responsiveness" to extraneous data, stemming from the LD child's inability to filter out the background information that should remain in the background. He is constantly exploring his environment—looking, listening, and touching. What should remain in the background often leaps to the foreground. We call him "stimulus bound"—he is at the mercy of all stimuli. When eating he will fidget with the glasses, napkins, silverware. When washing, he may begin an elaborate game with the soap. When writing, he may become overly attentive to the feel of the paper against his finger and the sight of the pencil as it moves through the air rather than concentrate on the task at hand. Lynn (1979, pp. 5-6) points out that "[the] child's attention is easily drawn away—by light and shadow, sounds, random movements, even by his or her own body sensations."

The second aspect of distractibility evolves from parts-whole confusion. The LD child does not always grasp the "wholeness" of what he sees and hears, but perceives only the parts. He may concentrate too much on one isolated letter instead of the entire word, on the metal tip of the shoelace instead of upon the complete act of lacing shoes, upon a relatively insignificant detail of a paragraph during a reading activity instead of upon the main idea of that selection.

There is a strong connection between incidental learning ability and attentiveness. Optimally a child should be proficient in both. Unfortunately, LD children usually are deficient in these factors. In all likelihood, true incidental learning is not subtractive but additive. It may connote the ability to pay attention to some background detail *while not losing sight of the foreground.* Nevertheless, at the extremes, the reciprocal relationship becomes evident: if the child pays attention to the task at hand completely, then he is not learning incidentally. On the other hand, if he does considerable—almost total—incidental learning, he is then, of course, not paying attention to the foreground. Very likely his inability to do two things at once hinders him. Ideally a learner should blend the two. Payne, Polloway, Smith, and Payne (1977, p. 24) believe "it is incumbent upon the teacher to provide a classroom environment that promotes acquisition of information in this fashion [that is, incidental learning] through bulletin boards, displays, and appropriate models. At the same time, this effort must be balanced against the desire to avoid distracting the child's attention from the instructional task."

In our endeavor to help the LD child improve in this area, we must realize that attention is multidimensional (see page 155). Some of these aspects of attention are: arousal time, focus, vigilance, attention span, scanning, pursuit, the quality of attention (e.g., can he maintain heightened attention or is it lackadaisical?), etcetera. Does he pay attention adequately to distal stimuli but find considerable problems with proximal ones—a condition typical of many LD children—or is the converse true? Is he confused, that is, overly stimulated by people as opposed to things? We must also seek to understand the difference between passive attention and active attention. For example, many LD children can watch television programs for hours on end behaving appropriately—that is, they seem like any other child watching T.V. shows. However, when called upon to converse with others, their attentional deficits leap to the forefront because they are expected to contribute something to the conversation, not just absorb sensory stimuli.

It should be pointed out that vividness of stimuli, per se, does not dictate whether or not that particular data is background or foreground. For example, Ross (1976, pp. 34–35) points out that ordinarily when reading, we tend to disregard defects in the face of the type; however, should the person be engaged in the actual task of proofreading, what was formerly irrelevant now becomes the chief area of concern. Motivation is a crucial factor for the LD child as well as for the nonhandicapped. Isn't the teenaged girl able to hear the "sweet nothings" that her dancing partner whispers above the blaring of the dance band? Doesn't the proud mother "only have eyes" for her child in the school play despite the fact that there are many possible sources of distraction—the stage settings, the lights, the rest of the cast, the audience, and so forth.

Impulsivity. There is a "driven" quality to impulsivity. "If you send [a LD child] upstairs for a handkerchief, he will race all the way, fling open the drawer, scatter its contents, and return with a dozen of them. If you tell him to wash his hands and face, he will dart into the bathroom, turn on all faucets full blast, splash about enthusiastically wetting the floors, walls and mirrors; then he will hurry out much wetter and, sometimes, a trifle cleaner.

He doesn't walk, he runs. He doesn't close doors, he slams them. He doesn't put his shoes in the closet, he throws them in" (Siegel, 1961, pp. 38–39).

The child who is reflective can wait, can delay, can postpone, can mull over answers and reflect upon a variety of solutions, whereas the LD child, since he is impulsive, often responds with the first, possibly trivial, unsophisticated or even irrelevant answer that pops into his head (Keogh & Donlon, 1972). Peters, Davis, Goolsby, Clements and Hicks (1973, p. 7) state: "The MBD child has difficulty holding back his talk or actions. If he thinks of something, he tends to blurt it out. If he sees a touchable object, he tends to reach out to handle it. ... He reacts before he has time to reflect, so that often he appears to be not thinking, guessing at answers from the first visual or auditory clues that present themselves."

Becker (1976) in an experiment involving "risk" and "non-risk" kindergarten children, learned that the risk children were more impulsive than the others. He further found them to be less flexible in that they were unable to alter their tempo—Becker refers to this as "conceptual tempo"—when going from simple to complex situations and when instructed to work faster or slower. Ross (1976) feels there is a strong relationship between impulsivity and selective attention—namely, if one is impulsive, he does not take the time to select the most relevant features from a perceptual field. Peters, Davis, Goolsby, Clements and Hicks (1973, p. 7) explain that ". . . such unchecked behavior is due to 'mild,' selective CNS damage, to minor genetic variations, or to extreme early deprivation wherein the more delicate inhibitory circuits of the brain are impaired or at least retarded in their schedule of development" (p. 4).

There are many ways in which the LD child's impulsivity will manifest itself both in the classroom as well as outside: guessing answers (whether oral or written), frequently missing the point (not taking the time to perceive and/or consider all the data which is available to him), interrupting others, motor-disinhibition (frequently reaching out to touch objects), rushing to be the first one finished in a test or to be first in a line, raising his hand feverishly even though he does not know the answer, changing the subject, speaking inappropriately (stemming from the inability to screen out his own inappropriate intrusive thoughts), and so forth.

Perseveration. Perseveration has often been defined as the tendency to continue with an activity long after there is any logical need to do so. The perseverative individual has been likened to a phonograph needle that gets stuck in one groove of the record and plays that portion over and over and over again. These children are thought to be perseverative owing to their neurological handicap: because they find it so difficult to integrate the myriad of sensory stimuli that impinge upon them into meaningful wholes, when they finally do structure a set of incomplete data, they seem reluctant to let go of this percept and begin another, more appropriate one. They cannot readily shift from one situation to another, so they *perseverate*—continue an activity that they are unable to cease or to modify although its appropriateness has waned. Smith (1978, p. 11) points out that LD children are frequently inflexible (another way of saying perseverative): "Swamped by an overload of sensations, in a world that often appears to him as an undifferentiated mass, he opts for one way to do things and rebels if there is to be a change. This child dreads the unknown and the unfamiliar. There is little that makes sense to him."

Perseveration is not a predictable factor. It can occur in a variety of situations and in different forms (Siegel, 1961, pp. 19-20). In writing a word, a perservative child may suddenly write one letter over and over again. In coloring with crayons, he may cover the entire page with a single color. Possibly stress plays a part in perseveration in that it tends to limit one's ability to interact *flexibly* with the environment. Thus, instead of confronting and integrating each new set of perceptual events, the LD child deals only with the original one. After all, it requires some degree of alertness and some effort to be able to manipulate abstracts and to reorganize incoming data continually. Ross (1976, p. 11) considers perseveration one aspect of deficit in selective attention. There may be additional explanations for perseveration other than the neurologically-based ones. Smith (1978, p. 11) states: "When we are most unsure of ourselves . . . we tend to become rigid and inflexible. When we are most confused . . . we tend to look for one answer. When we are overwhelmed . . . we want to cling to the familiar."

Whatever the cause, it is safe to say that the LD child's tendency to perseverate will hinder him in a variety of ways: socially (e.g., he may virtually ignore a third party during a conversation because he has fallen into the set pattern of conversing with only one other person); academically (e.g., he may continue to apply the addition process which was appropriate a few moments ago instead of now beginning subtraction) with respect to self-management in the classroom (e.g., continuing with the previous activity instead of beginning a new one which is now appropriate); and so on.

Disorganization. Disorganization is one of those traits that plague many LD children throughout their lives: in the playground, in school, in family living, at work. Disorganization can reflect the child's perceptual deficits. Authors (Smith, 1978, p. 2; Wilcox, 1970, p. 7) point out that the LD child's deficits in temporal orientation frequently render him disorganized. This can result in dawdling, chronic lateness, and, in general, "not getting with it." Moreover, it can show up in faulty spelling (wrong order of letters), reversal of words in reading, and errors in arithmetic (wrong order of procedural steps). Spatial orientation deficit can manifest itself in incorrect arrangement of written pages—for example, poor spacing, not centering titles, failure to keep margins, uneven columns, scattering various steps of arithmetic problems—as well as in untidy notebooks (Lehtinen-Rogan, 1971, p. 43).

To be organized, one must be adept in long-range planning, selective (able to discriminate between the important and the trivial) and flexible—qualities not generally attributed to LD children. Wilcox (1970, p. 8), in describing the LD adolescent, maintains that "time and sequence are his greatest enemies" and that "he lacks the inner direction to organize." Roa Lynn (1979, IX), a LD adult who has become a journalist-researcher-author, describes her problem:

> I have difficulty writing down the simplest note when someone gives me information—even a telephone number gets twisted in my hands. I am frequently bewildered by complex stimuli such as large parties, some kinds of music, and cluttered rooms. Although I have a good memory for events more than a few days old, I often cannot recall what I have most recently learned. When I move to a new city, it takes years before I can walk out the door confident that I will be able to find my way home.

Emotional Lability. LD children are frequently labile (i.e., changeable, unstable, prone to "slip") in the affect domain. Just as their physical movements are gross, sudden, jerky, and uneven, so too are their emotional displays devoid of any subtlety or smoothness. They laugh—or cry—too quickly. They talk too loudly. They move too suddenly. They react impulsively—not reflectively. In fact, they *overreact*. A relatively trivial event (e.g., not being able to find a toy, breaking a pencil point, learning that Uncle Henry cannot come over to dinner as planned) can set off what has been described as a "catastrophic reaction" (Strauss & Lehtinen, 1947) marked by tears and/or tantrum. Rappaport (1964, p. 47) describes one LD child who giggled and spoke rapidly whenever he felt uncertain about himself, and another who burst into loud sobs after completing some project upon which she had been working for several days—a simple sigh of relief would have sufficed. This type of behavior can be viewed as an emotional reaction to feelings of frustration, insecurity, and fear (Cruickshank, 1975, p. 262). LD children are often irritable (stemming from such factors as neurological overload, frustration, frequent failure in academic, social and perceptual-motor tasks, etc.) and excitable.

Emotional lability implies a degree of unpredictability. LD individuals are prone to "miss the point," that is, they do not readily assemble pertinent sensory data into valid Gestalts and they often misread nonverbal communication signals such as facial expressions and tones of voice. Therefore, their reactions are perceived by others as inappropriate and unexpected. Another factor could be displaced emotions—such feelings as anger and depression may become generalized and nonspecific, and hence, reactive behavior becomes directed toward "false" targets.

Some LD children are *destructive*. This can, of course, be a form of hostility—perhaps they opt to destroy things (i.e., visual stimuli) rather than risk being distracted by them. Frequently, though, it is a question of such deficits as poor spatial orientation (e.g., cramming books into a briefcase until it tears), impairment in kinesthesis (e.g., cleaning eyeglasses so vigorously and with so much pressure that they break), impulsivity (e.g., reaching for a glass of water so suddenly that it is knocked over and shatters), and/or perseveration (e.g., making the wheels of a toy truck go around more and more, faster and faster, until it breaks*).

Similarly, some LD children are *aggressive*. Again, this can be a manifestation of hostility; perhaps the child tries to fight his way into the group that has rejected him or has developed a style of lashing out indiscriminately at a world he finds threatening and punitive. It may, however, be "pseudo-aggressiveness" due to basic perceptual-motor problems and overall clumsiness. If I step on your foot accidentally (because I judged that I could walk between you and the table when actually there was insufficient room), it hurts as much as if it had been done on purpose. If I throw a ball to you with all my might (because I could not perceive that you were standing several feet away), the pain in you hand is just as intense as if I had thrown it deliberately to hurt you.

Anxiety. LD children are often besieged with anxiety and this has devastating effects upon the quality of their learning, thinking, behavior—indeed, upon their very personality. Bender (1949) contends that anxiety in brain-injured children arises from disorganization, frustration in reaching normal maturation, and unsolved motor problems. She further postulates that the earlier the cause, the more likely that the anxiety will be nonspecific. (This would apply to the majority of LD children since they have neurological impairment due to prenatal or perinatal factors.) To make it worse, this type of "free-floating" anxiety is apt to be internalized and therefore not likely to be articulated. Finally, Bender points out that this anxiety heightens all other psychological problems of brain-injured children—for example, their propensity for clinging to adult figures, to develop unpatterned impulses, and to accommodate these difficulties with further inappropriate and excessive activity. Bradley (1955, p. 91) maintains that the anxiety of the parents is often fed by—and subsequently feeds into—the anxiety of their LD children. Finally a vicious cycle is generated in that the LD child's inadequate performance

* LD children are frequently fascinated with moving parts.

(social, academic, motoric, etc.), his awareness of his poor showing, and the subsequent negative reaction of others toward him increase his anxiety, which in turn, results in even less adequate performance (Connolly, 1971, pp. 164–167).

Poor Self-Concept. Perceptual impairment is likely to be a major contributor to poor self-concept. In negotiating with his environment, the LD child forms an overall impression of "being in over my head." "Just everyday living in his physical-sensory world is too much—tense and disorganized, generally unsatisfying rather than pleasurable. This feeling of discomfort, of resultant anxiety, of being 'out of it' is likely to contribute to self-devaluation" (Siegel, 1969, pp. 56-57). Giffin (1971, pp. 27–28) explains: "These children, from the very beginning of their lives, are blunted, obtunded, wound up—in some way deficient in the potential for the building of a strong ego. They have a much harder time developing a personality structure."

Research continues to demonstrate that LD children are significantly less popular and more rejected by their peers than are the nonhandicapped (Bryan & Bryan, 1978, p. 122) and "there seems to be little question that the learning-disabled child is likely to be rejected by parents . . . and teachers [as well] " (p. 128). Isn't it possible that the LD child's poor *self*-concept and his *own* expectation that he will fail can serve to launch this very attitude in others? Certainly other *children* are quick to perceive this inherent weakness in the LD child. "One says that this child 'invited' the derisions, taunts, and hostilities . . ." (Siegel, 1969, p. 56).

Rappaport (1966) cogently sets forth the relationship of faulty neurology and the emergence of a poor self-concept:

> "In marked contrast is the child who is not born with an intact central nervous system [i.e., the LD child]. Primary ego functions, such as motility and perception, can develop only with the maturation of the central nervous system. Secondary ego functions, such as impulse control, while developing from the child's interaction with his environment, are rooted in and prerequire those primary functions so that they may develop adequately. Hence, lack of neurological intactness itself robs this child of the inherent opportunity to develop ego functions in the usual course of growing up. His attempts at mastery result not in success, but in frustration; not in self-esteem, but in self-derision; not in a sense of "I am one who can," but in a sense of "I am one who can *not*" (p. 3).

Gullibility. Clements (1966, p. 12) states that the LD child is "overly gullible and easily led by peers and older youngsters." Others seem to sense his weakness, his differentness, his vulnerability. This trait often continues into adulthood when the learning disabled is apt to be exploited by salespeople, coworkers, unscrupulous employers, even strangers. When he was younger, he was cheated of marbles; now it's money.

There are several explanations for his gullibility. He often exhibits perceptual impairment and conceptual inadequacies—he has been referred to as *dyslogic* (Wacker, 1975), a condition reflecting the brain's inability to compute incoming data correctly and to "print out" logical responses and reactions. He therefore misses the point in many situations. Deficits in reading nonverbal communication signals heighten the likelihood that he will not surmize the moods, the reactions, the true intent of others. It may also result from the fact that adults (especially parents) *reinforce* this guilelessness (that is, the openness, honesty, the total dependence) of children. Our own ego needs are met when children laugh uproariously at our jokes and slapstick routines, listen intently to our stories, watch our magic tricks with complete acceptance and without seeking explanation. Normal children, surviving this period successfully, move on to the next stage, but many LD children get hopelessly mired at this point of development, thus prolonging their dependency. Kronick (1975, p. 45) explains: "Human nature is ironic. If we fail to obtain ultimate satisfaction from a relationship or status state, instead of leaving it to seek a more rewarding relationship, we are loathe to part from it and keep 'bashing its door down' . . . . "

Guilelessness can also occur because the LD child makes a pact with himself, agreeing (generally at the unconscious level) to accept the jeers, barbs, and rebuffs of others since *any* attention is better than none. This "voluntary gullibility" is further crystallized since the LD child's low self-esteem may make him feel too weak, too unimportant, and too uncomfortable to challenge the exploiter.

Poor Motor Integration. Rappaport (1964, p. 47) points out that many brain-injured children, despite being able to walk and run adequately, still evidence difficulties in gross motor activities such as crawling, moving arms and legs upon command ("Angels-in-the-Snow"), and so forth. He contends that segmentation—that is, "the inability to move one's body or its parts in a synchronized and integrated fashion"—interferes with fine motor coordination, eye–hand coordination, postural adjustment, and balance as well as with some gross motor activities. Peters, Davis, Goolsby, Clements and Hicks (1973, p. 7) believe that MBD children frequently demonstrate: (1) clumsiness in movement of parts of the body (e.g., hands, fingers, mouth, tongue) rather than during movement of the entire body; (2) problems in the base as well as the moving part (e.g., holding the hand awkward when fingers are being moved); (3) extraneous movements (e.g., the head moving while the eyes track an object; movement by fingers on the left hand when the right hand is engaging in some motor task); (4) poor modulation (e.g., swinging arms too far and too fast, talking too loudly, exerting too much pressure on a pencil when writing, "overshooting the line" in copying some geometric form); and (5) poor motor planning (i.e., the element in the motor sequence being held in mind competes with the current movement, resulting in clumsiness and irregular movements).

Motor incoordination can affect the LD child at all ages. A "clumsy child syndrome" emerges (Arnheim & Sinclair, 1975): The MBD child with poor motor control ". . . falls a lot, is continually knocking into things and has bruises to show for it, drops things, and cannot keep up with the other children in physically active games. . . . Other children will not play [with him] because he is 'no fun,' [he] has difficulty in climbing, throwing and jumping, [and] . . . plays with children younger than himself. . . . He may have difficulty in writing, drawing, or copying; he has a self-defeating attitude" (p. 17). The range of risk activities extend from dressing to driving a car, from coloring with crayons to using a protractor, from finger painting to fixing a leaky faucet.

Conceptualization and Communication Deficits. LD children frequently have difficulty in the overall area of cognitive language—in fact the initials "SLD" stand for *Specific Learning Disabilities* and *Specific Language Disorders* interchangeably. One aspect of SLD (either connotation is applicable here) is a concrete style of thinking (and communicating)—that is, the LD child often can deal with real objects, with the "here and now" rather than with symbols and ideas.

Some additional examples of abstract thinking in which brain-injured children are often inadequate have been cited (Strauss & Kephart 1955, pp. 112-127). These include the ability to generalize (i.e., purposely ignoring superficial environmental variations while discerning basic conceptual similarities); to deal with possibilities as well as actualities; to be cognizant, as one looks at an object, of elements that are out of view (e.g., looking at a dime on "heads," but realizing that the hidden side is "tails"); the ability to manipulate past experiences freely.

Clements (1966, p. 12) characterizes the disorders of thinking processes frequently found in BI children as:

1. Poor ability for abstract reasoning.
2. Thinking generally concrete.
3. Difficulties in concept-formation.
4. Thinking frequently disorganized.
5. Poor short-term and long-term memory.
6. Thinking sometimes autistic.
7. Frequent thought perseveration.

Although learning generally aids thinking, some individuals engage in stereotyped thinking and find it hard to change the methods they use to solve problems (Forgus & Melamud, 1976). This is a common difficulty among LD children.

The communication deficits of the LD child include slight speech irregularities (mumbling, and conversely speaking too loudly; mispronouncing some words—e.g., "pit" for "put," "shicken" for "chicken," occasional drooling, mouth open during the listening phase of a conversation, etc.). In addition to these articulation and cosmetic deficiencies—and of far graver consequence to the LD child—is his faulty communication *style:* (1) Egocentricity results in too much talking about "me," and in ignoring the mood of the listener; (2) Overall errors in perception, conception, and in logical thinking are manifested by the individual frequently "missing the point"; (3) Perseveration can account for general talkativeness, talking about the same subject incessantly, asking questions—often the same one—repeatedly (even when the answers are known), holding onto and talking about a prior topic when it is no longer in order, talking a subject "to the hilt" instead of giving it the cursory attention it warrants, refusing to allow others to have the floor, etc.; (4) Impulsivity evidences itself in the LD child blurting out the first thing that pops into his head rather than modifying or curtailing his comment, in inappropriate actions instead of listening, and in the interruption of others; (5) Distractibility makes it difficult to pay attention to the speaker; (6) Excitability and irritability can further contribute to the unacceptability of the LD child's conversational rendering; (7) Concretism makes it difficult to see nuances and subtleties and to deal with multiple meanings of words, idiomatic expressions, simile and metaphor; (8) Poor self-concept often brings about inappropriate defense mechanisms such as:

taking an "oddball" position and holding onto it at all costs; clowning; adopting some psychologically subservient role such as the perennial "straight man" or the chronic devil's advocate; apologizing profusely and unnecessarily; and (9) Anxiety may make the LD child try too hard; hence, what he says will not "ring true."

For many reasons, LD children encounter great difficulty in nonverbal communication. Authorities agree that, in spontaneous informal conversations, the messages contained in nonverbal cues—e.g., eye movements, facial expressions, posture, gesture, tones of voice, space between speaker and listener—are of far greater significance than the words themselves (Mehrabian & Wiener, 1967; Mehrabian & Ferris, 1967; Giffin, 1971). Yet LD children find precisely these kinds of stimuli particularly confusing (Johnson & Myklebust, 1967; Wiig & Semel, 1976; Bader, 1975; Siegel, Siegel, & Siegel, 1978). Hence, they misinterpret the mood, the intent, the reaction of others (Gordon, 1969). Rejection occurs and a negative spiral ensues. Thus the very vehicle by which they could improve socially—namely, experience— is denied them, and so they continue to misunderstand and, in turn, to be misunderstood.

Is it any wonder that the LD child frequently communicates at the surface level? Giffin (1971, p. 26) observes, "When we look for a few moments at the most poignant experiences of our lives, we will realize that it is the visual sensitivity, the flick of the hand, the gesture, the humorous interchange that is really meaningful." We accuse the LD child of being emotionally shallow, when, in reality, because the messages fed into his system *seem* to be devoid of feeling, he responds in kind.

Social Immaturity. Besides being socially imperceptive (i.e., not adroit in interpreting—and expressing—nonverbal communication signals), the LD child is frequently immature socially. (The two are, of course, not unrelated.). Among some of the characteristics of social behavior and relationship capacities described by Clements (1966, p. 12) as typical of LD children are:

- Peer group relationships generally poor.
- Overexcitable in normal play with other children.
- Better adjustment when playmates are limited to one or two.
- Frequently poor judgment in social and interpersonal situations.
- Inappropriate, unselective, and often excessive displays of affection.
- Easy acceptance of others alternating with withdrawal and shyness.
- Excessive need to touch, cling, and hold on to others.
- Social competence frequently below average for age and measured intelligence.
- Behavior often inappropriate for situation, and consequences apparently not foreseen.

*   *   *

Since many of the traits listed here constitute perfectly normal behavior when they occur in young children, the appearance (from time to time) of these symptoms does not denote "LD behavior." Rather, the persistent manner in which they occur (i.e., continuing over a period of years), is the clue (Lynn, 1979, p. 5).

Interrelationship of Traits

Although the characteristics of LD have been listed singly, they are not independent factors; in fact, they tend to be interrelated, one characteristic frequently
influencing another (Myers & Hammill, 1976, p. 35): Perseveration can be seen as a
form of hyperactivity (needless repetition of a given activity—e.g., talking) as well
as a defense against distractibility. Impulsivity and hyperactivity are synonymous in
many instances (e.g., tapping of fingers on the table, out-of-seat behavior). Also,
impulsive, sudden actions contribute to motor incoordination. There is a strong link
between egocentricity and a concrete style of thinking; as a matter of fact, egocentricity can be seen as the epitome of concretism: What can be more concrete than
me?

One trait can often be viewed as both the cause and the effect of another. For
example, it is commonly stated that hyperactivity causes distractibility (that is,
the excessive energy level renders the LD individual incapable of attending to a
given set of stimuli for any appreciable time span). However, the converse may also
be true. Ross (1976, p. 52) contends that "attention to extraneous . . . stimuli leads
to extraneous responses." (Thus, a LD child in the classroom not only is distracted
by the sound of playground noises, but rushes over to the window to witness the
"action"). Similarly, Smith (1978, pp. 2-3) believes that distractibility causes disorganization, but can also reflect it. Hewett (1968, p. 51) further relates these two
traits by reminding us that it is often necessary to attend in a discrete order—e.g., in
reading we proceed word-by-word, line-by-line, left–right, and top–bottom. Impulsivity frequently results in disorganization, but it works the other way around too:
The LD child, prone to neurological overloading, is not sufficiently organized to do
two things at once. Namely, he cannot readily think about something *he is going to
do* and, at the same time, be involved in the process of conversing (or more precisely, listening), *so he does it now*. Poor self-concept and anxiety can readily be
generated by failure—academically, socially, motorically; once created, however,
they assume their own momentum, resulting in even lowered functioning.

At times, a single act can mirror a profusion of traits. Consider a LD child attempting to pencil in a predrawn outline of a square. He moves his hands frenziedly,
faster and faster (impulsivity, hyperactivity, emotional lability), does not seem to
pay attention to the borders (distractibility), performs in a tense manner (anxiety),
overshoots the boundary lines (visual-motor incoordination), and doesn't stop
(perseveration) until the pencil breaks and/or the page tears (impaired kinesthetic
perception, destructiveness).

Intragroup Variability

Considerable variability among the LD population exists for many reasons. First of
all, one must consider the degree of impairment: Any of the deficits—process impairment, disorder in learning, incoordination, behavioral traits (e.g., hyperactivity,
distractibility) can range from relatively severe to practically insignificant. Then,
too, there is the matter of attendant strengths: emotional adjustment, degree and
kinds of compensation and coping strategies, ability to socialize, intelligence
(Remember: There is no upper limit insofar as the IQ of any given LD child is concerned), general health, and so on. Also, it is a question of just which areas are impaired and which are intact: Although many LD individuals have auditory percep-

tual deficits, there are some with perfect pitch! As a group, LD children are tactually imperceptive, but studies have unearthed some BI subjects who soar above the average nonhandicapped child in tactual tasks such as two-point threshold discrimination (the ability to judge whether their palm is being touched by either one or two points of a caliper-like instrument as the two points come closer and closer together) (Siegel, 1966). Similarly, some LD children are intact visually and kinesthetically, and even have athletic ability and mechanical aptitude. Regarding underachievement, LD children do not always exhibit an across-the-board deficit in learning: Some are poor in reading, but excel in arithmetic; for others, the opposite is true.

Peters, Davis, Goolsby, Clements, and Hicks (1973) have focused upon three distinct groups of MBD (see Figure 3-2): The first type is *The Pure Hyperkinetic*. These are exogenous, do better in the Wechsler Intelligence Scale for Children's (WISC) Verbal subtest than in the Performance, and frequently evidence traits like distractibility, impulsivity, and hyperactivity. Problems in learning (reading, arithmetic, etc.) are less often present. The second group is *The Pure Learning Disability* type. They are endogenous, score higher on the WISC's Performance subtest than on the Verbal, and demonstrate learning problems rather than behavioral deficits. The third and most prevalent type is a mixture of the two: related to both endogenous and exogenous factors, scoring equally well (or poorly) on both portions of the WISC, but with a jagged profile for each, and *presenting various combinations of learning and behavioral deficits*. This model is an extremely useful one in that it is consistent with the unusually high degree of intragroup variability generally attributed to the LD population.

Clusters

There is a tremendous paradox regarding this range of differences found among the LD group: *Unlike other categories of exceptionality, there is not a single trait, per se, that holds this group together* (and broadly speaking, this includes underachievement as well, since it is well known that many BI individuals—even those with *provable* brain injury—need not have any learning disorders); yet, a sizable number of authorities continue to state—and, in many instances, to demonstrate—that they can recognize a LD person when they see one. The explanation probably lies in the fact that the traits seldom appear singly, but in clusters; those who seem able to identify LD children purely on the basis of a clinical observation of their behavior have probably internalized the concept of various subgroups among the LD population, and are familiar with each of them.

Bryan & Bryan (1978, pp. 136-137) point out that many traits (e.g., distractibility, clumsiness, emotional lability, poor academic performance, poor peer relationships, low self-esteem and irritability) are correlated with hyperactivity. Silver (1979) has called attention to two distinct patterns: One reflects deficits in perception, integration, and memory *visually*, and includes fine motor and visual-motor impairment, whereas the other demonstrates disabilities in perception, integration, and memory *auditorially*, encompassing expressive language disorders. Clements (1966) reassures us: "The situation . . . is not as irremediable as it might appear. Order is somewhat salvaged by the fact that certain symptoms do tend to cluster to form recognizable clinical entities. . . . Recognition and acceptance of

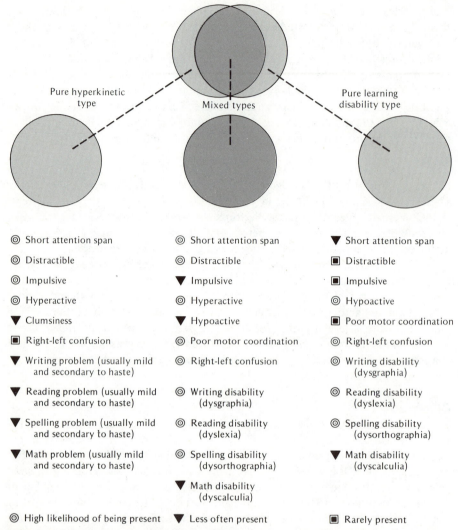

Figure 3-2. Three types of MBD. (From Peters, J. E. et al. *Physicians Handbook: Screening for MBD*. CIBA Medical Horizon 1973.)

these specific symptom complexes as subcategories, within the general category of minimal brain dysfunctioning, would facilitate classification and the development of appropriate management and education procedures" (p. 13).

Scatter, Inconsistencies, Opposites

In addition to the large range of differences found among the LD population, there is another aspect of variability which suggests scatter and inconsistent performance on the part of the individual LD subject. It can manifest itself in testing situations: Research has shown greater variability for BI subjects than for control subjects with respect to intertest subtests scores as well as for trial-to-trial scores within each subtest (Reichstein, 1963; Myklebust, 1954, pp. 165–166). Lynn (1979, p. 7) points out that the presence of learning disabilities necessarily lowers performance on some of the very tasks appearing on many intelligence tests. Inasmuch as definition-ally a LD person *must* achieve average or higher than average overall scores on these tests—otherwise he would be classified mentally retarded and not LD—he must actually demonstrate superior performance on some of the subtests to bal-ance his poor showing on others, thus producing the typical LD jagged strength-weakness profile. Besides evidencing itself during standardized testing, this incon-sistent performance is also found in less formal situations: (e.g., acting impulsively or perseveratively, spasmodically rather than consistently; sometimes reversing words in reading, but at other times reading them correctly.) McWhirter (1977, pp. 10–11), discussing his own LD son, cites additional examples of incongruent behavior such as being disinterested in reading yet liking to discuss ideas and concepts; following direction and completing tasks at home, but failing to do so at school; demonstrating fine muscle incoordination, impaired sense of balance, and general clumsiness, yet being an agile and graceful climber. In fact, two of the major traits of learning disabilities—distractibility (which can manifest itself in the aimless flit-ting from one stimulus to another) and perseveration (sticking to one activity purposelessly but relentlessly) seem to be mutually exclusive of each other, yet the same LD child frequently exhibits both. It is highly likely that the two behaviors are part of the same system: Distractibility is forced responsiveness to some passing stimulus, and perseveration occurs when the LD child becomes fixated upon it (Farnham-Diggory, 1978, pp. 14–15). This stimulus, no matter how trivial, tangen-tial, or inappropriate, continues to seduce his attention. The ease with which "stim-ulus bonding" occurs is matched only by the intensity of that bond.

Another reason for this category of exceptionality remaining somewhat of an enigma is the fact that some LD children have traits opposite to the ones usually cited for them. For example, many LD children are *hyperactive*, but a few are *hypoactive*—that is, they appear lethargic and generally exhibit a less-than-normal amount of motor activity and energy expenditure. (Interestingly, the theoretical neurological site of damage may be the same for both: in hyperactivity, the reticular sends all sensory data to the projection areas of the new brain indiscriminately without filtering out the superfluous ones; whereas in hypoactivity, it may be that all sensory data are "frozen" at the level of the reticular—hence the organism re-sponds as though no stimulation has occurred.) Some LD children are aggressive, irritable, explosive, and given to antisocial behavior, while others are "sweet and even tempered, cooperative and friendly" and "very sensitive to others" (Clements, 1966, pp. 12–13). Authors frequently write of LD children who are depressed (Gardner, 1973, p. 249; Lynn, 1978, p. 5); yet Smith (1978) reminds us of the "sheer joy . . . that many a learning-disabled child brings to life. He seems to em-brace life with an enthusiasm and jauntiness that most of us lose with maturity" (p. 35).

DIFFERENCES BETWEEN THE LD CHILD AND THE OLDER LD PERSON

In general one sees a lessening of the Strauss syndrome traits (including both fine and gross motor incoordination) as the child grows older (Wilcox, 1970; Gordon, 1975, p. 96; Siegel, 1974). These may never completely disappear, but they seem

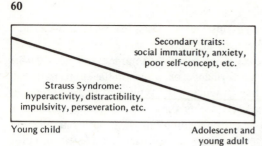

Young child   Adolescent and   **Figure 3-3.** Chronological course of
                                     young adult   characteristics.

to diminish. Coming to the forefront, unfortunately, are a host of secondary characteristics: poor self-esteem, anxiety, depression, social immaturity (see Figure 3-3).
Kronick (1975) adds anger, fear, loneliness, and feelings of unrelatedness and of
being lost and alienated.

Wilcox (1970, pp. 7–8) believes that disorders of memory and thinking are
most recognizable at the secondary level, manifesting themselves in lack of organization, unroutinized behavior, and poor study habits. Lack of resourcefulness
(Lehtinen-Rogan, 1971, p. 44) and meager ability to plan ahead and to make long-
range decisions (Anderson, 1963) are more pronounced as the LD child grows older.
(When he was younger, his parents and teachers made most of the decisions for
him, but now, he is more on his own and is frequently besieged with indecision and
inertia.) The younger LD child is open, naive, and gullible, whereas as he grows
older, he develops facades, subterfuges and coping mechanisms (often inappropriate
ones). He remains unsophisticated and vulnerable, but now he attempts to cover up.

Some of the characteristics they have as children "turn around"—but still
exist—in adulthood. Perseveration manifested itself in repetitive action of the LD
child; it shows up as talkativeness in later years. As a child, his gullibility made him
the butt of others' jokes and tricks; now he falls prey to the fast-talking door-to-
door canvasser. Distractibility and hyperactivity give way to more generalized tenseness, "edginess," and a demeanor that is seldom calm or relaxed.

Also, LD symptoms do not occur spontaneously, but are frequently a function
of external influence: A LD child may not have demonstrated any significant disorganization while at elementary school. Upon entering secondary school with its
departmental program, myriad of stairways and corridors, plurality of teachers,
huge school population, new school regulations, increased distance between school
and home, pressures of time such as due dates for book reports, and so forth,
the LD adolescent meets with an overwhelming format. Disorganization and confusion ensue.

RELATIONSHIP OF LD CHARACTERISTICS TO
EXPECTATION OF OTHERS

For a child to be labeled hyperactive, some influential person in his life would
have had to observe him and judge his activity level to be beyond the generally
accepted standard for that behavior (Ross, 1976, p. 87; Zentall, 1975, p. 549). We
tend to categorize a child as lonely when, in fact, he may *prefer* periods of privacy
(Siegel, Siegel, & Siegel, 1978). Many of the LD traits take on either positive or

negative valence, depending upon the values of the observer. Smith (1978) believes that impulsivity (a negative trait) can endear the LD child to us in that it often can be seen in "the spontaneous expression of feeling, the unedited comment, the untrampled-upon gesture" (p. 35). She further claims that because he doesn't see the whole picture (another negative trait), "There's a freshness which he conveys ... that turns our attention to experiences we have come to take for granted. In the midst of checking the route map, watching the road signs, estimating when the next gas stop must be made, our attention is suddenly diverted to an unexpected delight when the learning disabled child remarks: 'How fresh and good the grass smells!'" (p. 35). Distractibility (still another negative trait) can be used to advantage (Peters, Davis, Goolsby, Clements, and Hicks, 1973, p. 7; Siegel, 1972, pp. 121–122): "The [LD] perturbed girl with the storm cloud gathering around her can suddenly change into a sparkling delight if an adult strikes the right chord and provokes her to laugh by imitating her pouting. Within minutes her mood can change ..." (Smith, 1978, pp. 36–37). In considering a LD pupil's disability, Cruickshank (1975, p. 285) contends that sometimes we can "find ways of exploiting it to the child's advantage." He gives some specific examples: highlight the foreground stimuli, thus catering to the LD child's hyperactivity to stimuli; incorporate motor activities in the learning task, thus accommodating his motor disinhibition. Similarly, perseveration, despite its connotation of aimlessness and rigidity, does imply a capacity to "stick with it." If we start a LD child in some task that he is able to do and is motivated to do (and, of course, that we deem is in his best interests), then this very trait may redound to his benefit. In retrospect, it may be that when a LD child does something over and over again, and we don't like it, we label it perseveration, but if we approved of it, we call it perseverance.

Productive intervention will not occur as long as teachers continue to view the LD child's characteristic behavior as completely negative and detrimental to both the child's effort to learn and to the teacher's efforts to remediate. Moreover, negative feelings toward the child are likely to be generated, since it is a short step away from saying—or feeling—"I don't like anything he *does* or *says*" to "I don't like *him*." The key is to avoid using the child's deficits as an excuse for not teaching. ("I know how to teach, but he has too many problems to learn.") Instead, by seeking to use the child's weakness to advantage, the teacher succeeds in creating (*creating* is the proper term here, since it is the creative teacher who thinks along these lines) effective teaching tools out of hitherto hinderances to learning. Astute teachers are still committed to the long-range goal of remediating his disabilities, but, *in the meantime*, by capitalizing upon the LD child's current behavior and learning style wherever possible, they can maximize chances for his success—academically as well as affectively.

REFERENCES

Anderson, C. *Jan: My brain-damaged daughter.* Portland, Oregon: Durham Press, 1963.

Arnheim, D. O., and Sinclair, W. A. *The clumsy child: A program of motor therapy.* St. Louis: C. V. Mosby, 1975.

Ayres, A. J. Tactile functions: Their relation to hyperactive and perceptual motor behavior, *American Journal of Occupational Therapy*, January, 1964, *18*, 6–11.

Bader, B. W. *Social perception and learning disabilities.* Des Moines, Iowa: The Author and Iowa Association for Children with Learning Disabilities, 1975.

Beck, H. S. Detecting psychological symptoms of brain injury," *Exceptional Children*, September, 1961, *28*, 57–62.

Becker, L. D. Conceptual tempo and the early detection of learning problems, *Journal of Learning Disabilities*, Aug/Sept., 1976, *9*(7), 433–442.

Bender, L. Psychological problems of children with organic brain disease, *American Journal of Orthopsychiatry*, July, 1949, *19*(3), 404–414.

Bradley, C. Organic factors in the psychotherapy of children. In Paul H. Hoch and Joseph Zubin (Eds.), *Psychopathology of childhood.* New York: Grune & Stratton, 1955.

Bryan, T. H. and Bryan, J. H. *Understanding Learning Disabilities*, 2nd ed. Sherman Oaks, Calif.: Alfred Publishers, 1978.

Cartwright, G. P., Cartright, C. A., and Ward, E. M. *Educating Special Learners.* Belmont, Calif.: Wadsworth Publ. Co., 1981.

Chalfant, J. C., and Scheffelin, M. A. *Central processing dysfunction in children: A review of research* (NINDS Monograph No. 9.) Bethesda, Md.: U.S. Department of Health, Education, and Welfare, 1969.

Clements, S. D. *Minimal brain dysfunction in children: Terminology and identification* (Phase I, NINDB Monograph No. 3.) Washington, D.C.: U.S. Department Health, Education, and Welfare, 1966.

Connolly, C. Social and emotion factors in learning disabilities. In Helmer R. Myklebust (Ed.), *Progress in learning disabilities, vol. II.* New York: Grune & Stratton, 1971.

Cruickshank, W. M. The education of children with specific learning disabilities. In William M. Cruickshank and G. Orville Johnson (Eds.), *Education of exceptional children in youth, 3rd ed.* Englewood Cliffs, New Jersey: Prentice-Hall, 1975.

Davids, A. An objective instrument for assessing hyperkinesis in children. *Journal of Learning Disabilities*, November, 1971, *4*(9), 499–501.

Eisenberg, L. Behavioral manifestations of cerebral damages in children. In H. G. Birch, (Ed.), *Brain damage in children: The biological and social aspects.* Baltimore: Williams and Wilkins, 1964.

Farnham-Diggory, S. *Learning disabilities.* Cambridge, Mass.: Harvard University Press, 1978.

Forgus, R. H., and Melamud, L. E. *Perception: A cognitive-stage approach, 2nd ed.* New York: McGraw-Hill, 1976.

Gardner, R. Psychotherapy of the psychogenic problems secondary to minimal brain dysfunction, *International Journal of Child Psychotherapy*, 1973, *2*(2), 224–256.

Gibson, E. *Principles of perceptual processing and development.* New York: Appleton-Century-Crofts, 1969.

Giffin, M. How does he feel? In Ellen Schloss (Ed.), *The educator's enigma: The adolescent with learning disabilities.* Novato, Ca.: Academic Therapy Publications, 1971.

Gordon, S. Psychological problems of adolescents with minimal brain dysfunction. In Doreen Kronick (Ed.), *Learning Disabilities: Its implications to a responsible society.* Chicago: Developmental Learning Materials, 1969.

Haeussermann, E. *Developmental potential of preschool children.* New York: Grune & Stratton, 1958.

Hewett, F. M. *The emotionally disturbed child in the classroom.* Boston: Allyn & Bacon, 1968.

Johnson, D. and Myklebust, H. *Learning disabilities: Educational principles and practices.* New York: Grune & Stratton, 1967.

Keogh, B., and Donlon, G. Field Dependency, Impulsivity, and Learning Disabilities. *Journal of Learning Disabilities*, June–July, 1972, *5*(6), 331–336.

Kranes, J. E. *The Hidden Handicap.* New York: Simon and Schuster, 1980.

Kronick, D. *What about me? The LD adolescent.* Novato, Calif: Academic Therapy Publications, 1975.

Krupp, G. R., and Schwartzberg, B. The brain-injured child: A challenge to social workers' *Social Casework*, February, 1960, *41*, 63–69.

Lehtinen-Rogan, L. How do we teach him? In Ellen Schloss (Ed.), *The educator's enigma: The adolescent with learning disabilities.* Novato, Ca.: Academic Therapy Publications, 1971.

Lerner, J. *Children with learning disabilities*, 2nd ed. Boston: Houghton-Mifflin, 1971.

Lynn, R. *Learning disabilities: An overview of theories, approaches, and politics.* New York: The Free Press, 1979.

McWhirter, J. J. *The learning disabled child: A school and family concern.* Champaign, Ill.: Research Press Company, 1977.

Mehrabian, A., and Wiener, M. Decoding of inconsistent communications, *Journal of Personality and Social Psychology*, 1967, *6*, 109–114.

Mehrabian, A., and Ferris, S. R. Inference of attitudes from nonverbal communication in two channels, *Journal of Consulting Psychology*, 1967, *31*, 248–252.

Myers, P. I., and Hammill, D. D. *Methods for learning disorders*, 2nd ed. New York: Wiley, 1976.

Myklebust, H. R. *Auditory disorders in children: A manual for differential diagnosis.* New York: Grune & Stratton, 1954.

Payne, J. S., Polloway, E. A., Smith, J. E. and Payne, R. A. *Strategies for teaching the mentally retarded.* Columbus, Ohio.: Charles E. Merrill, 1977.

Peters, J., Davis, J. S., Goolsby, C. M., Clements, S. D., and Hicks, T. J. *Physicians's handbook: Screening for MBD.* CIBA Medical Horizons, 1973.

Piaget, J. *The origins of intelligence in children.* New York: International Universities Press, 1966.

Rappaport, S. S. (Ed.). *Childhood aphasia and brain damage: Habilitation, vol. III.* Narberth, Pa.: Livingston Publishing Co., 1966. (publ. by the Pathway School, Norristown, Pa.)

————. (Ed.). *Childhood aphasia and brain damage: Definition, vol. I.* Narberth, Pa.: Livingston, 1964. (published by the Pathway School, Norristown, Pa.)

Reichstein, J. Auditory threshold consistency—A basic characteristic for differential diagnosis of children with communication disorders. Ed.D. Dissertation. New York, Teachers College, Columbia University, 1963.

Roach, E. G., and Kephart, N. C. *The Purdue perceptual-motor survey.* Columbus, Ohio: Charles E. Merrill, 1966.

Ross, A. O. *Psychological aspects of learning disabilities and reading disorders.* New York: McGraw-Hill, 1976.

Siegel, E. A comparison of minimally brain-injured children of normal intelligence with nonhandicapped children, Ed.D. Dissertation. New York, Teachers College, Columbia University, 1966.

————. *The exceptional child grows up*. New York: E. P. Dutton, 1974.

————. *Helping the brain-injured child*. Albany, N.Y.: New York Association for the Learning Disabled, 1961.

————. The real problem of minimal brain dysfunction. In Doreen Kronick (Ed.), *Learning disabilities: Its implications to a responsible society*. Chicago: Developmental Learning Materials, 1969.

————. *Teaching one child*. Freeport, N.Y.: Educational Activities, 1972.

Siegel, E., Siegel, R., and Siegel, P. *Help for the lonely child: Strenghtening social perceptions*, New York: E. P. Dutton, 1978.

Silver, L. B. The minimal brain dysfunction syndrome. In J. Noshpitz (Ed.), *The basic handbook of child psychiatry*, vol. 2. New York: Basic Books, 1979.

Smith, S. *No Easy Answers: The Learning Disabled Child*. Wash., D.C.: Department of Health, Education, and Welfare Publication No. (ADM) 77-526, 1978.

————. *No Easy Answers: Teaching the Learning Disabled Child*. Cambridge, Mass.: Winthrop Publishers, 1979.

Strauss, A. A., and Lehtinen, L. E. *Psychopathology and education of the brain-injured child*, vol. I. New York: Grune & Stratton, 1947.

Strauss, A. A., and Kephart, N. *Psychopathology and education of the brain-injured child*, vol. II. New York: Grune & Stratton, 1955.

Wacker, J. The dyslogic syndrome. In *Texas Key*. State Newsletter of the Association for Children with Learning Disabilities, September, 1975.

Wiig, E., and Semel, E. *Language Disabilities in Children and Adolescents*. Columbus, Ohio: Charles E. Merrill, 1976.

Wilcox, E. Identifying characteristics of the NH adolescent. In Lauriel E. Anderson, (Ed.), *Helping the adolescent with the hidden handicap*. Novato, Ca.: Academic Therapy Publication, 1970.

Zentall, S. Optimal stimulation as theoretical basis for hyperactivity. *American Journal of Orthopsychiatry*, July, 1975, *45*(4), 549–563.

Etiology

4

Without definitive evidence of CNS damage, a history is used to identify children with behavioral characteristics presumed to be indicative of brain injury. ("Presumed" because many children with verifiable brain damage do not exhibit those characteristics (Birch, 1963).) Identification is complicated by the fact that, in moderate cases, results often do not become evident until the child is in school. Many data are lost because of this lapse of time. Moreover, when providing a history, the parents may not recall or may confuse details about pregnancy, delivery, and early childhood illnesses and trauma. An important factor may be overlooked while another is given undue stress. There also may exist the possibility of interactive effects of various factors which may be difficult to determine.

CAUSES OF NEUROLOGICAL DYSFUNCTION

The causes of neurological dysfunctions are as diverse as the population itself. Included among these factors are: a) a brain injury indicative of an insult (trauma) to the brain at any phase of development and can vary according to extent, type, and locus of damage and the duration and rate at which damage occurred; 2) a chemical imbalance within the brain; 3) impaired neurological development; and 4) a developmental lag. A genetic implication may give rise to the last three factors. In addition, environmental and emotional elements have also been considered to play either a primary or secondary role. The behavior patterns that result are not considered a direct consequence of any of the four factors, but are the product of the child with an impaired central nervous system interacting with his total environment—emphasizing the fact that there are many types and degrees of learning disabilities. Denckla (1978), noting the variations in cerebral organization, suggests the "D" in MBD be "stretched to encompass the full range from damage to difference" (p. 268).

The onset of many handicapping conditions may be obvious at an early age. However, the learning disabled child is generally not discovered until he has failed in the academic area. Because of this, among the major thrusts in the field of learning disabilities presently is the search for early identification of the child at risk. The need for greater attention not only to the first three years of life but also to the recognition and prevention of handicapping conditions before, during, and after birth is now recognized. Input from many disciplines will provide the knowledge that will foster early identification and treatment. Parents, too, will play a major part in the identification and education of the young child at risk (see Chapter 19).

Prenatal Factors

Injury to the brain can occur in prenatal, perinatal, and postnatal periods. In the prenatal period, the mother's health is an important factor. Poor maternal nutrition can lead to babies with a birth weight of less than 2,500 grams (5½ pounds) (Winick & Rosso, 1973), and premature births, a major contributor to learning disabilities. Koch (1967) believes that "a deficiency of vitamin B-12 in utero is damaging to the central nervous system."

Maternal toxemia, which can lead to premature delivery, may appear in the last trimester of pregnancy. It produces hypertension, headache, edema (swelling) and albuminuria (the presence of albumin in the urine). Generally good prenatal care can eliminate this condition which, if untreated, can result in convulsions, coma, and death. Koch (1967) reports toxemia to account for one third of maternal deaths.

Maternal infections usually do not harm the fetus but there are exceptions. Rubella during the first trimester can cause mental retardation, deafness, heart disease, eye problems, and growth deficiency. Babies who were exposed to rubella during the first trimester and present no major anomalies are apt to be premature and have below normal birth weight (Koch, 1967).

Drugs and medication of various kinds taken by the mother during pregnancy are transmitted through the placenta to the fetus and can be harmful. Hundreds of drugs have been found to produce anomalies in experimental animals, though no more than twenty have been definitely found to cause defects in the human fetus (e.g., quinine can cause deafness, thalidomide inhibits normal limb development in utero). While it is risky to make generalizations about humans based on animal studies, it seems logical that as long as the central nervous system is maturing, it remains susceptible to damage.

The newborns of drug-addicted mothers go through withdrawal symptoms (Blatman, 1974), but the effect of the drugs on the child's neurological development and functioning level has not been documented. The school-age children of alcoholic mothers have been found to have short attention spans, to be less goal oriented, more assertive, and less controllable than children whose mothers were not alcoholics (Omenn, 1974). Whether this difference is caused by alcohol, per se, or the home environment is not known. More research in both areas is needed.

Because the fetus is most vulnerable during the first few weeks after conception, and this is before most women realize that they are pregnant, drugs of any kind should be avoided by potentially childbearing women, as well as pregnant women, unless there are compelling clinical indications for their use (Robinson & Robinson, 1976).

The effect of emotional stress of the mother is not yet clear. Anxiety and stress, however, cause physiological changes in the autonomic nervous system of the mother which, in turn, may affect the activity level, heart rate, and birth weight of the fetus and may be manifested in the child in the form of neurologic dysfunction, behavior disturbances, and a delay in language development (Stott, 1973). Birth weight and fetal development also are affected by stress. The severity and duration of stress and the amount of personal support received during pregnancy appear to be important factors (Nuckolls, Cassel, & Kaplan, 1972; Stott, 1973).

Mothers who smoke tend to have LBW children and an increased rate of premature deliveries. According to a report of the United States Surgeon General, studies have shown that cigarette smoking during pregnancy may affect the physical and mental growth and behavior of children up to the age of eleven. The results of these studies have been questioned because other factors must also be considered, for example, the role of stress, use of alcohol, and so forth.

In recent years, attention has turned to the unwed teenager (Robinson & Robinson, 1976). These young mothers are often at a disadvantage nutritionally, socially, and psychologically with a high risk of prenatal complications and prematurity. Medical care frequently is sought late in pregnancy. They may be under a great deal of pressure—that is, stress—to make plans for the future. That more of their offspring may be at risk than offspring in the general population may account for the high number of adopted children identified as having learning problems (Silver, 1971). Hoffman (1971) compared 100 learning disabled students with 200 able students. Ten percent of the learning disabled children were adopted as compared with one half of one percent of the control group. Hoffman did not analyze the reasons for the difference. In addition to the fact that the children may be more at risk because of prenatal factors, other possibilities must be considered: The fact of being adopted may cause the child to feel different and/or be treated differently.

Perinatal Factors

Birth is a normal, though stressful, situation passed through successfully by most infants. Among the potential birth hazards linked to learning disabilities are: prematurity, caesarian section, low birth weight, anoxia, (and conversely, too much oxygen), and direct injury to the brain. The possible causes of these hazards are numerous (some of which were discussed in the section on prenatal factors). In some cases, an interactive process may be the cause of the damage leading to learning disorders; that is, mild problems at birth may assume greater importance if they occur to an infant who developed poorly during gestation. Dunn (1973) suggests that difficult deliveries may be the result of prenatal events.

Investigations of birth procedures that present hazards to the neonate and can cause permanent damage that affects functioning throughout its life have led to an amendment of Public Health Law 2503-a, which states that physicians must explain to expectant mothers what methods and procedures will be used during delivery and the expected effects on mother and child. This amendment has been supported by "parents who learned too late of the consequences of certain medications" (NYALD, 1979; p. 1).

Furthermore, although recognizing the possible necessity of use for medical reasons, the FDA announced a new labelling procedure which recommends that oxytocin products should not be used for *elective* induction of labor (NYALD, 1979). The chemical oxytocin stimulates contraction of the uterus and is used to induce labor and/or control postnatal hemorrhage.

Studies have shown that babies born of induced labor can suffer fetal distress from the drugs, can be premature because the length of pregnancy was miscalculated, and/or can have breathing problems. Though complications were not higher than for the population as a whole, this procedure is used mainly by middle-class families who ordinarily would have *fewer* birth complications (Pakter, 1976).

Prematurity and low birth weight (LBW) are major contributors to learning disability. Two groups of affected children can be identified: 1) the LBW child who was delivered prior to full term but was developing normally; and 2) the child who was carried full term but had a growth deficiency in utero. Most studies do not differentiate between the groups.

With improvements in postnatal care of LBW children, more are now surviving, even many weighing below 1,500 grams. These children are at even greater risk because of the immaturity of their organs and the increased incidence of major defects.

Many factors appear to be associated with prematurity and low birth weight, such as twinning, poor maternal nutrition, maternal illnesses, such as toxemia, heavy cigarette smoking, alcoholism, and so forth. Mothers from low socioeconomic classes tend to have a higher incidence of premature, low birth weight children, with poor nutrition, lack of good and consistent medical care, and economic factors as contributing agents.

The relationship between LBW and high risk for many handicapping conditions has been well documented. Research linking LBW and learning disabilities has been increasing, in order to discover early signs with high predictive value for indicating perceptual and cognitive difficulties (Daum, 1978).

Reviewing studies that examine the relationship between low birth weight and increased risk to the child, Robinson and Robinson (1976) report that the rate of definite neurological abnormalities was significantly higher for LBW children.

A strong relationship between prematurity and low socioeconomic class has also been noted (Robinson & Robinson, 1976; Hallahan & Cruickshank, 1973). The difficulty of lower socioeconomic families to obtain pre-, peri-, and postnatal medical services may account also for "the more striking disabilities" found in this group as compared to the specific learning disabilities found more frequently in the middle-class, at-risk child (Robinson & Robinson, 1976, p. 219).

Birth weight rather than gestational age has been proven a factor in psychological and educational impairment; that is, the lower the weight, the greater the impairment regardless of the length of the gestation period (Rubin, 1973; Daum, 1978). LBW males and small for date of birth boys and girls had a higher incidence of problems requiring special school placement and services than full birth weight children. The LBW children scored lower on all measures of mental development, language development, and readiness through age seven (Rubin, 1973).

During and/or immediately after delivery, oxygen deprivation can occur because of blockage of placental blood supply or the lack of spontaneous breathing causing anoxia. Controversy abounds on whether or not this deprivation causes permanent neurological damage in children, although animal studies support such a thesis (Robinson & Robinson, 1976). A study of preschool children was conducted by Graham, et al. in 1962, in which performance of 3 groups of children were compared: 159 children had been born full term and without complications, 116 children had been full term but anoxic, and 80 had suffered from varying complications at birth. The anoxic children had poorer performance than the other two groups in cognitive and perceptual functioning. They also exhibited more neurological deficits. No significant difference in the number of children who were considered hyperactive was apparent. A direct positive relationship appears to exist between the length of time of oxygen deprivation and the severity of brain damage.

Neurological damage caused by direct injury to the head and brain because of mechanical and physiological factors (e.g., forceps delivery, breech birth, separating placenta, etc.) are considered to be rare (Koch, 1967; Robinson & Robinson, 1976). Either a too prolonged or too precipitate delivery is more likely to be a factor.

Postnatal Hazards

A variety of postnatal factors are believed responsible for the neurological dysfunction that causes learning disabilities: direct damage, tumors, infections, anoxia, and malnutrition. Recently improper diet, allergens, and toxic substances have been suspected of also playing a role.

The effect of severe nutritional deprivation on neurological functioning remains unclear. Hallahan and Cruickshank (1973) reviewed several studies that investigated the relationship between nutritional factors and mental retardation and learning problems. The interrelationship between nutrition and social conditions is so entwined that it was difficult to infer a direct causality between learning disabilities and malnutrition. However, these researchers concluded that, (1) early malnutrition can retard physical and mental growth, (2) the severity of which varies according to the age when it occurs, and the degree and duration of the deficiency, and (3) the damage is probably permanent (pp. 35-36).

In an attempt to observe the effects of malnutrition uncomplicated by socioeconomic deprivation, Lloyd-Still, et al. (1974) studied middle-class children between the ages of two through twenty-one from middle-class homes who had malnutrition in infancy caused by cystic fibrosis. Compared to their nonhandicapped siblings, these subjects exhibited adverse effects upon intellectual development up to the age of five. Beyond that age, no difference could be found in intellectual and sensory-motor performance or in social adaptation. The initial poor performance results from the initial impact on the family of the disease and its prognosis.

Klein, Forbes, and Nader (1975) investigated the effects of pyloric stenosis (PS), which causes brief starvation in the first three months of life and is unrelated to socioeconomic status. Analysis of the data indicated that when the effect of starvation caused a reduction of 10% or more of body weight in the infant, associated deficits in short-term memory and attention at the time of the study (when the children were 5 to 15 years of age) occurred. There was no effect on subsequent physical development.

The relationship between neurologic dysfunction and allergies (especially in food) has been investigated because of the frequency with which both appear in the same individual. The "allergic tension-fatigue syndrome" can be manifested by pallor, fatigue, headaches, abdominal pain, hyperactivity, learning problems, depression, and obsessive-compulsive behavior, and is caused by intolerance to food coloring and other additives, drugs, pollen, dust, specific foods, and so forth. The effect of diet control on learning disabilities is discussed in Chapter 6.

A pilot project that investigated the effects of fluorescent lights on hyperactivity found less out-of-seat behavior and more attending behavior in classrooms where cool white tubes were replaced with full spectrum tubes (Ott, 1976). Ott suggests a relationship between the successes reported in the elimination of artificial food coloring from diets and this study. There is a "possibility of an interaction between wavelength absorption bands of synthetic color pigments and the energy peaks caused by mercury vapor lines in fluorescent tubes" (p. 420). By eliminating the food coloring, the absorbing material is not present and the fluorescent lights no longer affect behavior. More research is needed to test this hypothesis.

Head injuries are increasing problems at the present time. They can be caused in falls, automobile accidents, in sports, or by abusive parents. Any serious injury to the skull can cause brain damage. Brain tissue may be directly destroyed, or damage can result from a ruptured neural artery and/or a lack of oxygen available to the brain. While most head injuries are not serious, some children may show test scatter on intelligence tests which did not appear before the accident (Richardson, 1963). Others may develop impulsive behavior, short attention spans, and memory and cognitive deficits (Hjern & Nylander, 1962).

A study comparing brain-injured children with normal children and brain-injured adults was conducted by Ernhart, et al. (1963). They found that brain-injured children performed differently from normal children and brain-injured adults. The hyperkinetic syndrome, although manifested in some, was not typical of brain-injured children. The effects of the injury depend upon the age at the time of the injury and its extent. Some functions appeared less impaired when the immature brain is injured. The difference in the effect of early and late injury may "depend upon the 'uncommitted' structures in the immature brain and a reorganization of cerebral pathways" (Rudel, 1978).

Anoxia (lack of oxygen) can be a secondary effect to many episodes, including cardiac arrest, accidental drowning, and carbon monoxide poisoning. Any incident that causes a lack of oxygenated blood flowing through the brain is capable of causing brain damage. The length of deprivation is the critical factor.

A metabolic disease, hypoglycemia (low blood sugar) has been found to produce many of the *symptoms* of learning disabilities: for example, irritability, short attention span, and hyperactivity. Dietary changes (discussed in Chapter 6) can control the symptoms and enable such a child to participate in and profit from class activities. There are some children, not diagnosed as having hypoglycemia (blood sugar is in the normal range), who exhibit the same symptoms and respond to the same nutritional interventions. Katz (1975) cautions educators *"there is absolutely no evidence that low blood sugar causes either developmental hyperactivity, dyslexia, or other specific learning disabilities*" (p. 79). The term should be used with care. If hypoglycemia is suspected, the matter should be discussed with a physician and endocrinologist.

High fevers and childhood infections that cause inflammation of the brain (encephalitis) or of the membrane (meningitis) have been associated with brain injury. Robinson and Robinson (1976) report several studies indicating that in cases where mental retardation does not occur, sometimes other changes are noted; that is, changes in personality and abnormal EEG patterns. The link to learning disabilities has been suggested but not proven.

For over 60 years, it has been known that excess lead in children can cause neurological complications such as mental retardation, seizures, and cerebral palsy. However, the link between lead and learning disabilities, though suspected in the early 70s, remains uncertain. Samples of children's blood tend to reflect recent exposure and is not a reliable measure of previous exposure (Lin Fu, 1979). In addition, some studies used subjects from clinics and residential schools which made for a skewed, nonrepresentative sample of the general population. In some instances, inadequate handling of confounding variables affected results.

Early research and screening programs have involved the "lead belt," the industrial northeast. More recent investigations have found undue lead absorption in children in suburban and rural areas. Not all cases could be traced to lead paint which, in the past, has been considered the leading cause of lead poisoning among the urban slum children (Chisolm, 1976). Further investigation found high lead content in the soil and dust, which probably results from emissions from leaded gasoline and industrial pollution.

A well controlled and designed study conducted by Needleman, et al. (1979) has shown the link to learning disabilities to be real and pervasive, endangering children in the suburbs and rural areas as well as the inner city. None of the children in this study had any symptoms that would normally be considered signs of lead poisoning. An analysis was made of the dentine of shed teeth of 3,329 children in first and second grades in the years 1975 through 1978 in Chelsea and Somerville, Massachusetts. Subjects with a lead sample mean 20 ppm (parts per million) were classified as high lead. Low lead classification required a mean less than 10 ppm. Excluded from the sample were children whose parents did not wish to or were unable to participate, whose first language was not English, who had a low birth weight (<2,500g), or who had a history of head injury.

A comprehensive test battery included measures of intelligence; acquisition of conservation of number and substance (Piaget's classical experiments of the quantity of a piece of clay remains the same regardless of its shape); achievement in reading and mathematics; auditory discrimination; and visual perception and integration. Attentional performance was evaluated using reaction time under intervals of varying delay. Each child's teacher answered an 11-item, forced choice, behavior rating scale after the child was in the class for at least two months. The teachers were unaware of the lead level status of each child.

Analysis of the data showed deficits in verbal performance, auditory processing, and ability to sustain attention in children with high lead levels. The high level children also received negative teachers' ratings. The negative ratings increased with increasing dentine lead level, and children with the highest lead levels were rated poorest on nine of eleven items in the behavior rating scale.

Consonant with these findings, recent results reported by Silbergeld (1978) indicate that very low levels of lead can penetrate the neuron and affect it adversely. The pathways that mediate inhibition in the brain also appear to be sensitive to lead (Lin Fu, 1979).

The increase noted in the number of children with learning disabilities and hyperactive behavior may result from the increase of lead in our environment. Certainly this study indicates that lead absorption too mild to have been called "poisoning" can nevertheless interfere with mental functions and classroom performance.

Developmental Lag

The behaviors of many LD children are characteristic of the performance of younger children. It has been hypothesized that either neurological damage occurred at an early stage of development or that the rate of neurological development is slower than the norm. LD children described as immature perform as would a much younger child in motor skills, communication, and/or interpersonal relationships. Of course, not all children develop teeth at the same rate, walk at the same time, or speak at the same time. Development of some children is within the normal range, while others take even longer for physical development or the acquisition of skills. There are also differing maturational levels within the same child. That is, a child may be functioning within the normal range in some areas but there may be a lag in others. Such a child may be considered to have a specific developmental lag or delay.

Studies using electroencephalogram (EEG) tracings point to neurological immaturity as a factor in LD. Critchley (1970) reports that dysrhythmias, which are associated with cortical immaturity, are found in the brain waves of dyslexic children. Satterfield, et al. (1973) compared 31 children diagnosed as having MBD with 21 normal controls. They found there were significantly lower amplitudes and longer latencies (delay between stimulus and response) evoked by auditory stimuli in the MBD group as compared to the control group. It was also reported that excessive amounts of slow wave activity is the most common clinical EEG difference found in MBD children. Both of these findings evidence a maturational delay of the CNS which correlates with the reported immature behavior patterns of the MBD children.

Because of frequent reports of the small stature of LD children, Gold (1978), using data supplied by the Nassau County Growth Clinic, investigated the relationship between learning problems and a lag in physical development. Comparing children diagnosed as having constitutional growth delay (CGD) and those diagnosed as being of familial short stature (FSS), Gold found that a greater frequency of CGD children reported to have MBD and/or hyperactivity, with half the CGD group characterized by teachers as having immature behaviors. The schools reported that a significant proportion of the CGD children presented learning problems. Based on a study of learning in twins, in which it was found that those with academic problems had a slower rate of weight gain in the first two years, Dolan and Matheny (1978) suggest that growth delay may be an early indication of high risk.

Selective attention has been considered developmentally linked in that it can be shown to improve with age. Two studies of reaction time by Czudner and Rourke (1972), using auditory and visual stimuli, showed that the younger the group, the longer the reaction time. The young LD children performed poorest of all and the older LD performed better than the young, normal children. After studying LD children's ability to attend, using a reaction time task under distracting conditions, Dykman, et al. (1971) concluded that "The main cause of learning disabilities is a developmental lag. Neurological immaturity could well explain the attentional deficits . . ." (p. 88).

The search for an explanation of the cause of slow reaction time and delay in general processing tasks leads to an examination of the possibility of a lag in neurological development related to neural myelinization (see Chapter 2).

Geschwind (1968) hypothesized a linkage between the stages of psychomotor and language development and the sequence of myelinization. He also suggests that since boys tend to mature at a slower rate than girls, they are more vulnerable to injury in the unmyelinated areas, which may account for the preponderance of boys among the learning disabled.

Denckla (1978) views "Dysfunction/Delay", as one of the "Ds" in MBD. She cautions that "delay" or "lag" does not mean that the child will catch up. Improvement in one area does not mean improvement in all. Indeed, training in the areas of delay should be chosen carefully. While bicycle riding and handwriting should be trained to age level, other activities such as skipping and hopping do not seem to warrant the expenditure of time (p. 243).

Genetic or Endogenous Factors

During the last ten to fifteen years, the hereditary factors related to learning disorders have received new support although a genetic basis has been posited since the early 1900s when research describing multiple cases of word blindness in single families was reported by Thomas in 1905 and Stephenson and Hinshelwood in 1907 (ACLD, 1978).

Analysis of case data indicates that learning disabilities tend to cluster within families. It is not unusual to find a parent or sibling who has similar learning problems or exhibits a similar developmental lag. Because of the many manifestations of the disability, it can be assumed that there is a cluster of genes which, in the presence of predisposing factors, may emerge as a specific learning disability.

Many researchers (Orton, 1937; Bender, 1957; de Hirsch, Jansky and Langford, 1966) believe that language disorders—for example, learning to read, as well as deficits in verbal expression—are genetically determined. Orton theorized that incomplete hemispheric dominance or mixed dominance was genetically linked and caused language disorders. Bender and de Hirsch viewed the disability as caused by genetically based developmental lag.

Studies of parents and siblings, as well as adoptive and twin studies, have added data supporting the hypothesis that the hyperactive syndrome is of genetic origin (Cantwell, 1975a; Omenn, 1973). Comparing the prevalence rate of minimal brain dysfunction in biologic and nonbiologic families of adopted children with MBD, Cantwell (1975b) found an increased prevalence in the biologic families while the rate of MBD in the nonbiologic families was no greater than that found in the control groups.

Shaywitz, Cohen, and Shaywitz (1978) suggest that genetic factors affect the neurochemical mechanisms that lead to the array of symptoms called learning disabilities. The depletion of brain dopamine,* which may play a part in minimal brain dysfunction, appears to have a genetic base.

Interim reports from a longitudinal study being conducted at the University of Louisville using more than 300 twin pairs and their siblings, indicated a genetic influence on articulation and neuromuscular and cognitive development and the establishment of laterality (Matheny & Dolan, 1974).

The research found that identical (monozygotic) twins with academic problems had a slower weight gain the first two years and had poorer eating habits, greater emotional lability and poorer sleep patterns than their age-mates of fraternal (dizygotic) twins. As preschoolers they were found to be more active and less able to sustain interests. Bakwin (1973), Dolan and Matheny (1978) and Matheny and Dolan (1974) reported shared reading disabilities in monozygotic twins as compared to dizygotic twins.

Robinson and Robinson (1976) caution that twin studies have several possible sources of error. For example: Prenatal life may have been different with two amniotic sacs and a variable circulatory supply: twins usually develop language later; they are never "the only child" in the family; there is generally a shorter gestation period and they weigh less at birth. Compared with fraternal twins, identical twins tend to spend more time together and share the same friends. The psychological relationship also can be quite complex.

The interactive effect of environment and heredity in all children must not be neglected. Not only can environmental factors cause genetic changes (e. g. , radiation and chemical mutagens), but they can also affect "the expression of genetically determined biochemical functions" (Robinson & Robinson, 1976). The propensity toward a particular behavioral pattern may not become evident unless the environmental conditions make it possible. This interactive effect may account for the differences in children who manifest learning disabilities after a trauma while others evidence no impairment.

PREVALENCE OF LEARNING DISABILITIES

The estimates of the number of learning-disabled children vary from a low of 1% to 40% or higher. This wide variation has arisen because of the absence of a clear-cut definition and because large-scale, in-depth diagnostic precedures are expensive (Lynn, Gluckin, & Kripke, 1978). When PL 94-142 was enacted, it was specified that no more than 2% of the school age population (ages 5-17) could be considered learning disabled for purposes of funding. It was also stated that when the Commissioner of Education established specific criteria for learning disabilities, the 2% limit was lifted with the proviso that no more than 12% of all children could be

---

* Dopamine, an internally-produced substance is a neurotransmitter that carries impulses from neuron to neuron in the central nervous system. It is believed to mediate the interpretation of sensory perceptions.

considered handicapped, including the learning disabled. However, the definition that was adopted is open to interpretation and a wide range of estimates continues.

Some programs include children who are classified as having a mild emotional disturbance; others equate learning disabilities with hyperactivity or brain injury, even in the absence of learning problems; while still others include within the group children who are two years or more behind in reading or mathematics, whether or not there are any other symptoms, such as perceptual disorders, attention deficits, and so on. Children with language impairments are also equated with learning disabilities by some. Many studies also include educable mentally retarded children within the learning disabilities group (Kirk & Gallagher, 1979). After reviewing several studies of the prevalence of learning disabilities, Kirk and Gallagher (1979) conclude that "the best guess at this time is that learning-disabled children constitute 1 to 3 percent of the school-age population" (p. 294).

Learning disabilities is a comparatively new category of a handicapping condition which was not recognized thirty years ago. Since its beginning, the number of children classified as learning disabled has increased yearly. This increase may have occurred, in part, because programs are now funded, but it may also represent a true increase. More children with birth injuries or genetic defects now survive and are benefitting from supportive services which enable them to perform at higher levels than would have been expected in the past. In addition, increased environmental pollution may also be increasing the number of children who develop neurological problems (Lynn et al., 1978). Heightened awareness among professionals and parents may also lead to the identification of learning disabilities which were overlooked in the past.

An inverse relationship between socioeconomic status and the incidence of learning disabilities appears to exist. Poor health care before, during, and after birth, poor nutrition, and or deprivation during critical periods may account for this relationship.

Most studies report a higher incidence of boys with learning disabilities than girls (Cohen & Cohn, 1967; Silver, 1971; Hallahan & Cruickshank, 1973). More boys tend to be premature and have a low birth weight of less than 2,500 grams (5½ pounds). Males also are bigger babies, and in passing through the birth canal are more prone to brain injury. The effect of low birth weight and performance was discussed earlier in the chapter.

Boys tend to mature later than girls and tend to need large motor activities beyond the age that girls do. It has been suggested that, in general, if boys started school and/or learning to read a year later than girls, fewer boys would develop learning disabilities.

Differences in the number of reading disabilities appear to vary from country to country. Where there is more of a one-to-one correspondence between the spelling and pronunciation of words, the percentage of children with reading disabilities is relatively low. Other differences in incidence between countries may be due to differences in diagnostic methods and criteria and social expectations (Lynn, Gluckin, & Kripke, 1978, p. 161).

The review of the literature shows that the prevalence figures are only broad estimates. Until uniform criteria and diagnostic techniques are adopted, it will continue to be difficult to compare studies and plan for the future.

REFERENCES

ACLD *Newsbriefs*. Researching genetics as a causative factor. Dallas, Texas, September–October, 1978, vi.

Bakwin, H. Reading disability in twins. *Journal of Learning Disabilities*, 1973, *6*, 439–440.

Bender, L. Specific reading disability as a maturational lag. *Bulletin of the Orton Society*, 1957, *7*, 9–18.

Birch, H. G. The problem of brain damage in children. In Herbert G. Birch (Ed.), *Brain Damage in Children*. Baltimore: Williams & Wilkins, 1963.

Blatman, S. Narcotic poisoning of children (1) through accidental ingestion of methadone and (2) in utero. *Pediatrics*, 1974, *54*, 329–332.

Cantwell, D. P. (ed.) *The Hyperactive child: Diagnosis, management, current research*. New York: Spectrum Publications, 1975.

Chisolm, J. J. Jr. Current status of lead exposure and poisoning in children. *Southern Medical Journal*, 1976, *69*, 529–531.

Cohen, S. M., and Cohn, J. *Teaching the retarded reader: A guide for teachers, reading specialists and supervisors*. New York: Odyssey Press, 1967.

Critchley, M. *The Dyslexic child*, 2nd ed. London: William Hernemann Medical Books Limited, 1970.

Daum, C. Neurobehavioral assessment of the newborn. NYALD Annual Conference, New York City, December 9, 1978.

de Hirsch, K., Jansky, J. J., and Langford, W. S. *Predicting reading failure*. New York: Harper & Row, 1966.

Denckla, M. B. Minimal brain dysfunction. In Jeanne S. Chall and Allan F. Mirsky (Eds.), *Education and the brain*. Chicago: University of Chicago Press, 1978.

Dolan, A. B. and Matheny, A. P. "A distinctive growth curve for a group of children with academic learning problems." *Journal of Learning Disabilities* *11*(8), 1978: 490–494.

Dunn, L. M. *Exceptional children in the schools*. New York: Holt, Rinehart and Winston, 1973.

Dykman, R. A., Ackerman, P. T., Clements, S. D., and Peters, J. E. Specific learning disabilities: an attentional deficit syndrome. In H. R. Myklebust (Ed.) *Progress in learning disabilities vol. 2*. New York: Grune and Stratton, 1971:56–93.

Ernhart, G., Eichman, P. L., Marshall, J. M., and Thurston, D. Brain injury in the preschool child II: comparisons of brain injured and normal children. *Psychological Monographs*, 1963, *77*, 574.

Geschwind, N. Neurological foundations of language. In Helmer Myklebust (Ed.), *Progress in learning disabilities, vol. 1*. New York: Grune & Stratton, 1968.

Gold, R. F. Constitutional growth delay and learning problems. *Journal of Learning Disabilities*, 1978, *2*(7), 427–429.

Graham, F. K., Ernhart, C. B., Thurston, D., and Craft, M. Development three years after perinatal anoxia and other potentially damaging newborn experiences. *Psychology Monographs*, 1962, 76.

Hallahan, D. P., Cruickshank, W. M. *Psychoeducational foundations of learning Disabilities*. Englewood Cliffs, N.J.: Prentice-Hall, 1973.

Hjern, B. and Nylander, I. Late prognosis of severe head injuries in childhood. *Archives of Diseases in Childhood*. 1962, *37*, 113–116.

Hoffman, M. S. Early indications of learning problems. *Academic Therapy*, 1971, *7*, 23.

Katz, H. P. Important endocrine disorders of childhood. In R. H. A. Haslam and P. J. Valletutti (Eds.), *Medical problems in the classroom*. Baltimore: University Park Press, 1975.

Kirk, S. A. and Gallagher, J. J. *Educating exceptional children*. Boston: Houghton Mifflin Co., 1979.

Klein, P. S., Forbes, G. B., and Nadar, P. R. Effects of starvation in infancy (pyloric stenosis) on subsequent learning abilities. *Journal of Pediatrics*, July, 1975, *87(1)*, 8–15.

Koch, R. The multidisciplinary approach to mental retardation. In Alfred A. Beaumeister (Ed.), *Mental retardation: Appraisal, education and rehabilitation*. Chicago: Aldine, 1967.

Lin Fu., J S. Lead exposure among children: A reassessment. *The New England Journal of Medicine*, Mar. 29, 1979, *300*(13), 731–732.

Lloyd-Still, J. D., Shuachman, H. Letter: Intelligence after malnutrition. *Lancet*, Apr. 1974, *1*, 679.

Lynn, R., Gluckin, N. D., and Kripke, B. *Learning disabilities: The state of the field 1978*. New York: Social Science Research Council, 1978.

Matheny, A. P., and Dolan, A. B. A twin study of genetic influences in reading achievement. *Journal of Learning Disabilities*, 1974, 7(2), 99–102.

Needleman, H. L., Gunnoe, C., Leviton, A., Reed, R., Peresie, H., Maher, C., and Barrett, P. Deficits in psychologic and classroom performance of children with elevated dentine lead levels. *The New England Journal of Medicine*, March 29, 1979, *300*(13), 689–695.

Nuckolls, K. B., Cassel, J., and Kaplan, B. H. Psychosocial assets, life crisis, and the prognosis of pregnancy. *American Journal of Epidemiology*, 1972, *95*, 431–441. Cited in Halbert B. Robinson & Nancy M. Robinson, *The Mentally retarded Child*, 2nd ed. New York: McGraw-Hill, 1976.

NYALD, New restrictions on use of oxytocins. *The News*, July–August 1979, *18*(4), 1.

Omenn, G. S. Alcoholism: A pharmocogenetic disorder. *Modern Problems of Pharmopsychiatry*, 1974, *10*. Cited in Halbert B. Robinson and Nancy M. Robinson, *The Mentally retarded child*, 2nd ed. New York: McGraw-Hill, 1976.

———. Genetic issues in the syndrome of minimal brain dysfunction. *Seminars in Psychiatry*, 1973, *5*, 5–17.

Orton, S. *Reading, writing and speech problems in children*, New York: W. W. Norton, 1937.

Ott, J. N. Influence of fluorescent lights in hyperactivity and learning disabilities. *Journal of learning disabilities*, Aug–Sept. 1976, *9*(7), 417–422.

Pakter, J. Address at the American Public Health Association Meeting, Miami Beach Florida, October 20, 1976.

Richardson, F. Some effects of severe head injury. A follow-up study of children and adolescents after protracted coma. *Developmental Medicine and Child Neurology*, 1963, *5*, 471–482.

Robinson, H. B., and Robinson, N. M. *The mentally retarded child*, 2nd ed. New York: McGraw-Hill, 1976.

Rubin, R. A., Rosenblatt, C., and Balow, B. Psychological and educational sequence of prematurity. *Pediatrics*, 1973, *52*, 352–363.

Rudel, R. G. Neuroplasticity: Implications for development and education. In Jeanne S. Chall and Allan F. Mirsky (Eds.), *Education and the brain: The*

Seventy-seventh yearbook of the national society for the study of education part II. Chicago: The University of Chicago Press, 1978.

Satterfield, J. Lesser, L., Saul, R., and Cantwell, D. EEG aspects in the diagnosis and treatment of minimal brain dysfunction. In Felix La Cruz, Bernard Fox, and Richard Roberts (Eds.), *Minimal brain dysfunction*. Annals of the New York Academy of Sciences, 205, February, 1973.

Shaywitz, S. E., Cohen, D. S., and Shaywitz, B. A. The biochemical basis of minimal brain dysfunction. *Journal Pediatrics*, 1978, *92* (2), 179.

Silbergeld, E. K., Adler, H. S. Subcellular mechanisms of lead neurotoxicity. *Brain Research*, 1978, *148*, 451–467.

Silver, L. B. Familial patterns in children with neurologically-based learning disabilities. *Journal of learning disabilities*, 1971, *4*, 349–358.

Stott, D. H. Follow-up study from birth effects of prenatal stresses. *Developmental medicine and child neurology*, 1973, *15*, 770–787.

Winick, M., and Rosso, P. Effects of malnutrition on brain development. *Biology of brain dysfunction*, 1973, *1*, 301–317.

Diagnosis in Learning Disabilities

5

The diagnostic process introduced here is an integral part of the diagnostic-prescriptive teaching and programming approach to learning disabilities. This non-categorical model applies to any population.

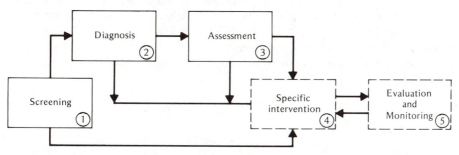

Figure 5-1. Steps in Diagnostic/Prescriptive Approach.

THE PROCESS

The diagnostic process constituting part of a diagnostic/prescriptive approach is viewed as a three-step procedure: the *screening* process utilizes gross measures from a variety of sources to determine if there are sufficient concerns about current and potential performance to warrant a more thorough diagnostic work-up. The screening process must be brief, inexpensive, and easily administered (e.g., it often consists of checklists of observed behaviors noted by teachers and/or parents) since its sole purpose is to provide general informaton about large numbers of children. All concerned must realize that screening tests do not make a diagnosis. *Diagnosis* represents, in this schema, activities carried out with the view of determining if there is a disability, which requires special education. The results of the diagnosis generally lead to a classification. Adelman (1979) notes a label itself has limited use and in some situations "classification (itself) may be a superfluous act" (p.61). *Assessment* is that part of the intervention process in which the data generated will be used to make decisions concerning educational placement and practices and long-and short-range goals. It is at this point that the Individual Education Program (IEP) is written (see Chapter 18). The diagnostic process leads to the fourth step, recommendations and implementation of program and *specific interventions. Evaluation and monitoring*, the fifth step, provides a feedback mechanism for change and revision. Federal mandate requires a review and updating of the IEP at least once a year. If these last two steps in the diagnostic/prescriptive approach are not implemented, the diagnostic process becomes an empty procedural performance.

For some children, fewer steps will be utilized. For example, the screening process suggests that there is a language deficiency which may be caused by environmental and/or experiential deficits. An intervention is planned that provides appropriate activities and situations for the introduction and use of expanded vocabulary. Evaluation at the end of a specified period will determine if the interventions were effective. If not, at that point it may be decided to return to the second step and perform a thorough diagnostic work-up.

Purpose of the Diagnostic Process

The data collected in each step of the diagnostic process are used: 1) to identify those children who have learning disabilities or, in the case of the younger child, who may be "at risk," and 2) to plan appropriate interventions, that is, specific services, programs, and instructional methods and materials. This is not a static process. The educational plan, and even the diagnosis, must be considered tentative. Modifications may be considered when the child's strengths, weaknesses, and potential are assessed as he matures and goes through the educational program. Data collection and interpretation are important aspects of each step in the total process.

SOURCES OF DATA

Case History

The case history contains data from many sources and provides information about the child's past, such as health, developmental milestones, and family and educational background. In a general screening procedure (upon entry to school), the case history data, in conjunction with other devices, should help detect high-risk cases.

Data can be obtained through an individual interview with the parent or by having the parent complete a questionnaire. A questionnaire can also be employed if an interviewer is used because it helps structure the interview session. Although an individual interview takes more time and is more costly, an added advantage is that the interviewer can go beyond the prepared questions and gather additional pertinent information. The screening interview and/or questionnaire asks questions concerning birth history, general background health information, early development, social and personal factors, educational background, and family relationships.

If the child has been in school, additional information for the history can be obtained from school files, test data, anecdotal records, and reports from and interviews with former teachers and other personnel. The teachers' reports should include, not only areas of perceived strengths and weaknesses, but also methods that were found to be successful.

When the case history is used as part of the diagnostic step, input from the obstetrician and the child's pediatrician may be requested. Their observations are helpful in corroborating the parents' information and in uncovering possible clues unknown to the parent.

Most districts develop their own questionnaires. They should not be complicated or lengthy but should be of sufficient detail so that the necessary data are generated.

Observation Scales

As part of the screening process, observation scales have been used to obtain teacher judgements of the child's functioning in several behavioral categories (Myklebust & Boshes, 1969; Kirk, 1966). Teacher ratings have been found to be a reliable means of identifying children with learning and behavioral problems (Lerner, 1981; Feshbach, Adelman & Fuller, 1974; Bower, 1969). Although there are published scales which have been used for this purpose—e.g., *Devereaux Behavior Rating Scale* and *Pupil Rating Scale*—many school districts and learning-disability specialists develop their own form suitable for the role of the classroom teacher in their district (Katz & Lopatich, 1978). Most of the scales include items that rate auditory comprehension, oral language, spatial orientation, behavior, and motor functioning.

Behavioral checklists and rating scales have also been developed to be completed by parents (*Louisville Behavior Checklist*, 1977; Klein, 1978b, 1980). The Klein scale, A-PART, is completed by parents of kindergarten and beginning first grade children. A pilot study using this scale found that not only were parent ratings consonant with teacher ratings but, in addition, the parents became more aware and understanding of their children's needs. They were able to take an active role, working cooperatively with the teacher and tutoring their children when the need was recognized.

Neurological Examination

When after the initial screening, a neurological problem is suspected (and remember, most definitions of LD include a neurological basis), the child is referred to the neurologist. The neurologist obtains a detailed medical history for clues in the child's background which may account for the learning difficulties. That is, the neurologist looks for clues that may indicate the possibility of brain damage before, during, or after birth or the presence of a familial disposition toward neurological difference. The developmental milestones (the age when the child crawled, stood, walked, spoke), feeding and sleeping patterns, and social and school experiences may also offer clues to the neurologist.

The conventional neurological examination includes; (1) evaluation of the function of the cranial nerve as it relates to hearing, vision, chewing, swallowing, taste, facial expression, and equilibrium; and (2) assessment of motor function and reflexes. Tests of perception and tactile stimulation evaluate the sensory nerves.

The electroencephalographic (EEG) recordings of the child's brain wave are no longer included in routine neurological examinations in the diagnosis of LD (Bryan

& Bryan, 1978, p. 265). Brain activity is detected by electrodes which are attached to different parts of the head. Analysis of the pattern produced on a chart can indicate if there are brain abnormalities. However, the relationship of such patterns to learning disabilities is not clear. Many children with learning problems have apparently normal EEG patterns while others with no learning problems may have abnormal patterns. In addition, researchers have been unable to link a particular EEG pattern to a particular learning problem.

Although the EEG, as part of a learning disabilities diagnosis, has been criticized and at present has not yielded much useful information for the educator, several researchers believe there are new possibilities of their use for diagnosis and even prediction when used in conjunction with computer analysis (John, 1977).

Because most learning-disabled children do not exhibit gross neurological abnormalities, an expanded neurological examination is used to detect the more subtle, or soft, signs.* The examiner looks for indications of motor coordination problems, awkwardness of movement, delays in language development, and perceptual-motor problems. Included in the exam are: hopping on either foot, balancing on either foot, gait, crossing the midline (touching the nose, than the left ear, the nose, right ear), alternating touch (nose, examiner's finger, nose, examiner's finger), and finger agnosia (with eyes closed, tell which finger the examiner touches). In most of these motor tests, the examiner looks for speed, accuracy, and fluidity.

Denckla (1979) includes in her neurological exam walking on heels and on toes and looks for feet-to-hands overflow of movement. While the child is sitting, he taps feet, alternates heel and toe, and performs movements of hands and fingers. The points of overflow, as well as overflow itself, are considered significant. Denckla recently added tongue wiggle from left to right and eye movements to the examination. These last two activities may lead to head movement overflow. Under the age of seven, this type of overflow is common.

Peters, et al. (1973) suggest that physicians—that is, pediatricians and family practitioners—can take a greater part in identifying children with minimal brain dysfunction by including in their office screening procedures a special neurological exam that focuses on motor signs found to be associated with learning problems. This exam reviews a group of motor behaviors that have been associated with minimal brain dysfunction. The evaluation of the items looks for smooth and rhythmic motion, maintenance of balance, cross-modality integration and ability to move in space.

Sensory Acuity

Because visual and hearing problems can interfere with a child's performance in school, two of the first areas to be evaluated when a child is having difficulty are visual and auditory acuity. Most schools have screening programs that provide screening for visual and hearing difficulties on a yearly basis. Children considered at risk in either or both areas should be referred to the appropriate specialist for diagnosis.

---

* Soft signs have been categorized as two types: developmental and neurological. Developmental soft signs are those appropriate in a younger child, i.e., articulation or a motor skill.

Neurological soft signs are not developmental but are subtle or "pastel" versions of known pathological conditions, i.e., choreiform movements, tremors, reflex differences, postural and gait anomalies, etc. (Kinsbourne, 1973).

Acuity problems are differentiated from discrimination and perception problems (discussed in more detail in Chapter 9). It should be noted, however, that one can have perfect acuity in vision and hearing and yet display visual and auditory imperception.

The basic screening test for visual acuity is the Snellen Wall Chart: The child is asked to read the chart (one eye at a time and then both eyes) from a distance of twenty feet. The letters decrease in size from the top of the chart to the bottom. For those unable to read, the Snellen E Test is used. The child either points in the direction the arms of the E point or he holds up a letter to match it. Both tests only assess central visual acuity and not far-point visual functions such as peripheral vision, depth perception or binocular vision, nor do they evaluate near-point acuity.

Problems can arise if the child cannot discriminate letters, if he memorizes the letters, or if he guesses the letters when he sees only a general configuration. Additional testing should be done as part of the screening process. The Keystone Telebinocular, the Bausch and Lomb Orthorater, or the Titmus Vision Tester can be used to assess near- and far-point vision, muscle balance, and other aspects of vision.

Group auditory screening tests, used widely in the past, have low validity and reliability (Salvia & Ysseldyke, 1981). Individual screening of children, using a pure-tone audiometer, has been found more effective. Earphones are placed over the child's ears and he is asked to raise his hand when he hears a tone. The loudness or intensity of the sound is measured in decibels (dB). Pitch or frequency is measured in Hertz (Hz) units, the number of cycles per second. Each ear is tested separately at 20 to 25 dB at varying frequencies (500, 1,000, 2,000, and 6,000 Hz and 30 dB at 4,000 Hz). If a child does not seem to hear a tone in either or both ears, he should be retested. If he fails the second screening, he should be referred for further testing.

Physical Anomalies

A relationship between minor physical anomalies (MPA) and learning-disabled children has been suggested by several researchers (von Hilsheimer, 1974; von Hilsheimer & Kurko, 1979; Firestone & Douglas, 1976; Waldrop et al., 1978). The anomalies noted include high steepled palate, furrowed tongue, malformed, low, or asymmetrical placement of ears, teeth, and toes, and fingers that show slight abnormalities in length and spacing, etc.

Most studies reported a positive relationship between learning and behavior problems and MPA, that is, the more numerous the anomalies, the more severe the learning and behavior problems. Waldrop et al. (1978) contends that the link is so strong that the presence of MPA at birth can be used to predict hyperactivity by the age of three. Of course, correlation does not *necessarily* imply causality. A possible third factor may produce the two conditions. Von Hilsheimer (1974) believes that the presence of MPA and learning disabilities are both rooted in biochemical processes and may be associated with nutritional deficiencies.

Despite the overall positive correlations, MPA was found to be more prevalent among the low socioeconomic groups, though most of the learning and behavior-problem children come from upper and middle-income groups (von Hilsheimer & Kurko, 1979). Perhaps this reflects the likelihood that learning disabilities will be misdiagnosed as mental retardation or simply overlooked inasmuch as the disadvantaged status often masks learning disabilities (Meyer & Moran, 1979).

Standardized Tests

Some of the formal assessments discussed in this and subsequent chapters are used to provide an overall appraisal of functioning (appropriate for screening) while others attempt to give a detailed analysis of strengths and weaknesses. In many instances, the validity and/or reliability of the tests and the applicability from one normed group to another have been questioned. Also, tests measure the child's performance at one point in time only.

Specific drawbacks of particular tests are noted in the discussion of their use in the diagnostic process. These tests are included because, at this time, we do not have more reliable or valid instruments. If used with caution, with the recognized limits, the data derived from these instruments together with data from the other sources described in this chapter can be used in the formulation of a diagnosis and an educational plan. A listing of the tests and their publishers presented in this and subsequent chapters is found in Appendix A and B.

Individual Intelligence Tests

The *Wechsler Scales* consists of three tests: the *Wechsler Preschool and Primary Scale of Intelligence* (*WPPSI*), the *Wechsler Intelligence Scale for Children-Revised* (*WISC-R*), and the *Wechsler Adult Intelligence Scale* (*WAIS*). Because of the wide use of WISC-R in learning-disability programs, it will be discussed more fully than the two other Wechsler scales.

The WISC-R is used for the assessment of intelligence of children aged 6 to 16. In addition to a total score, there are verbal and performance subtest scores. For students above the age of 16, the WAIS is used. WPPSI is intended for children between the ages of 4 and 6½. All three scales sample similar behaviors.

The verbal subtest includes:

- Information—Knowledge of information a person is expected to have learned in and out of school.
- Comprehension—The ability to understand directions and make judgments.
- Similarities—The identification of similar aspects of objects presented verbally.
- Arithmetic—Arithmetic problem solving. In the WPPSI, simple counting tasks are used. The other two scales require computation of difficult problems.
- Vocabulary—Word definition.
- Digit Span—Immediate recall of orally-presented digits.
- Sentences—Included only in WPPSI, the child is required to repeat sentences.

The Performance Subtests are:

- Picture Completion—The student identifies the missing parts in pictures.
- Picture Arrangement—Pictures must be placed in an appropriate sequence to tell a story.
- Block Design—Small, colored blocks must be used to reproduce a stimulus design.
- Object Assembly—The parts of a puzzle must be fitted together to form a complete picture.
- Coding—Symbols associated with other symbols must be copied on paper.

- Mazes—A path must be traced through more and more difficult mazes.
- Geometric Designs—Included only in the WPPSI, geometric designs must be copied.

Although the WISC-R is a widely used, individually-administered test, having satisfactory reliability and validity (Salvia & Ysseldyke, 1981), the full scale and verbal and performance subtest scores do not provide an adequate picture of the student's abilities. Although no evidence exists that scatter or pattern analysis indicates cerebral pathology (Simensen & Sutherland, 1974), performance on individual subtests, should be examined. That is, intertest scatter (the differences between subtest scores) as well as intratest scatter (failure on easy items and pass on some of the more difficult ones within the same subtest), can offer clues to a child's strengths, weaknesses, and learning patterns.

Three WISC patterns were identified by Clements (1964) as indicative of learning disabilities:

Pattern 1. Intertest and intratest scatter is found in verbal and performance scores. Frequently the final verbal and performance scores are equal and the scatter is ignored.

Pattern 2. The verbal score is 15 or more points higher than performance. These children usually have difficulty in perceptual-motor performance. Performance is frequently in the retarded range, though the full scale score indicates a normal I.Q.

Pattern 3. Performance score is 10-30 points higher than the verbal score. Children exhibiting this pattern have difficulty expressing themselves verbally. Clements found that this child frequently has a reading disability.

Bannatyne (1974) grouped several subtests to represent function in specific areas:

Spatial—picture completion + block design + object assembly
Conceptualization—comprehension + similarities + vocabulary
Sequencing—digit span + picture arrangement + coding
Acquired knowledge—information + arithmetic + vocabulary

The sum of the scaled scores of each group should equal 30 since the average scaled score on the WISC is 10. The composite scaled scores for the four groups can be compared and the child's strengths and weaknesses can be determined. Bannatyne reports that the majority of the children he has tested fit into these diagnostic profiles. Webb (1979) found that learning disabled young adults, who show strong performance on the Similarities and Block Design subtests of the WAIS, are good risks for college programs.

Stellern, Vasa, and Little (1976) have identified and described the performance areas that each subtest supposedly measures (p. 23), that is, the information and vocabulary subtests are considered to be dependent upon formal education; comprehension questions are based on practical experience; while arithmetic and digit span depend on the ability to concentrate. Subtest scaled score deviations are then used to identify the learner's strengths and deficits.

Denckla (1979) correlated performance on WISC-R with specific deficits, that is, a verbal score lower than performance score by at least 10 points may indicate a language impairment; low performance on arithmetic, coding, and digit span suggests an attention-disordered child. If, however, block design is also down, an attentional problem should not be assumed. Denckla also suggests that when errors are made in the information subtest, in order to ascertain whether the answer is unknown or if it is a retrieval problem, the child should be given a choice of answers.

The Stanford-Binet Intelligence Scale includes items ranging in difficulty from the two-year level to superior adult level. Two scores are obtained: an M.A. (mental age) and a deviation I.Q. Although it has a long history of use (it was originally designed in 1906) and has been revised many times, the stanford-Binet has not been used as frequently as the WISC-R or the WAIS in the diagnosis of learning disabilities. Salvia and Ysseldyke (1981) note that the new edition of 1972 provides too little data concerning standardization and no information regarding reliability or validity data, and therefore, its use is not warranted at this time. However, Stellern, Vasa, and Little (1976) consider the test the best available for children between the ages of two and six years, because it has a higher ceiling than other tests, thus enabling the testing of gifted young children.

Tests of Academic Performance

Tests of academic skills are of two types: (1) a general survey of basic skills that yield grade level or quantitative scores in broad areas (e.g., silent reading, arithmetic computation) and (2) diagnostic tests that provide information on the quality of performance in more specific areas (e.g., blending, sight vocabulary, and exchanging tens and ones). An in-depth discussion of tne use of both types of tests in language arts (including reading) and mathematics can be found in Chapters 12 and 13.

Motor-Performance Tests

Early identification screening batteries include general assessments of fine and gross motor skills (see p. 92). There are also tests that diagnose the components of motor functioning, such as the Lincoln-Oseretsky Motor Development Scale and the Purdue Perceptual Motor Survey.

The Lincoln-Oseretsky Motor Development Scale is an individually-administered test that examines a wide variety of motor skills arranged in order of difficulty by age. Depending on the age level, some tasks differ for girls and boys. The test was designed for children from age six to 14.

The Purdue Perceptual Motor Survey, an individual test for children four to ten years of age, assesses gross and fine motor performance. The survey is concerned with three major aspects of skill development: laterality, directionality, and perceptual–motor match. This test examines five areas: balance and posture, body image and differentiation, perceptual-motor match, ocular control, and form perception (visual-motor). The test is not used to grade or classify children, but to make a qualitative assessment of perceptual motor skills. The validity of the test has been questioned since there is little support on the necessity of the acquisition of such skills for academic success (see Chapter 9).

Visual-Motor Tests

Visual-motor tests are used to detect soft signs of neurological dysfunction. Tests in this category generally require the child to copy various geometric forms and are considered to assess the integration of visual reception and motor expression.

Several screening tests and motor tests include similar activities as part of the total evaluation. Most of the tests are intended to be used with children in the primary grades.

The *Bender Visual Motor Gestalt Test* for ages five through eleven is given on an individual basis. It consists of nine designs presented one at a time and must be copied on a sheet of paper. The figures produced are evaluated in terms of distortion of shape, object rotation, integration of parts, and perseveration (e.g., drawing more than needed). The Koppitz system for scoring the Bender is the most widely used.

Originally developed by Bender in 1938 to differentiate between brain injured and nonbrain-injured adults and to detect possible emotional disturbance, it has been used to measure intelligence, academic achievement, and visual perception and to identify damage and emotional disturbance. Salvia and Ysseldyke (1981) contend that the Bender Gestalt is just a measure of skill in copying designs. It should *not* be used to measure intelligence; to predict the academic performance of an individual child; or to identify emotional disturbance since it samples a limited perceptual-motor skill area, and has relatively low reliability and questionable validity. Research is equivocal as to its effectiveness in predicting academic success or identifying brain damage (Coles, 1978).

The *Developmental Test of Visual Motor Integration* (*VMI*) for children 2–15 years is a group test with high reliability requiring the student to copy 24 designs of increasing difficulties. Though it, too, measures a limited sample of behavior, the VMI provides a larger sample than the Bender Gestalt. The validity of the test has been questioned, but it has relatively high reliability (Salvia & Ysseldyke, 1981).

The *Developmental Test of Visual Perception* designed by Frostig, includes subtests the author considers to be necessary for acquisition of academic skills; they develop early in life; they are deficit areas of the neurologically impaired; they lend themselves to group testing; and they effect the total functioning of the child.

Eye-hand coordination examines the subject's skill in drawing lines and starting and stopping on target.

Figure-ground perception requires the child to identify figures imbedded in increasingly complex backgrounds and to discriminate intersecting figures.

Form constancy assesses the ability to perceive a geometric figure regardless of its size or orientation.

Position in Space examines the ability to find stimulus figures whether they are reversed or rotated.

Spatial Relations assesses skill in copying patterns. Dots are used as guide points.

The test is designed to be administered in groups or to individuals four to eight years of age. Remediation at preschool and kindergarten age is preferred since, according to Frostig, many problems will not appear when the child gets older. Based on the results of the test, the teacher is directed to use the Frostig materials to remediate the areas of deficit.

Though Salvia and Ysseldyke (1981) find the total test score indicative of overall visual-perception skill development, users are cautioned that the individual subtests cannot be used for diagnosis since their reliability and validity are questionable. They note that the authors' conclusions that five independent skills are measured are not supported by the data. Stellern, Vasa & Little (1976) also point out that while the test may reveal a weakness it does not reveal its cause. The teacher must "teach for transfer" to academic subjects if the intervention is to be successful (Frostig and Maslow, 1973).

The tests described above are among the most commonly used assessments of perceptual–motor performance. Others are: the *Memory for Designs Test*, *Lincoln-Oseretsky Motor Development Scale*, and the *Southern California Perceptual-Motor Tests*.

The use of perceptual-motor tests is based on the assumptions that 1) the tests can be used to identify brain damage and 2) academic success is linked to perceptual-motor performance. Many of the assessments lack the reliability needed for educational decisions and there is little support for the supposition that the training of perceptual-motor skills will improve academic performance. "Perceptual-motor training will improve *perceptual-motor* functioning" (Salvia & Ysseldyke, 1981, p. 367).

Tests of Auditory Perception

Several tests have been used to assess aspects of auditory perception such as discrimination, memory sequencing and blending (see Chapter 3). The *Auditory Discrimination Test* (Wepman, 1973) is a short, easily-administered test that requires the child to tell which of forty spoken pairs of words are the same or different. Thirty of the pairs differ either in the initial, medial, or final position, that is, tub-tug. The test has been criticized because a one item difference is used to distinguish between good discriminators and poor discriminators.

The *Goldman-Fristoe-Woodcock Test of Auditory Discrimination* uses word–picture associations. No verbal responses are required. It includes subtests that assess discrimination under controlled background noise conditions.

Auditory Memory is assessed by tests such as *The Oral Directions and Oral Commissions* subtests of the *Detroit Test of Learning Aptitude*.

Evaluation of auditory sequencing, the ability to remember and repeat in order words presented orally, is included in several tests: *Auditory Sequential Memory* subtest of the ITPA, *Digit Span* of the WISC-R, *Auditory Attention Span for Unrelated Words* in the *Detroit Test of Learning Aptitude*.

Sound blending is assessed in two subtests of the ITPA, *Sound Blending and Auditory Closure* and the *Roswall-Chall Auditory Blending Test*. Auditory training includes activities requiring the child to recognize the sounds in the environment, locate the source of sounds, attend to patterns of sound, and discriminate individual phonemes and words.

Language Tests

Many language tests are available for use in screening, diagnosis, and assessment. Several tests that assess various aspects of the language arts are discussed in Chapter 12. The early screening batteries (p. 92), the WISC-R and the ITPA also include language subtests that assess performance in expressive and receptive language.

The Goldman-Fristoe Test of Articulation is a criterion-reference test (assesses the extent to which specific objectives have been met) administered individually to assess the ability to articulate within simple and complex situations. Three parts comprise the test: (1) The sound-in-words subtest uses pictures as a stimulus; (2) The sounds-in-sentences subtest requires the child to retell the major aspects of stories that have been read to him, and pictures are available for prompts; (3) For children who make articulation errors, the Stimulability subtest has the examiner say the misarticulated consonant in a syllable. The child is asked to repeat the consonant. If it is done correctly, the examiner uses the sound in a word. If the child repeats it correctly, the examiner uses the sound in a sentence. This aspect of the test provides information for the speech therapist regarding the child's ability to respond to and benefit from therapy.

The Peabody Picture Vocabulary Test-Revised (PPVT-R) is a test of receptive language for ages two and one half through 40. Each of its two forms contains a series of plates in graduated difficulty. Each plate consists of four pictures. The examiner reads a stimulus word and the student points to, or otherwise indicates, the picture which represents the meaning of the word.

Illinois Test of Psycholinguistic Abilities (ITPA) is an individually-administered test designed to assess verbal and nonverbal communication along three dimensions: (1) levels of organization (automatic and representational), (2) channels of communication (input and output modalities), and (3) psycholinguistic processes—receptive, expressive, and associative. The test consists of 12 subtests, two of which are supplementary and used at the discretion of the examiner. Table 5-1 lists each subtest, defines the function that is evaluated, and provides a representative item.

Data derived from the ITPA provide age and scaled scores. The profile of performance of the normal learner is relatively flat and within the normal range for the age. The profile of a learning-disabled youngster shows areas of discrepancy with some scores falling within the normal range and others below.

Subscores can be analyzed in a variety of ways. They can be combined to compare the child's functioning on the levels of organization. That is, mean scores at the representational level can be compared to the mean scores at the automatic level. In the same way, the mean scores of the tests of different channels of communication can be compared. Comparison of the performance relative to the psycholinguistic processes—that is, reception, association, and expression—can also be contrasted. Such analysis will help highlight areas of strength and weakness.

Although the ITPA is a widely used test, the norms and validity have been questioned (Salvia & Ysseldyke, 1981). Research has not shown it to have predictive or diagnostic validity (Newcomer, 1975). Stellern, Vasa, and Little (1976) consider it to be a good instrument for identifying learning problems (a low score indicates a learning weakness), but not for the identification of causes. Presently no studies support the use of the ITPA for the selection of remedial programs (Bryan & Bryan, 1978).

Social-Maturity Assessment

Social maturity is usually assessed by the *Vineland Social Maturity Scale*. The parent, or another person who is knowledgeable about the student, is asked a series of specific questions about behaviors that evaluate eight areas of performance: (1) self-help general, (2) self-help eating, (3) self-help dressing, (4) locomotion, (5) occupation, (6) communication, (7) self-direction, and (8) socialization. The scale,

Table 5-1. The Subtests of the ITPA

Subtest	Process	Sample Items	Response Made
Auditory Reception	ability to comprehend what is said	Do dogs eat?	vocal (yes or no)
Visual Reception	ability to gain meaning from pictures	A picture related to a stimulus picture must be found from among a group of four	pointing
Auditory Association	ability to relate concepts presented orally, verbal analogies	A dog has hair; A fish has _____.	vocal
Visual Association	ability to relate concepts presented visually	Shown a stimulus picture and four options, the child must answer the question, "What goes with this?"	pointing
Verbal Expression	ability to describe objects orally	Child is shown an object, e.g., a button, and asked to "Tell me all about this."	vocal
Manual Expression	ability to express ideas and show understanding of the use of objects by using gestures	When shown the picture of an object, the child must demonstrate how it is used.	motor (gesture)
Grammatic Closure	ability to use the grammar and syntax of the English language	After being shown a picture and given an incomplete statement about it, the child completes the statement. This dog likes to bark. Here he is _____.	vocal
Visual Closure	ability to identify a common object when only part is visible	Estimates objects, e.g., fish, is seen in varying degrees within a drawing of a scene. The child is asked to point to all examples of that object with the drawing.	motor (pointing)
Auditory Sequential Memory	ability to remember and reproduce a series of digits which are spoken by the examiner.	5, 4, 3 _____ what did I say? _____	vocal
Visual Sequential Memory	ability to remember and reproduce a series of non-meaningful figures	After being shown a sequence of figures, which are then removed, the child is asked to reproduce the sequence using chips of the figures.	motor
Auditory Closure (Supplementary)	ability to fill in the missing parts of a word which were deleted by the examiner	What am I saying? bo / le tele / one	vocal
Sound Blending (Supplementary)	ability to blend the sounds of a word	Examiner Listen— c-a-t student "cat"	vocal

which extends from infancy through adulthood, yields a social-age score and a social quotient. The scale has been used since 1953 and it has been suggested that a revision is now needed. Several items are placed at age levels that seem inappropriate at the present time (Salvia & Ysseldyke, 1981).

Informal Tests

To be most effective, diagnosis must be continuous. Informal observation and testing permit immediate revisions of the educational plan as greater knowledge concerning the child's performance is gained during instructional periods and because the child himself changes as a result of interventions. The literature does not emphasize such an informal approach; however, for the teacher, it is most important since the skill can be examined in a real learning situation.

Bachor (1979) considers that students' classroom work is the most underutilized information teachers collect. Informal diagnosis supplements the information gathered from formal testing programs and from observation. The many advantages of informal testing and diagnosing include: (1) Error analysis provides the teacher with data for modifying the teaching program; (2) Interstudent as well as intrastudent error analysis, although time-consuming, allows the teacher to compare the performances of the children within the group as well as that of the individual student: Group analysis enables the teacher to evaluate teaching effectiveness while intrastudent analysis highlights individual patterns of error; (3) The testing atmosphere is generally more relaxed; (4) Specific subtest areas of deficit or strength can be assessed; (5) The diagnostician can ask questions about performance in order to determine how the child approaches a task; (6) The informal tests are generally constructed and administered by the teacher and can correspond to the specific classroom experience and better reflect the child's classroom performance; (7) The tests can be criterion-referenced.

Ideally, as Hofmeister (1975) says, the tests should be well integrated into the day-by-day school program so that they will not be considered a testing situation. The effectiveness of informal tests is limited, however, by the teacher's training in constructing and interpreting tests, lack of standardization, and teacher bias (test will include what the teacher thinks is important and may omit important aspects of a task).

Wallace and Kauffman (1978, pp. 61–62) suggest four types of informal evaluation which can be conducted by the classroom teacher: 1) seatwork exercises emphasizing a single task; 2) oral exercises; 3) informal lessons; and 4) individually-written assignments.

The trial lesson is another informal testing technique in which the teacher conducts individual mini-lessons using different techniques and approaches to find the child's best learning style. Two approaches have been designed for this purpose: the Mills' Learning Methods Test (1970) and the Roswell and Natchez technique (1971). An important caution should be noted: Do not assume that the child will use the same learning style in all subject areas and for all kinds of learning. Performance style in learning spelling is not necessarily the same one used in learning to compute in arithmetic. Nor can we assume that increasing on-task behavior in one academic area will generalize to another.

Informal testing methods such as the Informal Reading Inventory (IRI) and the Cloze method used in the language arts areas and informal arithmetic tests are described in Chapters 12 and 13.

Informal diagnosis and assessment should be part of every teaching session. As the lesson progresses, the teacher should be evaluating how and what the child is learning. Such an assessment "will yield results which suggest instructional strategies that are more educationally relevant and instructionally appropriate than strategies selected by a variety of other diagnostic approaches" (Poteet, 1980, p. 98). This implementation of the diagnostic/teaching approach, in a realistic, nonthreatening learning situation, enables the teacher to modify strategies on an on-going basis. As McLoughlin and Lewis (1981) note, the type of assessment used, whether formal or informal, depends on the assessment question to be answered.

Screening and Early Identification of Learning Disabilities

Screening at the kindergarten and first-grade levels for potential learning disabilities has become standard procedure in most school districts. Federal legislation also has provided the impetus for screening programs directed at the preschool, three to five-year age group. As part of the national child find project, each state has developed procedures for the identification of all unserved handicapped children, beginning from birth, in order to enroll them in appropriate programs as early as possible. Early identification enables the school and other agencies to institute intervention techniques designed to eliminate or minimize learning difficulties and their accompanying emotional problems. White (1975) has identified child development from eight months to three years as a particularly critical time.

In addition to the case history data that is gathered, several screening batteries are available for these early identification programs. Representative assessments are the *Meeting Street School Screening Test, Cognitive Skills Assessment Battery*, and *Developmental Indicators for the Assessment of Learning.*

The *Meeting Street School Screening Test* (*MSSST*) is an individually-administered test which includes three subtests: motor patterning, visual-perceptual-motor, and language. Each subtest samples input, integration, and output skills. Norms are provided for each subtest and for the total test at six-month intervals for ages 5-0 through 7-5. In addition, a behavior rating scale is included to be used to rate the child's test-taking performance.

The *Cognitive Skills Assessment Battery* for prekindergarten and kindergarten levels (CSAB) is a criterion-referenced test administered on an individual basis. It measures competencies considered by the authors to be needed for success in kindergarten and first grade. Instead of scores, a profile of strengths and weaknesses is developed. This profile indicates curriculum needs of the class as well as the individual child. The test samples performance in five areas: orientation toward the environment; coordination; discrimination; memory; and comprehension/concept formation. Response during the assessment procedure is also evaluated. The authors suggest the battery be administered at the beginning and end of the school year in order to identify areas of improvement and those still needing development.

The *Developmental Indicators for the Assessment of Learning* (DIAL) screening test is used to screen children aged $2\frac{1}{2}$ to $5\frac{1}{2}$ and can be administered by para-professionals. Six areas are assessed: 1) sensory (visual and auditory acuity), 2) motor (gross and fine motor activities), 3) conceptual (following directions, identifying concepts shown in pictures, counting, and so on), 4) language (describing pictures, answering questions, and the like), 5) affective, and 6) social. The last two areas, which use an observational rating form completed by the tester, assess the child's behavior during the screening session.

Other tests used in early identification screening programs are the *Boehm Test of Basic Concepts* (See Chapter 13), and the *Peabody Picture Vocabulary Test.*

Identification of a high risk factor through screening leads to the diagnostic phase and, most important, to the development of appropriate educational practice and intervention for each child. In practice, a label is usually attached at this stage. However, in view of the limitations of assessment tools and the lags mentioned earlier, at the preschool-age level it is frequently impossible to pinpoint a specific diagnostic category. Broad, cross-categorical terms such as *developmental disabilities* and *high risk* are used (Lerner, 1981). The diagnostic data need not be used to label; rather knowledge concerning the child's current functioning is used to select the suitable activities, programs, placement, and so forth, with modifications as the child changes.

Even though there are problems associated with early identification (see Chapter 19), many researchers are attempting to find ways of recognizing LD children before the age of three. Again, the hope is that the earlier the intervention programs, the fewer and less severe the learning problems. Because most clinical and behavioral observations do not identify underlying brain dysfunction, Cohen (1978) suggests that the next decade will see an increase in the use of the EEG to provide insight into brain function. While the cognitive behaviors themselves are not yet manifested, indicators of the functioning of these brain regions can be obtained by coupling EEG output with a computer, using a technique called "averaging." Although the present studies focus on normal adults, future research will examine normative development from infancy. Cohen states that these studies will provide information about the mechanism of learning disabilities, rather than only detect them, and will distinguish between maturational lag and neurological disorder.

E. Roy John (1977) reports that research that uses a Neurometric Battery has been conducted at the New York University Medical Center. The Battery measures evoked potentials (the responses of a region in the brain to sensory stimulation) using data from the EEG, which is analyzed by a computer. John reports that it is possible to discriminate learning-disabled children from those who are not disabled, and brain-injured children from those who have neurological dysfunctions from other causes. Patterns found in children younger than twelve years of age differed from those of teenagers. The patterns of children who were classified as verbal underachievers, arithmetic underachievers, and verbal and arithmetic underachievers differed from each other and from normal achievers. John has considered using this method for early identification of learning disabilities but notes that, because of the dangers of premature or mistaken diagnosis, caution is required.

* * *

The diagnostic process in the field of learning disabilities has been receiving much criticism. Part of the problem in attempting to diagnose learning disabilities is that no constellation of behaviors and characteristics is unique to the learning disabled. Some signs common in cases of learning disabilities are also found in the non-learning disabled so they cannot be relied upon, in and of themselves, as diagnostic signals. However, we contend that a group of specific behaviors, in conjunction with specific patterns of response on diagnostic assessments in the presence of learning problems, may indicate neurological dysfunctions and lead to diagnosis of learning disability.

The tests used in diagnosis and assessment have also been criticized, in large part because of the inability to distinguish learning disabilities from other disorders, which again leads us back to the lack of a precise definition as well as an inability, given the limitations of many of our current procedures, to definitively pinpoint the presumed neurological dysfunction.

For the teacher, parent and child, such circuitous discussions help little. We cannot wait until better tests are available. The problem is here, *now*, and we must meet it. We need not be locked into any test or score. Nor should we think solely in terms of groups of children; each child must be approached as an individual with unique needs. Use the data available from the diagnostic process (including his functioning in a testing situation) in order to develop the appropriate educational goals and program, and in so doing, ask, not only what can't the child do, but more importantly, what *can* he do and under what circumstances? At best, develop a hypothesis for this one child, based on the best data available, being fully aware that if it does not work, it can be changed.

REFERENCES

Adelman, H. S. Diagnostic classification of LD: A practical necessity and a procedural problem. *Learning Disabilities Quarterly*, Spring, 1979, *2*(2), 56–62.

Bachor, D. G. Using work samples as diagnostic information. *Learning Disabilities Quarterly*, Winter, 1979, Volume *2*(1), 45–52.

Bannatyne, A. Diagnosis: A note on recategorization of the WISC-scaled scores. *Journal of Learning Disabilities*, May, 1974, *7*(5), 272–273.

Bower, E. *Early identification of emotionally handicapped children in school*, 2nd ed. Springfield, Ill.: Charles C Thomas, Publisher, 1969.

Bryan, T. H., and Bryan, J. H. *Understanding learning disabilities*, 2nd ed. Sherman Oaks, Ca.: Alfred, 1978.

Clements, S. D., Lehtinen, L. E., and Lukens, J. E. *Children with minimal brain injury: A symposium*. Chicago, Ill.: National Society for Crippled Children and Adults, 1964.

Cohen, H. J. Early signs of neurological dysfunction: What do they mean? Presentation at New York Association for the Learning Disabled Annual Conference, New York City, December 9, 1978.

Coles, G. S. The learning disabilities test battery: Empirical and social issues. *Harvard Educational Review*. Aug. 1978, *48*(3), 314–340.

Denckla, M. B. The role of the neurological examination in the diagnosis of brain dysfunction in children. Workshop at Teachers College, Columbia University, April 7–8, 1979.

Feshbach, S., Adelman, H., and Fuller, W. W. Early identification of children with high risk of reading failure. *Journal of Learning Disabilities*, December, 1974, 7(10), 639–644.

Firestone, P. L., and Douglas, V. Hyperactivity and physical anomalies. *Canadian Psychiatric Association Journal*, 1976, 1(23).

Frostig, M., and Maslow, P., *Learning problems in the classroom*. New York: Grune & Stratton, 1973.

Hofmeister, A. Integrating criterion-referenced testing and instruction. In Wills Hively and M. Reynolds (Eds.), *Domain-referenced testing in special education*. Minneapolis: Leadership Training Institute/Special Education, University of Minnesota, 1975.

John, E. R. et al. Neurometrics. *Science*, 1977, *196*, 1393–1410.

Katz, S., and Lopatich, G. B. Assessment remediation series. In Herbert Goldstein (Ed.), *Readings in learning disabilities*. Guilford, Conn.: Special Learning Corporation, 1978.

Kinsbourne, M. Minimal brain dysfunction as a neurodevelopmental lag. In *Minimal Brain Dysfunction*, Felix de la Cruz, Bernard H. Fox, and Richard A. Roberts (Eds.), *Annals of the New York Academy of Sciences*, February, 1973, *205*, 268–273.

Kirk, W. D. A tentative screening procedure for selecting bright and slow children in kindergarten. *Exceptional children*, Dec., 1966, 235–242.

Klein, P. *A-PART*. Garden City, N.Y.: Adelphi University Mimeograph, 1978.

————. Cognitive performance of kindergarten children when tested by parents and strangers. Paper presented at International Conference on Early Childhood Education, Jerusalem, January, 1980.

Lerner, J. Children with learning disabilities, 3rd ed. Boston: Houghton Mifflin, 1981.

McLoughlin, J. A. and Lewis, R. B., Assessing Special Students: Strategies and Procedures. Columbus: Charles E. Merrill Publishing Company, 1981.

Meyer, E. L. and Moran, M. R. A perspective on the unserved mildly handicapped. *Exceptional Children*, April, 1979, *45*(7), 526–530.

Mills, R. E. *Learning methods test*. Fort Lauderdale: The Mills Educational Center, 1970.

Myklebust, H., and Boshes, B. *Minimal brain damage in children: Final report*. U.S. Public Health Service Contract 108-65-142, Department of Health, Education and Welfare. Evanston, Ill.: Northwestern University Publication, June, 1969.

Newcomer P. Construct validity of the Illinois test of psycholinguistic abilities. *Journal of Learning Disabilities*, April, 1975, *8*(4), 220–231.

Peters, J. E., Davis, J. S., Goolsby, C. M., Clements, S. D., and Hicks, T. J. *Physicians handbook for screening for MBD*. Ciba Medical Horizons, 1973.

Poteet, J. A. Informal assessment of written expression. *Learning disabilities quarterly*, Fall, 1980, *3*(4), 88–98.

Roswell, F., and Natchez, G. *Reading disability: Diagnosis and treatment*. New York: Basic Books, 1971.

Safford, P. L. *Teaching young children with special needs*. St. Louis: C. V. Mosby, 1978.

Salvia, J., and Ysseldyke, J. E. *Assessment in special and remedial education*, 2nd ed. Boston: Houghton Mifflin, 1981.

Simensen, R. J., and Sutherland, J. Psychological assessment of brain damage: The wechsler scales. *Academic Therapy*, Fall, 1974, *X*(1), 69–81.

Stellern, J, Vasa, S. F., and Little, J. *Introduction to diagnostic-prescriptive teaching and programming*. Glen Ridge, N.J.: Exceptional Press, 1976.

von Hilsheimer, G. *Allergy, toxins, and the learning disabled child.* Novato, Ca.: Academic Therapy Publications, 1974.

von Hilsheimer, G., and Kurko, V. Minor anomalies in exceptional children. *Journal of Learning Disabilities*, August 1979, *12*(8), 462–469.

Waldrop, M. F., Bill, R. Q., and Halverson, C. F. Newborn minor physical anomalies predict short attention span, peer aggression, and impulsivity at age 3. *Science, 1978, 199*, 565.

Wallace, G., and Kauffman, J. M. *Teaching children with learning problems.* Columbus, Ohio: Merrill, 1978.

Webb, G. Meeting at Curry College, April, 1979.

White, B. *The First Three Years of Life.* Englewood Cliffs, N.J.: Prentice-Hall, 1975.

Interdisciplinary Intervention

part Two

Biochemical Interventions for the Hyperactive Learning Disabled Child

6

Several treatment options have been suggested for the hyperactive learning disabled child (H-LD), but the choice of treatment is not easily determined. Hyperactivity is a collection of symptoms with a number of possible causes. A thorough diagnostic workup should be made by the physician so that hidden, treatable causes will not be overlooked (Walker, 1975). Special diets, medication, and behavior-modification techniques have their proponents and their detractors. The first two types of options are explored in this chapter; behavior modification is discussed in Chapter 8.

ALLERGY THERAPY

Allergies, a deleterious reaction to certain biochemicals in foods, is considered one cause of hyperactivity and of the newly defined "allergic tension-fatigue" syndrome (Chapter 4). Nutritional allergies have been recognized for many years to cause skin rashes, respiratory problems, headaches, stomachaches, and so forth. Only relatively recently have behavioral and learning problems been linked to allergies (Feingold, 1975, 1976; Crook, 1975; Adler, 1978; von Hilsheimer, 1974; Walsh, 1980).

Crook (1975) suggests testing for food allergies using an elimination diet beginning with milk (in all forms), chocolate, and cola. If no improvement in behavior is shown after seven to 21 days, the patients may return to their usual diets for a few weeks before other foods (cereal grains, eggs, and so on) are eliminated. Von Hilsheimer (1974) notes that stress reduction decreases the severity of allergic reactions.

The Kaiser-Permanente (K-P) Diet, designed by Feingold (1975), eliminates two groups of food: Group I is composed of fruits* and two vegetables, tomatoes and cucumbers, which contain natural salicylates. Group II consists of any foods that contain artificial colors or flavorings and, for some children, the food preservative, BHT. The child is placed on the diet for four to six weeks. If there is a favorable response, the restricted foods are reintroduced, one at a time for about four days. If no adverse response is noted, another food can be introduced. This procedure is continued until all the salicylates are tested and those that do not cause adverse effects are returned to the diet. The salicylates remain in the diet as long as no adverse reactions occur. The artificial food colorings and flavors are *never* to be added to the diet.

Diet therapy, particularly the Feingold (K-P) diet is popular with many parents of the H-LD. Parents have formed groups that try to have "junk food" (candies, sweets, and the like) removed from the schools and replaced with natural foods, free of food additives.

A 50% positive response of H-LD allergic children and 50-70% success with H-LD children is reported by Feingold (1975). He notes a sequence of improvement (1976). Behavior patterns are affected first, followed by better motor coordination. Perception and cognition show improvement next. The younger the child, the more rapid the change. Wright (1976) has found that a natural diet, free of artificial flavors, colors, and preservatives is successful with some hyperactive children, although the removal of salicylate does not help in most cases. Research by Connors (1976) indicated that while teachers reported a 15% reduction in hyperactive behavior, parents only noted a slight difference. A follow-up study of those children who had at least a 25% reduction in behavior problems showed that, a) the diet was most successful with younger children, and b) there was a sudden onset of symptoms after the artificial coloring and flavors were ingested, with the effects lasting up to three hours (Goyette, et al., 1978).

The cause-and-effect relationship between dietary regimens and hyperactivity has not been proven effective for large groups of children, although in individual cases the improvement is noteworthy (Harley, et al., 1978; Wunderlich, 1970).

Orthomolecular (Megavitamin) Therapy

Nutrition deficits caused by either an inability to properly metabolize particular nutrients or an inadequate diet have been linked to the hyperactive behaviors of some learning-disabled children (Adler, 1978; von Hilsheimer, 1974). Such deficits are frequently treated with megavitamin therapy, sometimes called orthomolecular therapy.

The orthomolecular therapy used by Cott (1977) is more than dispensing large doses of vitamins. It also includes diet controls and visual training, for approximately 90% of his patients (Lynn, 1978). Cott (1977) believes that orthomolecular intervention will help more than 50% of the hyperactive learning disabled. He reports that this therapy increases attention span and concentration and that the children seem more willing to cooperate at home and school. Cott (1972) found that youn-

---

* Almonds, apples, apricots, berries, cherries, grapes, nectarines, oranges, peaches, plums, and strawberries.

ger children (under seven years) respond better and faster than older children, with children in the 11 to 12 age group being the most difficult. Children who begin treatment early and continue it over a period of years progress the most.

Generally orthomolecular therapists prescribe only water-soluble vitamins which do not accumulate in the body (vitamins A and D are fat soluble and can build up in body tissue). Cott (1972, 1977) reports that B-6 (pyrodoxine) reduces hyperactivity. To prevent a depletion of magnesium when large doses of B-6 are given, magnesium is also added to the diet. Cott notes that magnesium appears to have a calming effect. Dosages are determined by body weight and can be administered in pill, capsule, or liquid form.

Some side effects have been reported: Niacin can elevate blood glucose and uric acid levels, cause nausea, flushing, and itching of the skin. These symptoms diminish with each succeeding day until, by the third day, they disappear. Headaches and nausea can appear with the use of niacinamide, and vitamin C can increase the frequency of urination and cause diarrhea. Lowering the dosages reduces these effects (Cott, 1977).

Kronick (1975) reports treating an LD child who exhibited emotional lability. The child was put on a high protein, sugar-free diet, but this was ineffective. Twenty-four hours after she was put on zinc tablets, no evidence of her former behavioral problems remained.

Krischer (1978) has found low blood zinc levels in children with allergies and those classified as retarded. In addition, these children usually exhibit high levels of copper, which is considered a CNS stimulant. Krischer hypothesizes that the high copper levels are responsible for the hyperactive behaviors found in these children. If dosages of zinc are administered, the effects of the copper appear to be reversed. Krischer also found that B-6 facilitates the utilization of zinc. Wright (1976) notes that B-6 may remove excess copper.

Diet control is part of the orthomolecular approach. A well-balanced diet which includes fresh whole foods and removes sugar and rapidly-absorbed carbohydrates is advised. Cott believes many H-LD children have a disturbance of glucose metabolism. Therefore, he recommends that sugar and refined carbohydrates, together with products containing caffein (cola drinks, tea, coffee, and chocolate) be eliminated from the diet. He, too, suggests the removal of artificial food colors and flavors.

Interestingly, some children who are allergic to wholesome foods respond with behavior disturbances rather than the usual allergic reactions of runny nose, rashes, and diarrhea (Cott, 1977). The foods most likely to cause what Cott calls cerebral allergy are wheat, milk, eggs, corn and beef. He recommends an elimination diet to determine which foods cause the problem.

Low serum calcium levels have been found by Walker (1975) to increase emotional lability and hyperactivity. By increasing the milk intake of a hyperactive child, Walker found the symptoms disappeared and the child was able to discontinue taking ritalin.

Adler (1978) stresses that the implementation of orthomolecular therapy should be under the guidance of a physician and/or nutritionist. This therapy is further recommended since it can be directed by parents or paraprofessionals with infrequent visits to specialists (Cott, 1977) and because it is relatively inexpensive and does not rely on complex equipment.

Although Cott (1972, 1977) has reported success with orthomolecular therapy, it has not been widely used, partly because the research results are not clearcut. The populations he treated are not well defined. Most of the children, though called LD, appear to be autistic and/or psychotic. The therapy is generally used in conjunction with other treatments, making it difficult to determine which is the most effective or if there is an interactive effect. Few double-blind studies have been conducted. Because children may possess different metabolic needs which can be obscured using group data, several researchers have been using clinical case studies where each child is his own control. Such studies generally report positive results with megavitamin treatment (Adler, 1978).

Hypoglycemia

Hypoglycemia is a condition of abnormally low blood sugar which can only be determined by laboratory tests (Katz, 1975). Hypoglycemic individuals have abnormal glucose tolerance with low blood sugar levels which fail to "nourish their brain optimally" (Heyman, 1975, p. 145). The outward symptoms are often subtle, for example, restlessness, sudden behavior changes, pallor, a tired or weak feeling. Although Katz stresses the fact that "there is absolutely no evidence that low blood sugar causes either developmental hyperactivity, dyslexia, or other specific learning disabilities" (p. 79), several researchers do link them (Cott, 1975; Heyman, 1975; Wright, 1976). Heyman, reporting on testing performed at the New York Institute for Child Development, notes that most hyperactive children are hypoglycemic and allergic and have enzyme and mineral imbalances. Walsh (1980) believes that an inability to absorb carbohydrates into the blood stream is the most common problem of the H-LD.

The hypoglycemic diet eliminates refined sugars, caffein (colas, chocolate, tea, and coffee) and limits the intake of carbohydrates. Rather than eating three full meals a day, the regimen generally requires three smaller meals and three snack periods—midmorning, midday, and bedtime. Meals and snack times should remain fairly constant; that is, the same schedule should be maintained daily. This will help keep a relatively stable blood sugar level. Most persons can control this metabolic problem through adherence to the dietary recommendations.

The schools can help the hypoglycemic child manage his diet by providing snack time in the mornings and afternoons. Snacks can include cheeses, vegetables (carrots, celery, and so on), fruits, nuts, and unsweetened crackers. Many teachers have reported to us that when they schedule a snack/rest time, it has a positive effect on most of the children, not just those diagnosed hypoglycemic. Possibly the change in pace and the opportunity to relax—and not the "healthy" snack—is responsible for the decrease in hyperactive behavior.

An analysis of the research indicates that no one factor is responsible for the H-LD. While there are children whose hyperactive behavior may be related to an inability to metabolize carbohydrates, the evidence indicates that there are many other possible causes. Katz (1975) cautions that only those children who have been diagnosed by means of a medical workup, including sugar-tolerance tests, should be labeled hypoglycemic.

Drug Therapy

Few interventions in LD are as controversial as drug therapy. Some researchers believe it should never be used, while others consider it the intervention of choice.

Part of the controversy relates to the inadequacy of research data. (The following research concerns, although discussed here in respect to the effects of drug therapy, are equally applicable to research in other areas.) As Ross (1976) notes, studies that examine the effectiveness of drugs with hyperactive children are difficult to compare. The first concern involves the definition of hyperactivity. Most samples are composed of children who exhibit varying symptoms in varying degrees.

It is difficult to measure improvement in behaviors which were ill-defined to begin with. Many of the studies do not use double-blind conditions (neither the child nor the dispenser of the pill should know which is the medication and which the placebo, an inert substance with no potency). Double-blind studies are important because the expectation of improvement will frequently bring forth improvement. In this case, unless double blind is used, either the child may improve spontaneously or parental behavior may change in anticipation of improvement.

In addition, the effect of the drugs on nonhyperactive children has not been studied, since giving medication to normal children raises ethical questions. This brief review of problems in drug-therapy research illustrates why the effectiveness of many treatments continues to be questioned.

The most frequently used drugs for reducing hyperactivity and increasing ability to attend and learn are two central nervous system stimulants: methylphenidate (ritalin) and dextroamphetamine (dexedrine). Penoline (cylert) is a relatively new CNS drug which is also being used. Other groups of drugs that are prescribed with less frequency are: antianxiety and antipsychotic drugs such as librium, thorazine, and mellaril; antidepressants, tofranil; and anticonvulsants, dilantin. If neither ritalin or dexedrine cause improvement, Millichap (1973) recommends that anxiety and antipsychotic drugs be tried. However, before changing medication, Silver (1978) suggests determining if the medication was taken as prescribed, if the behavior has a psychological basis, or if there are stresses at home or school such that medication alone cannot help.

Although in adults there is an increase in activity when CNS stimulants are used, they decrease the activity level in children. This was formerly viewed largely as a paradoxial effect; however, it is now believed that the medication increases (stimulates) the performance of the reticular activating system, enabling it to filter irrelevant incoming stimuli (Johnston, 1975). Stewart (1970) suggests that since amphetamines release norepinephrine, a neurotransmitter, at nerve endings, it may repair a deficit in norepinephrine activity or restore neurotransmitter balance (see Chapter 2).

Sroufe, et al. (1973) considered heart rate (HR) in anticipation of a stimulus to represent an attention process and hypothesized that those with attention deficits should exhibit less HR deceleration. Their research showed that H-LD given drug therapy showed greater change than those given a placebo. There was also an effect on reaction time: the greater the deceleration, the faster the reaction time. An age effect was also evident. The older the child, the shorter the latency, that is, the faster the reaction time.

There are many possible side effects and drugs must be monitored very carefully with respect to timing, size of dosage, and possible toxic reactions. Nervousness, insomnia, and anorexia have been reported as side effects of CNS stimulants. Skin rash and stomachaches have been reported among some children who take ritalin. Most side effects are transitory (Barkley, 1977). The choice of drugs depends on the doctors who prescribe them. Millichap (1973) prefers to recommend ritalin because there is less of a tendency to produce anorexia. Kaine (1977) recommends dexedrine because it can be given in spansule form which helps keep the amount of the drug in the bloodstream at a more even level. The effect of variation of high and low levels of the drug in the blood is more apparent when ritalin is used.

Although the literature recommends that there should be close communication among the school (teacher and nurse), the home, and the physician, studies indicate that this is not typical. A survey by Okolo, Bartlett, and Shaw (1978) of school personnel in 15 districts found that nurses were involved in the medication process but teachers were not. The teachers felt they were not adequately informed. Teachers and physicians had little contact once therapy had begun. These results are consonant with reports by Weithorn and Ross (1975) and Robin and Bosco (1973). The role of the teacher in a drug therapy program must be defined. Weithorn and Ross recommend that a simple communication structure be set-up to improve monitoring. A form or checklist that elicits information about concrete, observable behaviors can be completed by teachers and parents to provide useful information to the physician. Unless guidelines for observation are provided, there can be misinterpretation of behaviors and judgemental errors (Hollander, 1977).

Over time, the drug has a cumulative effect. The dosage should not be altered each time the child has a bad day, but the doctor should be notified if problems are generated over a long period; for example, the child appears glassy-eyed or overly lethargic or the hyperactive symptoms have returned. There are no predictors identifying which children will respond best (Whalen & Henker, 1976; Wender, 1971). Some show an immediate positive response; others exihibit a delayed response. Some children may respond negatively and others may have what Wender calls a "tolerant" response: they may respond positively and then revert back to inappropriate behaviors. If dosages are increased for the last group, positive behaviors may recur, but will revert again to negative behaviors. Silver (1978) indicates that some parents report increased emotional lability, including frustration and anxiety when the children receive medication. Decreasing or stopping the medication may be necessary. Omenn (1973) cautions that although in some cases hyperactivity and impulsivity appear to decrease, other children appear to suffer negative results (i.e., they become *more* hyperactive and impulsive).

Many researchers believe that physicians are not properly employing drugs. Solomon (1973) observes that physicians are pressured to attend LD children and are not adequately monitoring many of the children on drug therapy.* Toxic reactions can be subtle, and in addition to reports from home and school, blood tests must be given. Solomon believes that most physicians do not take the time needed.

---

* The schools should not pressure parents to have the child put on drug therapy. Such treatment should not be prescribed unless it is considered medically sound for the child.

Some doctors prescribe drugs as part of a diagnostic procedure for children in whom MBD is suspected. If there is a positive change (reduction in hyperactive behavior), the diagnosis is considered confirmed (Wender, 1971). The goal is to find the minimum dosage for optimal behavior. Many physicians suggest reducing or eliminating the dosage in the summer (Solomon, 1973; Lynn, 1978). However, others believe the child should receive medication daily to avoid the "yo-yo" effect. While many physicians prescribe medication only for school hours, Silver (1978) notes that the child may need it at other times so he can effectively take part in after-school activities, mealtimes, and so forth, since hyperactivity is often a 24-hour problem. Sometimes the stimulant causes sleeplessness and the afternoon dosage may have to be eliminated.

Suppression of weight and height gains have been reported by Safer, Allen, and Barr (1972) and Safer and Allen (1973). Aarskog, et al. (1977) noted that the level of growth hormone in the blood was lowered when dexadrine and ritalin were used. However, a recent report by Millichap (1978) indicates no suppression of growth in children who have been receiving five to 20 mg methylphenidate for an average of 16 months (with a six month minimum and 26 month maximum duration of treatment). The medication appeared to stimulate the growth of six children below eight years of age when daily doses of 10 to 20 mg were used. Treatment was not continued on weekends or during vacation periods. Aarskog, et al. (1977) suggest that the serum growth hormone response they noted indicates a possibility of long term adverse effects on the growth of the children, and they recommend caution in the use of drugs.

Some critics of drug therapy believe children will blame their behaviors on drugs (or the lack of them) rather than develop self-control (Whalen & Henker, 1976; Ross, 1976; Lynn, 1978). The possibility of abuse also exists. Many of the behaviors for which drugs are prescribed are important components of success in adults. Many critics fear drugs will be used to change or control individuals who are different, creative, or questioning. As Solomon (1973) notes, the physician makes a decision about prescribing drugs based on the results of a medical examination and data supplied by parents and teachers, whose reports are considered unreliable.

In a review of the literature concerning drug therapy, Whalen and Henken (1976) point out that the function of the drugs is not known and short-term improvement is not maintained after medication ceases. The drugs appear to help sustain attention, control motor responses, and reduce aggressive behavior and hyperactivity, but do not appear to improve social or academic performance.

Lerer, Artner, and Lerer (1979) found that ritalin improved the handwriting peformance of LD children in 52% of those studied. Their movements were smoother and more controlled and they appeared to be more at ease, that is, they used less pressure on the pencil. These gains tended to continue only as long as the children continued to receive medication.

A study conducted at the University of Illinois (Sprague & Sleator, 1977) found that maximum learning occurred when low dosages (0.3 mg/kg of body weight per day) of ritalin were administered, but social behaviors responded best to large doses (1.0 mg/kg of body weight per day). Levine (1978) hypothesizes that the minimum dosage may be effective in a one-to-one teaching situation, but in a classroom setting, a higher dosage may be necessary. He suggests that individual instruction of children who receive high dosages of ritalin should take place about three hours after the medication is received, when the blood levels are relatively low. The physician must balance the learning performance against social behavior and, to do this, data from many sources are needed (Sprague & Sleator, 1977). This again underscores the need for communication.

Wender (1971) found that medication increased the child's sensitivity to reward and punishment; that is, dependency needs and need for approval appear to develop. The child perseveres and tends to complete assignments and check work.

After reviewing the literature, Barkley (1977) reports that on a short-term basis, the use of drugs increases the child's ability to concentrate and reduces impulsivity in some settings. Drugs do not appear to ensure positive long term effects: LD adolescents and adults still score higher than normal individuals on measures of hyperactivity, distractibility, and aggressiveness. Peer status and academic achievement remain low. Wender (1971) found the prognosis poor for those with known brain injury and problematic for other LD individuals.

A different kind of drug therapy is being used by H. Levinson, a Queens, New York psychiatrist (Lynn, 1978). Because he believes that some LD is caused by an inner ear or vestibular dysfunction, he recommends the use of dramamine or marazine, medications for motion sickness. He reports success in 50% of the cases he selects for treatment (success is not defined) (Lynn, 1978).

Eisenberg (1964) suggests seven principles of drug treatment:

1. Drugs can be useful agents in managing pediatric psychiatric disorders when chosen appropriately and applied with discrimination . . .

2. Skill in using drugs requires knowledge of their pharmacologic properties and sensitivity to the psychologic significance . . .

3. No drug should be employed without firm indications for its use, without careful control of the patient, and without due precautions against toxicity . . .

4. An old drug is to be preferred to a new drug unless evidence of superiority for the latter is clear . . .

5. Drugs should be used no longer than necessary . . .

6. Dosage must be individualized . . .

7. The use of drugs does not relieve physician of responsibility for seeking to identify and eliminate the factors causing or aggravating the psychiatric disorder. (p. 170)

Medication is not a panacea and is usually used in conjunction with other interventions such as psychotherapy, behavior modification, and diagnostic/prescriptive teaching. Drugs used in low dosage and with careful monitoring do not appear to cause toxicity, nor have they been proven to cause drug dependency in later years. However, the authors believe that alternative procedures, environmental changes in particular, are preferable to drug therapy (see Chapter 9 on behavior modification, and Chapters 10 and 11 on educational principles). One thing, however, seems clear: It is as ill-advised to frivolously withhold drugs as to frivolously prescribe them.

REFERENCES

Aarskog, D., Fevang, F., Klove, H., Stoa, K. F., and Thorsen, T. The effect of stimulant drugs, dextroamphetamine and methylphenidate, on secretion of growth hormone in hyperactive children. *Journal of Pediatrics*, 1977, *90*, 136.

Adler, S. Behavior management: A nutritional approach to the behaviorally disordered and learning disabled child. *Journal of Learning Disabilities*, December, 1978, *11*(10), 651–656.

Barkley, R. A. A review of stimulant drug research with hyperactive children. *Journal of Child Psychology and Psychiatry*, 1977, *18*, 137–159.

Connors, C. K. et al. Food additives and hyperkinesis: A controlled double-blind experiment. *Pediatrics*, 1976, *58*, 154.

Cott, A. Megavitamins: The orthomolecular approach to behavioral disorders and learning disabilities. *Academic Therapy*, Spring, 1972, 7, 245–259.

_____. *The orthomolecular approach to learning disabilities*. Novato, Ca: Academic Therapy Publications, 1977.

Crook, W. G. *Can your child read? Is he hyperactive?* Jackson, Tenn.: Pedicenter Press, 1975.

Eisenberg, L. The role of drugs in treating disturbed children. *Children*, 1964, *2*(4), 167–173.

Feingold, B. F. Why your child is hyperactive. New York: Random House, 1975.

_____. Hyperkinesis and learning disabilities linked to the ingestion of artificial food colors and flavors. *Journal of Learning Disabilities*, November, 1976, *9*(9), 551–559.

Goyette, C. H., et al. Effects of artificial colors on hyperkinetic children, a double blind challenge study. *Psychopharmocology Bulletin*, April, 1978, *14*(2), 39–40.

Harley, J. P., et al. Hyperkinesis and food additives: Testing the Feingold hypothesis. *Pediatrics*, 1978, *61*, 818.

Heyman, R. They can make it now! *Prevention*, April, 1975, 139–145.

Hollander, S. K. Monitoring the medical management of students: The reading teacher, Oct., 1977, *31*(1):4–5.

Johnston, R. B. Minimal cerebral dysfunction: Nature and implications for therapy. In Robert H. A. Haslam & Peter J. Valletutti (Eds.), *Medical problems in the classroom*. Baltimore: University Park Press, 1975.

Kaine, R. A pediatrician looks at learning disabilities. Paper delivered at Florida AMA Family Practicioners Meeting, Miami Beach, May 5, 1977.

Katz, H. P. Important endocrine disorders of childhood. In Robert H. A. Haslam and Peter J. Valletutti (Eds.), *Medical problems in the classroom*. Baltimore: University Park Press, 1975.

Krischer, K. Copper and zinc in childhood behavior. *Psychopharmacology Bulletin*, 1978, *14*, 58–59.

Kronick, D. A case history: sugar, fried oysters, and zinc. *Academic Therapy*, 1975, *11*, 119–121.

Lerer, R. J., Artner, J., and Lerer, M. P. Effect of methylphenidate on handwriting deficits. *Journal of Learning Disabilities*, Aug./Sept., 1979, *12*(7), 450–455.

Levine, M. D. Dr. Melvin Levine Comments. *Pediatric Alert*, Feb. 2, 1978, *3*(3):12.

Lynn, R. *Learning Disabilities: The state of the field 1978*. New York: Social Science Research Council, 1978.

Millichap, J. G. Drugs in management of minimal brain dysfunction. In Felix de la

Cruz, Bernard H. Fox and Richard H. Roberts (Eds.), *Minimal Brain Dysfunc-ion: Annals of the New York Academy of Sciences*, February, 1973, *205*, 321–334.

———. Growth and methylphenidate. *Journal of Learning Disabilities*, November 1978, *11*(9), 567–570.

Okolo, C., Barlett, S. A., and Shaw, S. F. Communication between professionals concerning medication for the hyperactive child. *Journal of Learning Disabilities*, December, 1978, *11*(10), 647–650.

Omenn, G. S. Genetic approaches to the syndrome of minimal brain dysfunction. In Felix de la Cruz, Bernard H. Fox, and Richard H. Roberts (Eds.), *Minimal brain dysfunction: Annals of the New York Academy of Sciences*, February, 1973, *205*, 335–344.

Robin, S. S., and Bosco, J. J. Ritalin for school children, the teachers' perspective. *Journal of School Health*, 1973, *43*, 624–628.

Ross, A. O. *Psychological aspects of learning disabilities and reading disorders*. New York: McGraw-Hill, 1976.

Safer, D., Allen, R., and Barr, E. Depression of growth in hyperactive children on stimulant drugs. *New England Journal of Medicine*, 1972, *287*, 217–220.

Safer, D., and Allen, R. Factors influencing the suppressant effects of two stimulant drugs on the growth of hyperactive children. *Pediatrics*, 1973, *51*, 660–667.

Silver, L. B. *The minimal brain dysfunction syndrome–Section VI, disturbances of development*. Mimeograph updated March, 1978.

Solomon, G. Drug therapy: initiation and follow-up. In Felix de la Cruz, Bernard H. Fox, and Richard H. Roberts (Eds.), *Minimal brain dysfunction: Annals of the New York Academy of Sciences*, February, 1973, *205*, 335–344.

Sprague, R. L., and Sleator, E. K. Dose-related effects of methylphenidate in hyper-kinetic children. *Science*, 1977, *198*, 1274.

Sroufe, L. A., Sonies, B. C., West, W. D., and Wright, F. S. Anticipatory heart rate deceleration and reaction time in children with and without referral for learn-ing disability. *Child Development*, 1973, *44*, 267–273.

Sroufe, L. A., and Stewart, M. A. Treating problem children with stimulant drugs. *New England Journal of Medicine*, 1973, *289*, 407–413.

Stewart, M. A. Hyperactive children. *Scientific American*, April, 1970, 94–98.

von Hilsheimer, G. *Allergy, toxins and the learning-disabled child*. Novato, Ca.: Academic Therapy Publications, 1974.

Walker, S. III. Drugging the American child: We're too cavalier about hyperactivity. *Journal of Learning Disabilities*, 1975, *8*, 354.

Walsh, R. J. *Treating your hyperactive and learning-disabled child*. Garden City, NY: Anchor, 1980.

Weithorn, C., and Ross, R. Who monitors medication? *Journal of Learning Disabili-ties*, 1975, *8*(7), 458–461.

Wender, P. *Minimal brain dysfunction in children*. New York: Wiley Interscience, 1971.

Whalen, C. K., and Henker, B. Psychostimulants and children: A review and analysis. *Psychological Bulletin*, 1976, *83*, 1113–1130.

Wright, J. V. A case of hyperactivity. *Prevention*, November, 1976, 67–73.

Wunderlich, R. C. *Kids, brains, and learning*. St. Petersburg, Fla.: Johnny Reads, 1970.

Psychotherapy and Learning Disabilities

7

THE NEED FOR THERAPEUTIC INTERVENTION

The psychological factors in learning disabilities have been studied by many researchers (Rappaport, 1969; Gardner, 1973; Frostig & Maslow, 1973; Connolly, 1971). Two types of psychogenic problems have been identified in MBD children: a) those secondary to organic defects, such as timidity, insecurity, and withdrawal, and b) neurotic and psychotic symptoms to which any child is susceptible and would have arisen if no organic problem existed (Gardner, 1973). The disruption of neurological development interferes with total development and the child finds maladaptive ways to relate to his environment. This emotional overlay which accompanies LD usually appears at an early age and, unless the appropriate interventions are made (educational and psychological), will continue through adulthood, frequently becoming so debilitating that it can be more limiting than the original learning problems. The longer the maladaptive behaviors persist, the less adequate the LD child is in comparison to his peers (Rappaport, 1969).

Many common growth problems of children, such as anxiety, aggressiveness, and dependency, are magnified in the LD child. Maslow (1954) postulated that human behavior is directed toward the satisfaction of five basic needs which develop and are satisfied in a specific hierarchical order:

1. physiological needs (food, water, air, clothing, and shelter)

2. safety needs (physical and emotional). In a child, this may be seen as a need for a predictable, orderly world. When this need is met, anxiety levels are low.

3. a need to belong, to love and be loved. There may be a hunger for affection and friends.

4. esteem needs. Self-respect, recognition, and attention lead to feelings of self-worth, confidence, and adequacy. When this need is thwarted, feelings of inferiority, weakness, and helplessness may arise.

5. self-actualization (doing what one is fitted for or capable of becoming). It is related to self-expression.

The individual is dominated by unmet needs. Once these are satisfied, they are no longer needs. The high-level needs cannot be met until the lower level ones in the sequence are satisfied. Because of his learning deficits, the LD child may encounter difficulty in meeting any of the needs beyond the first level. The inability to satisfy these needs weaken the possibility of emotional adjustment. The gap in potential and performance is a particularly critical factor, and emotional and social problems often arise (Connolly, 1971).

The LD child's feelings of frustration frequently manifest themselves in aggressive behavior, that is, physical and verbal fights and disruptive acts. On the other hand, the very dependent child may seek close attention and physical contact with adults and yet be passive in his relations with other children. Some LD children exhibit extreme anxiety and often appear insecure and helpless. There may also be evidence of nervous habits.

The social and emotional problems of LD children may have their roots in brain dysfunction. For example, because of perceptual-spatial deficits, some LD children cling to their teachers or are reluctant to leave the classroom, fearing they may be unable to find their way (Denckla, 1978). Many children who were once thought emotionally disturbed are now recognized as having neurological dysfunctions of a minor nature which manifest themselves in learning disorders and lead to behavior problems in school (Connolly, 1971).

Some LD children overuse the denial mechanism and do not admit having any problems. Others wish for a magic cure. Because he is ill-equipped, the LD child frequently fears and withdraws from involvement with others. He is exposed to frustrations and humiliations that the normal child is not. He fears new activities and tends to generalize failure, even into areas where he would succeed. The child who withdraws is withdrawing from a real, hostile world because he has failed to acquire needed skills. The more he withdraws, the less he learns about—and how to handle—his world. Many of these children fixate or regress to a lower level of behavior which is incongruent with the relatively mild degree of their impairment. They may revert to clowning, temper tantrums, thumbsucking, or may refuse to perform age-appropriate activities. These behaviors are frequently reinforced by parents who allow them to continue. According to Rappaport (1969), LD children manifest two major disorders which appear with similar frequency: acting out and passive-resistive.

The LD child is sometimes characterized as having little motivation in regard to school (and, in adulthood, with respect to work) (Maslow, 1954). An important prerequisite for motivation is that the individual perceives the *possibility* of success. Generally, we desire what is possible to attain and will work to achieve it. If academic or job success seems unattainable (as it does to many of the LD), then motivation will be lacking.

With appropriate interventions, maladaptive behaviors can be redirected into the development of adaptive behaviors; that is, dependency can be used to help a child respond to reinforcers, a moderate amount of anxiety can facilitate performance, and self-assertiveness can be a positive outcome of aggressive feelings.

EMOTIONAL INTERACTION BETWEEN THE LEARNING-DISABLED CHILD AND HIS FAMILY

Parents' initial reactions to learning about any handicapping condition is usually characterized by feelings of shock, disbelief, anger, and guilt. Kronick believes that parents feel frustrated because their LD child fails where others succeed so effortlessly, because schools often appear unwilling—rather than unable—to accommodate the child, and because their own anxiety and impatience prevent them from conveying to the child that they really accept him (Kronick, 1975, p. 22). The child's learning and behavioral problems frequently create parental anxiety, but there is a reciprocal relationship as well: Dysfunctional parental attitudes can generate learning problems within the child, heightening attentional, academic, and perceptual deficits (Klein et al., 1981, p. 15).

Often parents of the preschool and elementary school child are easier for the schools to work with, partly because these parents see the future stretching before them, and they believe the child can grow and change, and become like others in time. A family with an LD child may be able to adapt to problems when the child is young, but as the child grows older and experiences difficulties with a peer group that does not accept him, and future education, employment, and living problems arise, the family's ability to cope may break down. At this time, the parents may become more demanding and dissatisfied with the schools and with the child.

Parents must be given a realistic picture and not false hope. They must be helped to realize that some LD persons will require support services and learning modifications throughout their lives. Many types of neurological dysfunctions are not and cannot be cured. As Denckla (1978) notes, "delay" or "lag" do not carry a guarantee of catching up and may lead to unwarranted optimism.

Some families become handicapped-child centered. The LD child demands more time, and parents feel guilty about the little time spent with their other children. Parents may also become overly protective. Fearful that the LD child will be hurt physically or emotionally, they keep him from engaging in activities that would give him opportunities to grow. Frequently, to assuage feelings of guilt, parents do too much for the child and expect too little from him.* Parents who become handicapped-child oriented often cause anxieties, problems, and resentments in all family members.

Many LD children become the scapegoats in families (Osman, 1979). This usually happens with the unconscious consent of the other family members. Siblings may goad the child who has poor ability to control his temper, and he is punished for outbursts of anger. He may be under constant criticism about how he eats, what he says, how he says it, how he dresses, and so forth. Siblings are often fearful that they, too, will develop problems. Frequently they are ashamed of their LD sibling yet feel guilty about this. They are afraid of what their peers think and may be ashamed at the way the LD sibling behaves in public. They may also feel guilty be-

---

* Parental guilt feelings should be taken into account in order to understand the reports they make in conjunction with the diagnostic process or when they are asked to evaluate the effectiveness of treatment.

cause they succeed and he cannot. Older brothers and sisters who have felt supplanted by the new baby may believe that their jealous feelings caused his problems.

FAMILY THERAPY

Because learning disabilities has an impact on all family members, most forms of interventions call for support services to parents and siblings, as well as the LD child (Rappaport, 1969; Bell, 1975). Ruth Mallison (1968), an educational therapist specializing in work with brain-injured children, incorporates home training as a significant component of her therapy. Cruickshank (1977) stresses the use of *family therapy* when children are referred for psychotherapy. The presence of organic causes of the child's symptoms does not contraindicate this type of therapy. Bell (1975) believes that the problems are symptomatic of family disturbance and, therefore, the family is the unit to be treated (p. 17). This method demonstrates the unity of the family and the mutual interdependence of the members. The family becomes conscious of the roles each plays in relation to the others.

Parents need opportunities to ask questions and vent their feelings; to become aware of the options that are available and future possibilities (Hatton, 1966); and to participate in the educational planning of their children (see Chapter 19).

The type of therapy, the setting, and the frequency are determined by the individual needs of the clients, as well as by the philosophy—and the availability—of the therapists. Although the approaches vary, the goals for everyone involved in working with the LD client and his family should include:

1. Helping the LD child understand his disability;
2. Helping the LD child understand how he is viewed by others;
3. Helping the LD child understand how he reacts to others;
4. Helping the LD child develop appropriate compensatory behaviors;
5. Helping parents work through their feelings about being parents of an LD child;
6. Helping parents learn how to deal with their child and his siblings;
7. Helping parents understand available alternatives;
8. Helping parents become more assertive regarding the rights of their LD child;
9. Helping siblings understand the LD child;
10. Helping siblings cope with their own feelings of guilt, shame, and so forth.

Parents of LD children generally do not require nondirective therapy. They need explanation, interpretation, guidelines regarding management, and "some forthright help with their feelings about the child" (Kurlander & Colodny, 1969, p. 142). Just as the LD child needs reassurance to relieve anxieties, so do his parents (p. 138). Considerable empathy is needed in counseling parents. Eisenberg (1967, p. 91) points out that the task of parenting a brain-injured child is difficult and that "a well-designed program of treatment requires that a good deal of effort be directed at the parents, who need support—yes, and acceptance—no less than the child."

THERAPEUTIC TECHNIQUES

Gardner (1973) uses a technique called *mutual storytelling*. A story is elicited from the child. Then, based on Gardner's interpretation of the psychodynamics, he tells a story using the same characters and setting that leads to a moral or identifies a problem area. Props such as dolls, puppets, and clay can be used. The child's parent or other adult caretaker remains in the room to audit the sessions; Gardner finds that it is meaningful to the parent and does not appear to impair the therapist/child relationship. The sessions are recorded on tape to be replayed at home for the child and/or nonattending parent. Gardner recommends that the child's disorders be discussed with him so that misconceptions can be rectified. In fact, he has written books about LD expressly for the child's own consumption: for example, *The Child's Book About Brain Injury*, (Albany: New York Association for the Learning Disabled, 1966. Reading level–about 4th grade).* By becoming informed about the nature of his problem, the brain-injured child's anxieties will not become global and pervasive (Rappaport, 1969, pp. 155–156).

The technique of *Bibliotherapy* can be used to enable the LD child to understand his problem. It involves selecting a story (or book) wherein the character's problems, fears, and anxieties, parallel those of the client. Lenkowsky and Lenkowsky (1978) report using this technique successfully with a LD adolescent.They contend that the therapeutic aspect is threefold: (1) *identity* (by identifying with the story's character or situation, the reader sees that he is not alone and begins to view his own life in proper perspective); (2) *catharsis* (through identifying with the events and the action, the reader's impulses and desires are gratified, resulting in anxiety reduction); and (3) *insight* (a more in-depth understanding facilitates modification of the reader's attitudes and behaviors). The authors further believe that bibliotherapy heightens self-esteem, which, in turn, promotes more effective learning.

According to Rappaport (1966), a school-related therapy program encompasses three stages in therapeutic treatment. The first stage focuses on the child as an individual, elicits information about what the child thinks his problems are, and teaches him the nature of his disability. The second stage broadens the child's understanding of himself in various situations and stresses interpersonal relationships. In the third stage, the child becomes a member of the community as a playmate and neighbor. During the first two stages, the child may need to be excluded from his classroom and worked with individually. He may require time out before he loses control. Although Rappaport found that group therapy is frequently more effective in helping a child relate to his peers and is highly beneficial in stages two and three, it should not replace individual therapy. Both are needed. The *life-space interview*

* Additional books directed toward LD children themselves are available. These include: Marnell Hayes' *The Tuned-In, Turned-On Book About Learning Problems*, Novato, Ca.: Academic Therapy Publications 1974 (reading level about 5th grade); Sol Gordon's *Living Fully*, New York: John Day, 1975 (reading level: secondary grades; written for handicapped– including LD–adolescents and young adults, their parents, and professionals); Richard Gardner's *MBD: The Family Book About Minimal Brain Dysfunction*, New York: Jason Aronson, Inc, 1973. (Part One is for parents; Part Two– on an elementary reading grade level–is for the LD child and his siblings.)

(Redl, 1959)* may help one child work through his disturbance after a crisis, while another child may simply need a truncated school day.

Reality therapy (Glasser, 1965) utilizes group therapy and deals with the "now," not the past or the "why." It has been recommended for use with the LD population (Glasser, 1965; Bassin, 1976; O'Donnell & Maxwell, 1976; Marandola & Imber, 1979). Reality therapy is concerned with two basic needs: to love and be loved, and to feel worthwhile to ourselves and others. These needs are similar to the higher-level needs postulated by Maslow (1954). The therapist in this model must become involved with the child and help him to face reality. The child learns better ways to behave as standards of behavior are acknowledged and irresponsible behavior is rejected.

Each student in reality therapy should progress at his own speed and experience success daily. Bassin believes it is the most effective way of working with students because each person in the group can act as a change agent. It is easier to accept peer explanations and perceptions than those of an authority figure. O'Donnell and Maxwell (1976) report that children with many types of handicapping conditions take part in the School Without Failure Approach (Ventura School, California), which utilizes class meetings as a vehicle for discussion about social, behavioral, and educational problems and for formulating their solutions.

Although formal psychotherapy is used in some schools, others employ "rap" sessions where LD students meet with a psychologist or their special education teacher and discuss problems of mutual concern. The leader helps the students focus on the problem and search for solutions. The method used is similar to the reality therapy approach.

Teachers can help improve a student's self-concept and reduce or prevent maladaptive behaviors by structuring the class for success (Frostig and Maslow, 1973) (see Chapter 10). The child should be helped to develop required skills or be taught how to cope with areas of deficit. Assignments should be geared to the student's functioning level and learning style. He should be made aware of his progress through the use of charts and graphs. His work should be compared to his previous performance and not to that of others. An attitude of mutual respect should be fostered and the teacher should be supportive but realistic.

Long, Morse, and Newman (1976) highlight 19 principles involved in the supportive psychoeducational environment. The principles relate in large part to: teacher/learner interactions that are reality-oriented, supportive, consistent, and flexible; curriculum that is relevant and reasonably challenging; peer group interaction that fosters feelings of mutual respect and sharing; and the development of self-awareness and personal responsibility.

TRADITIONAL PSYCHOTHERAPY FOR THE LEARNING-DISABLED CHILD

Some authors (e.g., Denckla, 1978; Osman, 1979; Bell, 1975) believe that because of the emotional overlays that usually develop, psychotherapy is needed for most LD

---

* In the life-space interview, the teacher has the student describe his perception of the problem (or incident). Questions are used to isolate the basic issue involved and the reality of what had occurred. The student's perceptions are accepted, but other alternatives are also explored. Possible solutions or plans of action are selected—e.g., who can help and how can they help.

children. Denckla advocates psychotherapy for those presenting significant second-ary emotional disabilities, with concomitant family counselling to help parents work out feelings of grief and guilt. She recommends that siblings be included in the ses-sions. Hatton (1966) feels that psychotherapy and parent counselling are increas-ingly important for children who are nine years or older. Kronick (1978) postulates that some LD adolescents will not benefit from academic intervention until some type of therapeutic intervention is offered.

However, there is a preponderance of opinion stating that traditional forms of psychotherapy are contraindicated for LD children (Gordon, 1975, pp. 10–11; Kur-lander & Colodny, 1969; Millman, 1972; Anderson, 1963). Inasmuch as traditional psychotherapy attempts to break down the ego to get to the unconscious, it is not considered the best therapy for children who already have ego insufficiencies (Con-nolly, 1971; Rappaport, 1969).

The child with neurological dysfunctions requires more directive and support-ive treatment. The therapist's role is to show the child that maladaptive behaviors are self-defeating. Because consistency is so important, Rappaport recommends that members of the team who work with the child meet frequently. Kurlander and Colodny (1969, p. 139) state: "We find no usefulness in the practice of drifting into open-ended psychotherapy [with LD children] and waiting for a diagnosis to ap-pear." They further argue, "No one has ever proved conclusively that insight (for which weary acquiescence is often mistaken) is the only cure for the painful symp-toms of anxiety."

Some authors advise psychotherapy for LD children but in conjunction with other therapies and in a relative order of priority. Gardner (1973) suggests that treatment include four avenues: (1) medication, (2) education, (3) parental guid-ance, and, (4) psychotherapy. The latter should be interjected only after the other three prove insufficient by themselves. Kurlander and Colodny (1969) recommend a remedial class and/or specialized tutoring as the first therapeutic mode, medication second, and psychotherapy as a "last and expensive resort" (p. 140). Even here, they state that this psychotherapy need not be intensive nor long: It should stress facts, not inferences inasmuch as "it is not his [the LD child's] motives but his machinery which does not work. He needs less to be inspired than instructed" (p. 142).

*   *   *

The psychotherapeutic techniques discussed in this chapter have proven effec-tive methods for helping the LD child. These approaches should not be used in iso-lation but in conjunction with a sound educational program which will develop the child's capacities to the fullest. Since there is tremendous intragroup variability among the LD population (and among their families as well), no single approach is recommended across-the-board. The choice of intervention (ranging from providing a structured environment coupled with simple direct counseling to the more non-directive, insight therapies) should depend entirely upon the individual case.

REFERENCES

Anderson, C. *Jan: My brain-damaged daughter*. Portland: Durham Press, 1963.

Bassin, A. IRT therapy in marriage counselling. In Alexander Bassin, Thomas E.

Bratter, and Richard L. Rochin (Eds.), *The reality therapy reader.* New York; Harper & Row, 1976.

Bell, J. E. *Family therapy.* New York: Jason Aronson, 1975.

Connolly, C. Social and emotional factors in learning disabilities. In Helmer R. Myklebust (Ed.), *Progress in learning disabilities,* vol. II. New York: Grune & Stratton, 1971.

Cruickshank, W. M. *Learning disabilities in home, school and community.* Syracuse: Syracuse University Press, 1977.

Denckla, M. B. Minimal brain dysfunction. In Jeanne S. Chall and Allan F. Mirsky (Eds.), *Education and the brain.* Chicago: University of Chicago Press, 1978.

Eisenberg, L. Psychiatric implications of brain damage in children. In Edward C. Frierson and Walter B. Barbe (Eds.), *Educating children with learning disabilities: Selected readings.* New York: Appleton-Century-Crofts, 1967.

Frostig, M. and Maslow, P. *Learning problems in the classroom.* New York: Grune & Stratton, 1973.

Gardner, R. A. Psychotherapy of the psychogenic problems secondary to minimal brain dysfunction. *International Journal of Child Psychotherapy,* 1973; *2*(2); 224–256.

Glasser, W. *Reality therapy: A new approach to psychiatry.* New York: Harper & Row, 1965.

Gordon, S. *Living fully.* New York: John Day, 1975.

Hatton, Daniel A. The child with minimal cerebral dysfunction. *Developmental Medicine and Child Neurology,* 1966, 8, 71–78.

Klein, R. S., Altman, S. D., Dreizen, K., Friedman, R., and Powers, L. Structuring dysfunctional parental attitudes toward children's learning and behaving in school: Family-oriented psychoeducational therapy, part I. *Journal of Learning Disabilities,* January, 1981, *14*(1): 15–19.

Kronick, D. *What about me? The LD adolescent.* Novato, Ca.: Academic Therapy Publications, 1975.

————. An examination of psychosocial aspects of learning-disabled adolescents. *Learning Disability Quarterly,* Fall, 1978, 1:86–92.

Kurlander, L. F. and Colodny, D. Psychiatric disability and learning problems. In Lester Tarnopol (Ed.), *Learning Disabilities: Introduction for education and medical management.* Springfield, Ill: Charles C Thomas, 1969.

Lenkowsky, B., and Lenkowsky, R. S. Bibliotherapy for the LD adolescent. *Academic therapy,* Nov. 1978, *14*(2): 179–185.

Long, N., Morse, W. C., and Newman, R. G. (Eds.), *Conflict in the classroom,* 3rd ed. Belmont, Ca.: Wadsworth Publishing Company, 1976.

Mallison, R. *Education as therapy.* Seattle, Wash.: Special Child Publications, 1968.

Marandola, P., and Imber, S. C. Glasser's classroom meeting: A humanistic approach to behavior change with preadolescent inner-city learning-disabled children. *Journal of Learning Disabilities, 12*(6): 383–392. June/July, 1979.

Maslow, A. *Motivation and personality.* New York: Harper & Row, 1954.

Millman, H. L. Treatment of problems associated with cognition and perceptual motor deficits. *Child Welfare,* July, 1972, *51*(7).

O'Donnell, D. J. and Maxwell, K. F. Reality therapy works here. In Alexander Bassin, Thomas E. Bratter and Richard L. Rochin (Eds.), *The reality therapy reader.* New York: Harper & Row, 1976.

Osman, B. B. *Learning disabilities: A family affair.* New York: Random House, 1979.

Rappaport, S. R. Comment's (a response to Gallagher). In William M. Cruickshank (Ed.), *The teacher of brain-injured children.* Syracuse: Syracuse University Press, 1966.

_____. *Public education for children with brain dysfunction.* Syracuse: Syracuse University Press, 1969.

Redl, F. The concept of the life space interview. *American Journal of Orthopsychiatry* XXIX, January, 1959, 1–18.

Behavior Modification Approaches and the Learning-Disabled Child*

8

Behavior modification offers the teacher systematic and structured techniques for improving academic and social performance within the classroom setting. We treat this approach in relation to the LD child from the perspective of three basic avenues, which is consistent with the current interpretation of the field in general (Thoreson, 1974; Kazdin, 1978) and learning disabilities in particular (Prout, 1977).

The first approach is *applied behavior analysis* (ABA), derived from operant conditioning (Skinner, 1938, 1953, 1968) and comprehensively articulated by Baer, Wolf, and Risley (1968). The second is *cognitive behavior modification* (CBM). CBM is distinguished from ABA in that, "Most cognition-based techniques stress the individual's perception and interpretation of external events rather than the direct influence of the surroundings themselves" (Kazdin, 1978, p. 307). The third is the *conventional* approach, based on the work of Pavlov (1960) and Hull (1943). It focuses on deconditioning interfering emotional reactions (such as excessive anxiety) and conditioning beneficial physiological states (such as deep muscle relaxation and optimal cortical arousal).

APPLIED BEHAVIOR ANALYSIS

The ABA approach focuses on observable and measurable behavior. Any behavior of interest may be targeted for modification. Behavior is analyzed quantitatively in terms of how frequently it occurs in a specific amount of time (rate), how long it lasts (duration), and how it is expressed (intensity). In addition, problematic behaviors usually involve an excess or deficiency which impairs an individual's ability

* By David Levinsky

118

Table 8-1.   Problematic Behaviors

Dimension	Degree	Examples
Rate	excessive	changes in task, repetition of same behavior, requests for repeats in directions, reversals, left–right errors, reading errors
	deficient	reluctant to comply with requests, inadequate manipulative play, limited initiation of contact with peers
Duration	excessive	dawdles getting dressed, prolonged time to complete homework, demands inordinate amount of attention from teacher
	deficient	lack of sustained on-task behavior, responds impulsively to aspects of task, volunteers before knowing what's required
Intensity	excessive	speaks too loudly, presses too hard when writing, cries and laughs to inappropriate degree
	deficient	weak motor responses (kicking a ball, swinging, etc.), speaks too softly, affect is very weak

to adapt to environmental requirements. Examples of problematic behaviors associated with the learning disabled are listed in Table 8-1.

Behaviors targeted for change are systematically observed to determine if events preceding the behavior (antecedents) or events following the behavior (consequences) are relevant. For example, antecedent events such as task difficulty, teacher instructions, and seating arrangements may be directly related to the behavior in question or consequences may be operating in the form of rewards and punishments. Their identification will suggest specific methods to deal with the situation. For example, appropriate behavior on the part of the child may go unrewarded while inappropriate behavior receives negative attention in the form of criticism and reprimands.

Baseline measures are taken on the behavior. For example, the rate of math problems completed with 100% accuracy is noted over four 10-minute tests. After baseline, a behavioral intervention is applied. Interventions may involve antecedent events and/or consequent events. Antecedent intervention typically involves providing a cue to appropriate behavior and systematically reducing the cue so that the behavior occurs independent of the teacher. For example, the teacher might assist the child by prompting all five steps in a math computation, then just the first four steps, then three, and so on.

Consequent events are classified as reinforcers or punishers. A reinforcer is any event that increases the behavior it follows. For example, a token may increase the rate of accurate math performance if it is given contingently (if–and only if–the targeted behavior occurs).

A punisher is any event that decreases the behavior it follows. Punishment is used as a procedure only when all positive means of effecting behavioral change have been exhausted. Punishment procedures require monitoring by appropriate committees set up to safeguard the rights of the children involved.

The success of the behavioral program will be reflected in the performance during intervention as compared to baseline. If the change is not in the desired direction, then a rethinking of strategies is in order.

The final consideration in any behavioral program is the maintenance and generalization of the effects. The child who has improved in his math performance should continue to perform at this level independent of any reinforcers. In addition, his performance should occur for other similar behaviors (e.g., math problems), in other settings (e.g., homework), and for other teachers. This is achieved by systematically and gradually reducing the amount of reinforcement external to the task (e.g., tokens), while grades and a sense of achievement acquire an internally-motivating quality.

Illustrative Studies

The following three studies illustrate the ABA approach. Each study attempts to deal with problematic behaviors by employing practical intervention available to classroom teachers. Two specific types of reinforcers—systematic praise and token programs—are examined.

Systematic Praise. A study designed by Hopkins and Conard (1976) sought to demonstrate the effectiveness of ABA procedures using systematic praise and other methods close to those available in the average classroom. The ratio of teacher to pupils was 1:20. The third-grade children represented a diversity of backgrounds and problems. Three of the children could have been labeled educable mentally retarded or learning disabled. Eight children had very short attention spans. Other problems noted were disruption of classroom activities and serious aggression. One child on the average of once a day would jab someone with a pencil or violently pull someone's hair. The very heterogeneity of academic and social behaviors made it an ideal testing ground for the generality of ABA procedures.

One third of the classroom was set aside for a free-play area. This resulted in some crowding but was conducive to teacher–pupil interaction (the teacher moved around the classroom to maximize contact).

Time in the free-play area could be earned by the pupils if they completed their individualized assignments. In the free-play area, activities such as making things out of cardboard, using glue, string, scissors, colored paper, games, and so on, were available in addition to a small record player and books. The children chose these materials and activities themselves. Any child who was disruptive in the play area was instructed to return to his seat. Aside from the granting of permission for free play, a number of other techniques were used which maximized the impact of the teacher on her class. Giving a pupil attention in the form of eye contact, proximity, verbal praise, physical contact, and so forth, was employed in the study as an integral part of the day.

The use of negative attention consisting of emotional and critical responses to child misbehavior was avoided. The teacher ignored incidences of misbehavior. She would praise children who were behaving appropriately and use one child's misbehavior as a cue for praising another child who was behaving appropriately (pointed or suggestive praise). The teacher also used descriptive rather than evaluative praise

(Ginott, 1972). This involved naming the behaviors involved in the praiseworthy situation, thus letting the child know exactly what he is being praised for. Examples are "Thank you for waiting quietly," "I like the way you have your hand up when you need help." Descriptive praise tends to condition a positive emotional reaction to a behavior, which makes that behavior more likely to occur in the future. In addition to praising good behavior and ignoring misbehavior, the teacher used sought-after privileges (e.g. distributing papers, lining up first for recess) and marked papers with positive comments, happy faces, and so forth.

Despite praising, ignoring privileges, marks, and free time, misbehavior still persisted on occasion. (Misbehaviors were defined for the children as not following specific rules, e.g., "Walk in hallways," "No talk except during free time," etc.) A simple punishment system was used when all else failed. It involved having the pupil put a point on the chalkboard. Each point represented a loss of five minutes of recess, during which the child had to sit at the edge of the playground for the specified amount of time.

The results of the study, which lasted two years and included an expansion to cover both the third and fourth grades, were noteworthy. Pupil performance was evaluated by weekly report cards which showed the progress in various academic subjects (pages worked in a programmed reader, percent of items done correctly, etc.). Group achievement tests indicated progress markedly above the national average in spelling, math, and reading. In terms of social behavior, attention to task increased from a baseline of 49.5% to 85.2%. Children dawdled less, got to work quicker, and took less time in transition from activity to activity.

What seems most remarkable about the study is the fact that the procedures, used with a heterogeneous group of 20 children, could be employed in just about any classroom. The pivotal position of the teacher as a manager of the contingencies of reinforcement was stressed. By employing rules, sensitive praising techniques, and a variety of additional uncomplicated behavioral procedures, the teacher was able to effect dramatic improvements in academic and social behaviors.

Token Programs. When procedures closer to the everyday classroom regimen fail, use of stronger systems can change behavior. One of the most popular behavior modification systems involves the use of tokens (point on a card, a poker chip, a card-punch, tickets, etc.), all of which are exchangeable for some back-up reinforcers. At least two types of token systems are available that bypass the issue of cost (a factor of concern to some teachers and school administrators), the use of home-based reinforcement, and the use of reinforcers naturally occurring in the classroom.

One program developed by McKenzie et. al. (1968) involved 10 students in a learning-disabilities class. There were eight boys and two girls ranging in age from 10 to 13 years, of normal intelligence with retarded achievement levels of at least two years in one or more academic areas. The children had a history of highly distractible and disruptive behaviors. The dependent measure was *attending behavior*, which was defined as orientation toward work materials including sitting at desk, eyes directed toward materials, and also appropriate requests for teacher assistance (e.g., raising hand). During group work, behavior was counted if attention was toward the student reciting, toward the teacher, or if the student himself was responding orally to the lesson.

Various reinforcements were already in use, including: earning recess by completing assignments; access to a free-play area; special privileges such as line leaders and monitors based on work improvements; teacher attention contingent upon appropriate behavior; eating lunch with the group as opposed to eating alone contingent upon appropriate behavior; and weekly grades. This latter procedure involved sending the child home with a weekly grade report which was signed by the parents and subsequently returned to the teacher by the child.

In the experimental intervention, all procedures used during baseline were continued plus one additional procedure (the experimental condition) was added: Grades were now exchangeable for money allowances which were tied to the specific performances of the children. Higher grades earned substantially more money. Parents sat down with their children each Friday and computed the amounts earned.

Results of the study indicated an increase from median percentage of attending to reading behavior of 68% during baseline to 86% during the token period. Similar results were indicated in arithmetic, from 70% baseline to 86% for token phase. In addition, by the end of the school year, all ten students had advanced one to four levels above baseline in all academic areas. Six of the ten students returned to the regular class at a level of one grade higher than the previous year. (The program was continued with the cooperation of the regular class teacher so that the students could be phased into the regular class setting.) Parent participation was crucial, and was maintained by frequent parent–teacher conferences.

A study by O'Leary et al. (1973) demonstrates the effectiveness of naturally-occurring reinforcers intrinsic to the classroom in modifying disruptive behaviors (out of seat, noise, aggression, touching other's property, not attending, turning around, playing, vocalizing). Subjects were 22 third- and fourth-grade children selected on the basis of homeroom teacher and principal recommendations, direct classroom observations, and teacher ratings. They were assigned to three resource rooms (depending on their area of academic deficiency) for one hour each school day.

The experimental condition consisted of setting up a token reinforcement program. The first 45 minutes of the hour in the resource room was a work period. Each child was given a worksheet listing his assignments and the number of points he could earn for completing his work. In addition, the worksheet had spaces for recording the number of points for work completed, coming to class on time, and appropriate behavior. Points were awarded daily at the end of the work period, each point redeemable for one minute of time in the activity area. Activities consisted of arts and crafts, games, and favorites brought from home by the children.

O'Leary found that points exchangeable for free play in an activity area were functionally related to consistent decreases in disruptive behavior. Following termination of the token program, Class B was observed for 20 days in the resource room. The behavioral gains were maintained, despite the discontinuation of awarding points. This token program demonstrates the effectiveness of free-play activities in reducing disruptive behavior. Setting aside areas of a classroom for activities, awarding points on a worksheet, and exchanging points for free-play time represent an accessible technology for teachers at a relatively minimal cost.

VARIATIONS OF APPLIED BEHAVIOR ANALYSIS

ABA has stimulated creative modifications of its own format and technology. Two examples of ABA variations are: *the engineered classroom* and *behavioral contracting.*

The Engineered Classroom

The LD child, like any pupil, functions in a milieu consisting of three major types of stimuli. Hewett and his colleagues (Hewett, 1968; Hewett et. al., 1971) have attempted to coordinate task, teacher expectancy, and environmental setting in order to maximize learning. The ultimate goal is to have each child function at least at his own grade level in the regular class setting.

The essential components of the engineered classroom are: task, teacher expectancy, environmental setting, and reinforcement.

Task Stimuli. These are arranged hierarchically into seven levels: attention, response, order, exploratory, social, mastery, and achievement.

Attention-level tasks are designed to minimize distractions, take a short time to complete, have a high degree of sensory stimulation, and be of a concrete nature. Any task that gains and holds the child's attention is of value.

Response level task performance should not be judged by a criterion for correctness, but should maximize the probability that the child will be successful. Success is critical so that tasks need to be programmed to assure this result.

Order level tasks involve becoming time-governed so that a task is initiated, carried out, and completed in some sequence that finally signals completion.

Exploratory-level tasks involve multisensory experiences with the world that enhance the child's knowledge of reality (how things work) and appreciation of his environment as predictable and pleasureable.

Social-level tasks involve social communication (talking and listening), interacting for the approval of others, and delay in gratification (increased tolerance for frustration).

Mastery-level tasks involve functioning independently in the community, home, and school. In addition, there are school-subject tasks requiring a criterion level of functioning such as a basic sight reading vocabulary, and so forth.

Achievement-level tasks involve learning for the reinforcement intrinsic in the tasks themselves. The curriculum challenges the student appropriately and allows him freedom to choose learning tasks and engage in critical thinking and maximal creativity.

Teacher-Expectancy Stimuli. Teacher-expectancy stimuli constitute the program's structure. The child's behavior is expected to conform to certain minimal standards even at the attention level. For example, a hyperactive child may be allowed to change activities as often as he likes but only within a circumscribed work area. In other words, contingencies are operative on all levels, but are geared to the unique characteristics of each child. At the response level, for example, responding successfully is of paramount importance. Yet at an order level, success of a response is determined by whether it follows a sequence and is completed, while at a mastery level success is based on a criterion of how well it is done.

Environmental-Setting Stimuli. In addition to tailoring the task to developmental ability and structure (in terms of teacher expectancies) to task performance, the classroom has been modified to enhance the learning process as well. There are three major centers in the classroom. The mastery center (mastery and achievement levels) involves rows of double desks where the students sit and pursue academic tasks. Study booths or "offices" are available for students requiring less distraction.

An exploratory center (exploratory and social levels) contains communication, science, and art areas. Activities appropriate here are arts and crafts, simple experiments, music, and social-skill interaction.

An order center (attention, response, and order levels) consists of double desks set up adjacent to each other and a storage cabinet where appropriate games, puzzles, and the like are kept.

Reinforcement. A work record card holder is placed near the entry to the classroom. The student picks up his individual work record card, which is divided up into 200 little squares. At the end of fixed periods of time and depending on the teacher's expectancy contingencies, checkmarks are given. These are exchangeable for rewards such as candy and trinkets, or special activities later on. In general, however, earning checkmarks is made easy for children involved in any aspect of the program. Any child unable to function at a higher level of expectancy for that day or time period is allowed to choose alternate, less demanding, and/or more interesting activities. A child need not stay in the mastery or exploratory area, for example, if he will function better (and earn checkmarks) in the order center.

The engineered-classroom concept has been extended to facilitate mainstreaming (Hewett et al., 1971) in terms of a learning-center concept. This involves gradations of four different levels of functioning with the highest level representing the regular classroom. This noncategorical approach serves children on the basis of their adaptive ability, which in turn determines the degree to which they can be integrated into the regular classroom. The engineering of space, activities, structure, and reinforcement remain consistent with the basic themes described above.

Contracting
According to Becker et al. (1975):

> Point contracts are specialized token reinforcement systems in which a written contract details the performance requirements and possible consequences. The students agree to meet certain requirements, and the teacher (or a parent) agrees to provide certain rewards if the requirements are met. The contracts function very much like those that are the basis for most adult exchanges of services and goods. A contract has four essential parts and a possible bonus clause:
> 1. Specification of responsibilities or performances to be reinforced.
> 2. Specification of privileges, or the rewards to be earned.
> 3. Specification of sanctions for failure to live up to the contract.
> 4. Specification of a monitoring system.

5. Specification of possible bonuses for going beyond contract requirements. (pp. 239–240)

Homme (1970) refers to his system as contingency-contracting. A contingency is a rule between a response and its consequence. The rules may vary depending on the circumstances. One rule may involve a specification of the number of responses required before a consequence is awarded (e.g., ten math problems for five minutes in a free-play area). Another may specify the time a specific response is to occur (e.g., every one must be seated by the second bell to receive a happy face). Whatever the contingency, the consequence is awarded if and only if the appropriate behavior occurs. This "if and only if" relationship makes the consequence contingent upon the behavior. The explicit stating of these contingencies constitutes the contract.

Contracting has been used for a variety of behaviors: corrective reading (Englemann et al., 1974; Pendrak, 1974), truancy (MacDonald et al., 1970), disruptive behavior (Lates & Egner, 1973), and in a total learning center (Cohen et al., 1974). The approach has special relevance to junior and senior high school students. These students receive the respect due their age for assuming their share of the responsibility of negotiating, monitoring, and fulfilling the contract agreements.

COGNITIVE BEHAVIOR MODIFICATION

The preceding studies and programs dealt with a specific behavioral approach in which the function of consequences (reinforcers, rewards, punishments, etc.) is stressed. A different approach, known as cognitive behavior modification (CBM) focuses upon the individual's *perception*—and *anticipation*—of the consequences. This is also referred to as social-learning approach (Bandura, 1977) and has been heralded as an alternative to the ABA.

CBM concerns itself with what goes on inside of the head of a person—the thoughts, fantasies, and rich symbolic processes that distinguish human beings from animals. What a person says to himself is a critical area of potential modification, as is illustrated in the following classical study.

Self-Instructional Training

In an important early study conducted by Meichenbaum and Goodman (1971), performance task problems in the LD were viewed as difficulties in one or more of the following areas: comprehending a task, planning appropriate cognitive approaches, and implementing these approaches in the process of guiding task-oriented performances.

Subjects were 15 second-grade children placed in a remedial class because of hyperactivity, poor self-control and/or low IQs (the minimal cut-off for the study was an IQ of 85). The subjects in the experimental group were seen individually for four half hour training sessions over a two-week period. Cognitive training consisted of the following:

1. The adult first performed the required task while verbalizing out loud (overtly) each of the task components.

2. Then the child performed the same task under the guidance of the adult who verbalized overtly each component.
3. Next the child performed the task while verbalizing overtly in the same way modeled by the adult.
4. Then the child did as in three above except his instructions to himself were in a whisper (lip movements).
5. Finally, the child performed the task without lip movements (covert verbalization).

The verbalizations consisted of focusing on the task ("Okay, what is it I have to do?"), comprehension of the task ("You want me to copy the picture with the different lines"), cognitive planning ("I have to go slowly and be careful"), self-guidance governed task implementation ("Okay, draw the line down, down, good; then to the right, that's it; now down some more and to the left . . . etc."), and self-reinforcement ("Good, I'm doing fine so far").

Included in the practice task performance was an intentional error. Meichenbaum and Goodman, in a previous study (1969), had noted that children with impulsive behaviors show marked decline in their performance following errors. In terms of the above task this involved self-instructional training as follows: ". . . Now back up again. No, I was supposed to go down. That's okay. Just erase the line carefully . . . Good. Even if I make an error I can go slowly and carefully" (p. 117). This same procedure was used with a variety of tasks from simple sensorimotor ones, such as copying line patterns, to complex tasks such as completing a picture series (taken from Primary Abilities Test). Results of the study indicated that self-instructional training increased performance considerably in desireable directions.

Guidelines in Modeling and Self-Instruction

Meichenbaum (1977) points out some additional considerations. First, the teacher implementing these techniques should recognize the need to generalize these strategies beyond the specific task or situation. The teacher should strive to promote an enduring change in cognitive style. Second, the importance of play as a vehicle for providing self-instructional training cannot be overlooked. This is particularly pertinent to the teacher and parent who have many opportunities throughout the day to model appropriate self-instructional practices. For example, in playing a game, it is advisable to choose one the child has had success with, rather than failures and frustrations. Meichenbaum (1977) described the adult's modeling response in relation to a game in which he fails to guide a ball through a maze covered with plexiglass:

> "This is just impossible. I can't do this. [The therapist begins to throw the maze game down when he says,] Just wait a second. Take a slow deep breath; good. Now, what is it I have to do? Go slowly, steady. Lower this hand, etc. Let me put on my thinking cap. [The therapist puts on his imaginary thinking cap and continues.]" (p. 85).

Note how important it is to include ways of coping with failure.

Third, affect is of critical importance in self-instructional training. The teacher or parent should model the appropriate affect and encourage practice in the process of matching self-statements by the child with proper inflection and feeling.

Fourth, the format should be flexible and geared to each individual child. Different children require different amounts of practice before they internalize these strategies (covert rehearsal). In some cases it may not be necessary to have the child self-verbalize aloud.

In general, self-instructional training should follow a shaping procedure in that adult modeling and child rehearsal follows an order from simple to more complex self-verbalizations. For the child who becomes embarrassed in using "thinking out loud" verbalizations, it is recommended that he be questioned by the adult about what he (the child) is telling himself. For older children this is particularly appropriate.

Finally, in terms of format, Meichenbaum (1977) cites Drummond (1974) who makes the following suggestions for working with groups:

1. Self-instructional training should occur early in the school day, before students become tired. This has the added benefit of giving students time throughout the school day for practicing and applying their skills.

2. Training with groups larger than three detracts from ease of management.

3. Videotape feedback and prerecordings of the child's own verbalization can provide additional media input which enhances the possibilities and promotes contrasting effects from different models.

4. Self-instructional training can be most effectively used with children in the early grades (less than third or fourth).

5. Self-instructional training with children can be embellished via the use of imagery. For example, a child who imagines he is a scientist while conducting an experiment can enhance the care with which he sets up and uses the materials. He may be instructed to picture himself working in a scientific laboratory where it is important to be quiet so as not to disturb other people's experiments, and so forth.

6. The child should be viewed by the teacher and parent as a collaborator in the total process. The child can tell much about his thoughts and feelings; he can also assist in developing and carrying out a self-instructional program.

THE CONVENTIONAL APPROACH

In addition to the ABA and CBM avenues of behavior modification, yet another branch exists. Termed the *conventional approach*, it attempts to more directly modify problematic emotions and muscle tension. These procedures, in one form or another, build on the conditioning model of Pavlov (1960). Through a process of conditioning, anxiety and muscle tension can come to be associated with key social and academic stimuli. Instead of engendering positive emotions and a moderate degree of appropriate tension, critical situations (such as interacting with others and studying) often elicit debilitating anxiety reactions and excessive muscular tension.

Three basic approaches directed at correcting these problems are *biofeedback*, *muscle-relaxation training* and *systematic desensitization*.

Biofeedback and Relaxation Training

Biofeedback is a procedure that involves giving a person information about his bodily processes via mechanical devices that heighten sensory awareness of minute fluctuations in these processes, thereby allowing individually-mediated control.

In an illustrative study, Braud (1978) worked with 15 hyperactive (age range 6-13) and 15 nonhyperactive (age range 6-15) children. In relaxation training, the subject is taught to discriminate between tense and relaxed states. This is done progressively through various muscle groups so that eventually the person can induce a state of self-directed relaxation in previously tense situations. The hyperactive group was compared with the nonhyperactive group in terms of muscular tension levels and several behavioral rating scales. In addition, the hyperactive group was randomly assigned to three conditions (biofeedback, relaxation, and control) of five subjects each.

After being outfitted with an electro-myographic monitoring device (EMG), the child was instructed that his objective for each session was to lower his overall body tension and that electrodes on his forehead measured that tension. He was told that as he relaxed his body tension, the lights on the console would change. (Red light = tension "much too high"; yellow light = "a little bit too high"; green light = tension so low that child was to try to keep the green light on as much of the time as possible.)

A shaping procedure was used to facilitate self-control of apparatus and progressive tension reduction. Initially, it was made very easy to keep the light green (by adjusting the gain on the apparatus). As the child relaxed by "trying to keep the green light on," gradually increasing degrees of muscle relaxation were shaped.

In one relaxation group children were given the same number of sessions as in EMG (12 sessions, two per week for six weeks). During each session the child listened to tape-recorded, progressive relaxation directions and followed the procedures set forth by Lupin et al. (1976).

Results of the study indicated that the hyperactive children as a group had higher muscular tension levels, more behavioral problems, and lower psychological test scores (Bender-Gestalt, Digit Span and Coding subtests on WISC, and Visual Sequential Memory subtest of ITPA). Within the hyperactive group, both EMG and progressive relaxation significantly reduced muscular tension, hyperactivity, distractibility, emotionality, aggressivity, impulsivity, explosiveness, and irritability.

Because of the relative ease of administration and comparable effects, relaxation is a superior technique. Finally, it is recommended that some sort of mental visualizations be included in relaxation training so that the mind can be tranquil along with the body.

Systematic Desensitization

When a negative emotion is conditioned, an individual seeks to avoid any situation containing conditioned stimuli that may elicit anxiety. Avoidance of these anxiety-arousing situtations may become a way of life impeding the person's growth and experience. Systematic desensitization, a technique developed by Wolpe (1969), attempts to neutralize the effects of conditioned stimuli to elicit anxiety. This is achieved by training the person in progressive deep *muscle relaxation*. Next the therapist breaks the target fear into subfears and begins treating the least innocuous first. Starting with imagining the lowest level, the subject relaxes deeply and progresses gradually through the hierarchy, substituting a relaxed response for the anxiety response—deep relaxation and anxiety are incompatible.

For example, in one clinical study (Coyle, 1968), an eighth-grade girl with anxiety over reading in front of the class was treated. The girl was 14 years old with WISC IQ of 78. She was seen for 11 weekly sessions and a three month follow-up.

Procedures involved teaching deep muscle relaxation and constructing anxiety hierarchies. The first list dealt with general school situations (the anxiety had generalized to situations associated with reading, e.g., the school) and the second list with reading itself. At first the therapist instructed the girl to *imagine* the situation. Later an "in-vivo" experience was included in which the girl read before increasing numbers of adults in the therapy situation. The level of difficulty of reading selections was also gradually increased. Results following termination and during follow-up indicated no further debilitating anxiety; in fact she was now volunteering to read before the class.

SOME CURRENT ISSUES IN BEHAVIOR MODIFICATION

Behavior modification is complex. Its principles seek continued empirical verification, particularly as they are extended to new and complex populations. The LD child will continue to challenge the creativity and ingenuity of behavior-modification personnel.

Reinforcement. In some recent work on reinforcement with the LD child, Douglas (1975) has suggested that reinforcement may actually interfere with performance if it is not used judiciously and contingently, or if it is withdrawn precipitously. Other researchers (Lepper et al., 1973) have considered an "overjustification" hypothesis, suggesting that the attributing of gains in learning to extrinsic awards may impair the child's sense of his own achievement, and when rewards are terminated he will have little intrinsic control to maintain these gains.

Surely, behavior modification does not rest on reinforcement alone. However, it would be hasty to disregard it given its long history of empirical verification. O'Leary (1973) has suggested minimizing the level of reward and also tying it into the intrinsic working of the classroom. The use of gradual fading of rewards according to specific types of schedules is a basic principle of behavior modification.

Finally, the approach of Cognitive Behavior Modification promises much in the way of dealing with reinforcement since it emphasizes internalization of both acquired skill and self-evaluative feedback.

Who Should Do the Modifying? Behavior modification has facilitated a democratization of the helping process. This has taken the direction (much in common with current legislative policies) of using parents as modifiers (O'Dell, 1974). In addition peers, siblings, and all manner of tutors have been employed in the process of helping. Some may lament this proliferation of interventionists. One wonders as to the minimal level of competence they should demonstrate before applying their techniques, even under the supervision of qualified professionals.

The fact is, however, that daily interaction between people—during formal or in addition to informal occasions—inevitably effects changes in one another's behavior. It is safe to say that we will go on modifying each other's behavior, whether mandated or not. Behavior-modification techniques, judiciously imparted through books, manuals, and college courses, with appropriate cautions and preferably supervised application, can greatly benefit as a mental-health system for the entire community.

Generalizing Results. The process of extending the positive effects of behavioral intervention is as important as the intervention itself. Acquiring a new behavior requires systematic programming as does generalizing that behavior across time, place, and person.

The preponderance of studies focus upon the acquisition of behaviors with little or no treatment of their maintenance. Research specifically attempting to validate procedures that promote long-term maintenance of behaviors in the learning disabled is needed.

Measurement. Measurement of targeted behavior has met with considerable resistance from even those behavior-modification users who testify to its efficacy. Teachers employ all variety of measurement techniques in the form of data from the child's tests and grades, attendance records, unusual incidence reports, and so forth.

Researchers have tried to simplify measurement techniques and make them practical for home and classroom use (Hall, 1974). As the information becomes more widely disseminated, hopefully more behavior modification personnel will use it for evaluating the effectiveness of their methods and curricula.

Behavior Modification and the Whole Person. It has been frequently observed that when one significant target behavior is changed for the better, many children begin changing in their general attitudes about themselves (Becker et al., 1975). Increasing positive experiences with competence tend to influence the child's overall self-concept. This is particularly true if the child is able to verbalize the relationship between his behavior change and his way of relating to the world (insight). Ryan et al. (1976), referring to the role of self-concept changes in behavior modification, state: "There is . . . a growing body of evidence that suggests these self-concept changes follow from, or even precede, changes in the targeted behaviors themselves and these self-concept changes may also have important consequences for maintaining and extending the effects of behavioral treatment" (p. 638).

Behavior modification has the potential to change the whole person—behaviorally, cognitively, and emotionally—an encouraging fact. However, the interrelationship between behavior change and the total child, particularly the LD child, requires a great deal more in the way of research and investigation.

REFERENCES

Baer, D. M., Wolf, M. M., and Risley, T. R. Some current dimensions of applied behavior analysis. *Journal of Applied Behavioral Analysis*, 1968, *1*, 91–97.

Bandura, A. *Social learning theory*. Englewood Cliffs, N. J.: Prentice-Hall, 1977.

Becker, W. C., Engelmann, S., and Thomas, D. R. *Teaching 1: Classroom management*. Chicago: Science Research Associates, Inc., 1975.

Braud, L. W. The effects of frontal EMG biofeedback and progressive relaxation upon hyperactivity and its behavioral concomitants. *Biofeedback and Self-regulation*, 1978, *3*, 69–89.

Cohen, S. I., Keyworth, J. M., Kleiner, R. I., and Brown, W. L. Effective behavior change at the Anne Arundel Learning Center through minimum contact interventions. In R. Ulrich, T. Stachnik, and J. Mabry (Eds.), *Control of human behavior, vol. 3*. Glenview, Ill.: Scott, Foresman, 1974.

Coyle, P. J. The systematic desensitization of reading anxiety, a case study. *Psychology in the Schools*, 1968, *5*, 140–141.

Douglas, V. I. Are drugs enough?–to treat or train the hyperactive child. *International Journal of Mental Health*, 1975, *4*, 199–212.

Drummond, D. Self-instructional training: An approach to disruptive classroom behavior. *Unpublished doctoral dissertation*, University of Oregon, 1974.

Englemann, S., Becker, W. C., Carnine, L., Meyers, L., Becker, J., and Johnson, G. *E-B Press corrective reading program*. Eugene, Oregon: E-B Press, 1974.

Ginott, H. *Teacher and child: A book for parents and teachers*. New York: Macmillan, 1972.

Hall, R. V. *Managing behavior, part 1: The measurement of behavior*. Lawrence, Kansas: H & H Enterprises, 1974.

Hewett, F. M. *The emotionally-disturbed child in the classroom*. Boston: Allyn & Bacon, 1968.

Hewett, F. M., Taylor, F. D., Artuso, A. A., and Quay, H. C. The learning-center concept. In R. H. Bradfield (Ed.), *Behavior modification of learning disabilities*. Novato, Ca.: Academic Therapy Publications, 1971.

Homme, L., Csanyi, A. P., Gonzales, M. A. and Rechs, J. R. *How to use contingency contracting in the classroom*. Champaign, Ill.: Research Press, 1970.

Hopkins, B. L. and Conard, R. J. Putting it all together: Super school. In N. G. Haring and R. L. Schiefelbusch (Eds.), *Teaching special children*. New York: McGraw-Hill, 1976.

Hull, C. L. *Principles of behavior*. New York: Appleton-Century-Crofts, 1943.

Kazdin, A. *History of behavior modification: Experimental foundations of contemporary research*. Baltimore: University Park Press, 1978.

Lates, R., and Egner, A. Teaching self-discipline through contingency contracting. In A. Egner (Ed.), *Individualizing junior and senior high instruction to provide special education within regular classrooms*. Burlington: University of Vermont, 1973.

Lepper, M. R., Greene, D., and Nisbett, R. E. Undermining children's intrinsic interest with extrinsic rewards: A test of the overjustification hypothesis. *Journal of Personality and Social Psychology*, 1973, *28*, 129–137.

Lupin, M., Braud, L. W., Braud, W. G., and Duer, W. F. Children, parents, and relaxation tapes. *Academic Therapy*, 1976, *12*, 105–113.

MacDonald, W. S., Gallimore, R. and MacDonald, G. Contingency counseling by school personnel: An economical model of intervention. *Journal of Applied Behavior Analysis*, 1970, *8*, 175–182.

McKenzie, H. S., Clark, M., Wolf, M. M., Kothera, R., and Benson, C. Behavior modification of children with learning disabilities using grades as tokens and allowances as back-up reinforcers. *Exceptional Children*, 1968, *34*, 745–753.

Meichenbaum, D. *Cognitive behavior modification*. New York: Plenum Press, 1977.

Meichenbaum, D., and Goodman, J. Reflection-impulsivity and verbal control of motor behavior. *Child Development*, 1969, *40*, 785–797.

————. Training impulsive children to talk to themselves: A means of developing self-control. *Journal of Abnormal Psychology*, 1971, *77*, 115–126.

O'Dell, S. Training parents in behavior modification: A review. *Psychological Bulletin*, 1974, *81*, 418–433.

O'Leary, K. D., Drabman, R., and Kass, R. F. Maintenance of appropriate behavior in a token program. *Journal of Abnormal Child Psychology*, 1973, *1*, 127–138.

Pavlov, I. P. *Conditioned reflexes*. New York: Dover, 1960.

Pendrak, M. Performance contracting and the secondary reading lab. *Journal of Reading*, 1974, *17*, 453–457.

Prout, H. T. Behavioral intervention with hyperactive children: A review. *Journal of Learning Disabilities*, 1977, *10*, 141–146.

Ryan, V. L., Krall, C. A., and Hodges, W. F. Behavior modification and self-concept. *Journal of Consulting Clinical Psychology*, 1976, *44*, 638–645.

Skinner, B. F. *The behavior of organisms: An experimental analysis*. New York: Appleton-Century-Crofts, 1938.

————. *Science and human behavior*. New York: Macmillan, 1953.

————. *The technology of teaching*. New York: Appleton-Century-Crofts, 1968.

Thoreson, C. E. Behavioral means and humanistic ends. In M. J. Mahoney and C. E. Thoreson (Eds.), *Self-control: Power to the person*. Monterey, Calif.: Brooks/Cole, 1974.

Wolpe, J. *The practice of behavior therapy*. New York: Pergamon Press, 1969.

Process Training

9

PERCEPTUAL-MOTOR SYSTEMS

Sensory-motor activity utilizes perceptual information which is correlated with motor performance. The importance of early sensory-motor (perceptual-motor) learning has been emphasized by Piaget and has found advocates in Barsch, Getman, Cratty, Kephart, Ayres, Doman, and Delacato, whose varied sensory-motor approaches are discussed in this chapter.

The background and training of these theoreticians are reflected in their views of perceptual-motor (P-M) testing and programming. Although most of their programs have aspects similar to other approaches—that is, all are concerned with patterns of development and view motor and perceptual functioning as the basis for cognitive performance—the stress of each system varies. As Tarver and Hallahan (1976) point out, Kephart, Barsch, and Getman were associated at various times with both Werner and Strauss whose influence is reflected in their theories. While Kephart and Barsch concentrate upon the role of movement, Getman, an optometrist, emphasizes the visual component. Cratty, from the perspective of a physical educator, focuses upon the need for movement games to improve perceptual-motor functioning. Ayres early training in occupational therapy is reflected in her stress on sensory integration and the belief that neurological dysfunction can be modified. Doman, a physical therapist, and Delacato, an educator, enlarged upon the views of Temple Fay, a neurologist, in developing the "patterning" theory of neurological organization. Each of these theorists believes that perceptual-motor performance can be evaluated and remedial interventions can be utilized which will improve the perceptual-motor functioning and academic performance.

The adoption of a "systems" approach to motor therapy is questioned by Smith (1968), who notes that choosing one system over another for the school program may cause experiential gaps for some LD children while requiring others to engage in unneeded activities. The motor experiences the child participates in should reflect his individual needs. In addition she cautions that unless motor therapy is supervised by a physical educator as part of a team approach, the activities engaged in may be more detrimental than therapeutic. Salvia and Ysseldike (1978) have found most perceptual-motor tests unreliable because their measures are inconsistent. They note that research fails to support the premise that perceptual-motor performance relates to academic performance. They belive reliance on P-M tests may lead to the assignment of children to relatively useless interventions.

Sensory-Integration Approach

Defects in cross-modal integration of visual, tactual, and kinesthetic perception caused by disturbances in the vestibular system are seen by Ayres (1972) as a primary cause of motor deficiencies and reading problems. The vestibular system is part of the brain that regulates balance and awareness of the body in space. Proprioceptors, located within muscles, tendons, and joints, respond to stimuli produced within the body. Vestibular-proprioceptive integration is responsible for eye movements, well-integrated posture, and the skilled movements used for writing. Ayres suggests that sensory information reaches the brain of the LD in a disorganized manner. Quirós (1978) states the vestibular-proprioceptor disassociation will affect spatial abilities, attention span, and acquisition of laterality.

According to Shaffer (1979), the inability to integrate vestibular input and maintain balance in opposition to gravity produces an emotional experience he calls "primal terror." Children with vestibular dysfunction find their daily world erratic and inconsistant, which can lead to tension, a lack of trust, a feeling of helplessness, constant anticipation of danger, a poor self-concept, and the belief that the world is a dangerous place. Vestibular dysfunction may cause the child to have frequent accidents, and to perform motor tasks so poorly that he cannot participate in childhood games (eg., baseball). This may be a contributing cause to the anxiety most authors associate with LD children.

Ayres presents a sensory-integration approach she contends can enhance the brain's ability to perform a variety of functions rather than train separate functions. She does not claim to eliminate the underlying causes but to alleviate some of the conditions that lead to learning disorders. Gearheart (1977), in discussing Ayres' theory, notes that this is a fundamental difference between Ayres' work and that of Doman and Delacato. Ayres recommends that a clinical evaluation of sensory integration include the Southern California Sensory Integration Tests (Ayres, 1972). The subtests are described in Figure 9-1.

Tonic neck and tonic labyrinthine reflexes are evaluated to determine the degree to which they have been integrated into the nervous system. Structured observations are used to determine muscle tone, the capacity to simultaneously contract antagonistic muscles, control of extraocular muscles, and integration of both sides of the body.

Quirós postulates that the visual proprioceptive and vestibular receptors balance or integrate with external and internal sensory receptors, thus providing complete information to the CNS which allows appropriate emotional, perceptual, and motor development. Well-developed vestibular-oculomotor pathways are needed

Space visualization: utilizes form boards to determine visual perception of form and space and ability to mentally manipulate objects in space

Figure-ground perception: involves use of stimulus figures, superimposed and imbedded so as to determine ability to distinguish foreground from background

Position in space: utilizes various simple geometric forms to determine ability to recognize such forms in different positions and orientations

Design copying: the child must duplicate a design on a dot grid

Motor accuracy: involves drawing a line over an existing (printed) line; the motor coordination component is the major component in this task

Kinesthesia: the child must place his finger on a point at which his finger previously had been placed (by the examiner) with vision occluded

Manual form perception: requires matching the visual counterpart of a geometric form held in the hand

Finger identification: involves ability to identify (point to) the finger on his hand which was touched by the examiner while the child was not watching

Graphesthesia: the child must draw a design on the back of his hand, copying a design drawn on the back of his hand by the examiner

Localization of tactile stimuli: the child must touch, with his finger, a spot on his hand or arm which was previously touched by the examiner

Double tactile stimuli perception: the child is touched simultaneously on either (or both) the cheek and the hand; he must identify where he was touched

Imitation of postures: the child imitates positions or postures assumed by the examiner

Crossing the midline of the body: the child imitates the examiner in point to one of the examiner's eyes or ears

Bilateral motor coordination: involves use of and interaction between both upper extremities

Right-left discrimination: the child must discriminate right from left: (1) on himself, (2) on the examiner, and (3) relative to an object (This test is the only part of the SCSIT which requires verbal responses.)

Standing balance, eyes open: indicates ability to balance on one foot with eyes open

Standing balance, eyes closed: indicates ability to balance on one foot with eyes closed

Figure 9-1. (Source: Published by Western Psychological Services.)

for fixations and the skilled movements of the eyes needed for reading. The lack of vestibular-ocular coordination can be determined using a provoked nystagmus examination with caloric tests. (Cold or warm water irrigates the external ear canal. Saccadic movements of the eyes toward the opposite side (nystagmus) can be seen.)

Both Ayres and Quirós stress that proper diagnosis is needed for appropriate therapy and remediation. The type of intervention depends on the particular problem. Some activities aim at modifying the vestibular system; others attempt to establish interaction between the vestibular and the muscle systems. Ayres believes her approach, while not eliminating the underlying causes, enables the LD child to benefit from special education (Lynn, 1979). To counteract the feelings of helplessness, fear, and poor self-concept stemming from vestibular inadequacies, Shaffer (1979) recommends positive emotional feedback, as well as well-structured activities.

Perceptual-Motor Theory

Newell Kephart, a leading advocate of perceptual-motor training, developed an intervention program based on the theory that the basis of all behaviors, including cognitive functioning, is motoric (1971). Development is viewed as a step-like process which is both quantitative (normative within a stage) and qualitative (between stages). He emphasized the importance of determining where development has been interrupted and restoring its normal course. If development is determined to be *delayed* (without evidence of neurological disturbance), he recommends that experiences that foster development be supplied. The enrichment program should be appropriate for the developmental level as well as the chronological level. In disruptive development, a stage has been skipped or one or more stages has been inadequately developed. It is necessary to solidify the incomplete or omitted stages after identifying them. (A hierarchy of stages of learning is postulated: gross motor → motor-perceptual → perceptual-motor → perceptual → perceptual-conceptual → conceptual (Ebersole, Kephart, & Ebersole, 1968). He cautions that no matter how poorly a new stage is achieved, the child will not behave as he did at an earlier stage. Therefore, when it is necessary to take a child back in order to develop the underlying skills, we cannot employ the same teaching methods used with a younger child who is ready for that stage.

According to Kephart (1972), development involves the acquisition of *generalizations* which permit the processing of data. Generalization is seen as a pattern whose function is to integrate data "on the basis of similarities, not on the basis of the situation in which they were acquired" (p. 51). This allows for a transfer of information and performance from one situation to another: the behavior becomes generalized. The inability to generalize is viewed as a basic deficit in many LD children. Learning appears to consist of specific discrete skills and information. The ability to organize and integrate data appears to be impaired, probably because of disturbances in the CNS (pp. 52–53).

The inability to generalize is also reflected in the acquisition of what Kephart calls a *splinter skill*. The child learns specific movements to perform a given task but is unable to use the skill to perform a related one. For example, a young child is taught how to copy his name but is unable to copy any other words. Kephart says the teacher must always be cognizant of the process or motor pattern the child is using and not stress the end result.

Generalization develops in three stages: 1) *initial datum*, e.g., a simple motor response; 2) *elaboration*, the addition of a number of similar experiences which result in the development of a pattern; and 3) *integration*, the process in which data from the elaboration stage is merged into a whole. The whole is made up of separate parts, each related to the other. Kephart recommends that integration be encouraged by introducing stimuli from many sources at one time, i.e., multi-sensory stimulation (MSS). Each stimulus must provide the same information simultaneously if the integration is to be effective. However, MSS must be individualized since some children may become confused and others may block out stimuli if more than one sensory channel is used.

The *perceptual-motor match* is a very important part of the learning process according to Kephart who uses the development of eye–hand coordination as an illustration. The first step is hand–eye. The child moves his hand and watches it as it moves. The eye follows the hand and begins to see what the hand feels. Because it is more efficient (it can move more quickly and supply more information), the eye begins to take the lead. The hand follows, confirming the results. The hand is used less and less. The second step is eye–hand. The eye begins to control the hand. The eye can then explore on its own and the hand can duplicate it. The perceptual data and motor data can be translated into the other. Both have the same meaning. Perceptual-motor match is now established. Perceptual data can appear distorted, a rectangular court on a playground may appear to be a trapezoid, but previous experience enables the child to interpret it as a rectangle.

Another major step in the learning process is the emergence of *figure–ground* relationships, which depend on the establishment of stable perceptual-motor match. The child learns to focus on pertinent aspects of the environment while the other parts become the background. Kephart relates the inability of hyperactive children to distinguish figure–ground, to the fact that they cannot differentiate their movements adequately and do not develop kinesthetic figure–ground.

The motor basis of learning involves four aspects: *posture*, *laterality*, *directionality*, and *body image*.

Posture provides the zero point for movement and enables us to maintain our relationship to our center of gravity. Flexible posture is needed in walking, running, and so on.

The second aspect, *laterality*, is learned. The child learns to use both sides of his body, how to know what side must be moved, and which side did move. In so doing, he learns to differentiate left and right sides. Some children become one-sided and do not differentiate the sides. Kephart believes that this restricts not only his movement, but also restricts learning.

Directionality, the third in the sequence of motor bases of learning, occurs when the child is able to project his inner awareness of left and right to the external world; for example, he realizes that a book is to the right of the pencil.

The last aspect is *body image*. The child learns where his body is, whether or not it is moving, how much space it needs, and so on, as he explores his environment.

After these four aspects have been mastered, the child can move about his environment, "*for the purpose* of contacting and interacting with the environment or parts of it" (p. 97). Balance and posture are prerequisite. Locomotion (walking, jumping, skipping, and so on) moves the child through space and he learns the relationship between objects. The child learns how long it takes to move to different places or to use a different means, for example, that running is faster. He learns to go around an object or pass between or under objects.

Contact with objects is another important step. The child learns to reach, grasp, and release. The child's movements should be fluid so that he concentrates on the object, not the motor activity.

The last phase of motor generalization is *receipt and propulsion*. He must learn to distinguish between his own movement and that of an object as he learns to catch a ball, dodge another child, and so forth. Throwing, batting, and pushing are propulsion activities. He learns how hard to throw in order to reach a target.

These movement generalizations (as well as the others mentioned earlier) are developed out of single movements and motor skills which must be elaborated and integrated. Programs of motor learning recommended by Kephart should start at the child's level and carry him through to the point of generalizations.

Kephart relates a time structure to motor learning. *Synchrony* (things happening at the same time) is needed in a variety of activities, such as running and jumping with two feet together. *Rhythm* is important in walking, running, marching, and talking, where consistent time intervals are desired. *Sequence* is the order of events.

Certain motor tasks require a specific sequence of movements, such as hitting the ball before running to the base.

In order to help children establish a secure base for learning, Kephart developed a program that tries to promote a better match between perceptual and motor development. The training program is individualized according to the evaluation made using the Purdue Perceptual Motor Survey. The program uses the walking board, balance beam, chalkboard exercises, rhythm activities, gross and fine motor activities, visualization, auditory-motor match, ocular pursuit, visual fixation, and varied form perception activities.

Movigenics

The Movigenic Curriculum designed by Barsch (1968) stresses the importance of movement patterns and efficiency. The ten principles which form the basis of this theory were set forth in his book, *Perceptual Motor Curriculum* (1967). According to Barsch, the movigenics curriculum enables the mover to develop a wide variety of motor patterns which must eventually become automatic so that he can concentrate on other things, that is, cognitive pursuits. The curriculum includes rolling, crawling, walking, jumping, metronomic pacing, and chalkboard activities and provides opportunities to explore near, mid-, and far space. In addition, Barsch recommends that the educational program provide training of all six perceptual modes. The teacher's role in this program is critical in assisting the child to explore body, time, and spatial relationships. Barsch cautions that this program is "not intended to exclude other activities in learning . . ." (p. 302). Though the tenth principle relates language development to movement development, no specific guidelines are provided.

Visuomotor Theory

Getman (1962) considers vision to be the basis for all learning and has recommended a program that emphasizes motor, sensory, and visual training. His model of the motor systems and their role in learning is primarily related to the development of visual perception (1965). He is concerned that many children are made to perform skills before they have developed an efficient use of the ocular-motor system. He believes the better the coordination, the better the opportunity for developing the perceptions needed for language and reading performance.

Six carefully sequenced training programs to implement his theory include practice in coordination, balance, hand coordination, eye movement, form recognition, and visual memory. The chalkboard, walking beam, and tachistoscope are used. The parents' role in strengthening the basic skill levels before the child enters school is also stressed by Getman (1962).

Motor Learning

Cratty (1969) considered motor games helpful in improving skills related to learning; for example, tension can be lowered, self-control and attention span increased, and the child will function better in social settings. He also notes that inability to perform adequately in playground games can be another link in ". . . a chain of failure. . . ."

Cratty describes a playground with six-feet by six-feet grids, containing one-foot squares, within which letters, numbers, and shapes have been painted. Games were played in which the child was instructed to jump from square to square, in different directions, thereby improving agility and the ability in spelling, arithmetic, and shape recognition. Although he stresses the fact that the human being "is an integrated organism," Cratty (1969) is careful to note the cause-and-effect relationship between movement education and intellectual improvement is only inferred and requires more research. Indeed, his analysis of several perceptual-motor programs points up the lack of research support (Cratty, 1970).

Cratty also developed a sequence of activities to improve balance, agility, strength, perception of the body in space, flexibility, and so on. He suggests that the training program also include the use of movement as a modality for developing academic concepts (Cratty, 1967).

Patterning

One of the most controversial interventions for treating neurologically-handicapped children is the Doman-Delacato method known as *patterning*. It is assumed, at least in part, that brain development is the *result* of body movement as well as the *cause* of body movement (Delacato, 1970). In addition, it is believed that as each person matures, he passes through the same developmental stages as the entire species in its evolution (ontogeny recapitulates the phylogeny). Thus for full neurological organization, development progresses from the lowest neurological level through the highest (Delacato, 1966; Doman, 1974), from the spinal cord and medulla, to the pons, the midbrain, and the cortex until the establishment of hemispheric dominance (Doman, 1974). That is, sequential development is dictated by each of these areas in succession. Failure to develop through each of these stages will result in problems in movement and/or communication. The goal of the patterning method is to bring each child to a sixth year neurological age. Even though a given child may be chronologically older and years behind his peers in experience and education, Doman believes that, in most cases, with intensive tutoring, he will catch up (Doman, 1974).

Doman and Delacato contend that by examining the level of neurological organization, they can determine which stages are poorly developed, and by prescribing specific activities can fill the gaps and improve neurological organization. They maintain that whether the movements are performed actively (under the individual's control) or passively (movement is provided by others), improvement in the neurological organization will occur (Delacato, 1963; Doman, Delacato and Doman, 1964).

After each evaluation, an individual prescription is prepared for each child which must be carried out on a daily basis. This prescription includes patterning exercises such as crawling, creeping, walking, sensory stimulation activities to improve awareness, breathing exercises, diet control (restriction of fluids, salt, and sugar), sleeping in prescribed positions (to be changed by parents), training of eye and hand use, and elimination of exposure to music so that the right hemisphere will not be stimulated, (Doman, et al., 1960; Delacato, 1970).

Central to this approach is the belief that the brain itself, rather than symptoms, is being treated. This is a cause of major criticism. In addition, there are no controlled studies that support the claims of Doman and Delacato (Hallahan &

Cruickshank, 1973; Zigler and Weintraub, 1980; Gearheart, 1977). There is also the concern that the demands of the program may lead to the neglect of other children in a family and, that since the role of the parents is so crucial in the therapy, severe feelings of guilt may develop if there is little or no improvement.

OPTOMETRIC-VISION TRAINING

The writings of many perceptual-motor theorists stress the visual component in learning disabilities (Kephart,1971; Barsch,1968; Getman,1965). The use of optometric training programs for the LD has grown rapidly since the sixties and with it a major controversy has also evolved. Optometric training programs form a continuum from specific treatment of the eyes to a whole-child approach. Keogh (1974) identifies three groups within the continuum: a) optometrists concerned with acuity and eye care; b) those who include orthoptic training, that is, eye exercises, in addition to general eye care; and c) optometrists who utilize a developmental vision approach and include gross motor, fine motor, and sensory-motor activities in addition to the procedures used by the other groups. Figure 9-2 lists behaviors that may indicate visual difficulties and help identify children who should be referred for professional evaluation of visual performance.

Vision therapies are introduced in order to improve visual and perceptual problems that may interfere with learning (Seiderman, 1979). The goal is to improve the child's visual performance so that he is more able to benefit from education. Seiderman suggests that the controversy of whether process-or-task-oriented training should be used is meaningless. He recommends that both types of training be instituted in those cases in which there are problems in visual and perceptual performance in addition to reading deficits.

After reviewing several studies of the effects of developmental vision training programs, Keogh (1974) reports that the results are equivocal. The methods used by each practitioner differ, with many types of activities including language-development activities lumped together so that the effect of a specific intervention cannot be determined. She believes that reports of success may be related to investigator enthusiasm.

Keogh also notes that the relationship between visual functioning and reading can be viewed in two ways. Reading can be considered a function of good visual perception. However, it can also be interpreted in another direction. As a child learns to read, he also learns to control his eyes in a coordinated manner and to scan in a left-to-right direction. A causal relationship is not easy to ascertain. The eye movements of normal adults and normal and reading-disabled children were compared in a study by Lefton, Lahey, and Stagg (1978). Compared to the others, the reading-disabled youngsters used an unsystematic approach when they were required to match samples with four alternatives and when attention had to be sustained more than five seconds. The researchers concluded that the deficit is more of a problem of attention or cognitive style than an inability to discriminate letters.

While some children do benefit from developmental vision training programs, these should be used judiciously and never to the exclusion of needed academic interventions.

EDUCATOR'S CHECKLIST

OBSERVABLE CLUES TO CLASSROOM
VISION PROBLEMS

Student's
Name _____ Date _____

1. APPEARANCE OF EYES:
   One eye turns in or out at any time _____
   Reddened eyes or lids _____
   Eyes tear excessively _____
   Encrusted eyelids _____
   Frequent styes on lids _____

2. COMPLAINTS WHEN USING EYES AT DESK:
   Headaches in forehead or temples _____
   Burning or itching after reading or desk work _____
   Nausea or dizziness _____
   Print blurs after reading a short time _____

3. BEHAVIORAL SIGNS OF VISUAL PROBLEMS:
   A. *Eye Movement Abilities (Ocular Motility)*
      Head turns as reads across page _____
      Loses place often during reading _____
      Needs finger or marker to keep place _____
      Displays short attention span in reading or copying _____
      Too frequently omits words _____
      Repeatedly omits "small" words _____
      Writes up or down hill on paper _____
      Rereads or skips lines unknowingly _____
      Orients drawings poorly on page _____
   B. *Eye Teaming Abilities (Binocularity)*
      Complains of seeing double (diplopia) _____
      Repeats letters within words _____
      Omits letters, numbers or phrases _____
      Misaligns digits in number columns _____
      Squints, closes or covers one eye _____
      Tilts head extremely while working at desk _____
      Consistently shows gross postural deviations at all desk activities _____
   C. *Eye-Hand Coordination Abilities*
      Must feel of things to assist in any interpretation required _____
      Eyes not used to "steer" hand movements (extreme lack of orientation, placement of words or drawings on page) _____
      Writes crookedly, poorly spaced: cannot stay on ruled lines _____
      Misaligns both horizontal and vertical series of numbers _____
      Uses his hand or fingers to keep his place on the page _____
      Uses other hand as "spacer" to control spacing and alignment on page _____
      Repeatedly confuses left-right directions _____

D. *Visual Form Perception (Visual Comparison, Visual Imagery, Visualization)*
   Mistakes words with same or similar beginnings _____
   Fails to recognize same word in next sentence _____
   Reverses letters and/or words in writing and copying _____
   Confuses likenesses and minor differences _____
   Confuses same word in same sentence _____
   Repeatedly confuses similar beginnings and endings of words _____
   Fails to visualize what is read either silently or orally _____
   Whispers to self for reinforcement while reading silently _____
   Returns to "drawing with fingers" to decide likes and differences _____

E. *Refractive Status (Nearsightedness, Farsightedness, Focus Problems, etc.)*
   Comprehension reduces as reading continued; loses interest too quickly _____
   Mispronounces similar words as continues reading _____
   Blinks excessively at desk tasks and/or reading; not elsewhere _____
   Holds book too closely; face too close to desk surface _____
   Avoids all possible near-centered tasks _____
   Complains of discomfort in tasks that demand visual interpretation _____
   Closes or covers one eye when reading or doing desk work _____
   Makes errors in copying from chalkboard to paper on desk _____
   Makes errors in copying from reference book to notebook _____
   Squints to see chalkboard, or requests to move nearer _____
   Rubs eyes during or after short periods of visual activity _____
   Fatigues easily; blinks to make chalkboard clear up after desk task _____

Figure 9-2. (Source: Copyright Optometric Extension Program Foundation, Inc., 1968, Duncan, Oklahoma. Reproduced by special permission of the Optometric Extension Program Foundation.)

Many LD specialists stress the perceptual inadequacies of LD children (Cruickshank, 1961; Lehtinen, 1965; Frostig and Maslow, 1973), while Johnson and Myklebust (1967) caution that the LD child should not be seem *primarily* as one with a perceptual deficit who needs to have a structuring of incoming stimuli. In fact, researchers note that the incidence of perceptual problems decreases among older LD students (Satz and Van Nostrand, 1972). One perceptual area in which this does not appear to hold true is social perception (see Chapter 17), a subject that only recently became the focus of interest of researchers and educational personnel (Siegel, 1974; Kronick, 1975).

EFFICACY OF THE PERCEPTUAL ORIENTATION IN LEARNING DISABILITIES

In a review of the literature concerning the effectiveness of perceptual-motor train-ing, Hallahan and Cruickshank (1973) note that only since the early sixties have controlled studies been conducted. They believe that such research was delayed because most of the major theorists were clinicians rather than researchers. How-ever, even these latest controlled studies have not yet definitively proven or dis-proven the perceptual basis of learning disorders nor the efficacy of perceptual-motor training for the learning disabled (Larsen and Hammill, 1975).

Mann (1970) considers most perceptual training to be unwarranted. He be-lieves that if the proper teaching methods are utilized, perception need not be taught. The deficit, not the "underlying process," should be remediated. Mann states "training in academics, development of art skills, increased proficiency in ath-letic games, are meaningful in and of themselves, whereas perceptual exercises. . . are of limited currency value" (p. 37). However, Bannatyne (1978) reports success when extensive training in basic deficits are taught "as elements within a compre-hensive (academic) program" (p. 96).

Rosen (1966) compared classes of children who received perceptual-motor training with Frostig materials to classes of children receiving only reading instruc-tion. The perceptual-motor skills of the Frostig-trained group improved. The largest gains in reading were attained by the children who spent equivalent time in reading instruction. Similar findings were reported by Wiederholt and Hammill (1971) for nonperceptually-handicapped children; that is, scores in the Frostig improved but not reading scores.

A pilot study by Painter (1966) introduced a sensory-motor program for ten children which included sequences of activities from simple to complex, based on the theories of Barsch and Kephart. Painter reports improvement in body and spa-tial concepts, motor performance, and in the auditory-vocal association subtest of the ITPA. There was no significant change in performance in the other ITPA sub-tests. Because the group was small and there was no control for the Hawthorne ef-fect, the results must be viewed with caution.

The naming and writing of letters and words as "reversal" has led many chil-dren to be placed in perceptual-training programs to improve visual discrimination skills. Several recent studies have questioned the assumption of a perceptual deficit (Deno & Chiang, 1979; Cohn & Stricker, 1979, Vellutino, et al., 1977). Deno and Chiang manipulated the learning environments of five children 9–12 years of age with severe learning disabilities. The children had to name correctly a sequence of letters half of which were b, d, p, q (no comments or rewards) and were given within alternated baseline and incentive phases (children were given colored beads for each correct response). Timed and untimed trials were also used. Accuracy in discriminating among b, d, p, and q was increased when incentives for correct per-formance were provided.

Research reported by Cohn and Stricker (1979) found that among over 400 first graders, a negative relationship between "perceptual" reversals and good letter recognition existed. When children were asked to name lower-case letters presented in fixed random order, more reversals were found in the responses of successful letter-namers. Cohn and Stricker conclude that poor letter-namers used gross cues to differentiate letters and only named correctly letters with unique characteristics while the more successful letter-namers, using more information, when incorrect, named letters resembling the ones they were looking at. Interestingly, few children consistently reversed; for example, although 376 children looked at q and said p, not one looked at p and said q.

Vellutino, et al. (1977) dispute those who assume that reading problems of the LD child are caused by perceptual disorders as evidenced by reversals of letters and words. Citing several studies they conducted, they report that children who call b for d or *saw* for *was* are perceiving them accurately but mislabel them.

The use of perceptual-motor (P-M) tests to identify children with deficits that will affect academic performance has engendered much debate. Salvia and Ysseldyke (1978) find that the most commonly used tests lack the necessary reliability. However, Saphier (1973) reports that "Despite their flaws, certain P-M tests have proven useful for early identification at kindergarten level . . . " (p. 590).

Harber (1979) investigated the usefulness of P-M tests to distinguish between LD and normal children. The performance of 55 LD children was compared with that of 54 normal children on four perceptual assessment measures: *The Motor Free Visual Perception Test*, the *Developmental Test of Visual-Motor Integration* (VMI), and the *sound blending* and *visual closure* subtests of the ITPA. In addition, the *Reading Recognition* and *Reading Comprehension* subtests of the *Peabody Individual Achievement Test* was administered. Analysis of the group data revealed no educationally-significant difference for the perceptual measures. However, the differences between the groups on the reading tests were found to be educationally significant. Based on her findings, Harber does not recommend the use of such P-M tests to classify LD children.

The educational advantages of several perceptual tests—*Wepman Auditory Discrimination Test*, and the *Auditory Sequential Memory*, *Visual Sequential Memory*, and *Sound Blending* subtests of the *ITPA*—were discussed by Larsen, Rogers, and Sowell (1976). Based on the data derived in their study, they concluded that the use of these tests for diagnosis and remediation was extremely limited. McCarthy (1976) questions their conclusions contending that 1) some of the subjects were beyond the recommended age for using the ITPA subtests and 2) the tests used were not "perceptual" tests; Larsen (1976b), however, reiterates the belief that, based on the work of researchers in the field, the tests used are "perceptual" and the population used was not too old for those measures.

Vellutino, et al. (1977) also questioned the concept of preferred learning modality, especially in remediation of reading deficits. They point out that whole word learning, sometimes called visual learning, and word analysis, referred to as auditory learning, are both visual-verbal learning which accent different cues. They suggest that educational interventions should not stress visual or motor training but should concentrate on analyzing reading deficits and skills and should provide direct instruction. For maximum transfer of skills, there should be a direct connection between the activities used in remediation and the skills to be taught; for example, use words and letters, rather than shapes, to develop discrimination skills.

With respect to the argument regarding whether perceptual deficits or verbal deficits result in reading problems, Fletcher and Satz (1979) believe it is not an "either-or" situation; rather, they contend *both* may be causal factors. They note that visual perception differences are found more often between younger reading groups. The linguistic skills tested by Vellutino, et. al., may be more important in late reading stages and would differentiate between older groups.

Other studies have investigated modality preference and instructional intervention. Sabatino and Dorfman (1974) determined the modality preference of educable mentally retarded children, grouped them according to modality strength, and then provided instruction using two curricula: The Sullivan Programmed Reading Series (visual emphasis) and the DISTAR Reading I Program (auditory emphasis). It was believed that the visual learners would show better performance than auditory learners when a program that emphasized visual input was used and the auditory children would show gains over the visual learners when the program emphasized auditory input. This hypothesis was not substantiated.

The effect of the mode of presentation in a paired-associated learning task with learning-disabled children, ranging in age from 8–12.5 years, was studied by Estes and Huizinga (1974). Ten-item learning tasks were presented in the visual and auditory modes. The initial learning was greater with the visual presentation; moreover, relearning, after a two-week period, was also faster when a visual presentation was made, regardless of the original learning modality. The preferred learning modes of the children were not determined. The data indicate that the visual presentation produces more learning.

A review of studies that examined the importance of auditory perceptual skills in reading was reported by Hammill and Larsen (1974). They concluded psycholinguistic training was not effective and did not support the view that particular auditory skills—auditory memory, auditory-visual integration, sound blending, and auditory discrimination—are essential for reading and that many children do not read proficiently because of deficits in these areas.

In a recent review of studies which examined the efficacy of psycholinguistic training, Kavale (1981) used a statistic, Effect Size, and concluded that such training was effective. In the studies under consideration, subjects who received training showed improvement in those abilities as measured by the ITPA.

A research project directed by Wilson, Harris, and Harris (1976) examined ways to improve auditory perception, reading, and spelling. The auditory-perceptual training program improved scores on measures of auditory perception, but no improvement in reading or spelling scores was found.

Torgesen (1979) compared the performance on memory tasks of good readers and reading-disabled children, who also scored low in tests of memory of digits, sequence of designs, serial order of pictures, paired associates, and order of events in a story. Both good readers and disabled readers were interviewed to determine the strategies they used to help them remember. Torgesen believes that many of the reading-disabled youngsters have difficulty not because they have structural deficits but because they have not developed ways to organize material to be learned.

Obviously the controversies surrounding perceptual approaches have not been resolved (Stephens and Magliocca, 1978). In our view, unless there are specific attempts to bridge the gap between such approaches and academic areas, for example, using the "process" format but substituting academic content,* the training will not remediate academic weaknesses. The effectiveness of perceptual training seems to be more apparent with the younger children (k-2), than with the older LD population although here, too, the improvements are tangential to academic performance. That is, the perceptual-motor programs appear to enhance the younger child's motor skills, enlarge the possibilities for play and recreation, and foster positive feelings about himself, rather than improve the ability to read, write, or do arithmetic. Again, we cannot stress it too often, direct remediation of the academic areas must occur for improved academic functioning.

REFERENCES

Ayres, A. U. *Sensory integration and learning disorders.* Los Angeles: Western Psychological Services, 1972.

Bannatyne, A. "Profiles: An interview with Alex Bannatyne." *Academic Therapy*, Sept. 1978, *14*(1), 95–98.

Barsch, R. H. *Enriching perception and cognition, Vol. 2.* Seattle: Special Child Publications, 1968.

————. *Perceptual motor curriculum, Vol. 1.* Seattle: Special Child Publications, 1967.

Cawley, J. F. Curriculum: One perspective for special education. In R. D. Needler and S. G. Traver (Eds.), *Changing perspectives in special education.* Columbus, Ohio: Charles E. Merrill, 1977.

Cohn M., and Stricker, G. Reversal errors in strong, average, and weak letter namers. *Journal of Learning Disabilities*, October, 1979: *12*(8), 533–537.

Cratty, B. J. *Developmental sequence of perceptual motor tasks.* Freeport, N.Y.: Educational Activities, Inc., 1967.

————. *Perceptual-motor behavior and educational processes.* Springfield, Ill.: Charles C Thomas, 1969.

————. *Perceptual and motor development in infants and children.* New York: Macmillan Publishing Co., Inc. 1970.

Cruickshank, W. A., et al. *A teaching method for brain-injured and hyperactive children.* Syracuse, N. Y.: Syracuse University Press, 1961.

Delacato, C. *The diagnosis and treatment of reading problems.* Springfield: Charles C. Thomas, 1963.

————. *A new start for the child with reading problems.* New York: David McKay, 1970.

————. *Neurological organization and reading.* Springfield, Ill.: Charles C. Thomas, 1966.

Deno, S. L., and Chiang, B. An experimental analysis of the nature of reversal errors in children with severe learning disabilities. *Learning Disabilities Quarterly*, Summer 1979, *2*(3), 40–45.

Doman, R. J., Spitz, E. B., Zucman, E., Delacato, C. H., and Doman, G. Children with severe brain injuries: Neurological organization in terms of mobility. *Journal of the American Medical Association*, Sept. 17, 1960: *174*(3), 119–124.

---

* Cawley (1977) uses the format of the ITPA but substitutes academic content. For example, he injects science content to train visual reception (the ability to gain meaning from pictures). The child is asked to select from among three pictures (a bear, a frog, and a horse) the one that belongs with the picture of a pond.

Doman, G., Delacato, C., and Doman, R. *The Doman-Delacato developmental profile*. Philadelphia: Institutes for the Achievement of Human Potential, 1964.

Doman, G. *What to do about your brain-injured child*. Garden City, New York: Doubleday, 1974.

Ebersole, M., Kephart, K., Ebersole, J. B. *Steps to achievement for the slow-learner*. Columbus, Ohio: Charles E. Merrill, 1968.

Estes, R. E. and Huizinga, R. J. A comparison of visual and auditory presentations of a paired-associate learning task with learning-disabled children. *Journal of Learning Disabilities*, Jan. 1974, *7*(1), 35–42.

Fletcher, J. M. and Satz, P. Unitary deficit hypothesis of reading disabilities: Has Vellutino led us astray? *Journal of Learning Disabilities*, March. 1979, *12* (3), 155–159.

Frostig, M., and Maslow, P. *Learning problems in the classroom*. New York: Grune & Stratton, 1973.

Gearheart, B. R. *Learning disabilities: Educational strategies*, 2nd ed. St. Louis: C. V. Mosby, 1977.

Getman, G. N. *How to develop your child's intelligence*. Luverne, Minnesota: G. N. Getman, O. D. 1962.

_____. The visuomotor complex in the acquisition of learning skills. In J. Hillmuth (Ed.), *Learning disorders, Vol. 1*. Seattle: Special Child Publications, 1965.

Hallahan, D. P., and Cruickshank, W. M. *Psycho-educational foundations of learning disabilities*. Englewood Cliffs, N. J.: Prentice-Hall, 1973.

Hammill, D. D., and Larsen, S. C. The relationship of selected auditory perceptual skills and reading ability. *Journal of Learning Disabilities*, Aug/Sept, 1974, *7*(7), 429–436.

Harber, J. R. Differentiating LD and normal children: The utility of selected perceptual and perceptual-motor tests. *Learning Disability Quarterly*, Spring, 1979, *2*(2), 70–75.

Johnson, D. J., and Myklebust, H. R. *Learning disabilities: Educational principles and practices*. New York: Grune & Stratton, 1967.

Kavale, K. Functions of the Illinois Test of Psycholinguistic Abilities (ITPA): Are they trainable? *Exceptional Children*, April, 1981, *47*(7): 496–513.

Keogh, B. Optometric vision training programs for children with learning disabilities: Review of issues and research. *Journal of Learning Disabilities*, April, 1974, *7*(4), 219–231.

Kephart, N. C. *The slow learner in the classroom*, 2nd ed. Columbus, Ohio: Charles E. Merrill, 1971.

Kronick, D. *The LD adolescent: What about me*. San Raphael, Ca.: Academic Therapy Publications, 1975.

Larsen, S. C. and Hammill, D. D. The relationship of selected visual-perceptual abilities to school learning. *The Journal of Special Education*, 1975, *9*(3), 281–291.

Larsen, S. C. Response to James McCarthy. *Journal of Learning Disabilities*, June/ July, 1976(b), *9*(6), 5–8.

Larsen, S. C., Rogers, D., and Sowell, V. The use of selected perceptual tests in differentiating between normal and learning disabled children. *Journal of Learning Disabilities*, February, 1976, *9*(2), 85–90.

Lefton, L. A., Lahey, B. B., and Stagg, D. I. Eye movements in reading: Systems and strategies. *Journal of Learning Disabilities*, November, 1978, *11*(9), 549–566.

Lehtinen, L. E. Have you ever known a perceptually-handicapped child? Monograph. Evanston, Illinois: Fund for Perceptually Handicapped Children, Inc. Revised May, 1965.

Lynn, R. *Learning disabilities: An overview of theories, approaches and politics*, New York: The Free Press, 1979.

Mann, L. Perceptual training: Misdirections and redirections. *American Journal of Orthopsychiatry*, January, 1970, *40*(1), 30–38.

McCarthy, J. J. The validity of perceptual tests: The debate continues. *Journal of Learning Disabilities*, 1976, *9*(6), 332–334.

Painter, G. The effect of a rhythmic and sensory motor activity program on perceptual motor spatial abilities of kindergarten children. *Exceptional Children*, October, 1966, *33*(2), 113–116.

Quirós, J. B. and Schrager, O. *Neuropsychological fundamentals in learning disabilities*. Novato, Ca.: Academic Therapy Publications, 1978.

Rosen, C. L. An experimental study of visual perceptual training and reading achievement in first grade. *Perceptual Motor Skills*, 1966, *22*, 979–986.

Sabatino, D. A. and Dorfman, N. Matching learner aptitude to two commercial reading programs. *Exception Children*, October, 1974, *41*(2), 85–91.

Salvia, J. and Ysseldyke, J. E. *Assessment in special and remedial education*. Boston: Houghton Mifflin, 1978.

Saphier, J. D. The relation of perceptual-motor skills to learning and school success. *Journal of Learning Disabilities*, November, 1973, *6*(9), 583–592.

Satz, P. and Van Nostrand, G. K. Developmental dyslexia: An evaluation of a theory. In Paul Satz and J. Ross (Eds.), *The disabled learner: Early detection and intervention*. Rotterdam, The Netherlands: Rotterdam University Press, 1973.

Seiderman, A. S. Visual function assessment. In William C. Adamson and K. K. Adamson, *A handbook for specific learning disabilities*. New York: Gardner Press, 1979.

Shaffer, M. Primal terror: A perspective of vestibular dysfunction. *Journal of Learning Disabilities*, February, 1979, *12*(2), 89–92.

Siegel, E. *The exceptional child grows up*, New York, Dutton, 1974.

Smith, H. M. Motor activity and perceptual development: Some implications for physical educators. *Journal of Health, Physical Education, Recreation*. February, 1968.

Stephens, T. M. and Magliocca L. A. The tenth myth: A rejoinder to Cruickshank's myths. *Journal of Learning Disabilities*, August–September, 1978, *11*(7), 8–9.

Strauss, A. A., Strauss, N. C., and Kephart, N. C. *Psychopathology and education of the brain-injured child, Vol. II*, New York: Grune & Stratton, 1955.

Tarver, S. G. and Hallahan, D. P. "Learning disabilities: An overview." in J. M. Kaufman and D. P. Hallahan (Eds.), *Teaching children with learning disabilities: Personal perspectives*. Columbus, Ohio: Charles E. Merrill, 1976.

Torgesen, J. K. Factors related to poor performance on memory tasks in reading-disabled children. *Learning Disabilities Quarterly*, Summer, 1979, *2*(3), 17–23.

Vellutino, F. R., Steger, B. M., Moyer, S. C., Harding, C. J., and Niles, J. A. Has the perceptual deficit hypothesis led us astray? *Journal of Learning Disabilities*, June–July, 1977, *10*(6), 375–385.

Wiederholt, J. L., and Hammill, D. D. Use of the Frostig-Horne perception program in the urban school. *Psychology in the Schools*, 1971, *8*, 268–274.

Wilson, S., Harris, C., and Harris, M. Effects of auditory perceptual remediation program on reading performance. *Journal of Learning Disabilities*, 1976, *9*, 670–678.

Zigler, E. and Weintraub, E. "A point of view—patterning: Unproved hope for brain-damaged children." *Education and Training of the Mentally Retarded*, December, 1980: 247–249.

Educational Interventions

part Three

Structure: A Basic Principle for the Education of the Learning Disabled

10

When authors enumerate a set of principles for the education of the learning disabled, the concept of providing the child with a structured environment invariably heads the list. So fundamental is this tenet, as evidenced by the number of authors who have focused upon it and by the many practitioners and administrators who have sought to implement it (via small class size, use of carrels, and consistent adherence to classroom routines), that we have decided to devote an entire chapter to this basic guideline. Additional principles—no less important than structure—will be dealt with in the next chapter.

STRUCTURE DEFINED

In the very beginning, when literature concerning the learning disabled (then referred to as "brain-injured") first began to appear, the concept of structure received prime consideration (Strauss and Lehtinen, 1947; Lewis, 1951; Strauss & Kephart, 1955; Kaliski, 1959; Lehtinen, 1959; Cruickshank, Bentzen, Ratzeburg, and Tannhauser, 1961; Barsch, 1965; Petersen, 1965; Hewett, 1968). More recent authors continue to refer to this need that learning-disabled children—or at least some of them—have for a structured educational environment (Golick, 1969; Smith, 1978, pp. 71-72, 84-85; Lerner, 1976, p. 113; Wallace and Kauffman, 1973; Denckla, 1978; Hewett & Taylor, 1980). Barry (1961, p. 21) set forth a precise, extremely clear, and well-written definition of structure:

> We mean putting things in order, we mean teaching limits and sequence, we mean clarifying, dramatizing, simplifying, concretizing. We mean bringing the foreground sharply into focus, blocking out non-essentials. We mean touching, and feeling, and looking, and listening, outlining, and underlining.

151

We mean performing a simple activity in deliberate, sequential steps, in response to deliberate, sequential commands such as, "Pick it up, look at it, where does it go?, put it there." We mean every technique, device, or trick that will help the child to hear, to see, to understand—to take meaning out of chaos—for until we structure the world for some of these children, it is just that—chaos.

A rationale for structure stems from the underlying neurological, perceptual, and psychological deficits of the learning-disabled child: he cannot readily filter out the extraneous sensory data (e.g., background sounds and sights); hence, we must highlight the figure and/or reduce the unnecessary stimuli. He encounters difficulty in checking his impulsivity, so we must cue him to slow down. He cannot process large doses of verbalisms, so we must speak less.

It is necessary to state that the need for structure is not the sole province of the learning disabled.* Interestingly, it is often recommended for the emotionally disturbed, as well (Hewett, 1968; Haring and Whelan, 1965; Haring and Phillips, 1962; Mercer and Mercer, 1981, p. 116). However, there may be different—or at least additional—reasons for this: Structure sets limits. It makes plain to the child what he can expect the consequences of a particular act will be. It reduces the anxiety that would ensue if no rules existed. It also proves to the child that the teacher and/or parent cares enough to say "no." Haring and Whelan (1965, p. 390) point out that "emotionally-disturbed children are, for the most part, controlling, disorganized, unproductive, and unilateral in their approaches to daily expectations, relationships to peers, and authority figures. A systematic, organized, planned routine . . . provides a pattern or model which enables disturbed youngsters to meet the responsibilities of daily living, as well as to take their place in the social community." Of course, one could add to this (1) the fact that excessive clutter coupled with ambiguity heightens anxiety, and (2) structure increases the likelihood that classroom success will occur, thus enhancing self-concept. It would be erroneous to conclude that all learning disabled and all emotionally handicapped need structure equally. A more reasonable perspective would probably be the one depicted in Figure 10-1 (showing the loci of the learning disabled and emotionally-disturbed populations along the structure-flexibility continuum).

The learning-disabled population is shown closer to the structure pole. This is so because, (1) most learning-disabled children probably benefit from structure more than they do from nondirectiveness, and (2) more authors advocate structure for the LD. For the same two reasons, the emotionally-disturbed population is placed roughly in the middle of the continuum, reflecting the notion that many of them need structure, but a significant number of them may well need its opposite, and also the fact that authors are pretty much divided on this point. For example,

---

* The topic of structure as it applies to the education of students demonstrating behavior disorders is treated in a remarkably comprehensive manner by Gallagher (1979); she describes procedures for structure in the order of their appearance: The teacher's employment interview for a position in a self-contained classroom, planning and preparation prior to the first day of school, the initial meeting with the class, ongoing educational diagnosis, selecting educational materials and setting up learning centers within the classroom, programming and sequencing of instructional tasks, establishing a behavior modification program, phasing out of dependent behaviors and strengthening maintenance, and finally, integrating the pupil in the regular classroom.

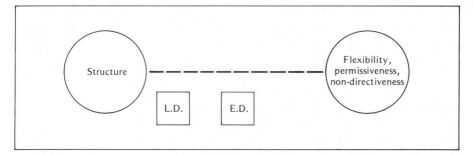

Figure 10-1. The location of learning disabilities and emotional disturbance along the structure-flexibility continuum.

Hewett (1968), Haring and Phillips (1962), and Haring and Whelan (1965) support the tenet of classroom structure for the emotionally disturbed; Bettelheim (1950), Newman (1956) and Axiline (1947) are often said to advocate greater permissiveness.* In fact, Mesinger (1965) warned against placing brain injured and emotionally disturbed in the same classroom (under the rubric of an early definition of learning disabled which encompassed both the brain injured and the emotionally disturbed), stating outright that the brain injured require structure whereas the emotionally disturbed require flexibility. A temporal factor may well exist here. Perhaps the typical learning disabled pupil needs a considerable amount of structure initially, but the long-range goal is to have him move—or rather *grow*—to the point at which he can handle some flexibility, nondirectiveness, and freedom of choice, thereby developing more self-confidence and a greater awareness of his own growth (Bradfield, 1965, p. 365). "Direction of the child's behavior, however, should eventually be effected from within himself rather than from externally regulated conditions. As the organic disturbances are lessened, the protections are removed . . ." (Strauss & Lehtinen, 1947, p. 135). The emotionally-disturbed child, on the other hand, may have to begin at the permissiveness end of the spectrum, but gradually develops a tolerance for limits and controls.

The mentally retarded can also benefit from structure. Frequently listed among the principles for educating them are use of repetition, concrete as opposed to abstract materials, and sequential approach. Clearly, these are all subsumed under structure.

---

* It should be pointed out that these latter authors do not admit to advocating a nonstructured classroom environment. For example, Bettelheim (1963, p. 329) in protesting the structure-permissiveness dichotomy alluded to by Haring and Phillips (1962), writes of ". . . having spent most of my professional life on structuring a very special environment that would further the education and rehabilitation of emotionally disturbed children . . . ." Hewett (1968, pp. 69-70) attempts to reconcile both points of view by explaining that "permissiveness is not synonymous with open license," and that both disciplines do, indeed, utilize structure, but the conceptual basis for each differs: Bettelheim's, generated by the psychogenic-interpersonal philosophy of intervention, focuses upon the child's *emotional needs*, whereas Haring and Phillips (and Hewett, too, for that matter), following the behavior-modification strategy, emphasize the child's *observable behavior*, the environment, and its attendant requirements for learning. Hewett further points out that, conversely, just as Bettelheim does not advocate total classroom freedom, neither does Haring's and Phillips' brand of structure constitute rigid and irrational authority: After all, ". . . they readily accepted the child's academic limitations and modified assignments when these tended to be conflictual" (p. 70).

Ways of Promoting Structure

Remove Excessive Stimuli. Obviously, this refers to extra sounds (noises outside the window, scraping of the chair against the floor, unnecessary talking, and so forth) and extra sights (too many posters and pictures, the teacher's jewelry, bright colors, too many examples on a worksheet, and the like). But it also pertains to excessive tactile and kinesthetic stimuli (tight—or too loose—clothing, the feel of one's wristwatch, eyeglasses, orthodonture braces). Cruickshank, Bentzen, Ratzeburg, and Tannhauser (1961) as well as Strauss and Lehtinen (1947) and others advocate the physical reduction of space—use of smaller classrooms, a carrel, and so on. However, some conflicting research regarding the necessity for stimuli reduction has emerged. Schulman, Kaspar and Throne (1965) found that the presence of neurological signs is more apt to correlate with *hypo*activity than with *hyper*activity. The clear implication here is that the teachers should arrange for more, rather than for less, stimuli to impinge upon the child. Gardner, Cromwell, and Foshee (1959) found that brain-injured subjects—as well as the control group—showed *less* activity (hence, less distractibility) with the *increase* of visual stimuli. In this experiment, the subject sat on a chair surrounded on three sides by a black screen seven feet wide. Long strips of brightly-colored cloth were attached to the top of the screen; each strip had toys and trinkets affixed to it (e.g., party hats, brightly-colored cards, costume jewelry). Several strings of multi-colored Christmas lights were also attached to the top of the screen. All of these stimuli could be folded so that they hung behind the screen, outside of the subject's view. At intervals, the examiners folded the strips to the front of the screen, thus creating sudden periods of increased visual stimulation. The activity levels of the subjects were measured. This study's findings of decreased activity under *increased* visual stimulation and increased activity under *decreased* visual stimulation (the hyperactive, brain-injured subjects showed a significant activity increase when confronted with the blank wall) flies in the face of the beliefs of Strauss and other pioneers in the field of brain injury/learning disabilities.

Gardner et. al. offer several possible explanations: When there is little or no sensory stimulation, particularly of vision and audition, the organism may attempt to provide his own by increasing his activity level. Another possibility is that the subject could attend to strong distal visual stimulation satisfactorily (i.e., without exhibiting any motor activity), but when this was minimized, there was a shifting of attention—accompanied by "gross motor or manipulative responses"—to proximal stimuli (p. 1033). In the same vein, Zentall (1975) suggests *increased*—rather than the generally recommended reduction of—stimulation for hyperactives, pointing out that they are more like normals during recess, transition periods, and free time. (All of these involve some movement.) However, hyperactivity peaks during such periods as waiting their turn in group situations. This is in consonance with a growing body of literature depicting LD children as *inactive*, externally-controlled learners—that is, they have an external locus of control, perceiving events stemming from their behavior as dependent upon others (Hallahan, Gajar, Cohen, & Tarver, 1978).

Those who suggest reduction of stimuli for the learning disabled do so in deference to the figure-ground confusion generally attributed to this population. The rationale, of course, is that the child is better able to attend to the task at hand when the irrelevant—that is, background—sensory input is lowered. More to the point, the *difference* in intensity between figure and ground is the essential consideration. If that is the case, cannot the same result be achieved by emphasizing the foreground? Many authors do, indeed, espouse highlighting as a way of promoting attention (Hewett, 1968, pp. 117-122. Bousfield, et al., 1957; Cruickshank et al., 1961). The valence of pertinent stimuli can be maximized via underlining, boxing in, using larger and/or darker print, employing color, increasing the volume of auditory stimuli, and so forth. In fact, Hewett (1968, pp. 119-120) found that underachieving adolescent boys were able to read phrases such as "heave this immediately" much quicker when the accompanying picture was that of a hand grenade rather than the more traditional—and sedate—football. The violent pictorial theme seems to heighten the vividness and impact of the visual stimuli (i.e., the words). Along the same line, albeit with less dramatic examples, Gallagher (1979, p. 91) suggests heightening interest in math problems by including such words as *10-speed bike, jeans, stereo tapes*, and *skateboards* as replacements for words like apples, balls and squirrels.

Certainly, the type of stimuli—distal or proximal—is one important criterion in deciding whether to increase or to decrease stimuli during instruction. Also, one must ask whether activity itself is a valid measure of attention. True, most authors would answer affirmatively, concurring with Dykman et al. (1971, p. 84): "There appears to be a reciprocal relation between motor restlessness and the physiological activities that underlie attention." Yet, Bryan and Bryan (1978, p. 135) point out that hyperactivity and distractibility do not correlate with one another. Still another consideration is the fact that attention is generally regarded as a single trait, when, in reality, it has a number of components: alertness, stimulus selection, focusing, and vigilance—and each may be independent of the other (Dykman et al., 1971, p. 57).

Also, one should note that both these key studies—Schulman et al. and Gardner et al.—utilized brain-injured subjects who were mentally retarded; this would be inconsistent with the current definition of learning disabilities.

A final point—which should be superimposed upon *any* statement made regarding the nature and needs of the learning disabled—is the extreme intragroup variability found in this population. To put it simply, some learning-disabled children require considerable reduction of stimuli and others do not.

Help the Child to "Slow Down." Impulsivity is a trait frequently assigned to the learning disabled (Bryan & Bryan, 1978, p. 35; Lynn, 1978, p. 5; Ross, 1976). Coupled with perseveration (another characteristic), impulsivity can account for a learning-disabled individual's persistent failure to "look before you leap," to "jump right in" without any planning, and once there, to continue in what has been described as a "driven" fashion (Strauss & Lehtinen, 1947, pp. 23, 155).

The teacher can help in many ways. She can present words tachistoscopically (using an actual tachistoscope or just plain "flash cards") at a reduced rate, thus forcing the learning-disabled child to read slower. Similarly, a rectangular slot cut out of an index card provides a frame which permits just one or two words to be seen at one time thus preventing the child from trying to read the whole page at once. Handing the child one peg at a time, utilizing a bank whose slot will admit just one penny at a time, requiring him to move one block at a time, are all techniques for reducing impulsivity when counting. Strauss and Lehtinen (1947, p. 155) suggest slowing the child down during counting by using a board with a row of holes drilled part of the way through. He is given screws and a screw-driver and is told to count each one as he screws it in. "Faced with the impossibility of rushing through the activity, the child can only do it slowly. At the same time, each count becomes separate and distinct and he realizes, often for the first time, what must be the goals of his efforts without such a device" (p. 155). The child who writes too quickly can be slowed down by the teacher rolling out some modeling clay in the bottom of a rectangular shallow pan and letting him write with a stylus (a wooden dowel shaped somewhat like a pencil and slightly thicker, sharpened at one end) (Siegel, 1961, p. 105; Strauss & Lehtinen, 1947, p. 186). Another technique—which has been around for a long time—is for the teacher to place her hand over the child's hand as he writes, thus offering physical guidance with respect to direction while simultaneously controlling the pace. The disinhibited, impulsive child who rushes to write a spelling word before thinking about it can be forced to pause by the teacher withholding the pencil during the "thinking" period and giving it to him only when it is time to write. The child who rushes through a test should be given one question at a time (perhaps on an index card); he is not handed the next question card until he has spent sufficient time on the first one.

The same principles apply to slowing the child down in social situations, such as during a conversation. A specific signal can be agreed upon which will denote that it is time to stop talking and to listen. Prompts, models and cues are useful. Group guidance lessons can give insight into the problem as well as suggest the means of amelioration. A tape recorder can be especially helpful in terms of monitoring, feedback, motivation, and simply for practice.

Clearly, impulsivity is a modifiable behavior. Hence, the teacher's familiarity with the techniques and principles of behavior modification can be crucial.

Establish Routines. All children, the "normal" as well as the learning disabled, need some routine, and they all acquire it via the same route—learning. There are no differences in substance, only in degree. The nonhandicapped, being less rigid, less impulsive, less anxious, more capable of "thinking on the spot," and of seeing cause-effect relationships than are the learning disabled, may not require as much routine. The learning-disabled child, on the other hand, experiencing difficulty in making spontaneous decisions, in organizing, in attending selectively, in processing competing stimuli, and in impulse control, has a heightened need for habit and routine.

Smith (1978, p. 3) believes that *disorder* is the chief characteristic of the learning-disabled child and that his learning disabilities flow directly from this. She points out that the learning-disabled child "lives in a world of disorder . . . cannot sort out that which is relevant or essential from that which is not . . . [and that] the child registers fragments of what is coming in, and what comes out is therefore fragmented, disorganized, irrelevant, disordered" (p. 1). She explains further that:

> For learning disabled children, the ability to organize has somehow been short-circuited, and normal learning cannot follow. If a child cannot be sure

what comes first, in the middle or last, then getting dressed is an ordeal, the days of the week stay jumbled, counting or reciting the alphabet becomes a hopeless chore, and reading is an impossibility.

No task is simple until it can be ordered. Growth is order, one step building to the next. Safety is order, with clearly defined limits. Order clarifies what is expected, what is to be done, where things belong, what goes together. An immature brain that lacks order cannot make sense of the environment—a huge handicap since "learning" begins with the organizing and ordering of messages coming in through the senses. Actions that seem simple to most people can be immensely complicated to a child who does not know where to begin, what order to follow, or when to end. (p. 2)

In fact, the very word "order'" has many different connotations. Yet all of them are highly significant in educating the learning disabled. These include: (1) arranging one's self and one's belongings with some degree of neatness and orderliness; (2) ordering in a series (e.g., alphabetical order, numerical order, nesting, size place); (3) following instructions; (4) obeying rules applying to conduct and manners; (5) ordering one's attention (e.g., reading from left to right, making eye contact with the speaker); (6) note-taking, studying, and test-taking in a *systematic* fashion—especially important for the learning-disabled child in secondary schools (Deschler, 1978, pp. 55, 57-59); (7) organizing one's time (e.g. allotting sufficient time for homework, starting book reports early enough, not dawdling on the way to school); (8) organizing spatially (e.g., writing headings appropriately on test papers and on homework assignments, placing arithmetic examples one in each box; (9) following a departmental schedule in junior and senior high schools; and (10) completion of educational tasks (Hewett, 1968, pp. 174-177).

In endeavoring to instill order and routine in the life of the learning-disabled child, one must realize that merely having the teacher state the rule is not enough. As a matter of fact, even when the *child* is able to state the rule (upon request), this does not guarantee that he can—or will—perform the behavior to which the rule applies; hence, a pupil may be able to recite various spelling rules perfectly, yet continue to be a poor speller (Johnson & Morasky, 1980, p. 320). Wallace and Kauffman (1973, pp. 49-50) stipulate three basic techniques for effecting appropriate classroom behaviors, which must be used in combination with each other: (1) stating the rules, (2) rewarding appropriate behaviors, and (3) ignoring inappropriate behavior. In addition, they should be relatively few in number, defined with clarity, posted, reviewed each day, and supported via appropriate consequences when violated (Payne et al., 1977, pp. 59-60). Moreover, the rules must be explained and "spelled out." Don't just command the child to fold his paper in half, but demonstrate and give the specific step-by-step details.

After a while, when this process has become habitualized by the child, the teacher's verbiage can be lessened. However, if the child has not yet internalized the means of implementing a "general" instruction, it is far better to give specifics. Egeland (1974) selected 72 children (aged: 6 years, 10 months to 8 years, 11 months) designated as "impulsive." They were identified on the basis of shortness of response time coupled with high number of errors, as evidenced on the Matching Familiar Figure (MFF) test. From this pool of subjects, two training groups (and one control group that received no training) were formed by random assignment.

Both experimental groups underwent training in five different exercises: (1) matching geometric designs, (2) matching nonsense words, (3) matching geometric designs from memory, (4) drawing geometric designs from memory, and (5) describing geometric designs. One training group was simply told to wait 10–15 seconds prior to responding and to "think about your answer and take your time." But the second training group was offered specific rules and strategies (e.g., attending to relevant features of the stimuli, comparing all alternatives with the standard, and looking for similarities and differences, successively eliminating those alternatives which differ from the standard. In other words, one group was told only to delay their responses whereas the other was given specific search and scanning strategies, that is, precise instruction in what to *do* during this delay time. When MFF tests were administered two months later, the group that had been given specific strategies showed a better performance than did the "general" training group.

The child's organization—or lack thereof—is very much a function of the teacher's pattern of self-organization. If the teacher is organized and systematic, this serves as a powerful model for the child. The child's chances for being better organized are infinitely enhanced if the teacher's desk is uncluttered; if her plan book and roll book are kept neat in appearance (e.g., clean covers, no loose pages falling out); if she distributes and collects materials systematically; if her lessons reflect careful planning; if she attends to such physical considerations as proper lighting and ventilation; if her chalkboard, bulletin board, and various charts are arranged orderly, and if she prints (or writes) sufficiently large and with correct letter formation; if she has formulated (often in concert with the class) a block program which is posted and followed; if she is methodical with respect to homework (writing the assignments on the board instead of merely giving oral instructions, ascertaining that the children know what to do and can do it, collecting the assignments and rendering appropriate and punctual feedback to the children); and if she takes the roll and prepares the class for dismissal in an organized and consistent fashion.

Besides the importance of the modeling factor, there is another consideration that makes the teacher's organized style of teaching redound to the benefit of the learning-disabled child. Moods (and demeanors), in some mysterious way, are contagious. We even use the expression, "infectious humor." Just as the teacher's own humor or depression, enthusiasm or listlessness, excitedness or calmness can be transmitted to the child, so, too, can organization—and, unfortunately, disorganization.

Consistency is an important feature of routine development. Since the learning disabled child has only a tenuous grasp of his environment with its competing sensory stimuli and ever-changing array of perceptual events, consistency becomes a prime means by which he is enabled to arrange incoming data into meaningful wholes. Consistency helps the lesson "take." The literature frequently lists consistency in relation to administering rewards (i.e., positive reinforcement) in the initial phases of any behavior modification program (Hewett, 1968; Haring and Phillips, 1962; Wallace & Kauffman, 1973, p. 114). A three-year demonstration project involving brain-damaged children in Columbus, Ohio, reported:

> Consistency in classroom procedures and routines was apparently a dominant factor in adjustment of children at all age levels. This was emphasized in re-

ports from all of the classroom teachers, by the itinerant teacher and several principals. It appears that this should be stressed in the organization, planning and operation of all future programs for brain damaged children. (Grover & Allen, 1962, p. 40)

Despite this plea for consistency, routines are best kept viable and relevant if some format for change is built into them. Payne et al. (1977, p. 60) believe that, at times, rules may be added, deleted, or changed; for example, as children mature, a "no talking while in the blue area" rule can be changed to "whispering allowed in the blue area." The teacher should be on the alert for rules that are "wearing out," and should be sufficiently flexible to alter a given routine to accommodate special conditions (Smith, 1970, p. 111).

A difference does exist between *planned* flexibility and inconsistencies which are happenstance and simply reflect the teacher's own disorganization. As Wallace and Kauffman (1973, p. 114) say: "Consistency does not mean rigidity. There are circumstances under which routines should be varied and rules should be broken. But if the classroom rules and routines are varied at the whim of either the teacher or the children, learning will not be optimal."

The establishment of routines can ameliorate an array of deficits—rather than the singular trait of disorganization. For example, routines and consistency play a major role in reducing anxiety. Relaxation is fostered when we set limits, let the child know what is expected, and clarify "how things are done around here." If he is less anxious, he will probably be better organized, and vice versa. Similarly, the establishment of routines can diminish the child's impulsivity, and reduced impulsivity, in turn, sets the stage for better organization. Finally, one must ask, "Is the learning-disabled child distractible because he is disorganized, or is he disorganized because he is distractible?" It doesn't matter. Either way, he wins via the propagation of pertinent, viable, "spelled-out" routines.

Give Few (or no) Choices. An extension of the concept of routines and consistency is the practice of *telling* the learning-disabled child what he must do rather than *asking* him what he would like to do. Instead of offering him choices, teachers are often advised to make the decisions for him (e.g., hand him a crayon, don't ask him which one he wants).

Learning-disabled children should not be kept in this routinized, overly-structured, authoritarian learning atmosphere forever. The practice of offering choices should be introduced gradually: "The autocratic nature of the parent [or teacher] as discipilinarian modifies and adjusts to the growing child's abilty to take on certain of the decision-making processes..." (McLaughlin, 1973, p. 21). Lewis, Strauss and Lehtinen (1960, pp. 100-101) advise that at first, 1) the choices should be rather easily accomplished; 2) they should be of the variety that carry no great consequences should the child opt for one rather than the other; 3) the child should be given a choice between only two possibilities rather than among many; and 4) when he grows older, reasons for the imposed choices should be explained to him.

It is especially important to avoid situations in which parents or teachers ask the child, "Do you want to . . . ," yet in reality offer no choice (Mallison, 1968, p. 63):

Any child should be allowed to make decisions only at a level he can easily handle and understand. Asking for "likes" when it is a matter of necessity is inappropriate. We do not ask unless he is capable of deciding, and then we are able to abide by his decision. When a child who has been offered a choice says "no," and we then proceed to make him do the very act against which he decided anyhow, he is not going to learn that we really mean what we say. If, in winter, we are going to make him wear his warmest jacket, why ask if he "wants to put it on" before going out.

Of course, a delicate balance does exist between "strictly reining him in and giving him total freedom" (Kronick, 1969, p. 21). In fact, freedom of choice is not always incompatible with structure. Schechter (1973, pp. 60-61) explains the fact that Montessori's principle of order did not preclude allowing the child to make choices: "I believe she means that freedom and liberty can only occur when rules and laws are obeyed. Within the framework of a clear-cut system of organization, the child is allowed complete freedom of choice of activities." The learning-disabled child who has begun to improve may benefit from the inclusion of some choice of experiences and activities instead of maintaining the status quo of always letting others decide for him. But the young brain-injured child, the one who has not yet started to compensate for his deficiencies, whose learning disabilities have not been overcome nor even ameliorated, whose perceptual distortion, ineffective processing mechanisms, anxiety, and rampant impulsivity still abound, is helplessly mired in an incomprehensible, ever-changing, unpatterned, chaotic environment. He needs stability, not democracy.

Ascertain That the Child is Paying Attention. Since attention is a significant prerequisite for learning, teachers must find some means of determining whether or not the pupil is paying attention to the task at hand. This is possible in a variety of ways, none of which are fool proof.

One way, of course, is to ask the child to repeat what has just been said (Gallagher, 1979, p. 111). Assuming that this auditory stimuli is sufficiently brief, simple, and delivered with appropriate tempo and volume, well within the limits of his processing abilities, *if he still can't repeat it*, the child was not attending. But the converse is not true. He may have been thinking about something else, and only giving peripheral (some call it unconscious) attention to the teacher. By calling the question, the teacher succeeds in jarring him back to reality for the moment and he is able to repeat what has just been said. *The point, however, is that he was not really listening.* The auditory stimuli—that is, the teacher's words—were never being processed, nor were images being generated; in fact, the data never left the reticular area and were well on the verge of being lost forever, when, just in the knick of time, he summoned them to the forefront.

Another way is to ask the child a question about what was just said. If he answers correctly, it's a good bet that he was attending, *providing that he did not already know the answer* (Ross, 1976, p. 38).

One may attempt to ascertain attention by requiring the child to perform some simple motor act—such as pushing a button—each time a predetermined stimulus appears. If he responds correctly, he was paying attention. But what if he doesn't?

Can we assuredly deem it an attention deficit? Not necessarily. Before we can do so, we must be able to stipulate that: 1) the motor response is within his repertoire; (2) the stimuli must be readily discriminable; and 3) the pupil must be cooperative and motivated (Ross, 1976, p. 43).

Most teachers feel that eye contact is a measure of attention (when they are addressing the child). This is probably so in a great many cases. Of course, most nonhandicapped children soon learn how to *look* like they're paying attention. (They may or may not have ever verbalized this discovery, but they certainly have internalized the principle that maintaining eye contact pleases the teacher.) Many learning-disabled children, however, have not arrived at this stage. Not only are they actually more distractible than their "normal" counterparts, but they do not even know how to *seem* to pay attention! To carry this further, then, if a *learning-disabled child* maintains eye contact with the speaker, the chances are good that he is, in fact, attending. Even this is not foolproof, however, for it does not take into account the learning-disabled child who is prone to neurological overloading, and who, in actuality, listens better to the speaker when *not* looking at her.

Although none of these methods are infallible indicators of attention in all instances, they certainly warrant the teacher's consideration. By being aware of their limitations, she will be in a better position to make the necessary modifications in individual cases, thereby maximizing their effectiveness. Moreover, often the very criterion for *measuring* can become the means of *promoting* attention. For example, asking the child simple, brief, but sufficiently frequent questions about what is being said not only helps the teacher pinpoint the degree of the pupil's attention, but primes the child to pay better attention. That is, it gives him an incentive to listen.

Provide the Child with Cues. There are various categories of cues: mnemonic devices; (e.g., *E*very *G*ood *B*oy *D*oes *F*ine and F-A-C-E for the musical scale's treble clef; rhymes (e.g., "When two vowels go walking, the first one does the talking"); songs (e.g., "I can say my A-B-C"); words within a word (e.g., remembering the difference between "peace" and "piece" can be facilitated with the cue of "a *piece* of *pie*").

Cognitive clues abound in arithmetic. For example, "doubles and near doubles" is the strategy in which the child's knowledge of 6 + 6 helps him remember 6 + 5. "Closing the tens" works on the principle that most children find it easier to add a number to ten than to nine. Therefore, 9 + ? can be cued by reminding the child to "first make a ten." That is, when *given* 9 + 7, *think* 9 + 1 = 10, 10 + 6 = 16. The ultimate extension of this cue is the simple "one less" strategy: Whenever the child is confronted with nine plus any single digit, he just has to "make the other number one less" and then add it to ten. Thornton, (1979, p. 8) suggests that the relatively difficult multiplication fact of 7 × 8 can be cued by "before you go to *7th* and *8th* grade, you go to *5th* and *6th*. Hence, 56 = 7 × 8. Similarly, the child can be taught to remember 12 = 3 × 4.

Other examples of cognitive clues would be context clues in reading, and word composition (in which reminders of prefixes, suffixes, and roots assist in deciphering new words.)

Visual associations are often helpful. In Penmanship, the written $\mathcal{Z}$ can be clued by the number 3. The written ℓ can be clued by: "Think of the ℓ. Now start it backwards ℓ. Then finish the ℓ" (Siegel, 1972).

The child's ability to differentiate his left from his right can be strengthened by use of the following visual cue: Hold both hands up with palms facing away, and thumbs pointed outwards:

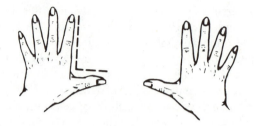

The letter L is formed by the left hand index finger and thumb.

An excellent visual cue for the child who knows the sounds of b and d, but has difficulty remembering which way each faces is the printed word "bed." Let the letters actually form a bed in which a doll is asleep:

If either—or both—of the letters were incorrectly faced, the doll would fall.

Auditory and visual associations frequently combine. For example, a snake makes a "s-s-s-s-" sound, and the letter S resembles a snake. A tired panting dog makes a "h-h-h-h-" sound, and this dog would like to rest on a chair whose shape h resembles the letter h. Stern's Structural Reading Program (Stern & Gould, 1965, p. 159) endeavors to facilitate sound-symbol matching by deliberately creating a key picture for each letter of the alphabet and imposing the letter upon it (see Figure 10-2).

Cues can be used in the secondary classes as effectively as in the elementary grades:

The Indian Chief named Soh Cah Toa can serve as a reminder for the trigonometric functions:

$$sine = \frac{side\ opposite}{hypotenuse}, \quad cosine = \frac{side\ adjacent}{hypotenuse}, \quad tangent = \frac{side\ opposite}{side\ adjacent}$$

The name S. P. COHN can help one remember the elements of protoplasm: sulphur, phosphorus, carbon, oxygen, hydrogen, and nitrogen.

Foreign language vocabulary memory can often be facilitated by providing word derivative cues linking the two words (Gagné, 1970, pp. 137–138):

French	Link	English
main	(manufacture)	hand
donner	(donation)	to give
froid	(freeze)	cold

Figure 10-2.   Key picture cues for symbol sound recall.

Recently, learning-disabled adults have begun to relate incidents of how they formulated their own cues to help them cope. One instance is that of a man who is still plagued with left–right confusion. One day, he hit upon the scheme of envisioning himself in his elementary classroom seat. Since the windows there invariably faced left, he was able to utilize this childhood memory as an effective clue to assist him with his current direction problem.

Jess Oppenheimer (1972), a successful producer and comedy writer who suffered from perceptual and equilibrium problems, devised various strategies that enabled him to cope in such diverse activities as catching a ball, judging distance for his Boy Scout tests, and driving a car.

Dian Ridenour, a professional social worker and co-founder of Time Out to Enjoy, an organization that provides services and support for learning-disabled adults, tells of using configuration cues to help her with decoding (Wilson & Ridenour, 1979, pp. 4-5).

> . . . I live in the Chicago area. If I have to go to Fullerton and Clark Streets, I know that "Fullerton" starts with an F, is a long word and ends with an n. "Clark" is a short word that starts with a C, has mostly long letters and ends in k. That's the way I get to where I'm going. I may spell the streets wrong, but I get there . . .

Teachers should try to select cues that are truly supportive, or they may fall into the trap of actually burdening the child with an *additional* memory chore. For example, in teaching laterality and/or directionality, many teachers use color cues, but they often choose the colors at random (e.g., a black spot of paint on the left hand and a white spot on the right hand.) The child can easily confuse the two, since no solid "memory peg" is provided. However, if the child has already developed a sense of phonics, the teacher might be more successful if she chose *r*ed for *r*ight. In other words, where possible, a cue is rendered more effective if it meets the criterion of exclusivity. True, many teachers seem to get around this problem by assigning a color to only one hand (e.g., the right hand is consistently given a spot of white paint, while the left hand gets none). Although this may prove more effective than the two colors (no phonic clues), there is still no solid reason why the child must associate the right hand, rather than the left, with the paint.

Children don't always wait for teachers to provide cues. At times, they devise their own, some of which may facilitate learning while others may further contribute to failure. Teachers should observe children engaged in various tasks and try to glimpse their coping strategy. (Asking them *how* they arrived at their answer is often a good means of learning the child's "system.") For example, a child may have picked up the trick of skimming word problems in arithmetic and automatically selecting the addition process (rather than subtraction) for those with more than two numbers, without even reading the problem. The concerned teacher can discover this and put the child on the right track with more effective cues (e.g., key words).

Other criteria for effective cues listed by Siegel (1972, pp. 104–5) are:

1. *The clue—or cue—must always be easier than the task itself.* (For example, in the *"piece* of *pie"* cue, the word pie is easier to read and to spell than is piece. In the penmanship cue, *3* is easier to form than is 𝟹.)
2. *The "performance" of (i.e., the understanding of, the mastery of, the ability to deal with) the cue must be within the child's repertoire.*
3. *The cues must not be too vague.*
4. *The cues should not serve as distractions.*
5. *Cues should be faded out.*

Sequence the Instructional Tasks. Sequencing is generally conceded to be an important element of structure (Peter, 1965, p. 37; Montessori, 1912; Barry, 1961, p. 21). Various connotations of sequencing exist, all of them significant in the education of learning-disabled children: arranging things and events in order according to size, number, shade of color, importance, chronology, and so forth; avoiding "overloading" and disorganization (that is, dealing with one thing at a time); avoiding failure by not presenting the child with tasks until he is ready for them.

Beyond all of these, sequencing is intimately linked with the topic of *task analysis*, an approach which goes to the heart of effective instruction, particularly for the learning disabled. Lerner (1976, p. 108) states unequivocally that task analysis is an approach ". . . designed to lead directly to appropriate teaching." Myers and Hammill (1976, p. 89) point out that the process of task analysis, enables the teacher "to know *what* he wants to teach, *where* he wants to begin, *when* he has succeeded, and *what* the next item should be." Kirk and Gallagher (1979, p. 411) believe that the overriding function of task analysis as a classroom procedure is to "establish goals and organize the tasks in small steps so that the child can experience continuous success."

In order to create an instructional sequence, the teacher must decide upon a behavioral objective. This should be stated clearly and concisely, and should specify exactly what the child is expected to *do* as a result of instruction. That is, the objective must be stipulated in terms of *observable* behavior. (For example, stating outcomes such as, "the child will recite," "will write," "will touch," "will point to," "will construct," "will measure," "will match," and so forth, are superior to those such as "will know," "will understand," "will learn." The ability to state specifically what it is that we are striving to teach the child is so crucial that several texts have been devoted solely to this topic: Robert F. Mager's *Preparing Instructional Objectives, Second Edition*, Belmont, Ca.: Fearon Publishers, 1975; Norman E. Gronlund's *Stating Objectives for Classroom Instruction, Second Edition*, New York: MacMillan, 1978.

Any behavioral objective, no matter how correctly worded, is nevertheless doomed to fail if it is not pegged to the child's entering behavior. The concept of "readiness" is apropos here (Siegel & Siegel, 1977, p. 44). For a behavioral objective (and its resultant instructional sequence) to be valid, the child for whom it has been selected must be ready for it—ready in every way: neurologically, perceptually, motivationally, physically, attention skills, academic levels—and especially in terms of his past learnings.

Traditionally, task analyses are written as a list of skills, arranged in hierarchical order of complexity, one being the prerequisite for the subsequent one, and terminating with the final goal (the stipulated behavioral objective). For example, Wallace and Kauffman (1973) suggest the following task analysis for a child in order for him to be able to follow the oral instruction, "Print your name at the top of the paper":

1. Interpret (understand) the task directions
2. Find the top of the paper
3. Hold the pencil in writing position
4. Form each of the manuscript letters in his name
5. Print the letters in his name in sequence (p. 105–106)

In teaching a child to subtract mixed numbers with exchange and with unlike denominators, a typical task analysis would be:

1. Demonstration of having mastered the concept of fractions; ability to select the numerator and the denominator of a given fraction; demonstration of the meaning of numerator and denominator; and so on
2. Show ability to handle fractional equivalencies:

$$\frac{2}{4} = \frac{?}{2}$$

3. Subtraction of fractions with like denominator:

$$\frac{3}{4}$$
$$-\frac{1}{4}$$

4. Subtraction of mixed numbers with like denominators and no exchange:

$$6\frac{3}{4}$$
$$-3\frac{1}{4}$$

5. Subtraction of mixed numbers with unlike denominators and no exchange:

$$6\frac{3}{4}$$

$$-3\frac{1}{8}$$

6. Subtraction of unlike denominators with exchange:

$$6\frac{1}{8}$$

$$-3\frac{3}{4}$$

Upon observing the preceding task analyses, it can be seen that the listing of the steps can serve as a checklist of prerequisite skills and as curriculum or (syllabus) guidelines. Also, ongoing experience in preparing them can make the teacher sensitive to the complexity inherent in tasks which, at first glance, may seem to be patently simple. Thus, the teacher becomes more empathetic to the learning-disabled child as he struggles to learn. However, it is equally clear that if the child's entering behavior ties him to a given step (e.g., suppose, in the task involving the ability to print one's name at the top of the paper, the child can do the first step, but fell down at the second), then the availability of the list in no way tells the teacher *how* to proceed—*it merely tells her where the child needs help but does not suggest a means of intervention.* In fact, if the child cannot do some of the initial steps, the teacher may have to abandon the original behavioral objective and backtrack to an earlier task (Siegel & Siegel, 1977, pp. 44–45; Myers & Hammill, 1976, p. 83).

Based on over a dozen years of teacher-training in which instructional sequences were considered, created, analyzed, evaluated, and refined, Siegel and Siegel (1977) set forth a method of devising instructional sequences—a method rooted in their observation that the best sequences always contained supportive sequential components. These were not listed, but were embedded in the sequences. Each component revolved around a specific variable: size of the material, weight, complexity, degree to which cues are used, degree of supervision, and so on. The "six factors in learning" espoused by Barsch (1965) can be regarded as typical variables upon which sequential components are formulated:

1. space (from more space to less space)
2. time (from brief tasks to lengthier ones)
3. multiplicity (from less stimuli—Barsch calls this "denuding the setting" (p. 336)—to more stimuli)
4. level (from lower performance levels to higher ones)
5. language (from simplified language—at times using "telegraphic speech" (p. 339)—to more elaborate communication)
6. relationship (from a close, intimate relationship, to a less personal one—or vice versa, for some children)

The key words for listing sequential components are "from" and "to." There are *general* components that obtain for many sequences (e.g., from concrete to abstract, from small initial doses to larger ones, from having a model on display to performing from memory, from use of cues to fading out the cues). Beyond these, there are sequential components indigenous to *specific* behavioral objectives. For example, in teaching a pupil to identify verbs appearing in a series of written sentences, the direction should be from action verbs to state-of-being verbs, from depicting action from which the pupil can actually observe to those which must be imagined, from using the terminology "action" word or "happening" word to using the more pedantic term "verb," and so on. In teaching the pupil to differentiate auditorially between the *long a* and *short a* sounds appearing in one-syllable words, the order should be from words in which the vowel sound is the initial sound (ache, ax) to medial (bake, tack) or possibly final placement. It should proceed from practice in discriminating the pure vowel sounds to isolating them in words, from use of a reference chart tying in a key picture for each sound (e.g., a picture of an apron for the *long a* and a picture of an apple for a *short a*), to producing the sound from memory. This sequence should also move from holding the word for a long time (trying to match the vowel sound being held with the chart's key sound) to pronouncing the word in a natural, nonexaggerated fashion.

Sequential components are just as relevant in junior- and senior-high school subject areas as they are in the elementary grades. In teaching typewriting, start with easily-fingered keys and gradually move on to the more difficult fingerings. Initially, offer verbal cadence ("a-a-a-space-d-d-d-space") and have a large keyboard chart posted in front of the room; later, both aids are removed.

When the instructional objective is to differentiate between simile and metaphor, teach the concept of simile first. (The simile is the basis for the metaphor. That is, an understanding of simile can facilitate the learning of metaphor, but the converse is not true). At first, remind the student to look for the clue words "as" and "like." Later, this support is withdrawn. The direction should be from recognizing metaphors which the pupil has observed the teacher creating from known similes (e.g., "as fast as lightning" → "Sugar Ray Leonard's lightning jab") to recognizing metaphors without alluding to their referent similes.

In teaching students to use a protractor for measuring designated angles, begin with angles in the upper right quadrant of the x-y axis graph. (The factor of not having to switch the protractor or the paper is supportive by virtue of its consistency.) Gradually angles in the other quadrants should be introduced. Initially it is less confusing to use only those angles of 10 and multiples of 10 before proceeding to the intermediate numbers (27, 68, etc.). Color cuing (a spot of paint—same color) the vertex of the protractor and the vertex of the angle is a supportive reminder which should be used preliminarily, then faded out.

Moyer and Dardig (1978, pp. 17-18) approach this topic of supportive sequential components with the concept of initially modifying—or simplifying—the conditions of the behavioral objective. For example, in teaching a child to cut along a 3″ line which has been drawn on a 4″ × 6″ piece of paper, they point out that, at first, the 3″ line could be shortened; it could also be widened (thus accommodating the novice's relatively large margin for error); the paper could be thicker at first (thereby minimizing crumpling); and so forth.

Regarding sequential components as the mortar for building instructional sequences, the following procedures for constructing these sequences emerge: (1) select an appropriate behavioral objective (based upon the entering behavior of the child), (2) compile a list of sequential components, (3) select the ones you wish to include in the sequence, (4) combine them into a sequence (all or most of them will appear in the first step), and (5) finalize them as you go along (that is, "any changes that are made in the conditions must be systematically eliminated before the learner can be said to have mastered the terminal objective," Moyer & Dardig, 1978, p. 18).

A sample sequence used in *Creating Instructional Sequences* (Siegel & Siegel, 1977) follows. A list of sequential components have been compiled, but only the checked ones have been included in the sequence.* All of them appear in step one of the sequence and are gradually finalized in the ensuing steps so that at step 5, the terminal objective has been reached.

Behavioral Objective:

When given several words written with a No. 2 pencil on a sheet of 8½" × 11" paper, the pupil will be able to erase them neatly using a regular pencil's eraser.

Entering Behavior:

Adequate fine motor control for grasping the pencil and for making the back and forth erasing strokes. Adequate eye-hand coordination.

Sequential Components:

√ 1. from small amounts to large amounts
√ 2. from erasing lighter writing to erasing darker writing
√ 3. from using art gum (sometimes called "soap eraser") to using the pencil's eraser
4. from using an eraser on a thicker pencil to one on a regular-size pencil
√ 5. from erasing on oak tag (the material of which file folders are made) to erasing on paper (paper is thinner)
√ 6. from the teacher's verbal cues to no cues
7. from drill in selecting a clean rather than a smudgy eraser to no drill
8. from the teacher physically guiding the pupil's hand to no guidance
9. from erasing words written in an open space to words written within a confined area
10. from erasing sand-writing (or chalk-writing) to erasing on paper

Instructional Sequence:

1. Write a small word with a light stroke (with a No. 2 pencil) on a piece of oak tag. Give the pupil an art gum eraser and instruct him to erase the word. Provide verbal cues (e.g., "Hold the oak tag"; "Rub back and forth lightly").

---

* It is a good practice to list each component as soon as it comes to mind, despite the fact that the teacher may later decide not to include it in the sequence. This insures that it will not be forgotten and it will at least be considered at the time of selection. It should be stated here also that the decision regarding which components to utilize and which to discard is a somewhat arbitrary one, varying from teacher to teacher. In other words, for any given behavioral objective, there is no such thing as a single *best* sequence, but a number of equally effective ones. Therefore, here, as well as in the additional samples appearing in the Appendix, the total pool of sequential components—those that will be used as well as those that will be omitted—has been listed; only the checked ones are included in the final sequence.

2. Write darker (still using a No. 2 pencil). Continue to use oak tag, a small word, an art gum eraser, and verbal cues.
3. Write several longer words with a dark stroke. Continue to use oak tag, art gum, and verbal cues.
4. Switch to a pencil's eraser and begin fading out verbal cues. Still use oak tag.
5. Switch from oak tag to paper and omit all verbal cues.

Another sample, dealing with differentiation between interrogative and declarative sentences, follows. The format is identical to the preceding sample with one major exception: Not *all*, but *most* of the selected (checked) sequential components appear in the first step of the sequence. Additional ones are introduced in intermediate steps. These, too, are gradually faded out so that by the last step, the behavioral objective has been reached.

Behavioral Objective: When given ten written sentences on or below reading grade level, half of them interrogative and half declarative in random order, the pupil will insert the correct punctuation mark (either a period or a question mark).

Entering Behavior: Adequate conversational skills (e.g., can generally differentiate between a complete and an incomplete sentence, but has received no prior training in grammar), a given reading grade level, sufficient motor ability to write the punctuation marks.

Sequential Components:

√ 1. from fewer sentences to more sentences
√ 2. from "who, what, when, where" questions to other kinds (e.g., Did you sleep?)
√ 3. from cur (reminding pupil of key words: *who, what, when,*) to no cues
√ 4. from cue ("Does it need an answer?") to no cue
√ 5. from drill in transposing questions into answers (and vice versa) to no drill
√ 6. from visual model on display to no model

What does Jack have?

Jack has a flag.

√ 7. from *naming* a telling and asking sentence (written) to *filling in* the correct punctuation mark
√ 8. from using the terms "telling" and "asking" to using "statement" and

"question" (This may be an extraneous component; however, some teachers may feel that knowledge of the term, "question," may cue the "question mark" response.

√ 9. from reminding the pupil of the vocal inflection cue to memory

10. from exaggerating the inflection cues to normal speech

√ 11. from oral sentences to written sentences

√ 12. from easy (brief and consistent) types of sentences to more difficult (varied) ones

√ 13. from using sentences based on visible objects (or people) to imaginary ones

√ 14. from composing telling and asking sentences to deciding whether a given one is a telling or an asking sentence. (Normally, composing a sentence is harder than using one that has already been supplied. However, this component can serve as an excellent initial training technique. For example, the teacher holds up a pencil and says. "*Tell* me about the pencil," eliciting such responses as "It is yellow," "It can write," "The pencil is in your hand." She then says, "Now *ask* me about it," eliciting such questions as "What color is the pencil?" "Whose pencil is it?" "Is it little?")*

15. from placing cut outs [●] [?] to writing the marks

Instructional Sequence:

1. Practice composing and labeling several oral telling and asking sentences based upon visible objects. Use brief and consistent types of sentences in which *who, what, when, where* appear. Point out the inflection cue, the key word cue, and the "Does it need an answer?" criterion. The model is on display throughout.

2. Same as above, but begin using other kinds of questions as well (e.g. Can Jerry jump?).

3. Gradually interject longer sentences with varied format, based upon imaginary—as well as visible—objects and people.

4. Provide special drill in transposing questions into answers (and vice versa). Gradually fade out the use of this drill during steps 5–10.

5. Same as 3, but instead of pupils composing sentences, the teacher will present them with oral sentences. They must state whether each is a *telling* or an *asking* sentence. Utilize cues and refer to model.

6. Fade out the "who, when, what, where" cue, the inflection cue, and the "Does it need an answer?" criterion. The model is still on display.

7. Same as 6. Gradually introduce the terms: "question" and "statement."

8. Teacher presents several written sentences. Pupils *tell* what mark should appear.

9. Teacher presents several written sentences. Pupils *write* the marks. (The model is still on display.)

10. Increase the number of sentences. Fade out the use of the model.

(Additional samples appear in Appendix C.)

Notice that at each step the child is expected to *do* something. This is a basic principle of instructional sequencing (Johnson & Morasky, 1980, p. 340). Not only

* This strategy is based upon a method developed by Sister Mary Consilia (1978, pp. 254, 255).

is this important in deference to the classic tenet of "learning by doing," but it enables us to witness whether or not the child has mastered that step.

Myers and Hammill (1976, p. 86) explain. "Sequentiality, as best it can be determined, is one of the most important principles of task analysis. The entire process is predicted upon the "building block" theory of skill learning, that is, that the skills one must acquire in learning a task are to be developed in a sequential order, that one must learn 'A' before 'B' and 'B' before 'C'."

CONCLUSION

Illustrations for providing structure discussed in this chapter are not exhaustive. Our intention has been to illuminate some of the major ingredients of structure that apply directly to the *teaching* process itself. That is, only those examples that mirror the "imparting of knowledges and skills" theme of education and whose sole raison d'être is to simplify instruction have been included. Other authors, however, considering structure from a more interpersonal point of view, have focused upon additional elements: For example, the selection of an appropriate reward and the schedule of reinforcement are set forth as crucial facets of structure (Wallace & Kauffman, 1973, pp. 113-114). Hewett (1968, p. 67) refers to this as the "limits or 'strings' the teacher . . . attaches to particular tasks assigned to the child." Some writers believe teacher-pupil relationships to be a vital part of structure (Wallace & Kauffman, 1973, pp. 113-114, Barsch, 1965, pp. 340-341; Haring & Phillips, 1962, pp. 9-10).

Rappaport (1966, p. R-1) uses the term *"relationship structure"* to denote "the ability of the adult to understand the child sufficiently well at any given moment, through verbal and nonverbal clues, to relate in a way which aids the child's development of impulse control and other ego functions." He further contends that ". . . the key to successful learning may be defined as a highly structured, methodical presentation of whatever is to be learned in a relationship that enables the child to feel supportive understanding and that allows him to borrow from the adult's inner strengths and goals until his own inner controls and motivations can be established."

REFERENCES

Axiline, V. *Play therapy*. Boston: Houghton Mifflin, 1947.

Barry, H. *Teaching the young aphasic child*. Washington, D.C.: Alexander Graham Bell Association for the Deaf, Inc., 1961.

Barsch, R. Six factors in learning. In Jerome Hellmuth (Ed.), *Learning disorder, volume I*. Seattle: Special Child Publications, 1965.

Bettelheim, B. *Love is not enough*. New York: Free Press, 1950.

––––––. "A noncontribution to educational research. *Harvard Educational Review*, 1963, *33*(1), 326-335.

Bousfield, W., Esterson, J., and Whitmarsh, G., The effects of concomitant colored and uncolored pictorial representations on the learning of stimulus words. *Journal of Applied Psychology*, 1957, *41*(3), 165-167.

Bradfield, O. The teacher at work, in Jerome Hellmuth (ed.), *Learning disorders, volume I*. Seattle: Special Child Publications, 1965.

Bryan, T. H., and Bryan, J. H., *Understanding learning disabilities, 2nd ed*. Sherman Oaks, Ca.: Alfred, 1978.

Consilia, Sister Mary. *The non-coping child*. Novato, Ca.: Academic Therapy Publications, 1978.

Cruickshank, W. M., Bentzen, F. A., Ratzeburg, F. H., and Tannhauser, M. T. *A teaching methodology for brain-injured and hyperactive children*. Syracuse, N.Y.: Syracuse University Press, 1961.

Denckla, M. B. Supervision, support, structure. *Perceptions: The newsletter for parents of children with learning disabilities*, Oct., 1978, *1*(4), 1, 6.

Deschler, D. D. Psychoeducational aspects of learning-disabled adolescents. In Lester Mann, Libby Goodman, and J. Lee Wiederholt (Eds.), *Teaching the learning-disabled adolescent*. Boston: Houghton Mifflin, 1978.

Dykman, R. A., Ackerman, P. T., Clements, S. D., and Peters, J. E. Specific learning disabilities: An attentional deficit syndrome. In Helmer R. Myklebust (Ed.), *Progress in learning disabilities, volume II*. New York: Grune & Stratton. 1971.

Egeland, B. Training impulsive children in the use of more efficient scanning techniques. *Child Development*, 1974, *45*, 165–171.

Gagné, R. *The conditions of learning, 2nd ed*. New York: Holt, Rinehart, and Winston, 1970.

Gallagher, P. A. *Teaching students with behavior disorders*, Denver, Col.: Love Publishing, 1979.

Gardner, W. I., Cromwell, R. L., and Foshee, J. G. Studies in activity level: II. Effects of distal visual stimulation in organics, familials, hyperactives and hypoactives. *American Journal of Mental Deficiency*, May, 1959, *63*, 1028–1033.

Golick, M. *She thought I was dumb, but I told her I had a learning disability*. Toronto: Canadian Broadcasting Corporation Learning Systems, 1969.

Grover, E. C., and Allen, A. A. *A demonstration project for brain-damaged children in Ohio*. Columbus: Ohio Department of Education, 1962.

Hallahan, D. P., Gajar, A. H., Cohen, S. B. and Tarver, S. G. The learning disabled as an inactive learner. *Journal of Learning Disabilities*, 1978, *11*(4), 231–236.

Haring, N. G., and Whelan, R. J. Experimental methods in education & management. In Nicholas J. Long, William C. Morse, and Ruth G. Newman (Eds.), *Conflict in the classroom*. Belmont, Ca.: Wadsworth, 1965.

Haring, N. G., and Phillips, E. *Educating emotionally disturbed children*. New York: McGraw-Hill, 1962.

Hewett, F. *The emotionally disturbed child in the classroom*. Boston: Allyn & Bacon, 1968.

Hewett, F. and Taylor, F. *The emotionally disturbed child in the classroom: The orchestration of success, 2nd ed*. Boston: Allyn & Bacon, 1980.

Johnson, S. W. and Morasky, R. L. *Learning disabilities, 2nd ed*. Boston: Allyn & Bacon, 1980.

Kaliski, L. The brain-injured child—learning by living in a structured setting. *American Journal of Mental Deficiency*, Jan., 1959, *63*(4), 688–695.

Kirk, S. A., and Gallagher, J. J. *Educating exceptional children, 3rd ed*. Boston: Houghton Mifflin, 1979.

Kronick, D. *They too can succeed*. Novato, Ca.: Academic Therapy Publications, 1969.

Lehtinen, L. E. The brain-injured child: What can we do for him?" *The Dallas Medical Journal*, Special Edition, March, 1959, 15–21.

Lerner, J. *Children with learning disabilities, 2nd ed.* Boston: Houghton Mifflin, 1976.

Lewis, R. S. *The other child.* New York: Grune & Stratton, 1951.

Lewis, R. S., Strauss, A. A. and Lehtinen, L. E. *The other child, 2nd ed.* New York: Grune & Stratton, 1960.

Lynn, R. *Learning disabilities—the state of the field 1978.* New York: Social Science Research Council, 1978.

Mallison, R. *Education as therapy.* Seattle: Special Child Publications, 1968.

Mercer, C. D. and Mercer A. R. *Teaching students with learning problems.* Columbus, Ohio: Charles E. Merrill, 1981.

McLaughlin, S. *Your special child.* Pittsburgh: Allegheny County Association for Children With Learning Disabilities, 1973.

Mesinger, J. F. Emotionally disturbed & brain damaged children—should we mix them? *Exceptional Children*, 1965, *32*, 237–238.

Montessori, M. *The Montessori method.* N.Y.: Schocken. 1912. (First Schocken Paperback Edition, 1964).

Moyer, J. R., and Dardig, J. C. Practical task analysis for special education. *Teaching Exceptional Children*, Fall, 1978, *II*(1), 16–18.

Myers, P. and Hammill, D. *Methods for learning disorders, 2nd ed.* New York: Wiley, 1976.

Newman, R. G. The acting-out boy. *Exceptional Children*, February, 1956, *22*, 186–190, 204–206, 215–216.

Oppenheimer, J. All about me. *Journal of Learning Disabilities*, August–September, 1972, *5*(7), 407–422.

Payne, J. S., Polloway, E. A., Smith, J. E., and Payne, R. A. *Strategies for teaching the mentally retarded.* Columbus, Ohio: Charles E. Merrill, 1977.

Peter, L. J. *Prescriptive teaching.* New York: McGraw-Hill, 1965.

Petersen, W. Classroom management for the neurologically impaired. In Jerome Hellmuth (Ed.), *Learning disorders, volume I.* Seattle: Special Child Publications, 1965.

Rappaport, S. *Perceptual problems* (Proceedings). Stratford, CT.: Connecticut Association of School Psychological Personnel. Fall Institute, 1966.

Ross, A. O. *Psychological aspects of learning disabilities and reading disorders.* New York: McGraw-Hill, 1976.

Schechter, M. B. Montessori and the child's natural development. In Harold A. Solan (Ed.), *The psychology of learning and reading disabilities.* New York: Simon & Schuster, 1973.

Schulman, J. L., Kaspar, J. C., and Throne, F. M. *Brain damage and behavior.* Springfield, Ill.: Charles C. Thomas, 1965.

Siegel, E. *Helping the brain-injured child.* Albany, N.Y.: New York Association for the Learning Disabled, 1961.

——— *Teaching one child.* Freeport, N.Y.: Educational Activities Inc., 1972.

Siegel, E., and Siegel, R. *Creating instructional sequences.* Novato, Ca.: Academic Therapy Publications, 1977.

Smith, S. L. *No easy answers: The learning-disabled child.* Washington, D.C.: Department of Health, Education and Welfare. Publication No. (ADM) 77–526, 1978.

Smith, W. I. *Guidelines to classroom behavior.* Brooklyn, N.Y.: Book-Lab, 1970.

Stern, C., and Gould, T. *Children discover reading.* New York: Random House, 1965.

Strauss, A. A., and Kephart, N. *Psychopathology and education of the brain-injured child, volume II.* New York: Grune & Stratton, 1955.

Strauss, A. A., and Lehtinen, L. E. *Psychopathology and education of the brain-injured child, volume I.* New York: Grune & Stratton, 1947.

Thornton, C. Parents can help: Success strategies—Basic arithmetic facts. *Perceptions: The Newsletter for Parents of Children with Learning Disabilities*, September, 1979, *2*(3), 1–8.

Wallace, G., and Kauffman, J. M. *Teaching children with learning problems.* Columbus, Ohio: Charles E. Merrill, 1973.

Wilson, M., and Ridenour, D. LD, adult and making it. *Perceptions: The Newsletter for Parents of Children With Learning Disabilities*, February, 1979, *1*(6), 4–5.

Zentall, S. Optimal stimulation as theoretical basis for hyperactivity. *American Journal of Orthopsychiatry*, July, 1975, *45*(4), 549–563.

Additional Principles for the Education of the Learning Disabled

11

Inasmuch as educators disagree violently regarding the very definition of learning disabilities, one would expect them to be at variance regarding the optimal instructional approaches. As Lynn (1978, p. 90) points out, "because so little is known about learning disorders at this point, the relationship between diagnosis and [educational] treatment is a weak one at best." The differences of opinion seem to mass along two major fronts: The first is the perennial controversy regarding the efficacy of task orientation as opposed to process orientation. That is, should we attempt simply to teach spelling, or are we mandated to concentrate upon "visual sequential memory?" (Siegel & Siegel, 1977, pp. 139-146; Larsen, 1976, pp. 501-503; Newcomer & Hammill, 1976). The second point of divergence is less of a direct issue than it is a question of degree. For example, some educators emphasize the remediation of the impaired modality (Strauss & Lehtinen, 1947, pp. 137, 139) whereas others stress utilizing the areas in which the child is better endowed, thus teaching "around the handicap." Some advocate an approach involving considerable multisensory experiences, while others prefer to use this approach sparingly. Some teachers believe that learning-disabled children should be given a very small number of situations requiring choices, but others feel that more decision making is preferable. The point is that rarely does any side approach it as an "either-or" proposition. In other words, some authorities recommend a lot of treatment X, others recommend less, and, still others who, owing to the large amount of diversity generally conceded to exist within the learning-disabled population (Peters et al., 1973; Siegel, 1969, 1974; Reichstein, 1963; Adelman, 1971), may be perfectly justified—*for some specific children*—in recommending none of it.

Notwithstanding these two concerns, there is surprisingly considerable consensus regarding the educational principles discussed in this chapter and in Chapter 10. Undoubtedly this is so because these principles essentially illustrate what most educators would consider "good teaching." It has been said over and over again that the learning-disabled field has given impetus to the emergence of those methods, techniques, and instructional strategies, which can redound not only to the benefit of the learning disabled, but to the mentally retarded, the emotionally disturbed, and to the "normal" child as well.

DIFFERENTIATE BETWEEN TEACHING AND OTHER PROCESSES

Teaching vs. Reviewing

To be sure, a good case can be made for giving learning-disabled children considerable opportunity for reviewing, practicing, and simply repeating what they already know. After all, they forget easily, they are inconsistent performers, they have attention problems, and may have missed some of the points from the original lesson. They also have secondary emotional disorders, notably a poor self-concept, and would hence benefit from "success-assured" activities. All of these statements are, of course, valid and the learning disabled do indeed require considerable practice and review. In fact, they need these more frequently than they need instruction of new material. The point, though, is that the *teachers* must know which of these the child needs and when he needs it, and must avoid pawning off practice as new learning simply because they, themselves, do not see the difference.

These two aspects of instruction—teaching something new and providing practice—relate to what the *teacher* does. The counterparts of these with respect to what the *child* does are (1) acquisition and (2) maintenance. Payne et al. (1977, p. 49) explain:

> Two specific stages of learning are important to differentiate, that is, acquisition and maintenance. Acquisition learning refers to the initial development of a skill or chunk of knowledge. Maintenance learning refers to the ability needed to retain this skill or knowledge over a period of time. It cannot be equated with memory because maintenance implies more than remembering. It takes the learner from the initial grasp of a fact, concept, or skill during acquisition to its solid establishment in his response repertoire over time. Perhaps it can best be viewed as a combination of *remembering* and *refinement* of the learned material.
>
> The differences between acquisition and maintenance learning result in several important teaching considerations. These include the determination of each stage's needs relative to consequences, antecedents, and their relationships to learning.

They go on to point out (pp. 49-50) three specific differences teachers should bear in mind. First, a continuous schedule of reinforcement works best during the acquisition stage, whereas intermittent schedules are effective for maintenance. Second, acquisition requires the presentation of frequent and varied stimuli (e.g., a vocabulary list could be taught via flash cards, a teaching machine such as a Languagemaster, or written and taught as spelling words) but once learned, they can be presented less frequently, perhaps merely by including them in some of the reading lessons. Finally, acquisition requires direct and complete teacher intervention but maintenance warrants less of this:

> ... based on the importance of continuous reinforcement and frequent, varied presentation of antecedents to learning, it follows that for *learning to be acquired it must be taught*. Exceptions to this rule may be infinite but educators, especially teachers working with handicapped learners, must assume the responsibility to teach whatever it is that should be learned. Only through direct teacher-student interaction can the requirements for consequences and antecedents be fulfilled. However during the maintenance stage the diminished needs for reinforcement and instructional stimuli lessen the importance of directive teaching. Indirect maintenance techniques, ranging from worksheets to student tutors, can play a valuable role when utilized properly. (Payne et al., 1977, p. 50)

If teachers fail to differentiate between these two stages and the teaching strategies indigenous to each of them, two problems can ensue (Payne et al., 1977, p. 50). The first involves "over-instructing" once acquisition has occurred, resulting in a waste of teacher time. Lindsley (1964) refers to this enforced plateau as the "acquisition hump." He believes that "it is almost as unkind to crutch-trap a handicapped person as it is to deny him a crutch in the first place" (1964, p. 65). The second potential problem is the converse of the first: It involves providing mere maintenance strategies when, in reality, the child is in the acquisition stage and therefore requires more direct teacher interaction.

Clearly, both mistakes—providing massive doses of teaching long after the child has already mastered that particular instructional frame, or expecting him to do what·has not yet been taught—can result in boredom, frustration, and behavioral problems.

Teaching vs. Testing

A second educational principle involves differentiating between teaching and testing. (Kirk & Kirk, 1971, pp. 119-121; Siegel, 1978). Asking a learning-disabled pupil who is a poor decoder to read orally, without providing him with any instructional strategies or cues, is testing, not teaching. The typical phonics workbook, in which the child is asked to encircle either *sh* or *ch* under each picture (e.g., shoe, ship, cherry) is another example of testing. In fact, any instance[*] in which the child is required to perform (e.g., measure with a ruler, copy from the chalkboard, punctuate a sentence, spell a word, recognize nouns) in the absence of any instructional strategies, prompts, reminders, models, cues, self-correcting materials, and the like is testing, pure and simple. The teacher must know "where the child is at" (the entering behavior of the child), but this is no excuse for repeated and continuous testing—which, in the case of the learning-disabled child, is an outright invitation to failure.

---

[*] It goes without saying that any of these testing situations can be transformed into illustrations of good teaching with the injection of *some* supportive methodology. Examples of these would be an illustrative algorism on the top of a workbook arithmetic page, a model of a letter correctly formed with arrows indicating the direction of its component lines, a reminder that saying *ch* words requires exhaling of more breath than do *sh* words (this can be felt by placing the back of the hand an inch from one's lips while saying the word.)

Teaching vs. Presenting

A teacher must also differentiate between teaching and presenting (Siegel & Siegel, 1977, pp. 32–35). Able learners may fare reasonably well despite receiving meager instruction. They can fill in the gaps, learn incidentally, and figure out things for themselves more readily than can their learning-disabled counterparts. Research demonstrates that the neurologically handicapped need more sensory data in order to derive meaning from their environment than do those with intact neurology. For example, Ross (1954, pp. 566–572) examined brain-injured adults, requiring them to recognize (by touch alone) thumbtack patterns of letters, numbers, and simple geometric design in progressive stages of completeness: the complete design, several tacks removed, more tacks removed, and so on. As anticipated, the experimental subjects required more tacks than did the nonhandicapped group in order to identify the design.

The teacher of an intact learner may find that, at times, a single presentation suffices. She demonstrates just once how to write the capital G, how to use a ruler for measuring to the inch and the half inch, what kind of sentence needs an exclamation point—and the child gets it! Not so with the handicapped learner. He needs more than that. He needs good teaching.

BECOME PROFICIENT IN TECHNICAL ASPECTS OF THE TASK

It is axiomatic that effective instruction rests to a large extent upon the teacher's thorough understanding of the instructional task in question. Despite its self-evidence, this is by no means a gratuitous statement. "Know that which you are endeavoring to teach" is easier said than done simply because *we do not know what we do not know*. In other words, the most conscientious teacher may *believe* that she is fully competent in all phases of the skill or knowledge being taught; yet, in reality, she may simply never have considered something about the task—some fine points, perhaps. Hence, the instructional intervention will not be as effective as it could be. The following are some examples of technical aspects which are often overlooked:

Blending Initial Consonants with Phonemes

Blending an initial consonant with a phoneme is facilitated if, in the beginning, we choose a letter that can be held a long time (e.g., s, m, l) instead of a plosive letter (e.g., p, t, k). That is, the child who is just beginning to learn to blend may well stumble on p-ay (because the p sound is over immediately after its production), whereas he is likely to be more successful with s-ay (since the s glides smoothly into the ay).

Vowels

When teaching vowels, most teachers—as well as textbooks, workbooks and phonic programs,—introduce the short vowels first, probably because 1) they generate a profusion of simple three-letter words, and 2) words with only one vowel are thought to be less confusing than those with two or more. However, a good case can be made for starting with the long vowels. First, there is a built-in cue (and most teachers are aware of this): The sound of the vowel is the same as its name. There is also another advantage: Each long vowel sounds markedly different from the others. This is not true in the case of short vowels, which leads to frequent confusion between *short a* and *short e* words (e.g., lag, leg), *short o* and *short u* words (e.g., cup, cop), and *short i* and *short e* words (e.g., pin, pen).

The *long i* and the *long u* sounds have inherent pitfalls and probably should be approached after the *long a* and *long o*. Each of these has *two* sounds (whereas the others simply "say their name.") The *long i* is different in p*i*ne than in *i*ce; similarly, there are two *long u* sounds: the *u* sound in words like r*u*le, tr*u*th, and t*u*ba is different than the one in c*u*te, m*u*le, and m*u*sic.

The *long e* has its own problem. Although it has only one sound (its name), and hence presents no difficulty from that standpoint, there are few instances in which it can be used in conjunction with the *silent e* rule. (*Pete* and *here* are a few of them, but there are not many others.) This places severe restrictions on the amount of illustrations and drills the teacher can use.

Consonants

In teaching the sounds of consonants, it is helpful to realize that the names of most consonants give a hint as to their sounds. The name of the letter T is somewhat similar to its sound. The same applies to $B, V, Z, D, F, L, M, N, S, R$, and many others. However, the letters W, H and G (as in *go*) have names which in no way give a hint as to their sound; hence, some children may find these more difficult.

Copying

A pupil learning to copy will probably find near-point (copying from the sample placed on his desk) easier than farpoint (copying from the chalkboard). For the latter, the distance itself can constitute a hurdle; also it requires the translation from the vertical to the horizontal plane; finally it necessitates the constant raising and lowering of the head, thereby introducing a choppy tempo and possibly contributing to fatigue.

Even when engaged in near-point copying, there is another technical aspect to consider: Experience has shown that it is easier to copy when the sample is placed directly above the pupil's work rather than to either side. For maximum support, if the sample is written on a large sheet of paper (i.e., $8\frac{1}{2}'' \times 11''$), fold it so that the model stimulus is placed as close as possible to the pupil's own writing, thereby reducing the amount of eye movement required.

Adding and Subtracting

Since a reciprocal relationship exists between adding and subtracting, many teachers instinctively approach these two processes in a totally symmetrical fashion. In many instances, this helps the child conceptualize the relationship between adding and subtracting, but at other times it can be confusing. For example, a perfectly legitimate way of nurturing the addition facts is to use two sets of materials and to give the child repeated practice in "discovering" (i.e., counting) the answer:

$$+\boxed{\substack{\cdot\ \\ \cdot}}$$

$$\boxed{\substack{\cdot\ \cdot \\ \ \cdot\ \\ \cdot\ \cdot}}$$

7

This works well for addition. However, it is ill-advised to show the two sets in subtraction. If presented with:

$$-\boxed{\substack{\cdot\ \\ \cdot}}$$

and told to "take two away from five," many children (especially learning-disabled ones) will simply remove the bottom set, producing the incorrect answer, five:

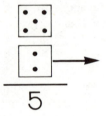

5

A better strategy would be to show the top set only and use the *numeral* for the subtrahend:

$$-\boxed{2}$$

3

(or simply *say* the subtrahend, witholding the visual representation.).

Fractions
In developing the child's concept of fractions, he needs a variety of materials. If we use circular parts (e.g., "pies") to exclusion, the learning-disabled child may not be able to transfer what he has learned regarding circles to other situations: e.g., $\frac{1}{4}$ of

a rectangle, $\frac{3}{4}$ of a square, $\frac{1}{2}$ of a bar of chocolate, $\frac{1}{3}$ of a triangle. Nevertheless, circular parts have a distinct advantage over the other shapes and teachers should take this into consideration. A half of a square, a fourth of a rectangle, an eighth of a cube, and so forth, all look complete. But in the case of a circle, *the part tends toward the whole*. That is, one can look at a half, a fourth, or three-fourths of a circle and immediately envision the entire circle:

Hierarchy of Number Complexity

The teaching of arithmetic is facilitated by teachers becoming more aware of the hierarchical complexity of numbers. For example, in teaching subtraction of two place digits with exchange, an example such as $\begin{array}{r} 82 \\ -\ 29 \end{array}$ is easier than $\begin{array}{r} 47 \\ -\ 28 \end{array}$ because the partial algorism, 12 – 9 is easier than 17 – 8. (If the child doesn't know the answers, he can count from 9 to 12 more readily than he can handle the interval from 8 to 17.) Similarly, in multiplying numbers like $\begin{array}{r} 75 \\ \times\ 3 \end{array}$, teachers should pay close attention to the intermediate algorism of adding the "carried" tens to the original tens:

$$\begin{array}{r} \overset{1}{7}5 \\ \times\ 3 \\ \hline 5 \end{array} \qquad \boxed{21 + 1 = \text{㉒}} \qquad \begin{array}{r} \overset{1}{7}5 \\ \times\ 3 \\ \hline 225 \end{array}$$

In selecting examples, intermediate algorisms involving addition within the decades (e.g., $\begin{array}{r} 72 \\ \times\ 8 \end{array}$ generates 56 + 1) are easier than those requiring exchange (e.g., $\begin{array}{r} 46 \\ \times\ 7 \end{array}$ generates 28 + 4). Even for those within the decade, there is a logical order. For example, $\begin{array}{r} 64 \\ \times\ 6 \end{array}$ generates 36 + 2, which is easier to handle than its commutation, 32 + 6 (generated by $\begin{array}{r} 48 \\ \times\ 8 \end{array}$).

The message, then, is this: Even if teachers have been getting favorable results, and are recognized as competent instructors (perhaps even as learning-disability specialists), they should still maintain an open mind, observe their colleagues' lessons, systematically monitor and evaluate their own teaching techniques, consider alternative approaches. Above all, they must relentlessly ask themselves, "Are there any aspects of this learning task, which can be hindering learning?—and, if so, can I select appropriate measures to counteract them?"

REDUCE ANXIETY

Many learning disabled children suffer from anxiety for a number of reasons (see pages 51-52), and this can seriously affect their academic, social, and emotional growth. Fortunately, the classroom teacher can plan to reduce anxiety in specific ways:

1. Provide pleasurable classroom experiences. Any approach that can make the classroom experience a more pleasurable one is apropros here. Use of humor, games (not just during recreation and physical-education periods, but concomitantly with academics—e.g., card games to develop basic arithmetic facts, "Concentration" in which the child must remember the location of pairs of word cards during a reading lesson, keeping score as a means of motivating arithmetic and handwriting), and activities with a high "relaxation index" (e.g., listening to music, listening to a story the teacher reads, "doing something with your hands" via some simple arts and crafts project) are all recommended. Puppetry can be helpful for many reasons: it allows the child to receive applause, and yet the audience does not stare at him but rather at the puppet; it literally allows him to eliminate his own tensions through the puppet; and it is fun.

2. Choose "failure-free" activities. For example, ask questions in which there are no wrong answers such as, "What season do you like best?" Start below the child's functioning level; have answers readily available.

3. Use formal tests sparingly. Make them untimed if possible, and, for some children, substitute oral tests for written ones.

4. Use short doses of activity. Barsch (1965, pp. 333, 334) has pointed out that a child's attention span is inversely proportional to the anxiety he is experiencing. That is, his attention span is shortened when he is anxious and lengthened when relaxed. Clearly, pushing him beyond his attention limits will serve to increase anxiety, thus igniting and fanning a vicious cycle. Modification is necessary. Instead of handing an entire workbook to the child, it is often wiser to start with a single page and present the remainder in small increments (Gallagher, 1979, p. 109): A short paragraph of silent reading may be more desirable than a whole page: one arithmetic problem on a separate index card is probably better than a page of them; three lines of handwriting, rather than a full page, may be all that a learning-disabled child can handle initially.

5. Avoid clutter. The LD student is often unable to ignore the presence of excessive amounts of instructional materials (papers, books, pencils, rulers, erasers) in or on his desk. He becomes confused, overwhelmed, anxious. Gallagher (1979, p. 111) recommends that materials which are not needed in a given lesson be stored in containers, on bookshelves, or in "in" and "out" trays—all located some distance from the student's desk.

6. Provide visible time clues. LD students frequently are disoriented with respect to time. They find it difficult to remember chronology of events, to judge how much time they will need to complete a task, and to estimate time intervals. Gallagher (1979, p. 49) recommends reducing time-related anxieties by placing a large clock with clear arabic numerals within easy sight of the student. She further suggests posting simple cardboard clocks denoting special time commitments near

Figure 11-1. Alleviating time concerns by use of clock displays.

the real clock to facilitate comparison to the actual time (see Figure 11-1). This is particularly helpful in secondary schools; it is here that LD students encounter the rigid time-adherence demands of departmental programming.

7. Raise self-esteem. A powerful means of reducing anxiety is to try to improve the child's self-concept. If he feels better about himself, he will not be constantly on guard, trying too hard, apologizing profusely (and inappropriately), and so on. In short, he will be more relaxed. Some means by which the teacher can help the child develop a more positive self-concept are:

• Recognize even small signs of growth and convey this to the learning-disabled child. However, praise ought not to be overdone, should be specific rather than general, sincere and never routine, and of course deserved.

• Avoid value judgments. The teacher should refrain from using such terms as "scribbling" or "sloppy" to describe handwriting: rather, emotionally-neutral descriptions such as "uneven" and "dark" are more desirable. Better yet, focusing upon the acceptable portion of the child's penmanship assignment serves the purpose of tactfully and unobtrusively calling the child's attention to his penmanship errors. Instead of telling a learning disabled, impulsive child who interrupts that he is "rude," it is better to tell him that he "forgot the rules."

• Encourage the child to take pride in his appearance. True, caring about one's appearance usually *follows* the development of a positive self-concept, rather than the converse. Nevertheless, if the teacher, through some means (say, behavior-modification techniques) could succeed in effecting this type of change in the child, others would recognize it, accept him more readily, thus enhancing the child's self-concept and thereby reducing anxiety. In other words, a child's concern for his appearance can be the cause—as well as the effect—of favorable self-concept and reduced anxiety.

• Carefully analyze a child's "wrong" answers. An answer can be totally correct but it may not be the one which the teacher had in mind. I (Siegel) once observed a student-teacher's lesson in which the teacher had drawn a large circle on the chalkboard and began eliciting from his pupils the names of the various vowels. Each one would become part of "Mr. Vowel's" face. When this much was completed,

the teacher said, "There's one more. Who knows it?" After some silence, one youngster enthusiastically blurted out, "No. That's the whole thing." The teacher virtually ignored him. Finally, another child said "o," whereupon the teacher completed the face, using an *o* for each ear.

The child who went beyond the pattern and realized that the original circle was an *o*, should have received an abundance of praise, but did not receive any recognition for a perfectly correct—*and creative*—answer.

Obviously, if the child is perfectly right, and the teacher doesn't recognize it, self-pride is diminished. But even in instances where he is only partially correct, or where his reasoning is evident (despite an incorrect response), if the teacher conveys to him that she sees and appreciates the correct portions and/or the child's logic, it makes him feel understood, important, and it takes the sting out of an otherwise wrong answer.

• Develop empathy. Things do not run smoothly in the life of a learning-disabled child. It is difficult to conform, to remember, to learn, to fit in. Because he is not mentally retarded and because he has so many strengths, it is easy for teachers and parents to conclude that "you could do better if only you tried." Often, if the teacher precedes some specific advice with, "I know it's difficult for you to do this, but . . .", the child feels that the teacher is on his side, is not rigidly demanding, is aware of his tribulations, appreciative of his efforts, and is considerate of his problem and of his feelings. Her patience, understanding, and compassion conveys to him that she *respects* him as a person. The latter point is crucial. Cohn (1979, p. 53) warns that "students who feel that others do not respect them are less likely to re-themselves."

Another aspect of empathy is to demonstrate sensitivity to the LD pupil's fragile ego. Because he often requires instructional materials designed for pupils in lower grades, he becomes vulnerable to negative reactions (e.g., jeers, teasing, raised eyebrows) by peers and/or siblings. To prevent this, Gallagher (1979, p. 109) recommends camouflage: Provide a colorful book jacket thereby disguising its grade level; those pupils who feel self-conscious when carrying books to and from school can be encouraged to utilize carriers such as large business envelopes. This is especially significant in the case of secondary students who are still functioning at elementary grade levels.

· Arrange for the learning-disabled child to help others (Siegel, 1969A, p. 55). He might be encouraged to tutor (drill or explain some point to a classmate in some area in which he excels). Time could be set aside for him to help younger children in lower classes by playing with them and reading to them. (It is well known that many learning-disabled children relate better to younger children than to their peers.) This opportunity to help others tends to diminish the learning-disabled child's preoccupation with himself, focuses upon his abilities rather than disabilities, and above all, makes him feel needed and important.

USE A MULTISENSORY APPROACH

There is historical precedence (Montessori, Seguin, Itard) for rendering multisensory training (i.e., educational intervention which uses two or more sense modalities simultaneously) to individuals presenting disorders in learning. The Visual-Auditory-Kinesthetic-Tactile (VAKT) system of Fernald (1943) is, perhaps, the classic illustration of this approach. Other advocates include Orton (1937), Spalding and Spalding, (1957), Gillingham and Stillman (1956), Strauss and Lehtinen (1947), and Cruickshank et al. (1961).

It is believed that a cross-modal approach (rather than relying on single modalities) enhances memory (Chalfant & Flathouse, 1971, p. 283; Bradfield, 1965, p. 370), nurtures attention, and promotes a high degree of understanding (Bradfield, 1965, pp. 369–370), and is necessary for us " in order to get and process the maximum amount of accurate information from the world around us" (Educational Staff, Marianne Frostig Center of Educational Therapy, 1972, Introduction). A basic premise is that the simultaneity of the strong sensory channel(s) collaborating with the weak one assists in the development of the latter, enabling the child to derive a greater degree of meaning through it (Gearheart, 1977, p. 92; Kirk & Kirk, 1971, p. 126).

The reason for espousing this approach for the learning-disabled population is twofold: First, many writers claim that this group is deficient in performing cross-modal tasks (Early et al. 1976–1977, p. 164; Deutsch & Schumer, 1967, p.20; Belmont, Birch & Karp, 1965). Second, multisensory functioning, being a developmental process, is vital in adaptive behavior and in the learning process. Birch and Belmont (1965, p. 135) state "the emergence of complex adaptive functions during childhood is dependent in large part upon the elaboration in development of increasing liaison among the separate sensory systems."

Putting these tenets together, namely that the learning disabled are poor in intersensory integration (and it is precisely this function which is so essential to learning, especially those tasks demanding higher cognitive skills), it is not surprising that the educational principle of using a multisensory approach prevails.

Frostig (Frostig & Horne, 1964, Getman (1962), and many others combine visual training with movement patterns. Glass analysis technique (Glass, 1973) trains reading decoding skills by combining vision and audition (see pages 217-218). In fact, it is safe to say that most classes for learning disabled—whether in public or private schools—utilize a significant amount of multisensory activities.

It is probably best to use this system of remediation judiciously. Some learning-disabled children may not be able to process the multiplicity of stimuli inherent in the multisensory approach; that is, their neurological circuitry is given to overloading (Johnson & Myklebust, 1967, pp. 30-32; Quirós & Schrager, 1978, pp. 79, 82; Kirk & Kirk, 1971, p. 125). Also combining a weak and intact modality may serve to weaken further the deficit area while strengthening the already intact one; thus instead of bringing the weak modality in line with the strong one, it might actually widen the gap (Kirk & Kirk, 1971, p. 126).

In addition, Bryan and Bryan (1978, pp. 175-176) point out that most research investigating cross-modal integration in handicapped learners does not clearly demonstrate that the learning problem reflected an intersensory integration deficit rather than impairment within a modality. Freides (1974) after reviewing the literature, refutes the commonly-held views that intramodal processing is less difficult than intersensory functioning (p. 287).

Notwithstanding this factor of inconclusive evidence, the use of multisensory experiences is widespread throughout education. Interestingly, it is recommended for emotionally-disturbed children, but for different reasons. Whereas learning-disabled children require it in deference to faulty neurology, the emotionally disturbed (as well as the mentally retarded and the disadvantaged) may well benefit from it in terms of heightened attention, motivation, and enrichment (Hewett, 1968; Hewett & Forness, 1974). Finally, in the education of normal children, the principle of providing intersensory experiences is bolstered by a pragmatic factor: In large classes of 30 or more, there is a high possibility—almost a certainty—that some students will function best via the visual channel whereas others will be auditory learners, and still others will prefer their tactile and/or kinesthetic modality. The multisensory approach can offer optimal accommodation for this diversity (Kirk & Kirk, 1971, p. 125).

UTILIZE BOTH WEAK AND STRONG AREAS

It is sometimes felt that a handicapped child should be encouraged to excel in the area in which he is well endowed as a compensation for the inadequate performance in his poorer areas. However, many learning-disabled children do not readily compensate for their deficits; this may be related to the fact that they are *mildly* impaired, and this echelon lives with considerable ambiguity. Strauss & Kephart (1955) emphasize this point in terms of compensatory mechanisms:

One paradoxical fact needs special mention. A major damage involving gross interference with function is frequently less disturbing than a minor damage which interferes only slightly. In the case of a major damage the disturbance is so gross that it is relatively easy to recognize and the individual develops compensatory activities which permit him to operate effectively without the necessity of using the damaged area. If, however, the damage is slight, its effects are not so easily recognized. The result is that a large number of activities are disturbed slightly, so little that the individual cannot recognize the disturbance. He therefore cannot develop the compensating activities which would allow him to operate, because he cannot locate the focal point of the difficulty" (p. 206).

Bateman (1965, p. 236) points out that in instances of severe, *across-the-board* pathology (e.g., autism drastically impairs one's ability to attend, to respond, to communicate, to express and receive affection), treatment must focus on the deficiencies: It must concentrate on speech development and nurturing of interpersonal relations. Yet in instances of severe deficit in a *circumscribed* area (e.g., receptive auditory impairment stemming from severe nerve damage), teaching to the strength (the intact visual modality) is recommended.

The learning-disabled child, being mildly handicapped, is an enigma. Typically, he does not have a crippling pathology (like autism) nor is he severely defective in a *sole* modality—hence, the dilemma of whether to concentrate on his strengths while ignoring his weaknesses, or vice versa.

Rarely do authors take an extreme position. Rather, it is a question of emphasis. Among those stressing a deficit-oriented approach are Strauss and Lehtinen, 1947; Bannatyne, 1978; Hallahan and Cruickshank, 1973; and Wallace and Kauffman, 1973, p. 87. Strauss and Lehtinen, besides advocating specific training in the weak modality, believe in *accommodating* (or *catering to*) the weakness where possible. For example, they recommend motor and manipulative activities during various lessons (e.g., math, spelling) in deference to the learning-disabled child's fascination with moving stimuli and his motor disinhibition (pp. 134, 136-137). Bannatyne (1978, p. 96) claims to "have had considerable success with programs involving an extensive training of those deficit areas known (*from research*) [emphasis added] to be the basic causes of learning disabilities in the vast majority of learning-disabled students." In fact, the whole field of diagnostic-prescriptive teaching is predicated on the principle of unearthing and remediating the internal defective process which causes failure in learning. Larsen (1976, pp. 501-503) points out that those who favor this "process" method believe that: (1) all learning-disabled individuals have an underlying process deficit (e.g., perception, language); (2) these can be identified diagnostically; (3) once identified, these disorders are amenable to training (that is, correcting), and (4) as a result of correcting the process disorder, the child will show improvement in reading, spelling, arithmetic, as well as in listening, thinking, and other areas. Pitfalls in utilizing the learning-disabled child's strong areas indiscriminately include: (1) "Exercising that which he already has and further weakening the deficient function through disuse" (Kirk & Kirk, 1971, p. 126), thereby furthering the gap, and (2) "The day or the task may come when the disability areas can no longer be circumvented or compensated for"

(Bateman, 1965, p. 237). Bateman offers the following example of this: A child with auditory perceptual difficulty, but with strong visual memory, is allowed to begin decoding via the whole-word approach. By the time he reaches fourth grade, too many new words are coming at him, especially in science and social studies, and he can no longer get by on visual memory alone.*

However, many researchers have set forth cogent reasons for emphasizing the child's strengths. Boder (1971, p. 310) believes that stressing intact areas insures success, thus fostering motivation and a positive attitude toward school. Hayes (1979) states that the learning-disabled child needs to view his intact modality as "an asset which can be of constant use," and that emphasizing *ability* rather than *disability* enhances his self-concept (p. 82). Maher (1979, p. 120), in writing about exceptional children in general rather than the learning disabled per se, makes a dramatic plea for the virtual exclusion of deficit training: "Teachers are told to look for the peaks as well as the valleys in individual profiles. What often happens, however, is that the valleys are so low and the weakness so noticeable that we find ourselves spending so much time in remediation that there is very little time left for developing the potential gifts and talents." She believes that stressing the child's talents can nurture career interests and hobbies and heighten self-esteem; she further states (as do many authors) that the impaired area can frequently be improved by working through the areas of strength. Owen, Braggio, and Ellen (1979, p. 326) make no bones about relegating the child's impaired areas to the back room: ". . . a particular clinical teaching strategy is effective only in attenuating the educational handicaps of the learning disabled child if the kind of task selected does not permit the disfunction to come to expression." Sabbatino & Streisguth (1972) provided A Word Form Configuration Training Program (hence, visual perception training) to two groups of learning-disabled children—*visiles* (strong visual perception), and *audiles* (strong auditory perception). The visile group—and not the audiles—made significant gains in reading achievement as well as in visual perception.

In reality it may not be so much a question of which avenue—the intact or the impaired areas—to use, as it is a matter of knowing *when* and *how* to use them. Some authors believe that the strong area should be used at first—that is, at the onset of some new instructional task (Educational Staff of Marianne Frostig Center for Educational Therapy, 1972, Introduction). Bateman (1965, p. 236) regards the strength as a "crutch" (asset) and presents, as an example, a child who has verbal strengths but visual-motor incoordination resulting in difficulty in printing; an astute teacher will initally encourage this child to "talk through" a letter (i.e., to verbalize his movements) as he prints it.

Johnson (1979, p. 8) believes that there should be a balance in the degree given to strengths and weaknesses, but that the impaired areas cannot, and should not, be avoided: The dyslexic child who is auditorially intact must still be instructed to read. The orally-proficient child must also learn to write. Children who are adequate socially only in one-to-one situations must also be instructed in group functions. Very often the weak area can be integrated into various units of instruction

---

* Fortunately, as a child progresses from first to fourth grades, he is better able by virtue of neurological maturity, to handle an auditory (phonics) approach. Moreover, his prior success with sight vocabulary has created a stockpile of words which can now be used as reference points for phonic acquisition.

instead of necessitating specific process remediation (Bannatyne, 1978, p. 96; Johnson, 1979, p. 283). At times the pupil's strengths and weaknesses will be tapped simultaneously. Yet at other times, they may alternate, Johnson (1979, p. 285) cites an example of a child who can grasp the concepts of mathematics but whose visual-motor deficits hinder him in writing. Until his coordination abilities improve, he should receive worksheets requiring him merely to circle a number; a rubber stamp set would enable him to "print" numbers. But in the meantime, his specific incoordination disabilities could be worked on by a clinical teacher.

Siegel (1972) has suggested that, at times, a weakness can be used to advantage: The teacher might be able to use a learning-disabled child's distractibility in directing his attention away from depression or a temper tantrum. Perseveration, though generally thought to be an undesirable trait, might nevertheless be put to good use. Since it signifies drive, the trick is to get the child started in something that he can do, wants to do, and that *we deem beneficial to him*—and he will stick to it. Over-meticulosity is a trait of many learning-disabled children (Strauss & Lehtinen, 1947, p. 25); they try desperately to combat the lack of order in their perceptual world by a superabundance of exactitude. Unable readily to assimilate incoming sensory data into meaningful wholes, systems, patterns, percepts, what they *can* systemitize, they do with a vengance! Hence, it is not unusual for a learning-disabled child to insist that corn flakes be eaten from a special bowl, tell you that he likes red first, blue second, green third, and so on. Some learning-disabled children can name mountain ranges in order, memorize baseball batting averages, recite the list of presidents in chronology. Clearly, all this has vocational implications: clerical, messenger, or shipping-clerk work, and, at higher levels, accountancy, librarian skills and computer programming.

The concensus seems to be that teachers should blend the two, ignoring neither the weaknesses nor the strengths. This moderate point of view gains considerable credibility when we consider that Tarver and Dawson (1978), in examining 15 published studies relating to the interaction between modality preference and efficacy of various methods for teaching reading, found strikingly little correlation either way. That is, neither principle, the deficit-oriented nor the strength-oriented was supported. Batemen (1965, p. 237) makes a good point: "Until research establishes the case more certainly, it seems reasonable to suggest . . . that the primary focus should be on teaching the child to do what he cannot presently do, and that whatever techniques assist in eliciting and strengthening their behaviors should be used."

USE AN EXPERIMENTAL APPROACH

The learning-disabled population is far from a homogenous group (see pages 56–57). The members differ among themselves in types of deficit; severity of impairment; strength-weakness profile; learning style; degree of motivation; attitude toward learning; self-concept; experience and prior learning; degree of anxiety, disorganization, dependency; and other variables. For this reason, one should not expect all of the principles listed here (and in the previous chapter dealing with structure) to apply equally to all learning-disabled children.

Remove excessive stimuli	
Help the child to "slow down"	
Establish routines	Structure
Give little (or no) choice	
Ascertain that the child is paying attention	
Provide the child with cues	
Sequence the instructional task	
Differentiate between teaching and reviewing	
Differentiate between teaching and testing	
Differentiate between teaching and presenting	
Become proficient in technical aspects of the task	Additional principles
Reduce anxiety	
Use a multisensory approach	
Utilize both weak and strong	
Use an experimental approach	

☐ General Principles: recommended for *all* children, but especially needed by the learning disabled

Specific Principles: recommended for *many*—but not all—learning disabled children as well as for some members of other populations

Figure 11-2. A differentiation of general and specific principles for educating the learning disabled.

Then, too, some of the principles were never meant to be used selectively—rather, they apply to *all* teaching-learning situations: For example, *no* child should be subjected to a chaotic, completely unroutinized classroom environment, confronted with confusing, out-of-sequence instruction, frustrated by being asked to perform that which he has not yet been taught, rendered overly-anxious by teachers insensitive to his fragile ego, nor taught by those who themselves are deficient in the very subject areas they are teaching. These principles are universal since they constitute "good teaching," pure and simple—precisely what the learning-disabled child so desperately needs.

Figure 11-2 illustrates all of the principles discussed here, depicting (1) those of special significance to *many* learning-disabled children (as well as to some members of other populations, including some of the nonhandicapped as well), and (2) those applying to *all* children.

The teacher, upon admitting a child who has been diagnosed as learning-disabled to her class, should be aware of all of these guidelines. Adhere to the ones that *all* children require, but experiment (initiate, observe, assess, refine, postpone and, at times, abandon) the others.

REFERENCES

Adelman, H., The not so specific learning disability population. *Exceptional Children*, March, 1971, *37*(7), 528–533.

Bannatyne, A. An interview with Alex Bannatyne. *Academic Therapy* (Profiles), September, 1978, *14*(1), 95–98.

Barsch, R. Six Factors in Learning. In Jerome Hellmuth (Ed.), *Learning Disorders, volume I*. Seattle: Special Child Publications, 1965.

Bateman, B. An educator's view of a diagnostic approach to learning disorders. In Jermone Hellmuth (Ed.), *Learning disorders, volume I*. Seattle: Special Child Publications, 1965.

Belmont, I., Birch, H. G., and Karp, E. The disordering of intersensory and intrasensory integration by brain damage. *Journal of Nervous Mental Disorders*, 1965, *141*, 410–418.

Birch, H. G., and Belmont, L. Auditory-visual integration in brain damaged & normal children. *Developmental Medicine and Child Neurology*, 1965, *7*, 135–144.

Boder, E. Developmental dyslexia: A new approach. In Helmer Myklebust, (Ed.), *Progress in learning disabilities, volume II*. New York: Grune & Stratton, 1971.

Bradfield, O. The teacher at work. In Jerome Hellmuth (Eds.), *Learning disorders, volume I*. Seattle: Special Child Publications, 1965.

Bryan, T. H., and Bryan, J. H. *Understanding learning disabilities, 2nd ed*. Sherman Oaks, Ca.: Alfred Publishing, 1978.

Chalfant, J. E. and Flathouse, V. E. Auditory and visual learning. In Helmer Myklebust (Ed.), *Progress in learning disabilities, volume II*. New York: Grune & Stratton, 1971.

Cohn, M. *Helping your teenage student*. New York: E. P. Dutton, 1979.

Cruickshank, W. M., Bentzen, F. A., Ratzeburg, F. H., and Tannhauser, M. T. *A teaching methodology for brain-injured and hyperactive children*. Syracuse, New York: Syracuse University Press, 1961.

Deutsch, C. P., and Schumer, F. *Brain-damaged children: A modality-oriented exploration of performance*. (Research Project 665 from the Vocational Rehabilitation Administration, Department of Health, Education and Welfare, Washington, D.C.) New York: Institute for Developmental Studies, New York University, 1967.

Early, G. H., Grisson, W. M., Labrentz, E. L., DeFelice, G., and McClain, N. J. Intermodal abilities as predictors of academic achievement. *Academic Therapy*, Winter, 1976–77, XII(2), 163–169.

Educational Staff: Marianne Frostig Center for Educational Therapy, *Visual sequential memory exercises*. Niles, Ill.: Developmental Learning Materials, 1972.

Fernald, G. *Remedial techniques in basic school subjects*. New York: McGraw-Hill, 1943.

Freides, D. Human information processing and sensory modality: Cross-modal functions, information complexity, memory, and deficit. *Psychological Bulletin*, 1974, *81*, 284–310.

Frostig, M., and Horne, D. *The Frostig program for the development of visual perception*. Chicago: Follett, 1964.

Gallagher, P. A. *Teaching students with behavior disorders*, Denver, Col.: Love Publishing, 1979.

Gearheart, B. R. *Learning disabilities: Educational strategies, 2nd ed*. St. Louis: C. V. Mosby, 1977.

Getman, G. N. *How to develop your child's intelligence*. Luverne, Minnesota: The Author, 1962.

Glass, G. *Teaching decoding as separate from reading*. Garden City, N. Y.: Adelphi University Press, 1973.

Gillingham, A., and Stillman, B. *Remedial training for children with specific disability in reading, spelling & penmanship, 5th ed*. Cambridge, Mass.: Educators Publishing Service, 1956.

Hallahan, D. P., and Cruickshank, W. M. *Psychological foundations of learning disabilities*. Englewood Cliffs, N. J.: Prentice-Hall, 1973.

Hayes, M. L. The auditory learner: In *Readings in learning disabilities*. Guillford, Conn: Special Learning Corporation, 1979.

Hewett, F. M. *The emotionally disturbed child in the classroom*. Boston: Allyn & Bacon. 1968.

Hewett, F. M. (with S. R. Forness). *Education of exceptional learners, 2nd ed*. Boston: Allyn & Bacon, 1974.

Johnson, D. J. Clinical teaching of children with learning disabilities. In Edward L. Meyen (Ed.), *Basic readings in the study of exceptional children and youth*. Denver: Love Publishing, 1979.

Johnson, D. J., and Myklebust, H. *Learning disabilities: Educational principles and practices*. New York: Grune & Stratton, 1967.

Kirk, S. A., and Kirk, W. *Psycholinguistic learning disabilities*. Chicago: University of Illinois Press, 1971.

Larsen, S. S. The learning disabilities specialist: Role and responsibilities. *Journal of Learning Disabilities*, October, 1976, *9*(8), 498–508.

Lindsley, O. R., Direct measurement & prosthesis of retarded behavior. *Journal of Education*, October, 1964, *147*(1), 62–81.

Lynn, R. *Learning disabilities: The state of the field 1978*. New York: Social Science Research Council, 1978.

Maher, C. J. Developing multiple talents in exceptional children. *Teaching exceptional children*, Spring, 1979, *11*(3), 120–124.

Newcomer, P. L., and Hammill, D. D. *Psycholinguistics in the school*. Columbus, Ohio: Charles E. Merrill, 1976.

Orton, S. T. *Reading, writing and speech problems in children*. New York: W. N. Norton, 1937.

Owen, J. A., Braggio, J. T., and Ellen, P. Individual diagnosis and remediation of educational handicaps manifested by learning-disabled children. In Edward A. Meyen (Ed.), *Basic readings in the study of exceptional children and youth*. Denver: Love Publishing, 1979.

Payne, J. S., Polloway, E. A., Smith, J. E. Jr., and Payne, R. *Strategies for teaching the mentally retarded*. Columbus, Ohio: Charles E. Merrill, 1977.

Peters, J., Davis, J. S., Goolsby, C. M., Clements, S. D., and Hicks, T. J. *Physician's Handbook: Screening for MBD*. CIBA Medical Horizons, 1973.

Quirós, J. B., and Schrager, O. L. *Neurological fundamentals in learning disabilities*. Novato, Ca.: Academic Therapy Publication, 1978.

Reichstein, J. *Auditory threshold consistency—a basic characteristic for differential diagnosis of children with communication disorders*. Ed. *D*. Dissertation, New York: Teachers College, Columbia University, 1963.

Ross, A. O. Tactual perception of form by the brain-injured. *Journal of Abnormal and Social Psychology*, October, 1954, *49*, 566-572.

Sabatino, D. A. and Streissguth, W. O. Word form configuration training of visual perceptual strengths with learning-disabled children. *Journal of Learning Disabilities*, August–September, 1972, *5*(7), 435–441.

Siegel, E. *The exceptional child grows up*. New York: E. P. Dutton, 1974.

————. The real problem of minimal brain dysfunction. In Doreen Kronick (Ed.), *Learning Disabilities: Its implications to a responsible society*. Chicago: Developmental Learning Materials, 1969.

————. *Special education in the regular classroom*. New York: M. John Day, 1969A.

_____. *Teaching one child*. Freeport, New York: Educational Activities Inc., 1972.

_____. "What did I teach today?" *Journal of Learning Disabilities*, November, 1978, *11*(9), 534–535.

Siegel, E. and Siegel, R. *Creating instructional sequences*. San Rafael, Ca.: Academic Therapy Publications, 1977.

Spalding, R. B. and Spalding, W. T. *The writing road to reading*. New York: Morrow, 1957.

Strauss, A. A., and Kephart, Newell. *Psychopathology and education of the brain-injured child, volume II*. New York: Grune & Stratton, 1955.

Strauss, A. A. and Lehtinen, L. E. *Psychopathology and education of the brain-injured child, volume I*. New York: Grune & Stratton, 1947.

Tarver, S. G. and Dawson, M. W. Modality preference and the teaching of reading: A review. *Journal of Learning Disabilities*, January, 1978, *11*(1), 5-17.

Wallace, G., and Kauffman, M. *Teaching children with learning problems*. Columbus, Ohio: Charles E. Merrill, 1973.

Methods for Teaching Language Arts

12

LANGUAGE DEVELOPMENT

Language development progresses in an orderly fashion and follows a specific pattern. From the babbling stage through single word, two and three word sentences, until the use of complete sentences, the child's speech is expanded without any formal lessons.

The field of psycholinguistics attempts to understand the totality of language processing. According to Chomsky (1957), human beings are born with an innate capacity to learn language. All children, regardless of culture, follow the same pattern, beginning with babbling, which leads to the understanding and generation of new sentences which they may not have heard previously. Because of the complexity of the task of language learning, Chomsky believes that given appropriate developmental and environmental situations, spoken language will emerge, a view somewhat analogous to a child's learning to walk. The human brain is equipped for development of language unless there is physical or mental impairment. Yet, according to Smith, Goodman, and Meredith (1970), if this were so it would not account for differences in the effective use of language among adults as well as children. Additional factors come into play: They posit an alternative view which holds there are ". . . four continuing cycles: increasing experience, increasing conceptualization, increasing communication, and increasing effectiveness in communication" (p. 17).

Marge (1972) believes three major variables affect the language acquisition of children: heredity, maturation, and environment (see Table 12-1), with each of the variables on a continuum from poor to good ". . . with a critical point below which the child's language development is seriously affected" (p. 79).

An understanding of the relationships among the language arts skills is of importance to the teacher of the learning disabled. The language arts skills include the

Table 12-1.   Significant Variables in Language Acquisition

---

1. Heredity
   a. Anatomical and physiological factors
   b. Innate capacity for language learning (assumed)
   c. Intelligence
2. Maturation
   Emergence of "readiness" stages for language acquisition
3. Environment
   a. Adult language used with the child
   b. Child-rearing practices
   c. Peer-group language used with the child

From Michael Marge, "The General Problem of Language Disabilities in Children." In Irwin & Marge (Eds.), *Principles of Childhood Language Disorders*. Englewood Cliffs, N.J.: Prentice-Hall, 1972, p. 79.

receptive aspects of listening and reading and expressive aspects of speaking and written language, including handwriting and spelling. Though these skills are interrelated and interdependent, there is a developmental sequence (see Figure 12-1) in which meaningful experience is the basis for all language development.

According to Myklebust (1954) a child integrates stimuli of various types (auditory, visual, tactual, olfactory, and gustatory) which are associated and become meaningful. Inner language, the language in which one thinks and which provides the basis for the meaning of words, develops from these experiences. "Word meaning must be acquired before words can be used as words" (Johnson & Myklebust, 1967, p. 36). Children with disorders of inner language may have difficulty in acquiring meaning itself. This is considered the most complex and the most difficult learning disability to remediate.

The ability to comprehend the spoken word is dependent upon the development of inner language. Furthermore, the development of both precedes expressive oral language and reading precedes written expression. Though both expressive and receptive abilities mature, with one enhancing the other (feedback), Johnson and Myklebust (1967) consider the receptive to dominate as in the case of the student who has a better receptive vocabulary (listening and reading) than an expressive vocabulary (speaking and writing). However, by the upper elementary and junior high school grades, the reading vocabulary extends beyond the oral vocabulary of daily usage.

In addition to the language arts skills discussed above, language development also can be considered to consist of four aspects:

   a. phonology—the system of speech sounds used to form words; progressing from babbling to imitation to fluency.
   b. morphology—the smallest meaningful units within a language; e.g., tenses, plurals, prefixes, suffixes.

Figure 12-1.   Sequence of language arts skill development.

    c. syntax—the branch of grammar dealing with word order (e.g., we say "the red house," not "the house red") and phrase structure and the transformations of these patterns (e.g., The dog is barking. Is the dog barking?).

    d. semantics—the branch of linguistics dealing with the meaning of words and syntactical patterns; i.e., the placement of words in a sentence in order to generate meaning and understanding within a context.

Although theorists disagree regarding the origins of language skills, all agree that language acquisition can be impeded by intellectual, physical, emotional, or environmental deficits or problems. Many learning-disabled children may not learn language spontaneously the way nonhandicapped children do because they lack either the perceptual ability to utilize language learning situations or because they lack the ability to generalize from the language samples to which they are exposed. "The fact that the child will not be able to take that step independently is what distinguishes him or her from the normal child" (Nygren, 1976, p. 7).

To remediate language disabilities, the teacher must be able to determine the basic problems involved and devise remedial activities to teach each specific subskill. The teacher must know the child's level of communication so that he can be helped to progress.

Nygren recommends that program development for language deficient children should be based on 1) a theoretical model of language acquisition, 2) normal language development, and 3) the type and extent of the handicapping condition. She cautions, however, that differences may exist in the way the nonhandicapped and handicapped learn. The handicapped may or may not progress through the same stages as the normal child, and even if he does, the amount of time needed to progress through a stage may differ.

Although this chapter is divided into units that discuss the remediation techniques for six aspects of the language arts—listening, oral language, reading, handwriting, spelling, and written expression—it does not preclude the use of a "whole-language" approach. All aspects should be integrated. "The challenge is to enthusiastically explore the possibilities of the whole-language approach while remaining sufficiently open-minded to use ideas and techniques from any teaching method. . . ." (Leigh, 1980, p. 69).

LISTENING SKILLS

Listening skills stand at the beginning of the language development hierarchy (see Figure 12-1) and are an important factor in the development of oral language and reading. Kellogg (1971) describes listening as "the first step toward maturity" and as "the process which provides the basic foundation upon which all other language skills develop" (p. 128).

The widespread use of mass media, that is, radio, television, audio tapes, and telephoning, proves that listening is an important skill within our culture. Visits to public schools indicate that listening (to teachers and other students) takes up more than 50% of the school day (Flanders, 1970, p. 101).

Three types of listening can be identified: attentive, appreciative, and background. Attentive listening is needed in order to get directions and information, for learning new things, and to take part in conversation. Often some response is required. One must think about what he hears in order to make judgments, draw inferences, and understand relationships. Appreciative listening requires less concentration than attentive listening. The listener is generally more relaxed and listens for the enjoyment of a story, poem, or music. Background listening occurs when we play the radio while we read, paint, sew, or play. The background music in a store is another example. In a clasroom, several groups of children may work at different things at one time (this is especially true in a resource room). The students must learn to attend to the sounds needed for their particular task and dismiss ambient or background sounds.

Kellogg (1971) identifies different levels of listening: auditory acuity, auditory discrimination, and auditory comprehension, the attentive listening skill discussed earlier. As does Lerner (1976, p. 221), we differentiate between hearing and listening, acuity being part of the hearing process not involving interpretation.

Because listening is a receptive process, it generally is judged by indirect criteria, namely by observing the *expressive* mode, that is, oral language, written expression, or another type of motor performance. The child is told to walk to the door and open it. If he does, it is assumed he listened and understood. However, although he may appear to be reacting appropriately, he may be responding to gestures or the situation itself, for example, the class preparing to leave the room.

Auditory discrimination and perception are emphasized for younger children or older children who perform at a lower developmental level. In general, if the child's oral language—for example, articulation and sound blending—is age-appropriate, it is assumed that auditory discrimination is adequate.

This section concentrates on comprehension, the attentive listening skill. A discussion of auditory discrimination and techniques for training perception can be found in Chapter 10.

In order to provide appropriate intervention, one must know the child's level of functioning. The subskills that generally must be stressed with learning-disabled children are: maintaining attention, following directions, repeating a message, discovering the main idea, relating what is heard to his own experiences, using context cues, differentiating between fact and opinion, making inferences, knowing what is relevant, and so forth.

Listening Tests

Compared to the number of tests available to evaluate a child's reading performance, there are relatively few tests to evaluate listening skills. As Alley and Deschler (1979) point out, researchers have disagreed on the definition of listening, critical factors for listening success, and the ways to measure them. The tests discussed below are used to measure aspects of listening comprehension. A listing of publishers and their addresses can be found in Appendix A and B.

Assessment of Children's Language Comprehension was designed to reveal levels of receptive difficulties in children with language problems. This easy-to-score test was designed for children from ages three to seven. There are four subtests that relate the ability to remember and understand the sequential elements of language input to language development and disorders. The first assesses the child's ability to identify pictorial representations. The subtests evoke single words as well as lengthier stimuli. According to Buros (1978), this test should prove useful to diagnosticians and clinicians.

The Sequential Tests of Educational Progress II (STEP) Listening subtest provides a measure of general listening comprehension for grades 4 through 12. The tester reads aloud different types of material: directions, explanations, narrations, arguments, and so on. The student answers questions about the material that measure comprehension, interpretation, and his ability to evaluate the passage, such as judging mood, recognizing intent, and judging sufficiency of detail. Questions have been raised about the validity of the test. (Does it test listening, or does it in fact measure other traits, such as hearing, intelligence, or aptitude?)

The *Brown-Carlsen Listening Comprehension Test*, developed for use with grades 9 through 13, is considered more appropriate for diagnostic measures than the STEP subtest (Alley and Deshler, 1979). In addition to measuring auditory recall, following directions, recognizing word meanings, and comprehension of lectures, it also measures reasoning and memory span.

The validity of the test (whether or not listening is being tested) has been questioned. Moreover, many of the items are phrased awkwardly in a way in which they are not likely to occur. Alley and Deshler also note that the items are presented in isolation and out of context, which is a more difficult task than when information is presented as part of a contextual framework.

The *Listening Comprehension* subtest of the *Durrell Analysis of Reading Difficulties* uses a series of graded paragraphs standardized for grades 1 through 6. For each grade level, there is one paragraph that increases in length (number of words in the paragraph) and complexity (syntactic level and vocabulary). The paragraphs are from six to eight sentences in length. The questions measure the child's ability to understand information from a verbal presentation.

Though designed as an intelligence test, the *Peabody Picture Vocabulary test* can provide a measure of receptive language development. A series of plates, each containing four drawings, is shown to the child who must choose the drawing that illustrates the stimulus word said by the examiner. No oral response is required. The child can point to the drawing he selects.

In addition to the tests discussed above, Wiig and Semel (1976) suggest evaluating auditory comprehension of paragraphs by using tests for the diagnosis of aphasia, such as the *Boston Diagnostic Aphasia Examination*, and the *Minnesota Test for Differential Diagnosis of Aphasia.*

Educational Interventions

Comprehension of Words. An essential requirement in listening is the development of vocabulary. Certainly, a child's vocabulary repertoire is a function of his experiential background. Hence, trips, visits to museums, nature walks, attending theater, going shopping, and similar activities should be encouraged. Beyond this, specific training activities have proven successful in the growth and expansion of vocabulary:

1. Begin with concrete words and use actual objects.
2. Verbs can be taught when the activity is performed. A simple game of charades can be used to reinforce the meanings.
3. After using real objects and activities, pictures can be introduced.

4. Descriptive words should be taught. Both concrete objects and pictures can be used. Not only synonyms, but also opposites, should be introduced.

5. To develop an understanding of concepts, use different versions of the same thing, e.g., cups of different sizes, colors, and shapes.

6. Categories such as vegetables, clothing, and furniture should be taught. The game, "I went to the store and bought _____" can be played by limiting the purchase to a specific category.

General Listening Comprehension. This skill combines listening with thinking. It is similar to reading comprehension with an auditory rather than a visual input.

1. Read or tell a story to the child. Ask questions about the story. Begin with factual questions that stress memory for detail. Then ask questions requiring the child to draw inferences. At the end of the story, ask the child what may happen next.

2. After reading or telling the child a story, show him pictures and have him put them in the order in which they occurred in the story.

3. Read directions for making something to the child. Have him perform the task by following the directions.

4. Teach the student to use verbal and nonverbal cues. This is especially important in the upper grades. Audio and videotapes can be used to teach identification of nonverbal cues, e.g., inflection of voice, pauses. Verbal cues include "in summary," "as a result," "There are five steps to follow."

5. The teacher can facilitate the student's learning of verbal materials by organizing oral presentations in a logical sequence and using verbal cues.

6. Encourage students to listen for mistakes when the teacher makes a presentation with planned errors.

7. When presenting an oral lesson, be sure there are no distractors on the child's desk and that background noise is at a minimum. As the child gains facility, the child will be able to screen out distractors automatically.

ORAL LANGUAGE

Normal Development

The acquisition of oral language is dependent upon inner language and listening skills and is itself the basis for reading and written language. Evidence exists that oral language develops within a predictable sequence and time frame.

Two basic theories of first (native) language acquisition have been postulated: an empiricist or learning theory based on the work of Skinner and a nativist theory of innate structures based on the work of Chomsky.

In brief, learning theorists believe that the pairing of verbal behavior with rewards, such as a smile, a hug, obtaining the desired object, reinforces the usage. Critics of this model, which is based on an expansion of the principles of operant conditioning, say it cannot account for the rapidity of the acquisition of complex grammars nor the comprehension of syntax.

Those who hold the nativist point of view assume there is an innate system which makes it possible to acquire language and "... provide a schema that is ap-

plied to data so as to determine, in a highly restricted way, the general form and
feature of the grammar that emerges upon presentation of language samples from
the environment" (Taylor and Swinney, 1972, p. 62).

Neither theory accounts for all aspects of language acquisition. A third theory,
a mixture point of view, is suggested by Taylor and Swinney, since such an integration would account for the many aspects of language development.

Oral Language Deficits of the Learning Disabled

The oral language problems of children with learning disabilities are complex and
multifaceted. These children may exhibit problems in language processing as well as
production. In addition, because oral communication is, in large part, a socialization
process, the language disabilities can also be caused by deficits in social perception
(see Chapter 17); for example, the child misinterprets a situation and responds inappropriately. In turn, the language disability can cause problems in socialization;
peers and adults tend to lose patience with children whose conversation is slow, dis-
jointed, or unsuitable. Thus a negative cycle ensues: the learning-disabled child, already deficient in social perception, is denied the vehicle by which he could improve—
namely opportunities to socialize.

Given the definition of learning disabilities currently in use, it is not surprising
to find that among this group language problems are diverse. The nature and degree
of the oral language deficits will vary from child to child. Wiig and Semel (1976)
consider language processing to be affected by "(1) the perception of the sensory
data, (2) linguistic processing . . . and (3) cognitive processing . . ." (pp. 23–24).
The linguistic aspect refers to speech/sound (phonology), word formation (morphology), sentence structure (syntax), and meaning (semantics) levels. Cognitive
processing refers to the use of words and concepts, verbal associations, verbal analogies, cause and effect, redefinition, and so on. In addition to these three areas, performance is also a function of auditory attention, short- and long-term memory,
and feedback.

Children who understand the spoken word but are unable to express themselves using spoken language are considered to have forms of expressive aphasia
(Johnson & Myklebust, 1967).

The oral language problems discussed below are frequently overlooked because
they tend to be subtle and are not totally crippling. They are manifested in the
following ways:

1. Incorrect grammar is used.
2. Words in the wrong order and/or incomplete sentences are found. Some
   learning-disabled children cannot originate correct sentence patterns because they are unable to remember the structure of sentences (Johnson &
   Myklebust, 1967).
3. There is a limited use of language, especially terms that express spatial and
   temporal relationships. They will frequently substitute another word for
   the term needed or they will give a functional definition. The word substitutions are generally of the same semantic and grammatical class as the intended one (Denckla, 1975; Wiig & Semel, 1976). They also may use a
   gesture or a nonsense word, e.g., "gizmo," instead of the word. Children

Table 12-2. Summary of Early Normal Speech and Oral Language Developmental Stages

Age	General Characteristics	Usable Speaking Vocabulary (Number of Words)	Adequate Speech Sound Production
Months			
1–3	Undifferentiated crying. Random vocalizations and cooing.		
4–6	Babbling, specific vocalizations. Verbalizes in response to speech of others. Immediate responses approximate human intonational patterns.		
7–11	Tongue moves with vocalizations (lalling). Vocalizes recognition. Reduplicates sound. Echolalia (automatic repetition of words and phrases).		
12	First word.	1–3	All vowels
18	One-word sentence stage. Well-established jargon. Uses nouns primarily.	18–22	
Years			
2	Two-word sentence stage. Sentences functionally complete. Uses more pronouns and verbs.	270–300	
2.5	Three-word sentence stage. Telegraphic speech.	450	h, w, hw
3	Complete simple-active sentence structure used. Uses sentences to tell stories which are understood by others.	900	p, b, m
3.5	Expanded grammatical forms. Concepts expressed with words. Speech disfluency is typical. Sentence length is 4–5 words.	1,200	t, d, n
4	Excessive verbalizations. Imaginary speech.	1,500	k, g, ng, j
5	Well-developed and complex syntax. Uses more complex forms to tell stories. Uses negation and inflexional form of verbs.	2,000	f, v
6–8	Sophisticated speech. Skilled use of grammatical rules. Learns to read. Acceptable articulation by 8 years for males and females.	2,600+	l, r, y, s, z, sh, ch, zh, th, consonant blends

*From Children with Oral Communication Disabilities, by Forrest M. Hull and Mary E. Hull, in *Exceptional Children in the Schools: Special Education in Transition* (2nd ed.), edited by Lloyd M. Dunn. Copyright 1963, 1973 by Holt, Rinehart & Winston. Reprinted by permission of Holt, Rinehart & Winston.

who can understand words but are unable to retrieve them spontaneously have problems in reauditorization (Johnson & Myklebust, 1967).

4. A small number of prepositional phrases are used.
5. There is a limited repertoire of adjectives and those used tend to be concrete. Subtle differences are rarely described. There is little use of abstract terms.
6. Words may be confused with their opposites, e.g., ". . . told me" instead of ". . . asked me."
7. They frequently repeat a question before attempting to answer it and there is a tendency to echo, vocally or subvocally, what others say. Repeating appears to allow thinking time for processing and interpretation.
8. Responses are delayed. Denckla (1975) found that learning-disabled boys above the age of eight had a longer response time in naming pictures and made more errors than normals of the same ages.
9. They will sometimes answer a question that was not asked instead of the one that was; e.g., "What time did you eat lunch?" "I had hamburgers and fries."
10. In class, they may raise their hands to answer but forget what to say.
11. In conversation, they jump from one topic to another. When telling a story, they frequently ramble on and lose the point (and the audience).

Assessment of Oral Language Performance

Many tests can be used to diagnose and assess oral language performance. Most of these tests require the child to answer with a word when presented with a stimulus. Some representative tests are described below.

The *Oral Vocabulary* subtest of the *Gates-McKillop Reading Diagnostic Test* uses multiple choice, sentence completion to assess vocabulary (ability to define words) of children above the third grade. Grade norms are available from grade 2, third month through grade 12, third month. Wiig and Semel (1976) consider it to be inadequate above the seventh grade since a difference of one raw score can cause a grade score difference of five months.

The *Social Adjustment* subtest of the *Detroit Tests of Learning Aptitude* (DTLA) requires the child to define twenty words that refer to the social environment. The responses are evaluated as to correctness, vagueness, generalizations, examples, explanations, and so forth. Though examples for scoring are included in the manual, scoring can be difficult and/or subjective. The *Likeness and Differences* subtest of the DTLA assesses the ability to define essential characteristics of objects, qualities, and ideas by telling what makes them alike and what makes them different. The examiner names two things (e.g., egg and apple). The student tells how they are alike (e.g., they are both food) and how they are different (e.g., the egg has a shell and the apple has a skin). A four-point scale is used in scoring. The norms from six years, nine months through 19 years are available.

The Auditory Association subtest of the *Illinois Test of Psycholinguistic Ability* (ITPA) requires the child to formulate verbal analogies by completing a sentence given orally, such as "I cut with a saw, I pound with a _____."

The subtest assesses verbal recall and verbal associations. It has been standardized for children from ages two years, four months to ten years, eleven months. Because performance on this subtest has been proven positively correlated with the *Peabody Picture Vocabulary Test* and the *Northwest Syntax Screening Test*, Wiig, Lapointe, and Semel (1975) feel it has predictive value.

The *Northwestern Syntax Screening Test* is used to screen children who may have deficits in grammar. Two parts comprise to the test. In the first part, twenty pairs of items are presented with a plate of four drawings for each pair. The child must point to the correct drawing after the examiner reads the sentence. In part two, there are two drawings on each plate. The examiner reads two sentences depicted by the drawings and asks the child, "What is this picture?" The child is supposed to repeat the sentence read by the examiner. Full credit is also given if the child uses the same grammatical structure and makes no grammatical errors.

Because no reliability data are given, the number of items is limited, and the norm group is small, Salvia and Ysseldyke (1978) suggest the test should be considered experimental.

The *Test of Language Development* (TOLD) is used to identify children who have problems understanding or using spoken language. Administered individually, it measures seven components of spoken language in seven subtests: picture and oral vocabulary, grammatic understanding, sentence imitation, grammatic completion, word articulation, and word discrimination. Language ages and scaled scores are available for children between four and eight years, eleven months. The test was standardized on a random sample of 1,014 children. Validity and reliability was established using normal children. A study analyzing the performance of language-impaired children with that of normal children support the test's validity and reliability when used with language-impaired children (Newcomer & Hammill, 1978).

In addition to using standardized assessments, tapes of a child's language can be made and analyzed. Salvia and Ysseldyke (1978) suggest obtaining a consecutive sample of 50 to 100 sentences, spontaneous or prompted by a stimulus, such as a picture. Informal analysis can determine vocabulary usage, sentence structure, grammar, hesitations, types of adjectives and adverbs, plurals and tenses, and ability to stay on topic. The data derived from examining the child's taped responses, used in conjunction with standardized tests, can guide the teacher in planning appropriate remedial activities.

EDUCATIONAL INTERVENTIONS

Language Programs

Several commercial language programs are available for use with children who have problems in verbal expression. Three programs in general use are described below.

The *DISTAR language* program (Engelmann, Osborn & Engelmann, 1969) was originally developed to teach language skills to disadvantaged preschool children. It is a highly-structured program with lessons taught in a specific sequential fashion. Daily lesson plans are provided. The teacher demonstrates the verbal behavior desired and asks the child to imitate it. Corrective feedback and positive reinforcement follow. The procedure is repeated several times.

Two parts comprise the program. Language I emphasizes familiar objects, prepositions, pronouns, superlatives, same/different, categories, plurals, verbs, tenses, colors, patterns, shapes, if/then, one, none, and comprehension. Language II stresses questioning skills, following instructions, synonyms, antonyms, analogies, classification, definitions, functions, problem solving, vocabulary. A question-answer instruction method is used. Children who have basic language concepts can begin with the second part. The program, which depends on a great deal of drill, has been recommended for primary-school children and older children who exhibit language deficits (Hammill & Bartel, 1975).

The four *Peabody Language Development Kits* revised (Dunn & Smith *et al.* 1981) are recommended for preschool and primary-level children and for older children with language deficits. Each kit contains a variety of materials (hand puppets, pictures, cover the objects, etc.) which can be used to develop and stimulate expressive languages, listening skills, nonverbal communication, as well as other language skills. Each kit contains 150 detailed lesson plans for the teacher and suggestions for followup activities. No reading or writing is required. Active participation by the children is stressed. The program, which appeals to children, is easily implemented.

The *MWM* program (Minskoff, Wiseman, & Minskoff, 1973) provides activities to remediate the psycholinguistic areas tapped by the ITPA: auditory reception, verbal expression,* visual reception, auditory sequential memory,* visual sequential memory, grammatic closure,* auditory closure, visual closure, sound blending, manual expression, auditory association,* and visual association. A wide range of materials is included such as workbooks, tape recordings, puzzles, and blocks. The teacher's manuals describe recommended strategies and activities which are presented sequentially in order of difficulty.

Instructional Activities

The following activities are illustrative of the many types of activities found to be successful in improving the oral language skills of learning-disabled children. They can be modified to meet the needs of children of different maturational, social, and chronological ages and can be used in a less formal manner than the commerical materials.

Problems with word retrieval. As noted earlier, many learning-disabled children with deficits in oral language have problems with word retrieval. As a general principle, the teacher must slow down the rate and amount of input. The student should not be rushed to respond nor rushed when he is making a response. The demands for oral language should be reduced at the onset of remediation and increased gradually. A supportive atmosphere should be provided. Cues must be used to help the child recall words. The teacher must determine which cues are best for individual students, that is, visual cues, a partial sentence, an associated word, the first sound of the word.

Developing vocabulary.

1. Pictures or objects placed in a "surprise" box can be used in many ways. The child chooses and names the objects or the items in the pictures. Different shapes can also be used, e.g., circles, squares, triangles.

* Recommended for oral language deficits.

2. Riddles can help the child become aware of the attributes of an object. The riddle describes the object and the child must name it.

3. The teacher or another child acts out a movement (charades) and the child names the action, e.g., running, eating, skiing.

4. "What Do You Call Them" (Consilia, 1978) is helpful in expanding vocabulary. First child: "I am thinking of pencils, pens, and crayons. What do you call them?" Second child: "I call them things to write with." If the child cannot think of things to categorize, provide them with pictures, e.g., hats, coats, socks. The child names them and asks for the category.

5. The concept of opposites can be nourished in a "Contrary Mary" game. First child, "I am *happy*." Second child: "I am *sad*." If the children cannot think of words, they can select either a word or a picture from a pack of cards that name or illustrate one of a pair of opposites and proceed as above.

6. "Supermarket" or "Department store" can help children learn to categorize. The child tells what items he expects to find in the dairy section, the furniture, or clothing department.

Developing sentence skills.

1. Place several objects or pictures in the "Surprise" box. Have a student take one from the box without showing the others. He should describe the object so that the other children can guess what it is.

2. Provide puppets for free play as well as for group and individual lessons. The children can make their own puppets out of various materials, e.g., paper bags, socks, paper on sticks. Puppet construction also provides opportunities to develop language. The students can describe their puppets, tell the steps used in construction, and dramatize stories or situations.

3. Flannel-board material can also be used to illustrate a story as it is being told or read. Original stories should be encouraged.

4. Show a picture to the student. Ask him to describe what happened before the picture was taken and to project what will happen afterward.

5. Give the child a group of pictures or illustrations that depict a sequence. Have the child put the pictures in the correct order and describe what was happening.

6. Present a basic sentence and help the student change and/or expand it. Several such exercises are suggested by Lerner (1976) and Consilia (1978). The examples below are a few suggestions.
   a. Teacher: I walk to school.
      Changes: I run to school. (change in verb)
                I ride to school. (change in verb)
                The boys walk to school. (change in subject)
                The girls walk to school. (change in subject)
                The boys and girls walk to school. (combining sentences)
                Do boys walk to school? (statement to question)
   b. Continue the exercise by having the child tell *when*:
      I walk to school in the morning.

I walk to school every day.
  c. Have the tense changed.
     I walked to school yesterday.
     I will walk to school next week.
  d. Continue changing subjects, verbs. Have them use other phrases that
     tell *where*:
     I walk to the store.
     I walk to my friend.

7. Consilia (1978, pp. 239–240) recommends "Word substitution for improved sentences." The stimulus is a simple sentence written on the
   board. The children supply new words for the subject, verb, and object.
   Stay on each category until the group has no other terms to use. The
   number of substitutions will vary according to age and ability.

The	*train*	ran	through the town.
	locomotive		
	diesel		
	pullman cars	rolled	
	(etc.)	zipped	
		zoomed	over the new steel bridge
		(etc.)	across the beautiful fields
			(etc.)

Consilia reports that the children find it fun to do and that slower children learn from listening to the others. She recommends it for grade 2
through 12. This can also be made into a written exercise.

8. Give the child a phrase, e.g., "in the desk," and have the child use it in as
   many sentences as he can create.

9. Positional words such as *on*, *in*, and *under* are difficult for some learning-
   disabled children because of their basic deficits in directionality and
   spatial orientation. Give the child a pencil and have him put it in different places in the classroom. Have him describe its location: "The pencil
   is on the desk." "The pencil is under the paper."

10. While reading a story, stop and have the child supply the next word so
    that it fits the sentence and the story. Encourage children to retell stories
    to other children.

11. Have the child explain how he performs familiar tasks, e.g., washing
    hair, frying an egg, peeling a banana.

12. "Twenty Questions" can help the child learn to formulate questions.
    An object or picture of an object is concealed. The child must ask ques-
    tions about the object that can only be answered with either "yes" or
    "no." When the child thinks he has enough information, he guesses the
    name of the object. He can use three guesses but may ask no more than
    twenty questions. This can be beneficial for learning-disabled children,
    since it encourages planning, organization, categorizing, and "narrowing
    down" possibilities rather than impulsively blurting out wild guesses.

13. The following activities adapted from Oral Communication, Grades K-6

(1976), are used to strengthen conversational skills, a deficit area of many learning-disabled children.

a. Have the students practice making introductions. Set the stage and structure the situation; e.g., "A school friend comes to visit you at home. Your mother never met him before, so you will have to introduce them to each other."

b. Play a tape of prerecorded conversations. Have the children discuss the differences between good conversations and poor conversations. Your prepared tapes should include such items as: one person mumbling and the other asking him to repeat himself; several people talking at the same time; one person saying only "aha" or "m-m-m" not really responding to the other person; and two people discussing a topic when a third person interrupts with irrelevant remarks. Be sure one sample is of a "good" conversation.

c. Provide opportunities for practice in speaking on the telephone. Many telephone companies will provide, free of charge, teletrainer equipment. Discuss and then have the child practice conversing. One person may have a prepared dialogue, while the other speaks spontaneously. Some suggested topics are: inviting a friend to a birthday party, taking a message for Mother, calling the fire department to report a fire, calling home for permission to eat dinner at a friend's house.

14. Teach rehearsal strategies. Alley and Deschler (1979) recommend this particularly for adolescents. They suggest four steps: 1) Consider the situation carefully. Determine if what is to be said is based on fact or opinion, on own experience, hearsay, or noted authority. 2) Student should discuss with others what he wants to say and ask for feedback. 3) Based on feedback, modifications should be made. 4) Determine the order of the presentation and rehearse the main points. Alley and Deschler suggest this sequence can be used in informal and formal situations.

The role of teacher questions. The amount and quality of student verbalizations can be influenced by the type of questions the teacher asks: Four types have been classified (Aschner, 1963): 1. *Cognitive-memory* questions require little thinking. Recall of known material is stressed (What was the name of the boy in the story? What did you eat for breakfast?). 2. *Convergent* questions lead to one expected answer and require the child to compare, contrast, see relationships, and draw conclusions (What can we say about all the words in the list? What is the same about bat, bear, and baseball? Why is it important to have a weather report?). 3. *Divergent* questions require the child to develop new ideas in a data-poor situation where there is more than one acceptable answer (What would happen if our country ran out of oil? Suppose there were no schools, how would you learn about the world? What other title can you give the story?). 4. *Evaluative* questions ask the child to make judgments based on specific criteria (What did you enjoy about the trip? Would you rather play for a little while now or have a long play time this afternoon?).

Minskoff (1974) suggests that for children with learning disabilities in verbal expression, cognitive-memory questions should be used at the beginning of training, with the other question types used when his expressive abilities are better established. She stresses the importance of divergent questions because lengthier verbalizations are generated.

Concept formation involves enumerating facts, grouping and categorizing, seeing relationships and making inferences, and labeling and generalizing. ". . . questions should be used in appropriate sequence to enable the students to learn to organize facts into more complex ideas and arrive at generalizations" (Gold, 1979, p. 43).

READING AND READING DISORDERS

Reading has long been acknowledged as a major source of information and pleasure in our society. The knowledge that is gained from reading helps an individual choose and maintain a job, understand the world around him, extend his interests, broaden his goals and spend leisure time enjoyably and productively (an important consideration for so many learning-disabled children who, because of rejection and/or lack of resourcefulness, have significant number of empty hours thrust upon them).

While we can learn and get emotional satisfaction from television, radio, movies, tapes, and listening to others, there are limiting factors. Though much can be presented in this way, these media have a temporal or instantaneous existence. It is difficult to remember accurately everything that is said or, with the exception of tapes, return to the presentation for clarification or renewal of pleasure at our own convenience.

The person who reads gains a degree of independence she will not have if she does not develop this skill. The person who cannot read or reads poorly must rely on others to interpret directions at home and at work and translate the myriad instructions, information, and descriptions found in newspapers, ads, social and business letters, and so on.

As limiting as the factors above seem, perhaps the most devastating is the effect on the self-concept of a poor reader in a reading society. This may well account for emotional overlays in many learning-disabled children.

Bryant (1969) notes that the child who cannot learn by one method is not necessarily a disabled reader if another method is used. However, Bryant also found that a child having difficulty using one method will probably also experience difficulty with others.

Framework for Intervention

To develop an effective intervention for the learning-disabled child, the teacher must know not only how the child learns and what the task requires but also what performance is expected in the regular grades.

Fortunately the recent mushrooming of mainstreaming has encouraged collaboration between regular and special teachers, thereby giving the former more insight regarding special-education approaches while making the latter more aware of the goals of the regular teacher.

Any discussion of remediation of reading disabilities must define "reading." In this text, reading is considered to be divided into two major components: the ability to pronounce the words (decode), and comprehension of words, sentences, and longer selections. Deficits in either of these areas will impede reading ability.

Additional skills can be identified. Those listed below have been categorized as decoding skills, comprehension skills, and study skills, all of which should be included in an integrated reading program. (Study skills, though listed separately, can be considered a subskill of comprehension.) Lack of study skills will not cause a reading disability but will impede satisfactory progress in academic subjects. Further refinement of these skill areas can be made (Ekwall, 1976, pp. 59-61). These skills should be extended and reviewed until they are firmly established by the child. In general, the comprehension and study skills receive the most stress from the intermediate grades through high school. Though decoding skills are usually mastered in the primary grades, this is often a deficit area in the older learning disabled child.

Decoding Skills
 visual perception of letters and sequence of letters
 auditory perception of sounds and words
 grapheme-phoneme correspondence
 phonetic analysis
 structural analysis
 basic sight vocabulary
 configuration cues
 suffixes and prefixes
Comprehension Skills
 understanding a stated fact
 understanding a sequence
 making inferences
 cause and effect
 drawing conclusions
 predicting endings
 noting and remembering details
 following a sequence
 skimming for information
 problem solving
 evaluating validity of information
 appreciating stories, poems, humor
Study Skills
 ability to alphabetize
 use of dictionary: guide word, stress and accent syllables, pronunciation key,
   selecting appropriate meaning
 knowing and using parts of a book: table of contents, index, glossary
 using encyclopedia: index, cross reference
 choosing appropriate reference books
 reading maps, charts, graphs, diagrams, tables
 use of library card index
 using bibliographies
 outlining
 summarizing

A hierarchy of skills has been identified by Wiener and Cromer (1967) and expanded upon by Ross (1976): 1) selective attention, 2) sequential scanning, 3) discrimination, 4) decoding, and 5) comprehension. A problem at any one of the levels will affect the performance of all the higher-level skills.

1. Selective attention—This level in the hierarchy is considered by Ross (1976) to be a major factor in a child's ability to develop adequate reading skills. Many stimuli, internal as well as external, compete for attention and only a finite number can be processed at one time. The individual must not only be able to select those stimuli upon which he wishes to focus but must decide to attend to those that are relevant to the school task at hand. Obviously failure in either will cause the child to experience difficulty in learning to read.

2. Sequential scanning—The second step refers to the learned, systematic eye movements, generally from left to right, required for reading. Research has shown that the development of these scanning strategies is delayed in learning-disabled children. Based on a study that compared nonreading kindergarten children with readers in the third grade, Nodine and Lang (1971) concluded that these strategies developed as a result of cognitive control over eye movements. This facilitates the ability to attend selectively to the reading material.

3. Discrimination—The third level, discrimination learning, is the ability to tell letters apart when shown the visual symbol, e.g., *b* or *d*. Failure to perform this skill will result in misread words which in turn lead to misunderstanding of written material.

4. Decoding—This fourth skill requires the reader to take the visual stimulus and translate it into a verbal equivalent. This is the acquisition of phoneme/grapheme (sound/letter) correspondence, a paired-associate learning task. We separate meaning from decoding because it is possible to mouth (orally decode) words that are not understood. However, decoding is frequently aided by context clues, i.e., the meaning of the rest of the passage helps identify the word in question. This brings us to the last step in the hierarchy.

5. Comprehension—This fifth step is the object of all reading. There are many types of comprehension skills which must be developed, as mentioned earlier (p. 209). In addition to the child's acquiring competency in the four skills listed above, the ability to comprehend written material is also predicted on the facility the child has in oral language and his experiences. The more limited the child's language and experiential background, the more limited the reading comprehension level.

The reading-disabled child is not a single entity. Children falling within this group are varied. There are many degrees, types, and combinations of this disability. A reading disability represents the interaction of several factors: a basic cause (neurological dysfunction): a secondary effect (emotional overlay): a contributing difficulty (decreased motivation); a correlated resultant (the neurological dysfunction also caused poor coordination); incidental factors (home environment); and expectations of performance (of child, family, culture) (Bryant, 1969). All these factors must be considered when developing an intervention strategy.

Dyslexia is a frequently used label for children with a severe and persistent inability to read, although no specific criteria have been developed. The population of children given the label is currently recognized as a heterogeneous group. Johnson and Myklebust (1967) describe two types of dyslexics, auditory and visual. Auditory dyslexics are unable to reauditorize (remembering what has been heard) and visual dyslexics are unable to revisualize (remembering what has been seen). Using a total language evaluation, Quirós (1964) also identified two groups based on auditory and visual processing deficits. Boder (1971) describes three subgroups who exhibit differing reading and spelling patterns. Diagnosis based on identification of such patterns enables ". . . teachers to play a key role in early identification of children in need of remedial teaching" (p. 294).

The first group Boder identifies, dysphonic dyslexia, is similiar to Johnson and Myklebust's auditory dyslexia. The reading pattern shows a limited sight vocabulary, the ability to read words better in context than in isolation, no word attack skills, and inability to decode simple words. The spelling pattern is characterized by an inability to spell phonetically, the addition and/or omission of letters, syllables, or both. The dysphonic dyslexic cannot analyze spoken words into component sounds or syllables. The second group, dysdeidetic dyslexia (Johnson and Myklebust's visual dyslexia) consists of children who read laboriously and have a lower sight vocabulary than those in the first group. Some do not recognize letters until fourth or fifth grade. Those in this group are analytic readers who seem to read by ear. They read phonetically, missing words which have irregular spelling; for example, laugh becomes "lag," bird becomes "by erd," and all letters are sounded (talk becomes "talek"). Spelling is performed phonetically—words that are unfamiliar but phonetic will be spelled correctly while words in their sight vocabulary that are nonphonetic will be spelled incorrectly.

The third group, mixed dysphonic/dyseidetic dyslexia, has problems in both auditory and visual analysis. Because these children have no area of strength, they are the most difficult to teach. They are unable to spell and show marked confusions in reading and writing.

According to Boder, one of the three patterns is consistent in all severely retarded readers who have been labelled dyslexic. In addition, she says that none of the patterns are found in children who read at or above grade level. Her study also found a high correlation of similar patterns in other family members, suggesting the possibility of a genetic basis.

The screening process can be done by teachers and other members of the multidisciplinary team. The pattern of errors reflects the specific deficit. "In the milder and transient forms, developmental dyslexia may represent a normal variation in psychoneurological maturation, e.g., a maturational lag in reading readiness" (p. 315).

Prognosis appears to be more favorable for groups one and two. Most of the children Boder studied were in group one, dysphonic dyslexia. The reading ability in that group tends to approach normal as sight vocabulary increases, though spelling tends to remain poor. Those in group two generally remain slow, laborious readers. Their spelling, however, shows more improvement than group one.

Diagnostic Reading Tests

Many diagnostic reading tests are used in evaluating the reading performance of learning-disabled students. Those discussed below differ in their approaches and the behaviors they sample. We include them because they represent tests that are frequently part of the diagnostic batteries administered in learning-disabilities clinics and the schools and because we believe the teacher, as a consumer of test data as well as test administrator, must know the reliability, validity, and limitations of the tests. Since most tests do have limitations—for example, errors that reflect limited experience rather than reading difficulty—the teacher should select instruments that seem to have minor drawbacks or that, when used with other diagnostic techniques and teacher observation, can provide the information needed to develop an appropriate instruction program.

Individual tests. Though time-consuming to give, individual tests do provide the teacher the opportunity to observe the student as he performs the tasks, thereby providing much more information than his recorded answers. Such tests also allow the measurement of oral reading as well as silent reading.

The *Botel Reading Inventory* consists of four subtests: word recognition, word opposites, reading and listening, and a phonics-mastery test. Word recognition, for pre-primer to fourth grade, consists of 20 words in eight reading levels. The test begins with a level at which the child is likely to know all the words. He continues reading the words until he falls below 70% on two successive levels. The last level is considered the instructional level. The word-opposites tests consist of ten levels from first grade to high school. The child must find the opposite of a stimulus word from among four choices. The test is administered orally as a measure of word-opposite listening. Developed for grades one through four, the phonics mastery test requires the child to listen to words and then write initial sounds, consonant blends, consonant diagraphs, words that rhyme, indicate short- and long-vowel sounds, and circle the number of syllables heard in the words read to him. Before giving the phonics mastery subtest to fourth graders, they are asked to pronounce nonsense words using the phonetic spelling and accents which are given. If the child performs well, the phonics mastery test is not given.

Two forms of the test are available. Both are quickly administered and easy to score. Because no norms or data concerning validity or reliability are given, Spache (1976) questions the use of the test battery. "The inventory may be a measure of some facets of reading, but the author has not yet demonstrated this fact" (p. 154). Ekwall (1976), however, suggests the administrations of the Botel nonsense words as a quick way to screen out children who have adequate word attack skills.

The *Durrell Analysis of Reading Difficulty* for ages six to eleven consists of several subtests that measure recall for: oral and silent reading; listening comprehension, visual recognition of letters and words; ability to sound letters; blends; and spelling.

According to Heilman (1967), this test has several limitations: there is only one form; the norms are based on rate only; and the comprehension questions mainly stress recall of detail. In scoring, any hesitations or repetition of a word is counted as an error. Harris and Smith (1972) believe that such factors should only be considered as errors if they interfere with the meaning of the passage.

Spache considers the supplementary test of letter-naming to have little value since the names of the letters are not part of reading. He also says that apart from correlations of validity found for the oral reading (.90–.92) and the words lists subtests (.92–.96), no other reliability or validity data are available.

If, rather than using the scores, the test data are analyzed qualitatively, the test can be useful in gaining information about the child's reading problems (Salvia & Ysseldyke, 1978).

The *Gilmore Oral Reading Test* is a short, easily-administered test used to evaluate three aspects of oral reading: comprehension, rate, and accuracy of oral reading. Two forms are available. In order to make the test similar to reading a story, each form is composed of 10 paragraphs describing different episodes in the life of a family.

In scoring, omissions or additions of one or more letters, errors on vowels or consonants, and wrong accent are considered to be mispronunciations. Errors in omissions and additions relate to whole words only. Hesitations of two or more seconds and failure to observe punctuations are also counted as errors, although the scoring of hesitations has been found difficult to do (Spache, 1976). Credit is given for comprehension of scorable paragraphs with additional credit for comprehension of paragraphs above the attempted level. Self-correction is also considered an error. Separate scores (grades and stanine) are derived for each area measured. Buros (1978) questions the procedure of equal weight being given in scoring to all errors, regardless of type.

The *Peabody Individual Achievement Test* (PIAT) consists of five subtests, two of which are in reading: Reading Recognition and Reading Comprehension. The subscores as well as the total score can be converted to grade and age scores, percentile ranks, and standard scores.

The recognition subtest is basically a measure of sight vocabulary. The comprehension subtest consists of single sentences presented one at a time. After reading each sentence silently, the child is shown a new plate and must choose one of four pictures that represents the meaning of the sentence. No writing is required. While this subtest indicates understanding of single sentences, the author does not offer any data to indicate that this skill relates to the sustained silent reading which is usually performed in school.

No validity data are available in the manual. The reliability coefficients adequate in the lower grades, especially for the recognition subtest, tend to decrease with grade level. More studies are needed "before the PIAT can be accepted as a valid test" (Buros, 1978, p. 19).

The purpose of the *Slingerland Test of Specific Language Disability* according to the developer is to identify children who have perceptual-motor deficits which may interfere with the acquisition of reading, writing, and spelling, and to determine modality strengths and weaknesses (Slingerland, 1970). Information on modality preference is to be used when selecting reading methods and materials.

There are four sets of tests for grades one through five and a prereading screening test. Each test has eight group subtests which examine the same areas. A ninth subtest is optional, to be given if performance on subtests six through eight is poor.

The scoring of some items is difficult. The manual includes suggestions for interpreting the scores, though no validity or reliability data are available. The manual suggests that the child's performance be compared with peers in the school or the district. The value of the test is that it uses school-related tasks and it can be administered to a group.

Subtest	Performance
1	Far-point copying from a wall chart.
2	Near-point copying from a page in the test booklet.
3	Visual perception-memory of words, letters, numbers (recall). No writing is required.
4	Visual matching of words from among groups of words on a page.
5	Visual perception/memory (writing from memory) after exposure on a card.
6	Auditory perception and memory. Groups of letters, numbers and words are dictated to be written on test page.
7	Auditory discrimination of single sounds within whole words (initial and final sounds).
8	Auditory perceptual memory of words, numbers and letter groups in association with visual patterns. A word, letter or number group is dictated and must be located from among several in the test page.
9	Word repetition, sentence completion, retelling a story.

The *Wide Range Achievement Test* (WRAT) is made up of three subtests: word recognition, spelling, and mathematics. The mathematics subtest is discussed in the next chapter.

The reading test is composed of two levels. If under twelve years of age, the child begins with Level I. This level requires the child to write his name, name two letters in it, and name 13 capital letters. If the last task is not completed successfully, the child is asked to match capitals. The child must also read a list of words aloud. Those on Level II read the words asked for at that level. The word items correct are those pronounced correctly according to the key given.

A correlation of .91 between the Gilmore Oral Reading Test accuracy score and the WRAT is reported by Gilmore (1965). This tends to support the belief that the test measures a narrow aspect of the reading process, "... a skill that is highly relevant to ordinary reading performances only at primary levels" (Spache, 1976, p. 193). The scores on the WRAT tend to be high in many cases and have limited use.

Informal testing procedures. The informal testing procedures introduced here can be used to estimate the instructional level and to isolate specific deficits. They require little special training for administration and interpretation. The child is usually at ease because he is not in a formal testing situation and he knows the tester. These procedures are also helpful inasmuch as they can be used at frequent intervals to provide information regarding the student's progress.

The *Cloze Procedure*, an informal test of reading level and comprehension, involves the reading of passages of from 250–275 words in length in which words are systematically deleted, usually every fifth word. The child writes in the missing word. Spache (1976) suggests that different types of deletions can measure different aspects of reading; that is, every fifth or tenth deletion of words (excluding nouns) measures detailed comprehension while deleting every fifth or tenth noun tends to measure understanding of ideas.

In scoring, the correct responses are recorded as a percentage of the total responses required. Usually only the exact word is counted as correct. The child is considered at an independent level if he scores 61% or more, at the instructional level if the score is between 60% and 41%. Lower scores indicate the frustration level (Rankin & Culhane, 1969). The procedure is considered inappropriate for children below a fourth grade reading level (Guszak, 1972). Besides obtaining a reading and comprehension level, the test can be used diagnostically to determine patterns of error. The procedure can also be used as a teaching device; for example, discuss why one answer is preferred to another. It is also helpful in selecting graded materials for students.

The *Informal Reading Inventory* (IRI) is administered by the teacher to determine the level at which the child is reading and to aid in the selection of materials. Passages of approximately 100–200 words are selected from different levels of a graded series of readers. The child is asked to read each selection aloud and answer comprehension questions. The comprehension questions should include a variety of types, such as cognitive-memory, convergent, divergent, and evaluative, and elicit levels of thinking based on Bloom's taxonomy (1956), that is, knowledge, comprehension, application, analysis, synthesis, and evaluation. Guidelines for constructing questions can be found in Valmont's article, "Creating Questions for Informal Reading Inventories" (1972).

Three levels of functioning can be determined: independent, instructional, and frustration. A child is considered to be at the independent level if the oral reading is well phrased and comprehension is at least 90%. At the instructional level, the comprehension score should be at least 75% with no more than one error out of 20 words in word recognition. When comprehension is 50% or less and there are many errors in word recognition, possibly coupled with signs of nervousness or tenseness, the child is at the frustration level. To gain the most information from the inventory, a qualitative analysis must also be made to determine the types and patterns of error. Gonzales (1975) found that while rereading of the passages lowers the number of errors, the pattern of errors remains the same.

Because the information gained from an Informal Reading Inventory depends upon the teacher's skill in constructing it and because development of a good inventory is time-consuming for individual teachers, several specialists have published materials that can be used for the same purpose (Hollander and Reisman, 1970; Sivaroli, 1973, Woods and Moe, 1981).

Miscue analysis is a qualitative, systematic analysis of oral reading errors (Goodman, 1965). According to Goodman, the errors or miscues the child makes provide information about the child's skill in reasoning and decoding, and his language pattern. To Goodman reading is a selective, anticipatory process. Readers use three types of information: graphic input, syntactic structure, and semantic interpretation. The less skillful reader relies more on graphic input and his errors affect meaning. Syntactic structure and semantic interpretation are utilized more by the skillful readers. The errors these readers make do not tend to change meaning. Yetta Goodman (1970) stresses the need to analyze, rather than just count, the number of errors a child makes. By analyzing the miscues, the teacher can better determine the mental processes the child is using to perform the task of reading. The type of errors made in oral reading rather than the number relates to comprehension.

The *Reading Miscue Inventory* (Goodman and Burke, 1972) can be a major aid in analyzing the child's miscues. Among the factors examined in this analysis are: dialect, intonation, graphic similarity, sound similarity, grammatical function, correction, grammatic acceptability, semantic acceptability, meaning change, comprehension, and grammatical relationships.

An additional procedure to determine comprehension is to have the child retell the story he read orally. Credit is given for plot, theme, specifics, generalization, major concepts, character analysis, and events.

The Inventory should be used with other assessments. According to Buros (1978), much of the scoring is subjective and it lacks standardized directions and specific criteria for cut-off points.

Reading Programs and Materials

The literature generally suggests that reading-disabled students require unique programs in order to learn to read. The programs described in this section were designed, in general, to teach beginning reading skills, and stress "breaking the code." The teacher must become aware of the limitations of each of these methods for specific children. Most were developed primarily for the elementary school age child, however, many are applicable for the secondary-level student.

Though the reading problems of the older student may be similar to the younger learning disabled child (Gillespie and Sitko, 1978), their problems have continued over a longer period of time, spilling over into other academic areas. Furthermore, a strong emotional overlay caused by years of frustration results in a lack of motivation. Indeed, only the rare reading-disabled adolescent would approach the task with any enthusiasm.

Several cautions must be exercised in selecting programs for the older child. The interest level must be high. The materials should relate to the student's current needs and interests. Comprehension, rather than word recognition, should be stressed. The format of the material and the physical appearance should appeal to an older child.

In addition to the specialized reading approaches, the other, more traditional reading programs—such as basal series and language experience, which were developed to meet the needs of the general school population—can be modified for the learning-disabled student. Frequently the specialized reading programs can be used in conjunction with the other approaches. This is especially feasible in a mainstreaming situation.

Distar. The Distar program (Engelmann & Bruner, 1969) was designed to teach reading to disadvantaged children. The program uses a behavioral approach and follows a detailed, structured format stressing immediate correction and reinforcement. Distar, designed to be used with small groups, concentrates on sequencing, left-right progression, sound-symbol association, and blending. Some of the symbols used differ from traditional orthography in order to reduce visual confusion. These differences are gradually faded out.

The program is presented in two levels and is expected to take two years to complete. Both levels contain a detailed teacher's guide, skill books, and materials to be used at home daily to reinforce the concepts learned in school.

The Distar developers believe all children should progress through the same steps in learning to read with only a difference in pace. Research is needed in order to determine the effectiveness of this program with learning-disabled children.

Fernald method. Developed as a remedial technique for students who did not learn to read, the Fernald method is a multisensory approach using visual, auditory, tactual, and kinesthetic inputs. As described by Fernald:

> The essentials of our technique consists of (1) the discovery of some means by which the child can learn to write words correctly, (2) the motivating of such writing, (3) the reading by the child of the printed copy of what he has written, (4) extensive reading of materials other than own compositions." (1943, p. 33)

In a truly individualized approach, the child chooses the word he wishes to learn. The teacher writes the word on a card with crayon, generally using large cursive writing, although manuscript writing can also be used. The child traces the word as he says it, then writes it without looking. He then checks it with the original. This sequence is repeated until the child can reproduce the word from memory. As the child builds up a vocabulary, the word cards are filed in alphabetical order. When the child has several words, he is encouraged to use them to write stories. If he needs additional words for his story, the teacher writes them. The child uses the same procedures to learn the new words. Fernald stresses four points. 1.) finger contact in tracing; 2.) when writing a word, the copy should not be seen; 3.) all words must be written as a unit. If an error is made, the whole word must be rewritten; 4.) the words must be meaningful to the child.

In the second stage, after the child has built up a large number of words, he should be able to eliminate the tracing of the word but continue the other steps, write his stories, and maintain the word file. During the third stage, the child looks at the word, pronounces it, and writes it from memory. He is now ready to read books. The Fernald method does not teach phonics directly. The child learns to read new words by comparing them with familiar words. Because the stress is on the *child's* reading, he is not read to by *teachers or parents* until he can read by himself. The success-oriented method uses immediate feedback.

Glass analysis for decoding only. As the title indicates, Glass Analysis is used to develop one aspect of reading: decoding. The method, a perceptual-conditioning approach, is based on the theory that "decoding is primarily a visual perceptual process that extracts from the whole word those clusters which are formed from contiguous letters within whole words" (Glass, 1977, p. 7). It deals with the complexity of the structure of words and not their meaning.

The method utilizes a behavioral approach. The objectives are defined in behavioral terms and there is immediate reinforcement on a predetermined schedule. A stimulus-response bond is developed so that the student is conditioned to form visual and auditory responses to the structures in the word. The material is contained in two sets, each of which contains 30 booklets. Sixty clusters are introduced in Set I and 59 additional clusters are found in Set II. The words for each cluster are introduced "in order of apparant difficulty" (Glass, 1976, p. 1). The teacher is encouraged to modify the order of presentation according to the needs of the students. Because the stress is on decoding, Glass says the words used need not be words familiar to the students. Any word that is appropriate from a visual or auditory point of view can be introduced.

Glass (1976) stresses that the goal of the system is to develop conditioning for the letter clusters, not to build a sight vocabulary. To insure transfer, Miccinati (1981) recommends oral reading immediately after a training session and at intervals during the day.

Neurological impress method. The Neurological Impress Method (NIM) has been described as another approach to teaching reading-disabled youngsters (Heckelman, 1969; Langford, Slade & Barnett 1974; Lerner, 1976). The student and teacher sit close together and read a selection in unison, the teacher speaking directly into the child's ear.* The reading is done at a rapid pace while either the teacher or student points to the words as they are read. There is no introduction to the selection. Theoretically, the auditory feedback from the student's voice coupled with the voice of someone else reading the same passages reinforces the learning. Hollingsworth (1970), using a tape-recorded variation, and Lorenz and Vockell (1979) found no difference between those using NIM and those who did not. However, Lorenz and Vockell report that the teachers taking part in their study noted some positive results: an improved attitude toward reading, better fluency in oral reading, and improvement in left-right progression and visual tracking. "... it should be noted that these positive results are subjective opinions, not the outcome of an impartial, objective analysis" (p. 422). Thus, until the effectiveness of this method is clearly established, it should be used cautiously.

Orton Gillingham approach. Based on Samuel T. Orton's work, Gillingham and Stillman (1966) developed a remedial program emphasizing phonics and focusing on reading, spelling, and handwriting.

The method uses a multisensory approach and follows a highly-structured sequence. It stresses the association of visual symbol with the letter name** and sound. At the beginning, individual letters and sounds are taught using phonetic drill cards. When these have been learned, the child is taught to write the letters. The child says the letter and the sound as he traces it. The letter is written from memory. Then the child writes the letter after the teacher gives the sound. Several consonants are taught and then the short-vowel sounds. The single sounds can then be blended into words which are also traced and written. The child builds up word cards he puts into his "jewel box." Additional letters, then words, and phrases are taught in the same manner. When the child has many words, he uses them to build his own sentences and stories. Outside reading is delayed until almost the end of the program.

Material included in the remedial kit are: phonics drill cards for reading, spelling, and writing, graded stories, and exercises on syllabification and the use of the dictionary.

* This is similar to "shadow" reading described by Frostig and Maslow (1973, p. 13). Here, too, the teacher reads with the child. The teacher fades her voice when the child reads with confidence but increases volume and maintains the pace if the child falters.

** The letter name is taught because "... the letter *name* must also be available for the child to use in oral spelling ..." (Orton, 1937, p. 160), and not to improve facility in reading.

This method appears appropriate for children who have visual processing and memory deficits because of the emphasis on phonics. However, because of the simultaneous use of the auditory, visual, kinesthetic, and tactile modalities, care must be taken to select children who can also tolerate several modality inputs at the same time.

Peabody Rebus reading program. The Peabody Rebus Reading Program (Woodcock & Clark, 1969) uses rebuses (a picture or symbol) in place of printed words. It is based on the belief that the bridge between the spoken word and the written word is more easily made when the child begins to read using a vocabulary of rebuses rather than printed words. An initial reading approach, the programmed reading materials allow the child to proceed at his own pace through the program. A special answer-marking system is used. The child chooses a response in each frame. He applies water to his answer, which turns green if correct and red if wrong.

The rebuses are gradually faded out as words are introduced in the five workbooks which comprise the program. Supplementary materials (rebus and sentence cards, answer strips, and review masks) are available for use with Books One and Two. Sentences as well as individual words are taught. At the completion of the program (end of Book Five), over one hundred words have been introduced.

The novelty of the material may make it an effective introductory approach for some learning-disabled children.

Sullivan programmed readers. The Sullivan Programmed Readers (Buchannon & Sullivan, 1963) were developed for grades 1-6. They utilize a linear-program format in which discrete units of reading skills are presented one at a time in a precise order regardless of the child's responses (a branching program sends a child along alternative steps depending on the answer).

The child must learn the letter names and how to print letters before the materials are used. The program follows a linguistic approach. Single-letter sounds are introduced and combined with sounds learned earlier. Short vowel and consonant sounds are taught first. In addition, some sight words are presented (*the, is*) so that sentences can be used. The program emphasizes the visual modality.

The child can proceed at his own pace with little direction from the teacher since self-marking sheets are available for immediate feedback. However, this can result in problems because a child may use the answer sheet to complete the blanks rather than trying to answer on his own and then correcting his work. Additional disadvantages are suggested by Gillespie and Johnson (1974). "... the material is not highly motivating or interesting to all children; children frequently obtain the correct answers without understanding the reason for them" (p. 212).

Words in color. This approach, introduced by Caleb Gattegno (1962), the developer of cuisinaire rods, uses color cues in addition to auditory, visual, and kinesthetic modalities. Each phoneme, no matter what the spelling, is printed in a different color on large wall charts (e.g., the letters in italics are all colored green: t*a*ble, th*ey*, s*ay*, gr*ea*t, fr*eigh*t). Colored chalk can be used in writing on the board. All other printed materials are in black and white so that the child does not only rely on color cues.

A specific sequence is used. Only the sound, not the letter name, is used. Short-vowel sounds are introduced first. The teacher introduces the phoneme from the chart, then says it, and writes it on the board. Next the children say the sound and write it in their notebooks. After the short vowels are mastered (the children can write them from dictation and say the sounds when they are shown the letter), several consonants are introduced. The consonants are always shown with a vowel, such as *pa*, *ap*, *ip*, *it*, *tap*, *pit*. This eliminates the aspirant that is heard when a consonant is introduced alone (*puh*, *tuh*) and makes blending more natural.

Much drill is used to develop automatic oral and written responses. Several word games are introduced. As the child learns to decode new words, he begins to write and read simple sentences. The beginning materials resemble stories found in linguistic readers. In order to force decoding rather than guessing, the books contain no pictures or illustrations.

Words in Color is not a total approach to reading. It is a method used to teach decoding skills.

The research concerning the efficacy of the method is equivocal. Some studies found the method improves reading scores (Hinds, 1966; Dodds, 1966), while others find no difference between the performance of groups that used Words in Color and those that did not (Kauffman, 1972; Lockmiller & Di Nello, 1970).

General Strategies for Teaching Reading

The following suggestions relate to the beginning stage of reading, decoding, and word-recognition skills. They are not meant to be exhaustive but illustrative of the types of activities that can be fostered regardless of the reading method used.

1. Teacher-made bingo and matching games can be used to reinforce grapheme/phoneme correspondence, sight vocabulary, rhyming words, and so on.

Weiss and Weiss (1979) describe a modification of the game, concentration to reinforce sight words. Word cards are turned face down and the child selects two cards and says the word or word part. If they are the same (makes a pair), he keeps them and has another turn. If not, they are turned over and the next child continues the game. Limit each deck to between ten and fifteen pairs so that the game is not confusing with too many cards. Two-syllable word cards can also be paired, for example, | mis | | ter |; and | ta | | ble |; as can compound words: | news | | paper |; | chalk | | board |.

2. For the child who has difficulty focusing on words in sequence, or who is easily distracted, a slotted card can help keep his place. The upright part of the card is moved along to the right until it is at the end of a word or phrase. Thus words are exposed in the correct sequence.

3. The Language Master can be used for simultaneous auditory/visual presentation. Commercially-prepared cards are available or the teacher can design and record cards with letters, letter names and/or sounds, words, or sentences to meet a specific child's needs.

4. If visual tracking is erratic, teach the child to move his finger across the line of print in a smooth pattern without stopping and pointing at each word. The child who points word by word tends to read word-by-word rather than in meaningful phrases.

5. Anagrams and word and letter-cube games can be used to build vocabulary and sentences.

6. Slotted cards with letter and word or cluster strips can be used for reinforcement. They are simple to construct and use. The word that appears in the slots is to be read. Either strip can be moved to make new words.

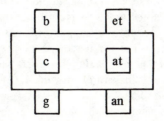

7. Prepared phrase cards can be used to help the child perceive phrases and groups of words rather than individual words. The phrase cards can then be used tachistoscopically, speeding up the presentations as more fluency is developed.

8. In general, oral reading should be on the independent reading level with time to prepare (prereading). Some older children who read fluently only on a low level may be asked to read to younger children. This can be a reinforcing activity and build up the child's self-concept.

Most reading programs suggested for learning-disabled children with reading deficits emphasize beginning reading skills. However, most LD children, whether or not they have difficulties in the initial stages (decoding and word recognition), have deficits in comprehension which may not become apparent until the upper grades. The importance of developing comprehension skills cannot be overemphasized. The activities discussed below have proven helpful in nurturing these skills.

1. Choose reading material whose topics are familiar and interesting for the pupil (e.g., reading the driving manual is very reinforcing for adolescents).

2. Structure silent reading by giving questions concerning the selection prior to the child's reading. Have the child read short passages first, gradually increasing the length. The pupil should read to answer the questions, *who? what? where? when? why? how?* Factual questions should precede inference. Using multiple-choice questions at first is more supportive than other types (e.g., true-false, sentence completion) since recognition is easier than recall. Some children may benefit initially by being given a choice of only two answers instead of the customary three or four.

3. Encourage the pupil to tell what he thinks happened after the story ended. He should be able to support his ideas from within the story.

4. To develop the skill of following a sequence, provide sentence strips with events or instructions in scrambled order and have the child assemble them in the correct sequence. If strips are numbered correctly on the back, the child can correct his own work by checking the number. Have the child read and follow directions to complete a model car or airplane, fold paper, or go on a treasure hunt. The driver's manual can also be used to stress sequence.

5. Do not teach reading in isolation. Show its relevance in and out of school. Many learning-disabled children think we read from 9:30 to 10:45 a.m. and nothing else is reading. Teach reading in the content areas. Introduce the vocabulary of the other academic areas. Material in the science books can be used to teach sequence and help the child learn to draw conclusions from the facts presented. The material in the social studies books can be used to find the main idea, understand relationships, and draw conclusions.

6. Many comprehension activities require children to answer questions based on written materials. To inhibit guessing, a simple technique has been suggested by Siegel (1972). The pupil is instructed to place the number of the question in the margin next to the part of the text that supports the answer.

7. Use a variety of material for reading. Newspapers and magazines provide high interest. Many children enjoy reading the sports pages. Have the children keep a list of all the ways wins and losses are reported; e.g., Mets *upset* Phillies; Dodgers *beat* Yanks; Giants *overcome* Jets.

8. Crossword puzzles can be used to increase vocabulary and understanding of synonyms and antonyms.

9. To develop study skills, teach outlining. Practice in selecting the best title for a story or paragraph or writing their own titles helps to develop an understanding of the main idea. Outlining is an important prerequisite for developing skills in notetaking, a process in which many learning disabled high school and college students are deficient.

10. The SQ3R method (Survey, Question, Read, Recall, Review) can be introduced to develop good study habits. The survey (S) is a rapid overview of the material, that is, introduction, first sentence in each paragraph, any visual aids (e.g., maps, graphs, pictures). The question (Q) consists of converting each subtitle or initial sentence of each paragraph into a question. The remaining portion (3R) denotes Reading the material to find the answers to the questions; Recall by answering the questions and summarizing each sub-section of the selection; and Review by writing the major ideas found in the selection. Harris and Smith (1972) caution that students frequently find the activities redundant and suggest some of the activities can be used with groups and under teacher direction until the strategy becomes "part of the child's skills due to repeated exposure to the model" (p. 428).

11. Reinforce correct responses and completion of work. It is better to give short assignments which can be accomplished and gradually increase the length and complexity.

12. The language experience/cloze technique has been found to be a useful procedure for developing comprehension skills (Lopardo, 1975). A language sample, written or dictated by the child, is typed and kept as a model. A cloze passage is prepared with every fifth word deleted. The passage is completed by the child and compared with the original sample. Differences are then discussed by the child and teacher. Lopardo cautions that not all language samples lend themselves to this technique and should be chosen judiciously.

HANDWRITING

Three main types of writing disorders have been identified (Johnson and Myklebust, 1967): dysgraphia, a disorder of visual-motor integration; revisualization deficits, an inability to remember the forms in order to reproduce them; and a deficiency in formulation and syntax, an inability to organize thoughts for written communication. The first two disorders will be discussed in this section; the last is included in the section on language disorders.

Dysgraphia

Children with dysgraphia may be able to speak and read but are unable to produce the motor patterns needed for writing. They cannot write spontaneously nor can they copy letters, numerals, or figures. Vision and motor skills appear to be intact; the deficit lies in the ability to integrate the two modalities.

Starting from the scribbling stage, the normal child, as he matures, learns what movements to make in order to reproduce a particular line, form, or pattern. Dysgraphic children do not learn to make these associations.

Though thought processes are intact, when the child concentrates on the production of written forms, the content of the written material frequently suffers. Sentences tend to be short with simple ideas, vocabulary, and syntactic patterns. It is as if all the child's energy is involved in the physical act of writing with little left over for the cognitive aspects of the task.

In arithmetic, disturbances are noted in writing numerals and putting them in the proper place on the page. The child may also have difficulty in understanding concepts of time and space.

Because he cannot determine which movements produce which results, the child may be unable to reproduce the sequence of movements needed in a game or dance. He may further be hindered in such subjects as physical education, home economics, industrial arts, and typing, as well as in daily-living skills.

As with other disabilities, there are degrees of involvement. Some children literally do not know where to begin the task of writing; others can copy moderately well if there is no time pressure.

Educational Interventions. Three sequences to develop nonverbal visual-motor patterning have been described by Johnson and Myklebust (1967): 1) visual to auditory to visual-motor. A pattern is presented followed by a verbal description of the movement required. The child watches and then imitates. 2) Kinesthetic to visual-motor. The child closes his eyes and the teacher guides his hands. The child then opens his eyes and watches as the action is repeated. 3) Kinesthetic to auditory to visual-motor. The procedure is the same as the second but the teacher also verbalizes the movements while the child's eyes are closed.

The sequence chosen depends on the extent and types of other learning disabilities present and whether the child can handle a multisensory approach. The cues should be reduced as the child gains competence.

For the child who cannot integrate the visual and kinesthetic modalities, it is suggested that each be presented separately and that the child then be helped in coordinating the two. The visual presentation is made first. The teacher draws a model on the board. It remains there as she slowly draws another. This is done several times. To heighten the effect, a flashlight beam can be used to trace around the shape. As the beam is directed around the figure, the teacher can verbalize what is happening.

In the kinesthetic phase, the child's eyes are closed and the teacher moves his hand over the figure on the board. She continues to guide him until he can do it alone. If the child will benefit, a verbal description can be used at the same time.

The last step is to have him draw the figure himself, first with his eyes closed and then with them open.

Other procedures can be used to reinforce visual-motor pattern learning; for example, templates and stencils, copying using tracing paper, tracing folds in paper.

The tracing of designs and preletter forms before introducing letters and numerals has been recommended by several authorities (Johnson and Myklebust, 1967; Frostig and Maslow, 1973; Siegel & Siegel, 1977).

When teaching letters, start with those that are easiest to copy. Similar letters are taught together but those that are easily confused (b, d, p. q,) should not be taught in succession. Break the letter into its simplest parts and show how they fit together. Begin with a strong stimulus or cue and then fade it. If the teacher must physically guide the movement, she should gradually lessen the pressure until the child can perform it himself. Several types of cue fading are suggested by Siegel (1977). If tracing is being used, the following sequence can be followed. It may take some children several days to go through this sequence, though the time should lessen as the child gains ability to integrate the modalities.

The child traces over the first letter several times. When his lines appear steady, he traces the letter in the second box several times. The child continues in the same fashion in boxes three and four. He writes the letter in the last box from memory and compares it with the model. Tracing paper overlays can be used also.

The teacher can verbalize the movements as the child writes the letter in box one. The child should be encouraged to continue verbalizing if it helps improve his performance. This, too, should be faded.

Some children require additional strategies and materials before writing letters with paper and pencil, such as writing in the air, painting the letter on large sheets of newsprint. For those who benefit from strong tactile feedback, fingerpaint and sandpaper letters can be used. Haptic feedback (tactile and kinesthetic) is provided by writing with a finger in wet sand and finger paint and with a stylus in clay. Sunken script letter board can also be used. Wet sand and clay is especially useful for "... it slows down the pupil who does things in a driven, impulsive fashion" (Siegel and Siegel, 1977, p. 82).

Other effective cues are colored dots and directional arrows denoting starting and stopping points. After individual letters are learned, the child should be taught to write whole words and sentences. Now spacing between letters and words becomes an important factor. If cursive writing is being used, the linkage between let-

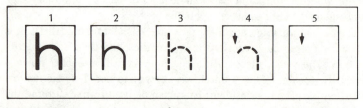

Figure 12-2.

ters must be taught. Note that letters change their form somewhat when they are connected to *o* and *v* (*n-on*; *e-ve*).

Be sure the child's writing posture is good; that is, feet flat on the floor; correct grasp of pencil between thumb and middle finger and index finger on top; the nonwriting hand should hold the paper in position (masking tape on the desk can mark the initial placement). The left-handed child should position the paper without a slant for manuscript writing and slanted to the right for cursive writing. A rubberband placed around the pencil, above the sharpened area, can help the child hold the pencil in the right place.

Lined paper should be used to help the child keep the writing in alignment. Paper with different widths of spacing between lines should be available. If the child has difficulty staying within the lines of the paper, the task will be easier if colored markers or crayons are used to make dark, heavy lines. As with other cues, these will eventually be faded.

Most dysgraphic children can develop legible handwriting if they are given consistent, sequential instruction with much practice and immediate feedback and reinforcement. While the child is learning, however, the demands for writing should be lessened. Tests should be given orally and untimed, or multiple-choice questions should be used. A buddy system can be instituted so that assignments for homework and class notes can be written in duplicate (using carbon paper). The typewriter can be used by some children who do not learn to write legibly or who write very slowly. Because these children will require special instruction, programs have been designed which modify basic typing programs (Davis, 1971; Heller, 1979).

Deficits of Revisualization

The child who cannot write because he cannot revisualize has a memory problem. He may be able to read, speak, and copy but he cannot write spontaneously or from dictation. Examination of the child's drawings may show a lack of detail. He may be unable to describe in any detail a familiar object. Occasionally, this problem occurs together with visual dyslexia but it can appear alone. When it is an isolated disorder, the scores in written spelling will be lower than in oral spelling and reading can be at or near grade level.

Educational Interventions. The objective of training is to develop the child's ability to revisualize and stresses visual memory activities. Johnson and Myklebust (1967) report success using a sequence which *"works from recognition to partial recall to total recall"* (p. 222).

Recognition is stressed when the child does not have to write a response but can indicate the correct answer from among several that are presented; for example, a stimulus is shown and then removed. The child is given a list of four possibilities and he indicates the one that is the same.

Partial recall is the ability to revisualize the whole figure when only part is shown (closure). Children with severe disabilities should be told what the figure is before they are asked to draw the missing part. Many such exercises should be given before the child is asked to complete figures without being told what they are.

All materials used should be sharp and clear. Large type is helpful. The child should have his own copy of letter and number charts at his desk for easy reference, near-point copying being an easier task than far-point. Color cues should be used to enhance the visual stimulus. Tactile writing exercises, such as sandpaper letters, can be used. To draw the child's attention, a flashlight can focus on the letter or word. Tachistoscopic presentations can be made with the speed increased as he becomes more successful. If the child benefits from reauditorization, he should be encouraged to say or spell what he wants to write as he writes it. To prevent frustration any tests given to children with this deficit should be of the multiple-choice type.

Manuscript or Cursive?

The choice of the type of writing depends on the nature and extent of the child's disability. It has been recommended that cursive writing be taught first to all children (McGinnis, 1963). Cursive writing has been used as a remedial method because words are written as units and a rhythm can be developed which facilitates performance. Lerner notes that "errors of reversal are virtually eliminated" (1976, p. 254). However, we have had students (including one in graduate school) who frequently wrote inversions, such as h for y, b for g.

Others prefer manuscript writing because the movements are less complex, basically straight lines and circles, and there are fewer changes of letter forms (Johnson & Myklebust, 1967). Though they recognize that spacing and letter alignment present difficulties, Johnson and Myklebust feel these can be overcome by the use of appropriate teaching techniques. Noting that the decision to shift to cursive writing depends on the individual child's abilities and the nature of his problems, they stress the importance of learning one form of writing thoroughly. ". . . they are taught one form for both reading and writing until they can read it successfully" (p. 213).

Spalding and Spalding, (1962) observed that only six types of pencil strokes are needed for making lower case manuscript letters and also suggested that cursive writing can be adapted from manuscript writing by using only five types of connective strokes, thereby simplifying the transition.

Siegel and Siegel (1977) suggest that when a lower-grade child has mislearned manuscript, it is best to begin to teach cursive writing since unlearning poor motor habits is difficult (p. 57).

Whichever form is used, it is taught the same way. Posture, letter forms, spacing, relative sizes, and slant are stressed. Letters are broken down into simple components and then blended together.

The teacher's own handwriting should be a model for the children. She should evaluate her own writing for spacing, slant, letter formation, size, and proportion. If improvement is needed, a student's workbook can be used to provide practice. Zaner-Bloser, Inc. publishes self-guiding workbooks for manuscript and cursive writing designed for teachers' use. In addition, for a small fee they provide a handwriting evaluation service.

SPELLING

Spelling, a tool subject, receives relatively little emphasis in the schools. The main teaching method stresses memorization of lists of words. Though frequently viewed

as a relatively simple skill, the spelling task is complex, requiring ". . . more auditory and visual discrimination, memory, sequentialization, analysis and synthesis
and integration simultaneously than perhaps any other skill" (Johnson & Myklebust,
1967, p. 239). It is not surprising then that most learning-disabled children have
deficits in spelling.

Spelling errors can be the result of discrimination, revisualization, and reauditorization problems or difficulty in establishing grapheme/phoneme correspondence. There is a strong linkage between reading and spelling. Children who have
difficulties in the first phase of reading, decoding and word recognition, also have
problems in learning to spell. Johnson and Myklebust suggest that the remediation
begin with the identification and improvement of the basic deficit, for example, revisualization or reading and that this will develop increased proficiency in spelling,
When revisualization problems occur in isolation, all academic areas may be at grade
level save written spelling, which is often three or four grades below the expected
level. Oral spelling and scores on multiple choice spelling tests will be higher than
scores in written spelling (1967, p. 218).

Informal teacher assessment can provide the information needed to institute
an appropriate spelling program. An analysis of errors will determine if a pattern
exists. Error patterns found in children's spelling have been identified by Edgington
(1967, p. 59). Some of the error patterns are listed below:

- Addition of unneeded letters (for example, *dressses*).
- Omissions of needed letters (*hom* for *home*)
- Reflections of child's mispronunciations (*pin* for *pen*).
- Reflections of dialectical speech patterns (*Cuber* for *Cuba*)
- Reversals of whole words (*eno* for *one*).
- Reversals of vowels (*braed* for *bread*).
- Reversals of consonant order (*lback* for *black*).
- Reversals of consonant or vowel directionality (*brithday* for *birthday*).
- Reversals of syllables (*telho* for *hotel*).
- Phonetic spelling of nonphonetic words or parts thereof (*cawt* for *caught*).
- Wrong associations of a sound with a given set of letters, such as *u* has been
  learned as *ou* in *you*.
- "Neographisms," such as letters put in which bear no discernible relation-
  ship with the word dictated.
- Varying degrees and combinations of these or other possible patterns.

Educational Interventions

Many spelling programs and methods have been suggested for the learning-disabled
child. Differences of opinion about basic approaches exist. Before deciding which
to use, the teacher should become familiar with the basic goals and approaches.
Most programs will not be able to meet the needs of all children with learning disabilities in a classroom. Some can be used in conjunction with individual remedial
techniques. The words chosen for the remedial spelling program should be words
which the child can read and will be able to use in his stories, letters, and other
written work.

Johnson and Myklebust (1967) suggest teaching phonetic words by stressing
reauditorization. Letter cards and anagrams are used to develop analysis and syn-

thesis. Separate the letters of the word so that different groupings can be seen. Say the word as the letters appear; for example, *m-a-n*; *m-an*; *ma-n*. Have the child repeat them as they are presented. Dictate slowly and have the child write the word.

They suggest that nonphonetic words should be taught using the steps discussed under revisualization (p. 225) for handwriting. Words should be written as wholes. Next letters are omitted from various parts of the word. Finally the child is expected to spell the entire word. Almenoff and Dallari (1977) have a graded series of prepared spelling sequence strips which can be used alone or with a slotted folder, called the Spelling Sleeve. First the whole word is shown through the slot. As the strip is moved, the word is shown with blanks in place of some of the letters. There are several exposures of each word with the blanks in different places. The child writes the missing letter(s). The last step in the sequence requires the child to write the whole word. A modification of this aid that has been found effective is to leave the model word on display (just above the slot). This provides visual-memory practice since he can alternate his focus between the complete word and partial word as long as necessary.

Barsch (1967) emphasizes the visual-spatial aspect of spelling (the order and sequence of the letters) saying, "In final analysis, an auditory approach to spelling has only a limited value" (p. 6). To remediate deficiencies in spelling, the teacher should provide activities to develop visualizing skills.

Visualization has three components or levels: visual comparison, visual memory, and visual imagery or projection (Hendrickson, 1967). Training of these components will develop the ability to visualize. In the sequence suggested, the child first looks at objects and compares them in size, shape, and color. He looks for similarities and differences. At the second level, the child is shown pictures and is asked to describe them. He is asked to draw from memory. Another activity suggested for this level is to have the child repeatedly trace words while saying the name of the letters. Writing in the air is also done. The third level, imagery, is the ability to describe something no longer in view. The child is asked to describe something for the teacher to guess. He is also asked to describe places or the way to go from one place to another.

The Cover-Write Method is a six-step procedure described by Edgington (1967). A word is written in very large letters on a card.

1. The child looks at the word and says it aloud.
2. Using unlined paper, the child writes the word while saying it. He is instructed to look at the sample and not his paper while writing.
3. The child compares his results with the model (visually).
4. If written correctly, steps two and three are repeated four more times.
5. The child covers all the words. He writes the word and says it. The results are compared as in step three.
6. Repeat steps one through five.

After practice, Edgington recommends that each word be written in a sentence. The teacher should dictate all the words learned during the week at the end of the week.

The Fernald method, which was described in the section on reading (p. 217), teaches spelling together with reading. In brief, the child chooses the word he wishes to learn, traces the teacher's sample (while saying it), and then writes it from memory. At later stages, he looks, says, and writes the word, until he can spell it after only looking at it.

The Gillingham Approach also teaches spelling in conjunction with reading. Sounds are built into words using visual, auditory, and kinesthetic associations. After establishing sound/letter association, a visual-memory pattern for a word is established which is reinforced through writing.

Oral spelling should not be stressed since there is little need for it (other than spelling bees). Many children will spell well orally but cannot pass a written test nor spell the words correctly when writing spontaneously. The written form should be encouraged since it is needed for everyday life. Some children will benefit from saying the word and/or spelling aloud as they write it. This input should be faded as the child becomes more proficient.

Weiss and Weiss (1979) describe a learning-disabled adolescent whose spelling pattern included syllable omission (especially in the medial position), transposing of sounds, and the phonetic—but incorrect—spelling of words. However, he improved considerably when he was *allowed* to repeat the word (which the teacher dictated) prior to writing it. "It was as if the verbalizing and hearing of his own voice say the words facilitated recall within himself of the correct phonetic or nonphonetic pattern . . ." (p. 20).

The spelling program should be integrated with the other language arts. Doing otherwise will limit its effectiveness. Children are motivated to acquire this skill when they realize it has a natural and necessary place in their lives.

WRITTEN EXPRESSION

The last of the language skills to be developed (see Figure 12-1), written expression, involves oral expression, skill in reading and spelling, legible handwriting, some understanding of written usage rules, and something to write about. Because of the many elements that must be combined, Lerner (1976) considers problems in written language to be the most prevalent of communication disabilities. Difficulties in any one of the hierarchy of language skills will limit the normal development of written language.

Disorders of written expansion are not evidenced until the child has developed some skill in reading, spelling, and handwriting. He is then expected to write his own stories, write answers to questions on tests, and to use the skill in a functional way, such as writing letters. It is at this point that some learning-disabled children exhibit problems in composing meaningful sentences or stories, such as difficulties in syntax. Though oral language may be intact, they are unable to translate their thoughts into written symbols.

Diagnostic Tests

Among the most commonly used standardized tests to determine written language performance are: *The Picture Story Language Test* (PSLT) and the *Sequential Test of Educational Progress II*—Subtest G (STEP).

The PSLT, for use with children aged seven to 17 measures productivity (word count and number and length of sentences), correctness (word usage, word endings, and punctuation), and meaning. An abstract-to-concrete scale measures ability to abstract. The levels are described in the following interventions section. Age equivalents, percentiles, and stanines can be derived from the test scores. Scoring is involved and subjective.

The STEP evaluation of the mechanics of writing, for grades four through twelve presents written material containing errors in spelling, capitalization, and punctuation which must be identified by the students. Corrections must be chosen from among several alternatives. The student's own writing sample is not analyzed. The test yields grade scores.

The reliability and validity of both instruments have been questioned. However, Alley and Deschler (1979) suggest that the components measured by both should be used as guidelines for informal teacher assessment.

Educational Interventions

The need to use written language becomes more acute as the pupil progresses through the grades. The teacher's primary consideration should be to reduce the anxiety about writing and to avoid the child's feelings of discouragement.

1. To stimulate the production of ideas to write about, provide experiences for the child. These can be in the form of class trips or classroom activities, some of which may be related to other subject areas such as science or social studies.

2. Develop group stories based on such experiences. Teacher questions can lead the student to make comparisons, see similarities and differences, recognize a sequence of activities, draw conclusions, and so on. Pictures and photographs can also be used to stimulate group and individual stories. Begin with oral discussion before asking the children to write a story or theme.

3. Have the students dictate their own stories either to the teacher, aide, or a tape recorder. The teacher or aide can transcribe them. The stories should then be read and discussed. When the student is able, he can transcribe his own stories from the tape.

4. The oral expression of many learning-disabled youngsters is considered appropriate for their age but the written language is more limited, similar to the writing of a much younger child. A method using four sequential levels of abstraction which are used in scoring the PSLT can be adapted to remediate this problem (Myklebust, 1965).

At the first level, *concrete-descriptive*, the child is encouraged to describe the things he sees, using simple sentences and a few adjectives. The next level, *concrete-imaginative*, requires the child to infer from a situation or experience. Shown the picture of a ball, the child should say something about the ball which does not appear in the picture, such as, "The ball belongs to a little boy." Some learning-disabled children find this difficult to do because they are stimulus bound and can only react to what is actually seen. This has also been described as concrete behavior.

In the third level, *abstract-descriptive*, stories that emphasize time and sequence are developed. Sequence pictures are helpful at this stage. It may be necessary to teach transition words such as next, later, before.

At the highest level, *abstract-imagination*, stories are developed that have plot, use figures of speech, and have continuity. The teacher can ask open-ended questions to help the child imagine relationships.

5. When written assignments are given, stress the ideas and content rather than the mechanics. Many children limit their efforts to simple vocabulary and sentence structure in order to avoid making mechanical errors. Their writing lacks any interest and creativity. Lerner (1976) suggests either only grading ideas or giving two grades, one for content and the other for mechanics.

6. Teach the student how to edit his own work for capitals, punctuation marks, spelling, and grammar. Establish the idea that the first effort need not be perfect, that errors can be corrected. A sequence of four steps can be used to accomplish this:

a. The teacher should read aloud, one at a time, sentences written by the child.

b. The child identifies the error in each sentence and corrects it on his paper. When this is mastered, the student can proceed to the next step.

c. The child reads his work aloud, sentence by sentence, and corrects his errors.

d. The last step is to have the child read silently and make corrections.

7. Many learning-disabled children have a limited vocabulary, making it difficult to express their thoughts in a clear manner. Increase the student's vocabulary by teaching synonyms and antonyms, prefixes and suffixes. Encourage the student to build lists of synonym words and phrases; for example, all the ways to say "hot."

8. To guide student note taking, the teacher should list the major points of the lesson on the board. Verbal cues should be used in lecturing, "The first point is . . . ," "Next we find . . . ," "The author listed four important factors . . . ."

9. Written tests are frequently required in the regular grades. Often two modifications are made for the learning-disabled students: the tests are given orally or they are given untimed (the student has unlimited time to read the questions and write the answers). Alley and Deschler (1979) suggest specific steps to be taken by high-school students to prepare for exams.

a. The student should ask his teachers what material will be on the test, the types of questions that will be used (essay, short answer, true-false), and what material will be covered from the text and class notes.

b. The student should ask to see previous exams in order to see the format and areas that were stressed.

In order to avoid cramming for tests, the student should be taught to set up and follow a study schedule. They should also be taught the terms used in tests, such as "compare," "contrast," "define," "describe," "briefly describe," "give a detailed explanation."

Because reading the question first may cause the student to panic and forget what he learned for the test, Alley and Deschler recommend that when taking an essay test, before reading the questions, the student should first write down brief outlines about what he knows. These outlines can be referred to during the exam.

REFERENCES

Alley, G., and Deschler, D. *Teaching the learning disabled adolescent: Strategies and methods*, Denver: Love Publishing, 1979.

Almenoff, P., and Dallari, E. D. *The spelling box*. Freeport, N.Y.: Educational Activities, Records, 1977.

Aschner, M. J. The analysis of verbal interaction in the classroom. In A. A. Bellack (Ed.), *Theory and research in teaching*. New York: Teachers College, 1963.

Barbe, W. B. *Zaner-Bloser handwriting workbook: Manuscript cursive*. Columbus, Ohio: Zaner-Bloser, Inc., 1977.

Barsch, R. H. A visual-spatial concept of spelling. *Academic Therapy Quarterly*, Fall, 1967, 5–8.

Bloom, B. B. (Ed.) Condensed version of the taxonomy of educational objectives. In *Taxonomy of educational objectives: Handbook I, cognitive domain*. New York: David McKay, 1956.

Board of Education of the City of New York. *Oral communication: Grades K-6*. Curriculum Bulletin 1976–1977, Series No. 2 Division of Educational Planning and Support.

Boder, E. Developmental dyslexia: Prevailing diagnostic concepts and a new diagnostic approach. In Myklebust, H. R. (Ed.), *Progress in learning disabilities: Volume II*. New York: Grune & Stratton, 1971.

Botel, M. *Botel reading inventory*, Chicago: Follett Publishing, 1962.

Bryant, N. D. Learning disability in reading. In Newman, H. (Ed.), *Reading disabilities: Selections in identification and treatment*. Indianapolis: Bobbs-Merrill, 1969.

Buchannon, C. D., and Sullivan Associates. *Sullivan programmed readers*. New York: McGraw-Hill, 1963.

Buros, O. K. (Ed.), *Eighth mental measurements yearbook. Vol. I and II*. New Jersey: Gryphon Press, 1978.

Chomsky, N. *Syntactic structure*. The Hague: Mouton, 1957.

Consilia, Sister Mary. *The non-coping child*. Novato, Ca.: Academic Publications, 1978.

Davis, M. *Typing keys for the remediation of reading and spelling*. Novato, Ca: Academic Therapy, 1971.

Denckla, M. Paper presented at the International Conference of ACLD, New York City, 1975.

Dodds, W. A longitudinal study of two beginning reading programs—words in color and traditional basal readers. Doctoral dissertation, Case Western Reserve University, 1966.

Dunn, L. M., Smith, J. O., Dunn, L. M., Horton, K. B. and Smith, D. D. *Peabody language development kits (revised)*. Circle Pines, Minn.: American Guidance Services, 1981.

Durrell, D. D. *Durrell analysis of reading difficulty*. New York: Harcourt, Brace, Jovanovich, 1955.

Edgington, R. But he spelled them right this morning! *Academic Therapy Quarterly*, Fall, 1967, 58–61.

Ekwall, E. E. *Diagnosis and remediation of the disabled reader*. Boston: Allyn & Bacon, 1976.

Engelmann, S., and Bruner, E. C. *Distar reading: An instructional system*. Chicago: Science Research Associate, 1969.

Engelmann, S., Osborn, J. and Engelmann, T. *Distar language:* Chicago: Science Research Associates, 1969.

Fernald, G. *Remedial techniques in basic school subjects.* New York: McGraw-Hill, 1943.

Flanders, N. A. *Analyzing teaching behavior.* Reading, Mass.: Addison-Wesley, 1970.

Frostig, M., and Maslow, P. *Learning problems in the classroom.* New York: Grune & Stratton, 1973.

Gattegno, C. *Words in color.* Chicago: Learning Materials, Inc., 1962.

Gillespie, P. H., and Johnson, L. J. *Teaching reading to the mildly retarded child.* Columbus, Ohio: Charles E. Merrill, 1974.

Gillespie, P. H., and Sitko, M. C. Reading problems. In L. Mann, L. Goodman and J. L. Wiederholt (Eds.), *Teaching the learning-disabled adolescent.* Boston: Houghton Mifflin, 1978.

Gillingham, A., and Stillman, B. W. *Remedial training for children with specific difficulty in reading, spelling, and penmanship, 7th ed.,* Cambridge, Mass.: Educators Publishing Service, 1966.

Gilmore, J. V. and Gilmore, E. C. *Gilmore oral reading test.* New York: Harcourt, Brace, Jovanovich, 1965.

Glass, G. G. *Glass analysis for decoding only: Teacher guide:* Garden City, N.Y.: Easier to Learn, 1976.

————. *The process of decoding for the teacher of reading.* Instructional/Communications Technology, Inc, I/LT Teacher Education Monograph No. 6, 1977.

Gold, R. F. *Basic instructional module (revised).* Mimeograph. Garden City, N.Y.: Adelphi University, 1979.

Gonzales, P. C., and Elijah, J. D. D. Rereading: Effect on error patterns and performance levels on the IRL. *The Reading Teacher, 28*(7): 647–652, April, 1975.

Goodman, K. S. A linguistic study of cues and miscues in reading. *Elementary English, 42:*639–643, October, 1965.

Goodman, Y. M. Using children's miscue for teaching reading strategies. *Reading Teacher. 23*(3): 455–459, February, 1970.

Goodman, Y. M. and Burke, C. L. *Reading miscue inventory manual procedure for diagnosis and evaluation.* New York: The Macmillan Company, 1972.

Guszak, F. J. *Diagnostic reading instruction in the elementary school.* New York: Harper & Row, 1972.

Hammill, D. D. and Bartel, N. R. *Teaching children with learning and behavior problems.* Boston: Allyn & Bacon, Inc., 1975.

Harris, L. A., and Smith, C. B., *Reading instruction through diagnostic teaching.* New York: Holt, Rinehart and Winston, 1972.

Heckelman, R. G. A neurological impress method of remedial reading. *Academic Therapy,* 1969, *4,* 277–282.

Heilman, A. W. *Principles and practices of teaching reading, 2nd ed.* Columbus, Ohio: Charles E. Merrill, 1967.

Heller, J. *Typing for individual achievement.* Wantagh, N.Y.: Special Education—Step by Step, 1979.

————. *Typing for the physically handicapped.* New York: McGraw-Hill, 1979.

Hendrickson, H. Spelling: A visual skill. *Academic Therapy Quarterly,* Fall, 1967, 39–42.

Hewett, F. M., with Forness, S. R. *Education of exceptional learners.* Boston: Allyn & Bacon, 1974.

Hinds, L. R. An evaluation of words in color or morphologico-algebraic approved to teaching reading to functionally illiterate adults. Doctorial dissertation. Case Western University, 1966.

Hollander, S., and Reisman, M. *Pupil placement tests.* Boston: Houghton Mifflin Reading Program, 1970.

Hollingsworth, P. M. An experiment with the impress method of teaching reading. *Reading Teacher*, 1970, *24*, 112–114.

Hull, F. M., and Hull, M. E. Children with oral communication disabilities. In Dunn, L. M. (Ed.), *Exceptional children in the schools: Special education in transition (2nd ed).* New York: Holt, Rinehart and Winston, 1973.

Irwin, J. V. and Marge, M. (Eds.), *Principles of childhood language disabilities.* Englewood Cliffs: Prentice-Hall, 1972.

Johnson, D. J., and Myklebust, H. R. *Learning disabilities: Educational principles and practices*, New York: Grune & Stratton, 1967.

Kaufman, M. *Words in color for intensive remedial instruction.* Boston: Northeastern University, 1972.

Kellogg, R. E. Listening. In Lamb, P. (Ed.), *Guiding children's language.* Dubuque, Iowa: William C. Brown, 1971.

Langford, K., Slade, K. and Barnett, A. An explanation of impress techniques in remedial reading. *Academic Therapy*, Spring, 1974: *9*, 309–319.

Leigh, J. E. Whole language approaches: premises and possibilities. *Learning Disabilities Quarterly*. Fall, 1980, *3*(4), 62–69.

Lerner, J. *Children with learning disabilities, 2nd ed.* Boston: Houghton Mifflin, 1976.

Lockmiller, P., and Di Nello, M. C. Words in color versus a basal reader program with retarded readers in grade 2. *Journal of Educational Research*, 1970, *63*, 330–334.

Lopardo, G. S. LEA-cloze reading materials for the disabled reader. *The Reading Teacher*, 1975, *29*(1), 42–44.

Lorenz, L., and Vockell, E. Using the neurological impress method with learning disabled readers. *Journal of Learning Disabilities*, June/July, 1979, *12*(6), 420–422.

McGinnis, M. *Aphasic children.* Washington, D.C.: Alexander Graham Bell Association for the Deaf, Inc., 1963.

MacDonald, J. D. Environmental language intervention. In Withrow, F. B., and Nygren, C. J. (Eds.), *Language, materials, and curriculum management for the handicapped learner.* Columbus, Ohio: Charles E. Merrill, 1976.

McCarthy, J. M. Evolution of my involvement with learning disabled children. In Kauffman, J. M., and Hallahan, D. P. (Eds.), *Teaching children with learning disabilities.* Columbus, Ohio: Charles E. Merrill, 1976.

Miccinati, J. "Teach reading disabled students to perceive distinctive features in words," *Journal of Learning Disabilities*, March, 1981, *14*(3): 140–142.

Miller, W. H. *Diagnosis and correction of reading difficulties in secondary school students.* New York: The Center for Applied Research in Education, Inc., 1973.

Minskoff, E. H. Remediating auditory-verbal learning disabilities: The role of questions in teacher-pupil interaction. *Journal of Learning Disabilities*, Aug/Sept 1974, *7*(7).

Minskoff, E. H., Wiseman, D. E., and Minskoff, J. C. *The MWM program of developing language abilities.* Ridgefield, N.J.: Educational Performance Associates, 1973.

Myklebust, H. Auditory disorders in children: A manual for differential diagnosis. New York: Grune & Stratton, 1954.

Newcomer, P., and Hammill, D. D. Using the test of language development with language-impaired children. *Journal of Learning Disabilities,* October, 1978, *11*(8), 521–523.

Nodine, C. F. and Lang, N. J. Development of visual scanning strategies for differentiating words. *Developmental Psychology* 5, 1971: 221–232.

Nygren, C. J. Language development. In Withrow, F. B., and Nygren, C. J. (Eds.), *Language, materials, and curriculum management for the handicapped learner.* Charles E. Merrill, Columbus, Ohio, 1976.

Orton, S. T. *Reading, writing and speech problems in children.* New York: W. W. Norton, 1937.

Quirós, J. de. Dysphasia and dyslexia in school children. *Folia Phoniatrica,* 1964, *16*, 201–222, as cited by Boder, E. *op cit.*

Rankin, E. F., and Culhane, J. W. Comparable close and multiple-choice comprehension test scores. *Journal of Reading, 13,* 1969, 193–198.

Ross, A. O. *Psychological aspects of learning disabilities and reading disorders.* New York: McGraw-Hill, 1976.

Salvia, J., and Ysseldyke, J. E. *Assessment in special and remedial education.* Boston: Houghton Mifflin, 1978.

Siegel, E. *Teaching One Child.* Freeport, N.Y.: Educational Activities, Inc., 1972.

Siegel, E., and Siegel, R. *Creating instructional sequences.* Novato, Ca.: Academic Therapy Publications, 1977.

Sivaroli, N. J. *Classroom reading inventory, 2nd ed.* Dubuque, Iowa: William C. Brown, 1973.

Slingerland, B. H. *Slingerland screening tests for identifying children with specific language disability, 2nd ed.* Cambridge, Mass.: Educators Publishing Service, 1970.

Smith, E. B., Meredith, R. and Goodman, K. S. *Language and thinking in the elementary school.* New York: Holt, Rinehart and Winston, 1970.

Spache, G. D. *Diagnosing and correcting reading disabilities.* Boston: Allyn & Bacon, 1976.

Spalding, R. B., and Spalding, W. T. *The writing road to reading.* New York: William Morrow, 1962.

Taylor, O., and Swinney, D. The onset of language. In Irwin, J. V., and Marge, M. (Eds.), *Principles of childhood language disabilities.* Englewood Cliffs, New Jersey: Prentice-Hall, 1972.

Valmont, W. J. Creating questions for informal reading inventories. *The Reading Teacher,* March, 1972, *25,* 509–512.

Weiss, M. S., and Weiss, H. G. *The basic language kit: A teaching-tutoring aid for adolescents and young adults.* Great Barrington, Mass.: Treehouse Associates, 1979.

Wiener, M., and Cromer, W. Reading and reading difficulty: A conceptual analysis. *Harvard Educational Review,* 1967, 620–643.

Wiig, E. H., Lapointe, C., and Semel, E. M. Relationship among language processing and production abilities of learning-disabled adolescents. Paper presented at the Annual Convention of the American Speech & Hearing Association, Washington, D.C., 1975, as cited in Wiig and Semel.

Wiig, E. H., and Semel, E. M. *Language disabilities in children and adolescents.* Columbus, Ohio: Charles E. Merrill, 1976.

Woodcock, R., and Clark, C. L. *Peabody rebus reading program.* Circle Pines, Minnesota: American Guidance Service, 1969.

Woods, M. L., and Moe, A. J. *Analytic reading inventory*, *2nd ed.*, Columbus: Charles E. Merrill, 1981.

Methods for Teaching Mathematics

13

Until recently, little emphasis has been placed on the diagnosis and remediation of disabilities in the area of mathematics. As used here, the term mathematics refers to the study of quantities, space, and form, and their relationships as expressed by numbers and symbols. After reviewing current literature, we must conclude that the evidence and extent of the problem of a specific mathematics disability are relatively unknown.

Analysis of arithmetic errors among learning-disabled children has led many educators to identify several general, as well as specific, problem areas (Johnson & Myklebust, 1967; Bartel, 1975; Lerner, 1981). The general areas include the inability to count meaningfully, establish one-to-one relationships, associate numbers with numerals, perform arithmetic operations, understand mathematical signs and symbols, follow a sequence of steps (and discover or generalize mathematical concepts). Difficulty in telling time, using money, interpreting maps and graphs, understanding when to use a particular process would be examples of a specific problem area.

The term *discalculia* has been used to indicate global deficits in the area of arithmetic and mathematics (Lerner, 1981; Bryan & Bryan, 1978) while others limit the term to a partial inability to perform calculations (Faas, 1976). Kosc (1974) defines discalculia as "a disorder of the maturation of mathematical abilities" (p. 166). Stressing the developmental aspect of the term, he suggests its use only for children "showing a distinctly lower than average level of mathematical age in relation to his normal mental age" (p. 166). He further defines six types of discalculia:

a. verbal—inability to apply a name or label to quantities, numerals, symbols, or to give an oral response.
b. practognostic—inability to manipulate objects in order to show mathematical concepts.

   c. lexical—inability to read mathematical symbols, e.g., numerals, operational signs.

   d. graphical—disability in writing mathematical symbols.

   e. ideognostical—problems in understanding of mathematical concepts and mental computation.

   f. operational—disability in performing operations, e.g., adding instead of subtracting. Child tends to prefer written to mental computation although the task is within his repertoire.

Clinical data suggest degrees of disability as well as various combinations of types. We identify two basic types of disabilities, primary and secondary. Primary refers to those who have a specific mathematics disability with deficits in understanding mathematical concepts, reasoning, and application. A secondary disability refers to a functional deficit. The concepts are understood but performance is poor because of the effect of learning-disabilities correlates (Figure 13-1). Still a third type would be those who exhibit a combination of primary and secondary performance.

DIAGNOSIS OF MATHEMATICS ABILITIES

The development of a comprehensive, individual mathematics program requires data that take into consideration the pupil's present general functioning level across broad conceptual areas and can be used to pinpoint gaps within areas, recognize the way the child learns best, and indicate how the child attacks word math problems in general (e.g., selecting the proper process to use) and in particular (e.g., difficulty in understanding that "comparing" implies subtraction). To determine educational needs, the diagnostic team must ask assessment questions that determine the level of achievement, strengths and weaknesses. (McLoughlin & Lewis, 1981). Because relatively little attention has been given to the dynamics of specific mathematics disabilities, few tests have been developed or adapted for the identification and diagnosis of the problem. At present, those most frequently used are: *Keymath Diagnostic Arithmetic Test, Peabody Individual Achievement Test (PIAT), Wide Range Achievement Test (WRAT), Boehm Test of Basic Concepts, Stanford Diagnostic Arithmetic Test, and System Fore.* Cawley, et al. (1976–77) developed the *Mathematics Concepts Inventory* (MCI) of Project Math for use with older learning disabled students.

Though other tests are also used to assess functioning levels, the preceding will be discussed in more detail because they are representative of the tests available and are used frequently in diagnostic settings. A listing of the publishers and their addresses can be found in the Appendix.

Keymath Diagnostic Arithmetic Test

Keymath is based on the developmental sequence of mathematics skills and provides an assessment of performance in three areas: content, operations, and applications. It yields a total score, with grade equivalents, a general pattern associated with each of these areas, and a profile of strengths and weaknesses across 14 subtests. Though developed primarily for preschool through sixth grade, there are no upper limits for remedial use. A study by Greenstein and Strain (1977) found that the Keymath could discriminate adolescent LD performance from normal performance.

The test is given on a one-to-one basis. Little reading or writing is required with most responses being oral. Only one form is available. It is called a diagnostic test, but because of the limited number of sample items, it should be used only for gross screening.

Peabody Individual Achievement Test (PIAT)

The mathematics portion of the PIAT is a frequently used test. This section, as well as the others (see Chapter 12), was designed for grades K–12. Four types of scores are derived: grade equivalents, age equivalents, percentile ranks, and standard scores, providing a profile for easy identification of strengths and weaknesses. The items, which are arranged in order of difficulty, require only an oral or pointing response. One form of the test is available. According to Buros (1972), the test-retest coefficients for mathematics are high at most age levels. The PIAT can be used for screening, but not for diagnosis. "Often it will be used to suggest the point at which a more comprehensive test may be employed, should a more reliable and thorough estimate be desirable" (Buros, 1972, p. 18).

Wide Range Achievement Test (WRAT)

The WRAT is widely used, largely because it is easily administered and scored. The test measures achievement in written spelling, oral reading, and arithmetic. Each subtest has two levels: Level I for ages five to 11 years, 11 months; and Level II for 12 years or older. An oral pretest can be used with children whose chronological age or performance is below a minimum point. Results are given in grade-level scores.

The arithmetic subtest measures computation in arithmetic. Stellern, et al. (1976) consider the test to be useful in measuring achievement. However, it has limited use for diagnostic purposes. "... one would hestiate to count on it for the accurate diagnosis of ... arithmetic disabilities" (Buros, 1972, p. 39).

Boehm Test of Basic Concepts (BTBC)

The Boehm Test of Basic Concepts surveys the understanding of concepts related to mathematics, that is, space, quantity, size, and directionality. It does not yield any scores or grade level but indicates mastery of concepts considered necessary for academic achievement. Those concepts not learned should be included in the child's individual curriculum.

The test is used to screen groups in grades K–2, but can also be used with older learning disabled youngsters. Buros (1972) considers that "... the test is too easy to be of great value for first graders from middle or higher socioeconomic levels or for second graders of any social class" (p. 336). Though cautionary about the lack of validation studies and reports of test-retest reliability, Proger (1970) suggests its use in remedial work with implications for the disadvantaged and handicapped. A recent study by Beech (1981) comparing the performance of kindergarten children on the BTBC and the Test of Auditory Comprehension of Language, the Carrow

Elicited Language Inventory and five of Piaget's tests of cognitive abilities, show the BTBC to be an appropriate screening tool to identify high-risk kindergarten children.

No reading is involved. The child places an X on a picture illustrating the concept. Incorrect answers here do not, in themselves, reveal the reasons for the error. Follow-up activities must be used to pinpoint the source. The child may be performing inappropriately because 1) the concept is not understood or 2) he has difficulty in interpreting it on a two-dimensional plane. This latter relationship may need be taught rather than the concept itself.

Stanford Diagnostic Arithmetic Test (SDAT)

Designed as a diagnostic test which focuses on numbers and computation, the SDAT has two levels which overlap (grades 2.5 to 4.5 and 4.5 to 8.5) with two forms for each level. The tests can be administered to groups or individuals. The test derives stanine, percentile, and grade-level scores.

The diagnostic value of the test is considered limited since "Little research on the effectiveness of group diagnostic tests in arithmetic has been reported" (Buros, 1972, p. 529).

System FORE

The mathematics section of *System FORE* is a criterion-referenced test divided into three strands: geometry/measurement, numbers/numerals, and operations/applications. The program consists of 32 levels to be used with children ranging in age from 18 months to 14 years, that is, levels 1–4: 18 months to five years; levels 5–18: five years to 10 years; levels 19–32: 10 years to 14 years.

Each short-term objective is defined, materials needed are listed, and the number of correct items needed to meet the criterion are noted. A skill key is provided which can be used to analyze patterns of strength and weakness.

Mathematics Concepts Inventory (MCI)

The Mathematics Concepts Inventory is a criterion-referenced test of selected mathematics concepts. It is recommended as a screening device, especially for LD adolescents, to determine areas of strength and weakness. There is a curriculum available which can be used to follow-up the results of the assessment (Cawley, 1978). The MCI contains at least one test item for each concept included in the curriculum.

Informal Teacher Diagnosis

Informal diagnosis plays an integral part in the development of an educational program (see Chapter 5). Together with formal standarized procedures, informal testing is used to measure the child's present performance, analyze how the child learns, and under what conditions he learns. "Very little has been done in mathematics to develop techniques for constructing, administrating, and integrating an informal arithmetic inventory" (Russell & Dunlap, 1977, p. 11).

Informal tests of mathematics performance should concentrate on specific skill areas using several items for each skill being examined. In addition to teacher-made tests, many mathematics programs and texts contain diagnostic tests and surveys which can be used for this purpose.

Informal diagnosis is a basic part of a strategy developed by Johnson (1979) relating arithmetic difficulties to learning disabilities. The diagnostic strategy incorporates seven general steps:

1. Looking for signs of problems in regular classroom work.
2. Using material designed to elicit behavior for diagnostic analysis.
3. Searching for nonarithmetic examples of deficit behavior in areas to which the problem may have generalized.
4. Deciding on whether or not to seek outside help.
5. Establishing a remedial objective.
6. Preparing and using remedial materials.
7. Revising and reworking the prescriptive diagnostic process. (p. 69)

Interventions

Many learning-disabled children have problems affecting mathematics proficiency which are directly related to the understanding of concepts and numerical reasoning (primary type). Indeed, children with this specific disability may even be good readers. Others have many of the characteristics of learning disabilities—deficits in attention, memory, visual and auditory perception, spatial organization, visual-motor integration, and directional orientation, which directly affect the acquisition of knowledge and skill in mathematics, as well as in reading, writing, language, and social skills. Several correlates of learning disabilities and the areas of mathematics that are affected are listed in Figure 13-1. Children who manifest these behaviors may not have specific disability in mathematics but functional deficits which "spill-over" into this and other academic areas (secondary type).

Instruction that takes learner characteristics into account and provides an

Secondary Mathematics Disability

A. Correlates of Learning Disabilities	B. Performance effected
1. *Attentional deficits:* distractibility impulsivity perseveration	1a. Guessing answers 1b. Completing work 1c. Repetition in writing numbers 1d. Repetition of computation
2. *Memory deficits:* auditory visual	2a. Oral problems 2b. Revisualization of numbers
3. *Visual-motor disorders:*	3a. Writing numbers 3b. Erasing numbers
4. *Visual-spatial deficits:*	4a. Distinguishing size, shape, length, amounts 4b. Estimating time, chronological sequence 4c. Writing columns
5. *Orientation disorders:*	5. Spatial and directional concepts

Figure 13-1. Effects of learning disability correlates on mathematics performance.

adaptive, sequential approach can do much to foster acquisition of computational and problem-solving skills. Because all children do not manifest the same problems, educational intervention must be specific for each child.

General Suggestions

The following suggestions are general guidelines to be used in a remedial session.

Directions should be concise and clear. Some children benefit when they are asked to repeat the directions. Children who rely on visual cues may profit from written instructions.

As the child works through a problem, have him verbalize the thought processes. This gives the teacher added insight, in addition to helping the child who must "talk through" his performance. (This may be ill-advised for certain LD children who are prone to "overloading.")

Especially when working with an older child on a one-to-one basis, it is helpful if the objective for the lesson is given, and the link to previous lessons explained. This helps a child to see the relationship between lessons. Unless this is pointed out, many children approach each lesson as though it is discrete and do not recognize the continuity of the subject matter.

Become cognizant of general mathematics teaching deficiencies. An examination of the methods, materials, and organization of the remedial lesson may help pinpoint aspects of the instructional sequence which should be changed and/or modified. Cawley, et al. (1979) discuss four aspects of instructional failure teachers should know.

> ". . . instruction is inappropriate, incorrect, or too limited to develop the skill or concept being taught . . . allowing a youngster to progress to a more difficult set of tasks without having mastered prerequisites (see p. 177, Chapter 11, Payne et al., maintenance versus acquisition) . . . tendency to over correct," and ". . . faulty or incomplete ability to relate assessment to instruction." (pp. 31–33)

Remediating the Effects of
Learning-Disabilities Correlates

The improvement of the mathematics performance of learning-disabled students (secondary type) requires specific interventions. This listing is not meant to be exhaustive but rather illustrative of the kinds of modifications which can be made. The interventions are for problem areas noted in Figure 13.1, column B.

1a. Guessing answers, impulsive responses. Prevent impulsive responses by reinforcing correct responses rather than the number of items completed. Do not present many examples or problems at one time. Some children respond to "so much work" by racing through, trying to get it over quickly. For these children, withhold their pencil, while they think through the problem. For oral responses, encourage "thinking time," rather than speed of response.

1b. Difficulty in completing work. Many workbooks have too much material on them, causing distraction. For this child, too, fewer items should be presented at one time. A cardboard window can be used to frame each example or problem while blocking out the others on the page. Behavior modification techniques can also be helpful.

1c. Repetition in writing numbers. Some children tend to perseverate and continue writing a response beyond what is appropriate. This happens frequently when drilling in writing of numerals. Structure the assignment or page so that repetition will not be encouraged. Do not have the child write the numeral more than once before introducing another numeral.

1d. Repeating a computational operation. To prevent continuation of operations, alternate operations required so that a pattern is not established. In some cases it may be necessary to alternate modes of responses or materials.

2a. Auditory memory deficits. Visual presentations can be linked with the auditory, so that the child is not limited by the weaker modality. The visual representation can be stressed.

2b. Visual memory problems. Children who have difficulty revisualizing numbers can learn to use verbal prompts or mediators. Some respond best if a motor cue is taught. Color cuing can sometimes be utilized. The process signs can be written in different colors. Problems can be given orally.

3a. Dysgraphia. When children have difficulty in writing numerals, alternatives must be considered. Writing should be kept to a minimum. Printed or duplicated materials can be used so that only answers need be filled in. In some cases, the child can be directed to underline the correct response from among three or four. A stamp pad and numeral stamps can be provided so that the child need only stamp in the correct answer. Answers can be given orally to the teacher or aide, or on a tape recorder.

3b. Erasing difficulties. This is a problem, though minor, which can adversely affect children's written performance (see appendix). Frequently they do such a poor job, they cannot separate what was rewritten from what was erased. Another factor should also be considered. Some children are fearful of making errors. By teaching them how to erase an error, we are also saying that mistakes can be undone.

4a. Difficulties distinguishing size, shapes, lengths, and/or amounts. Provide a variety of real materials for comparison to arrange in order of size, length, weight, and so on. All senses should be utilized: touching, looking, counting aloud. Such activities can be done simultaneously with some children but with a single sensory approach with others. Stern blocks and pattern boards or Cuisinaire rods can be used to build trains and stairs so the children can compare size, lengths, and numerical combinations.

Concept words such as heavy-light, bigger-smaller must be taught specifically. Things that go together related to size can be taught using cut-out dolls, photos, and so forth. Ask questions such as: "Which clothes will fit which doll?" "Which car is the right size for the garage?" Children also need experiences in weighing and measuring items. The child should initially learn to feel the difference between one pound and five pounds; then finer discriminations should be learned.

Puzzles and form boards provide cues to shapes. Discuss the shape needed to fill the space. Have the child feel and describe the shapes without looking at them. Many LD children have verbal strengths and these should be tapped in various learning situations (Johnson & Myklebust, 1967, p. 254). Large outlines of shapes can be placed on the floor. The children can trace the shapes as they walk along the edges.

4b. Deficits in estimating time and/or chronological sequence. Have the child estimate how long he thinks an activity will take. Have him show on a demonstration clock what it will look like when the time will be up. Compare the time on the demonstration clock with the actual time.

Use a timer and have the child attempt to complete a task before it rings. The teacher should integrate the use of time concepts in natural classroom situations: e.g., "We have five minutes to clean up before it is time to go to lunch."

To facilitate memory of sequence of steps, verbal or visual cues can be used. Charts can show step-by-step procedures. Verbalizations should be clear and concise. This skill is important in learning to follow directions in a recipe but also in performing computations and in doing two- and three-step word problems.

4c. Difficulties in maintaining columns. Writing numerals in columns can be aided by providing a strong visual and possibly tactile stimulus. The space for writing the examples can be set off by a heavy line or a raised barrier (cardboard frame). Colored lines on the paper can set off the place-value columns. Using ruled paper with the lines running vertically can also provide the needed structure. As proficiency is developed, the stimulus should be faded.

5a. Orientation problems. The concepts right-left, up-down, in-out, under-over, and so on, should be used in real situations in the classroom and then applied to workbook or other two dimensional planes. Because of the concrete thinking of many LD children, they have difficulty transferring concepts understood in the "real world" to the two dimensional world of their texts and workbooks. Specific teaching of the relationship between the real and representational frequently has to be provided. Cues such as a color or a shape may be used to show directions. Arrows can be used to indicate the direction in which to work calculations or where to "carry."

Fostering Acquisition of Mathematics

Though mathematics generally has a scope and sequence which is defined by the school district or by the textbook company, teachers should be free to modify the sequence to meet the specific needs of specific children.

> "The role of the teacher is one of a guide. A good guide uses judgment about when to take a detour and how to return to the main road after a detour. Knowledge of which skills have certain prerequisties is required on the part of the teacher. You cannot learn long division without knowing place value, multiplication, and subtraction. You can delay long division and detour to geometry, fractional numbers, or measurement" (May, 1974, p. 2).

No text or course can give all the answers for teaching all children. The skilled teacher should know many methods and materials for teaching a skill or concept and must be flexible in order to prescribe alternatives, choose and/or adapt materials. Criterion-referenced tests can be used to pinpoint the student's strengths and weaknesses. The child's unique pattern of performance provides the framework for the interventions which are chosen.

The evaluation plan should provide the teacher and child with information to be used in planning future lessons and should be based on the individual improvement and functioning rather than to compare children's performance. Whenever possible the student should be included in developing broad goals, work schedules, and so on. Though originally developed to be used with reading, the application of

Tannenbaum's taxonomic analysis (Fig. 13-2) can help the teacher choose, not only the appropriate teaching material, but also the most effective setting, response medium and modality for teaching and reinforcement in the area of mathematics.

Readiness for Instruction

Readiness for instruction is of particular importance in this academic area. Attainment of specific stages of development as defined by Piaget (1952; 1953; 1963; 1969) are needed if the child is to deal effectively with mathematics concepts. The interaction of maturation, experience, and education enables the child to progress through the four stages in the development of mental structures; that is, sensorimotor, preoperational, concrete operations, and formal operations. Though the sequence of acquisition rather than specification of absolute age level is of prime importance, Copeland (1979) notes:

> Since around seven years of age is a critical development time, one might be justified in concluding that the six to seven year old is in reality a preschooler as far as systematized instruction in mathematics is concerned. The six year old is more like the five than seven year old. The first grade as well as the

COMPREHENSIVE TAXONOMY

Strategy

Instructional Setting	Instructional Mode	Communication Input	Communication Output
1. Teacher— Total Class	1. Exploration	1. Visual	1. Oral Response
2. Student Self- Instruction	2. Problem Solving (Divergent)	2. Auditory—Visual	2. Motoric Response (Marking and/or Writing)
3. Teacher— Subgroup	3. Testing Recall	3. Auditory	3. No Response
4. Teacher—Student	4. Problem Solving (Convergent)	4. Motoric (Haptic, Tactile, Kinesthetic)	4. Oral—Motoric (Marking and/or Writing)
5. Student—Student Parallel	5. Exposition	5. Auditory—Motoric	5. Motoric Response (Gestures and/or Movement)
6. Student—Total Class	6. Game Competition Standard	6. Visual—Motoric	6. Oral—Motoric Response (Gestures and/or Movement)
7. Student— Subgroup	7. Game Competition Player	7. Auditory—Visual- Motoric	
8. Student—Student Tutorial	8. Game Competition Field	8. Self-Stimulation	
9. Student Self- Directed	9. Game Competition Team		
10. Student—Student Interactive	10. Role Playing		
11. Group Self- Instruction	11. Programmed Response		
12. Group Self- Directed	12. Patterning		

Figure 13-2. The "how" of instruction. (Source: A. J. Tannenbaum. Taxonomic Teaching Project, R & D Center, Teachers College, Columbia University, 1971. Revised 1980.)

kindergarten should probably be devoted to readiness activities as far as mathematics is concerned. . . . There should be more work with concrete material and less work with mathematical symbols, such as +, -, ÷. (p. 296)

In the preoperational period (ages 2-7) as defined by Piaget, the child begins to use symbols in a limited way. He is able to relate symbols without having to handle them physically though he deals with them mentally, visualizing this manipulation. Not until the concrete period (ages 7-11) do three changes important to the acquisition of mathematics concepts take place in the child's thinking. 1) He becomes less egocentric and begins to view the world from vantage points other than his own; 2) he understands the reversibility of processes, 3) enabling him to conserve. That is, he understands that changes in shape do not signify changes in mass. In general, children develop the ability to conserve between five and eight years. Until this level is reached, the child will be unable to comprehend the invariance of number. The teacher must provide an environment for it to develop. Knowledge of these levels should ". . . *serve as a guide for instruction, not as a basis for curriculum*. The teacher who is familiar with the stages of development as described by Piaget will at least know what *not* to teach" (Gearheart, 1976, p. 122).

When number concepts are introduced too early, children tend to learn splinter skills which they cannot yet apply to appropriate situations. As an example, consider the child who learns the two times table but cannot tell 4 X 2 because "We haven't learned that yet."

Almy (1967, p. 35) recommends using an interview technique similar to Piaget's rather than diagnostic tests to ascertain children's progress because it reveals how the child arrives at the answer to the problem. In addition to the tests referred to earlier, The Piagetian Attainment Kit (1978) can provide useful information pertaining to the acquisition of specific concepts related to mathematical performance.

Just as there is a readiness sequence for a child's level of acquisition of a concept according to Piaget, so too are there hierarchies of knowledge, skills, and of knowing. Knowledge, skills, and broad concepts can be developed by proceeding through a sequence which moves from the real or concrete through representational and abstract levels of presentation and, if approached properly, of understanding and application. According to Bruner (1963) the acquisition of concepts proceeds through seven stages of knowing: enactive, intuitive, concrete (iconic), representation, abstract (symbolic), application, and communication. A child may be at different levels in mathematics depending on the concept; for example, he may be at the communication level in addition while still at the concrete level in subtraction.

Many mathematics programs include at least three steps in concept development: concrete, representational, and abstract, with a fourth step, application, assumed (Fig. 13-3).

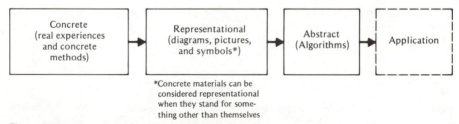

*Concrete materials can be considered representational when they stand for something other than themselves

Figure 13-3. Steps in arithmetic concept development.

The average teacher or learning-disabilities specialist has little difficulty in using the concrete and representational levels in teaching mathematics. Most texts stress the concrete thinking of the learning-disabled child and concentrate on ways to develop and select teaching methods and materials that enable the child to "see" the concept. Frequently the child is kept at the concrete level beyond what is appropriate. Little stress is given to developing strategies that go beyond the concrete to bridge the gap between that level and the abstract stage. Most often the abstract level is neglected because, "LD children find it difficult to abstract." The lack of emphasis of research on teaching strategies for problem solving by LD students has contributed to our poor record in this area. While it may be true that severely or moderately disabled youngsters may be unable to achieve at this higher level, the paucity of research with even the mildly handicapped leaves this an area of conjecture.

A five-step spiral for concept development has been suggested by Sharma (1978) to lead to abstract thinking in mathematics without undue reliance on manipulative material.

1. *Free play*—The children should be given time to interact with and explore the concrete materials before the concept is introduced.
2. *Primary operations and concepts*—Review the preceding or basic concept upon which the current concept is based.
3. *Manipulative activities*—The concept under study should be taught using hands-on experience.
4. *Recording of the concrete experiences*—The child should use symbols to illustrate concrete experiences.
5. *Experiences at the abstract level*—After "enough" experiences at level 4, the child should be given abstract problems "to translate in concrete experimentation and vice versa."

The same steps would be followed for teaching the next concept in the sequence or for a different sequence of concepts. The amount of time and number of activities at each level vary according to individual needs.

The Role of Practice

Though there are educators (Stern, 1971) who believe that mastery of arithmetic and the development of mathematical thinking can be achieved without the use of drill, many, such as Ausubel (1966), believe repetition consolidates learning. Practice, when used in conjunction with methods that emphasize the structure of the discipline and the relationship of numbers, helps develop facility in the use of learned material.

"To place primary emphasis on understanding, then, does not preclude the necessity for practice; it merely changes the position of drill in the learning sequence, with consequent changes in its nature." (Marks, et al., 1975, p. 20).

Several principles should be followed:

1. Practice or drill is not to be used to teach, only to reinforce.
2. Understanding must precede practice. Unless this is done, the child who forgets an answer will be unable to figure it out.

3. Practice must be spaced in order to avoid fatigue and maintain interest.
4. A variety of activities should be used. Care must be taken to avoid gimmicks or game rules that overpower the skill to be reinforced.
5. Practice must be supervised to assure the use of correct methods and responses, thus preventing practice of error.

Materials

Most math-disabled youngsters in grades K–8 will receive remediation each day in a resource room. Some will also be expected to take part in math lessons within the regular class. Generally, in grades 9 to 12, students with specific disabilities in math will receive instruction in a resource room or in a special track math class. Depending on the functioning level, these will either be classes where the curriculum stresses survival skills or classes for "applied" geometry and/or algebra.

No matter which settings are used, a wide variety of real and concrete materials and teacher-made materials, in addition to the commercially available texts, teaching systems, and games, must be available.

Capps and Hatfield (1979) suggest the following questions to enable the teacher to become aware of the attributes of the materials to be used. "Are there any irrelevant features which may be a distractor or serve as a hindrance to concept formation? Does the material clearly represent the concept to be extracted? Does the material provide for easy individual manipulation by the child? Does the device explore as many senses as possible? Does the device allow for abstraction" (p. 287)?

Basic materials for these classrooms are listed in Figure 13-4 and discussed below. These materials enable the child to apply concepts and work out problems within a concrete context to introduce, reinforce, and/or review concepts. They can be used with the teacher or alone by the student.

Counting Materials. For the students who are in the lower grades or are performing at a lower level, materials are needed that can be counted and used to reinforce 1 : 1 correspondence. Chips, counting frames, and bundling sticks can serve this purpose. Special care should taken in selecting materials for the older child who is performing at a lower level. Different sizes of hair rollers and nuts and bolts are more readily accepted by the older child. (Selection of these motivational materials is analogous to the concept of high interest/low reading level materials for the reading-deficient older student).

Abaci[*]. There are many types of abaci, such as nine-bead and 19-bead expanded. The expanded abacus contains 19 beads in each column, with the tenth bead of a contrasting color to stress the bridging of tens. It is more adaptable than the nine-bead abacus wherein the ones column must be cleared to all beyond nine, causing confusion. Also, the nine-bead closed abacus cannot be used for regrouping in subtraction.

---

[*] There is a difference between an abacus and a counting frame (although many teachers and texts, in error, continue to use these terms synonymously). In a counting frame, each bead is worth the same as any other bead—that is, one. With the abacus, place value is represented by column (hence, one bead in the tens column is equal to ten beads in the one's column).

Cuisinaire Rods. The Cuisinaire rods are wooden rods which can be used for all computation processes of whole numbers and of fractions. Length and color assume a value. White, the smallest rod, is one centimeter square. The rods increase in length by one centimeter, the largest being 10 centimeters. Activity books that explain how to use the rods are available.

Stern Materials. Like the Cuisinaire rods, the Stern blocks are also color-coded. However, a further cue is provided: each block is ruled to indicate individual cube units. The blocks vary in size from one to ten units. The student develops number concepts through the manipulation of the blocks together with counting boards, pattern boards, number cases, and so forth. Stern's structured approach to arithmetic is explained in detail in *Children Discover Arithmetic* (Stern & Stern, 1971). The program was developed for use in kindergarten through grade 3.

Montessori Materials. The basic set of Montessori materials includes geometric shapes, bead chains, counting boxes, sandpaper numerals, counting frames, and arithmetic frames. They can be used to develop many concepts; that is, 1 : 1 correspondence, comparison of size, shape, volume, and length, place value, and the four arithmetic processes. The Montessori program uses these materials within a specific developmental sequence.

Geoboard. The geoboard can be used to explore geometric relationships, introduce measurement of perimeter, and area of geometric figures. The geoboard can be made by placing rows of nails equidistant from each other on a wooden board. The distance between each nail is the unit. Rubber bands are fitted on the nails to form geometric figures. By counting the number of units around the figures, the perimeter is found. The students can also make a large rectangle and use additional rubber bands to divide the interior into square units. They can then see how many square units are inside the rectangle. Much practice with geometric figures of varying sizes will enable the students to generalize rules (formula) for finding the perimeter and the area of the figures.

Squared Materials. Squared materials are made easily and cheaply. Duplicate many sheets of paper divided into squares (approximately $\frac{1}{2}''$). Cut out squares that are 10 units by 10 units, single strips of 10 units, and many single units. The materials can be used to represent numbers and to make computations involving all four processes when renaming is required. This material has many benefits: it is cheap and easy to construct; it is adaptable for many types of examples; it is stored easily; and it does not make noise when it falls on the floor.

Pocket Chart. Column headings on the pocket chart indicate place value. Paper cut-outs ▯ or ◯ represent the numbers in the examples. Some teachers use different colored cut-outs to represent hundreds, tens, and ones.

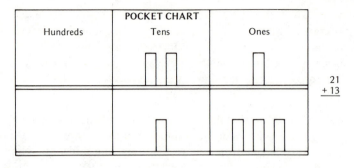

Number Line. The number line enables the student to see the numbers in sequence, and shows a continuous magnitude. All processes can be demonstrated using the number line, for example:

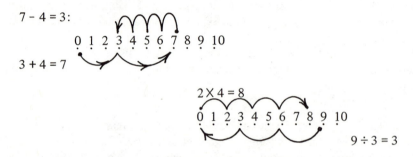

Measurement Materials. A variety of materials listed in Figure 13-4 relate to measurements of various kinds. Many of these materials are appropriate for children who are developing the concepts of conservation. In addition, they can all be used to help learning-disabled children understand their environment, become better consumers, and develop skill in measurement which will enable them to perform daily living tasks more effectively.

Found Materials. A representative sample of found materials is included in the chart. Many others can be added. These materials—the menus, advertisements, and time tables—can be used to develop mathematics skills within meaningful contexts. The scope and interest level are limited only by the imagination and skill of the teacher.

Calculators. There has been much discussion, though little research, about the use of calculators in the schools. In general the rule has been to allow their use after the child has good facility in performing computations. Although Schmoly (1978) says, "... the calculator must be acknowledged as the most efficient and the usual method of computation," she also emphasizes the need to develop children's skill in estimating and the ability to use algorithms. Strict adherence to this rule can be a disservice to some learning-disabled children. Indeed, it places a severe restriction on them. If the child has access to other aids—such as abacus, number line, etc.—a

Chips (discs) for counting	Geometric shapes
Number line	Geoboard
Squared material	Thermometers
Place value chart	Clocks
Pocket chart	Clock replicas
Abacus	Calendar
Counting frames	Scale rulers (varying sizes)
Bundling sticks	Containers of different liquid measures
Cuisinaire rods	Protractor
Stern materials	Compass
Fraction parts	Measuring cups
Montessori math materials:	Calculators
"Found" materials	
Menus	
Train and bus schedules	
Ads and circulas for sales	

Figure 13-4. Basic materials for mathematics.

good case can be made for including the calculator. Children with memory problems may be prevented from developing an understanding of the concepts if they are not allowed to proceed beyond their ability to compute on their own. Use of a calculator can speed up the rote process and enable the student to concentrate on problem solving. Though a calculator is used, the child still must determine the appropriate process. Moreover, the novelty aspect coupled with greater likelihood for success are powerful motivational ingredients. Instant feedback is provided—a tenet consonant with behavior-modification theory. Kasnic (1978) found that the use of calculators in problem solving helped low ability math students compete more successfully with higher-ability students.

Before deciding whether a calculator should be used, Teitelbaum (1978) suggests determining whether you are teaching a computational skill or problem solving. When application and problem solving is stressed, the use of the calculator by students frees time for teaching. When computational skills are being practiced, calculators can be used to check answers.

Care must be taken in the selection of a calculator. Portability is important. Many on the market are small and fit easily into a pocket or purse. The display board should be clear and easy to read, and should not be "loaded" with symbols and processes beyond the level of the student. In addition, too many symbols on the board will make it difficult for the student to locate the keys he needs. Some displays are too small or the keys are too close together for a child who has difficulty with eye/hand coordination. A stylus can be used to facilitate ease in plugging in data. It is best to avoid calculators that do not provide tactile or auditory feedback when data figures are entered. Instruction in the use and care of the calculators must be provided. The students must learn how to enter data and how to read the display panel and/or printout.

TEACHING TECHNIQUES

It is impossible to cover all aspects of teaching children with a primary mathematics disability in one chapter. We include the following because they represent techniques proven successful in the remediation of common errors.

Place Value

The concept of place value can be introduced and reinforced in many ways with many materials. A place value chart with columns labeled tens and ones can be used for placement of numerals. They are then read and discussed. When a student is writing numbers on a page or when doing simple problems, columns can be drawn and the child writes the numerals in the appropriate columns.

$$
\begin{array}{c|c}
\text{tens} & \text{ones} \\
4 & 3 \\
+\,1 & 3 \\
\hline
5 & 6
\end{array}
$$

When two place numbers are mastered, introduce the concept of hundreds and add a column to the chart. Children with more advanced skills, generally toward the end of the intermediate grades, can use a chart that extends to millions.

Millions			Thousands			Units		
Hundreds	Tens	Ones	Hundreds	Tens	Ones	Hundreds	Tens	Ones

Renaming

The student functioning on the intermediate level should be taught to rename the number of tens in hundreds, the number of hundreds in thousands: for example, there are 63 tens in 634. Renaming (regrouping, exchanging) was found by Cox (1975) to be an area of frequent error of computation for all processes. Many concrete materials can be used to illustrate the concept: abacus, Cuisinaire rods, Stern blocks, squared materials, bundling sticks, and so forth. These materials stress equivalences and utilize the idea of exchanging tens for ones, hundreds for tens. The sticks can be "bundled" into groups of ten or "unbundled" when it is necessary to exchange. The hundred squares of the squared material can be exchanged for ten strips and the ten strips can be exchanged for ones. The act of physically exchanging the material is reinforcing. The use of dollars, dimes, and pennies can enhance motivation.

The most common type of systematic error is inversion error in subtraction (Cox, 1975). This error occurs when, rather than regrouping (renaming), the minuend is subtracted from the subtrahend: e.g.,

$$\begin{array}{r} 42 \\ -\ 6 \\ \hline 44 \end{array}$$

Blankenship (1978) suggests using demonstration plus feedback to remediate this error: 1.) The teacher demonstrates the correct way to do the problem; 2.) the student solves a second problem, 3.) if correct, the student is told it is correct and additional problems are given; 4.) if incorrect, the student is told so, and the teacher demonstrates another problem. Steps 2 and 3 are repeated. Using this approach, Blankenship found that generalization to noninstructed problem types took place as well as maintenance of the newly acquired skill.

Weill (1978) reports success using "the hill method" for subtraction when the minuend is greater than 10 but less than 20.

a	b	c	d	
	↗15	↗15	Ask: How many steps to 10?	2
15			How many steps from 10	
− 8	8	8 10	to the number?	5
	Write 10 in the middle.		e. Add the steps for the	
			answer.	7

Many similar examples are practiced. The children are then encouraged to visualize the hill and talk through the process.

Operations

Many LD children confuse arithmetical operations and do not know whether to add, subtract, multiply, or divide. Vocabulary must be stressed with key words emphasized: for example, adding, plus, sum, total, altogether. Provide practice in associating the visual symbol with the spoken word and synonym. Teacher-made games such as Bingo can be used. A word card indicating a process is called. If the child has the process sign on his card, he covers it with the word card. The game continues (as in bingo) until a complete row is covered.

Rote Counting

Some learning-disabled children rely heavily on counting in order to add or subtract. While this is appropriate in the early stages of learning, it causes difficulties later. Materials that encourage counting, such as the abacus and counting sticks, should be phased out. Capps and Hatfield (1979) offer two suggestions. Tachistoscopic exercises using dotted flash cards will help decrease the reliance on counting. The cards are flashed briefly and the child tells how many dots were seen. The viewing time is gradually decreased as the child gains fluency. (A by-product of tachistoscopic activities is that attention skills are nourished). Because Cuisinaire rods are not scored to indicate units, they can also be used to decrease the reliance on counting.

Learning the Addition and Subtraction Facts 1–10

Numerous techniques for teaching this basic knowledge exist. Counting by one is related to adding one to or subtracting one from any number. Learning to count is a step away from understanding of number sequences with respect to directionality. ("What comes *after* six?" "What comes *before* nine?" etc.). This, in turn, can be applied to adding (or subtracting). If seven comes after six, then 6 + 1 = 7; if eight comes before nine, then 9 - 1 = 8. (A number line is a tremendous help here.) This relationship between number sequence and addition of one more (or subtraction of one less) seems self-evident, and indeed, most children, by the time they enter first grade, have already "figured it out" by themselves; LD children, however, may have to be given specific instruction in this area.

Similarly, counting by two's facilitates adding (and subtraction) of two's. The child who can recite, and count two—four—six—eight—ten is ready to learn such facts as 8 + 2 = 10, 6 - 2 = 4, and so on.

Fingers can be used to assist the child to acquire many of the number facts, but especially 5 + 1, 5 + 2, 5 + 3, 5 + 4, 5 + 5. A nickel and five pennies can be used as well.

The child's knowledge of 4 + 4 can lead to his learning 4 + 5, and 4 + 3 (the so-called "doubles and near doubles" cue).

A highly effective method that improves visualization, involves physical manipulation of objects (an approach especially recommended for LD children, Strauss and Lehtinen, 1947, p. 137), provides instant feedback, can be used with all of the addition and subtraction number facts (1-10), and is novel and "fun" is the Cover Up method (Siegel, 1961, p. 110). Place some chips (or pennies) on the table; count them with the child; cover them with your hand (it helps if they were arranged in domino pattern—thus facilitating recognition and memory). Slide some more chips under your hand. Ask the child how many there are now. Remove your hand to verify. Start with three or four chips at first, and gradually increase to ten. Subtraction is taught by removing some (instead of sliding in additional ones) from the initial array of discs. This is always done in full view of the child. Thus, the fact that he has just finished looking at the original set is a crucial factor. In other words, this activity utilizes, as well as develops, visual memory. Thornton (1979, p. 1) suggests a similar activity using counters and a butter tub to hide them.

A grid system can be used to provide a visual representation of multiplication facts (Hayes, 1975). For example, to show 5 X 3, five vertical lines are crossed with three horizontal lines. The intersections are counted to find the product.

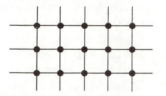

The Chisanbop Finger Calculating Method has been suggested as a computing aid for learning-disabled children (Lieberthal & Pai, 1977). In this method, numerical values are assigned to the fingers and thumbs. Numbers can be represented in various ways by pressing down combinations of fingers and thumbs. Greater speed ensues as the presses become more automatic. Though stressed as a supplementary mathematics program, Greenwood (1979) points out that the sequence of teaching computations differs from most mathematics curricula. Additions and multiplication are taught before subtraction and division. The focus on regrouping fives and using the nine complement for subtraction involves abstractions difficult for children to grasp. It is Greenwood's contention that the method does not enhance the comprehension of number but, ". . . it actually *requires* such an understanding" (p. 19). In addition, good psychomotor coordination and manual dexterity are essential. These frequently tend to be areas of deficit for the learning-disabled child. Greenwood cautiously suggests the use of Chisanbop in grades 4–10 as an alternative to performing whole number computation and as a possible remedial program when "It is assumed the students have acquired number and place value concepts . . ." (p. 21). Until research demonstrates the effectiveness of this approach for learning-disabled students, teachers should be cautious in implementing such a program.

Word Problems

Problem solving receives little emphasis in many programs for the learning disabled. The students are asked to "do" examples but are rarely asked to solve word problems. Rather than omitting word problems because the students do them poorly, emphasis must be placed on teaching how to solve them.

The word problems should be motivating and relate to real experiences or realistic situations set up by the teacher. "Students must feel that their efforts to solve mathematics problems have some important ends. The essential elements appear to be that the student feels the problem can be solved and that the solution has application outside the assignment" (Alley and Deschler, 1979, p. 173). A common experience can be the basis for problem solving in classes where children perform at different levels. The suggested "found materials" (Figure 13-4), that is, menus, ads, train schedules, can provide data for the problems.

Visualization of the situations presented in the problems can be aided by the use of drawings, diagrams, or, if necessary, concrete materials. Generally, concrete materials are used when a new concept is being introduced or when the student has difficulty in conceptualizing the word problem.

Cawley, et al. (1979) developed materials in Project MATH that present problem-solving situations that can be used with groups of children of varying abilities. "Problem solving offers a unique opportunity to integrate a host of learner needs into a cohesive activity. Rather than excluding problem solving, programs should emphasize this topic in order to meet the needs of the learning disabled" (p. 41). Children who cannot read should not miss out on the opportunity to learn how to solve the problems. They can be given the problems orally or with a minimum of verbiage. Though initially the problems should be written simply, the students should be taught how to extract the important data and omit extraneous information from more complex presentations.

Mathematics skills must be used every day, at home, on the job, and in social situations, for example, telling time, planning a schedule, using money, balancing a checkbook, paying bills, measuring amounts and distances, buying food, fuel, clothing, planning a trip, and preparing a meal. The learning-disabled must develop the abilities necessary to perform these daily living skills or they will be truly handicapped. Learning-disability specialists and general-education teachers must work together to implement strategies to build and strengthen these basic competencies.

REFERENCES

Alley, G., and Deschler, D. *Teaching the learning disabled adolescent: Strategies and methods*. Denver: Love Publishing, 1979.

Almy, M. *Young children's thinking*. New York: Columbia University: Teachers College Press, 1967.

Ausubel, D. P. A teaching strategy for culturally-deprived pupils: Cognitive and motivational considerations. In Frost, J. L., and Hawkes, G. R. (Eds.), *The disadvantaged child*. Boston: Houghton Mifflin, 1966.

Bachor, D. G. Using work samples as diagnostic information. *Learning Disabilities Quarterly*, Winter 1979, *2*(1), 45–52.

Bagai, E. (Ed.). *System FORE, mathematics*. North Hollywood, Ca.: Foreworks, 1977.

Bartel, N. R. Problems in arithmetic achievement. In Hamill D. D., and Bartel, N. R. (Eds.), *Teaching Children with Learning and Behavior Problems, 2nd ed*. Boston: Allyn & Bacon, 1978.

Beatly, L. S., Madden, R., and Gardner, E. F. *Stanford diagnostic arithmetic test*. New York: Harcourt, Brace, Jovanovich, 1966.

Beech, M. C. Concurrent validity of the Boehm Test of Basic Concepts. *Learning Disabilities Quarterly*, July, 1981, 4(1) 53–60.

Blankenship, C. S. Remediating systematic inversion errors in subtraction through the use of demonstration and feedback. *Learning Disabilities Quarterly*, 1978, *1*(3), 12–22.

Bruner, J. S. *The process of education*. New York: Vantage Books, 1963.

————. *Toward a theory of instruction*. Cambridge, Mass.: Harvard University Press, 1966.

Bryan, T. H. and Bryan, J. H. *Understanding learning disabilities, 2nd ed*. Sherman Oaks, Ca.: Alfred Publishing Company, 1978.

Burk, D. *Piagetain attainment kit*. New York: McGraw-Hill, 1973.

Buros, O, K. (Ed.). *Eighth mental measurement yearbook*. New Jersey: Gryphon Press, 1978.

————. *Seventh mental measurement yearbook*. New Jersey: Gryphon Press, 1972.

Capps, L. R. and Hatfield, M. M. Mathematical concepts and skills: Diagnosis, prescription, and correction of deficiencies. In Meyen, E. L., Hergason, G. A., and Whelan, R. J. (Eds.), *Instruction planning for exceptional children*. Denver: Love Publishing Company, 1979.

Cawley, J. F. An instructional design in mathematics. In Mann, L., Goodman, L., and Wiederholt, J. L. (Eds.), *Teaching the learning-disabled adolescent*. Boston: Houghton Mifflin Company, 1978.

————. Youth and mathematics: A review of characteristics. *Learning Disabilities Quarterly*, Winter, 1979, *2*(1), 29–44.

Cawley, J. F. Fitzmaurice. A. M., Shaw, R. A., Kahn, H., and Bates III, H. Mathematics and learning-disabled youth: The upper grade levels. *Learning Disabilities Quarterly*, Fall 1978, *1*, 37–52.

Cawley, J. F., Fitzsimmons, A. M., Shaw, R. A., Kahn, H., and Bates, H. Math word problems: Suggestions for learning-disabled students. *Learning Diabilities Quarterly*, Spring, 1979, *2*, pp. 25–41.

Cawley, J. F., Goodstein, H. A., Fitzmaurice, A. M., LePore, A. V., Sedlak, R., and Althaus, V. *Project Math. Levels I, II, III, IV*. Tulsa: Educational Development Corporation, 1976–1977.

Connolly, A. J., Nachtman, W., and Pritchett, E. M. *Keymath diagnostic arithmetic test*. Circle Pines, Minn.: American Guidance Service, 1967.

Copeland, R. W. *How children learn mathematics, 3rd ed*. New York: Macmillan, 1979.

Cox, L. S. Systematic errors in the four vertical algorithms in normal and handicapped populations. *Journal for Research in Mathematics Education*, 1975, 6, 202–220.

Dunn, L. M., and Markwardt, F. C. *Peabody individual achievement test*. Circle Pines, Minn.: American Guidance Service, 1970.

Faas, L. A. *Learning disabilities: A competency-based approach*. Boston: Houghton Mifflin, 1976.

Gearheart, B. R. *Teaching the learning disabled: A combined task-process approach*. St. Louis: C. V. Mosby, 1976.

Greenstein, J., and Strain, P. S. The utility of the key math diagnostic arithmetic test for adolescent learning disabled students. *Psychology in the Schools*, July 1977, 14(3), 275–282.

Greenwood, J. Critique on the chisanbop finger calculating method. *Arithmetic Teacher*, March, 1979, 18–21.

Hayes, M. L. *Somebody said learning disabilities*. San Raphael, Ca.: Academic Therapy Publications, 1975.

————. The visual learner. Readings in Learning Disabilities. Guilford, Conn.: Special Learning Corporation, 1978: pp. 76–79.

Jastak, J. F., and Jastak, S. R. *Wide range achievement test*. Wilmington, Delaware: Guidance Associates, 1965.

Johnson, D. J., and Myklebust, H. R. *Learning disabilities educational principles and practices*. New York: Grune & Stratton, 1967.

Johnson, S. W. *Arithmetic and learning disabilities: Guidelines for identification and remediation*. Boston: Allyn & Bacon, 1979.

Kasnic, M. J. The effect of using handheld calculators on mathematics problem-solving ability among sixth grade students (Doctoral Dissertation, Oklahoma State University, 1977). *Dissertation Abstracts International*, 1977 38A, 5311, March 1978. No. 7801276.

Kosc, L. Developmental dyslexia. *Journal of Learning Disabilities*, March, 1974, 7, (3) 165–177.

Lerner, J. W. *Children with learning disabilities, 3rd ed*. Boston: Houghton Mifflin, 1981.

Lieberthal, E., and Pai, H. Y. *Teachers manual of chisanbop finger calculations*. Mt. Vernon, N.Y.: Chisanbop Enterprise, 1977.

Marks, J. L., Purdy, C. R., Kinney, L. B., and Hiatt, Q. A. *Teaching elementary school mathematics for understanding, 4th ed*. New York: McGraw-Hill, 1975.

May, L. J. *Teaching mathematics in the elementary school, 2nd ed*. New York: Free Press, 1974.

McLoughlin, J. A. and Lewis, R. B. *Assessing special students: strategies and procedures*. Columbus: Charles E. Merrill, 1981.

Piaget, J. *The child's conception of number*. New York: Humanities Press, 1952.

————. How children develop mathematical concepts. *Scientific American*, November 1953, pp. 74–79.

Piaget, J., and Inhelder, B. *The child's conception of space*. New York: Humanities Press, 1963.

_____. *The early growth of logic in the child*. New York: W. W. Norton, 1969.

Proger, B. B. *Test Review No. 2 Boehm Test of Basic Concepts Journal of Special Education*, Spring-Summer 1970, *4*(2), 249–251.

Russell, S. N., and Dunlap, W. P. *An interdisciplinary approach to reading and mathematics*. Novato, Ca.: Academic Therapy Publications, 1977.

Schmoly, S.P.R. Calculators: What difference will they make? *Arithmetic Teacher*, December, 1978, 46–47.

Sharma, M. C. How to take the child from concrete to abstract. Wellesby, Mass: *The SLD Gazette*, Massachusetts ACLD, 1978, *1*(5), 4–7.

Siegel, E. *Helping the brain-injured child*. Albany: New York Association for the Learning Disabled, 1961.

_____. *Teaching one child*. Freeport, N.Y.: Educational Activities, 1972.

Smith, S. L. *No easy answers: The learning-disabled child*. Washington, D.C.: DHEW Publication No. (ADM) 77-526, 1978.

Stellern, J., Vasa, S. F., and Little, J. *Introduction to diagnostic-prescription teaching and programming*. Glen Ridge, New Jersey: Exceptional Press, 1976.

Stern, C., and Stern, M. B. *Children discover arithmetic*. New York: Harper & Row, 1971.

Strauss, A. A., and Lehtinen, L. E. *Psychopathology and education of the brain-injured child, Volume I*. New York: Grune & Stratton, 1947.

Tannenbaum, A. J. *Taxonomic teaching project*. Columbia University, Reading and Disabilities Center, 1971.

Teitelbaum, E. Calculators for classroom use. *Arithmetic Teacher*, November, 1978, 18–20.

Thornton, C. A. Parents can help: Success strategies. *Perception: The Newsletter for Parents of Children with Learning Disabilities*, September, 1979, *2*(3), 1, 8.

Weill, B. Mrs. Weill's hill: A successful subtraction method for use with the learning-disabled child. *Arithmetic Teacher*, October, 1978, 34–35.

Weiss, H., and Weiss, M. *A survival manual: Case studies and suggestions for the learning-disabled teenager*. Great Barrington, Mass.: Treehouse Associates, 1974.

Science and Social Studies

14

Because the LD child has substantial deficits in the basic skills, the other subject areas are often downgraded. This can easily be seen by examining special-education texts, college-course outlines, topics presented at professional conferences, and so on. The "three R's" (and process training) get their due, but there is a void with respect to science, social studies, and the other school subjects. Special education teachers probably spend a significantly larger proportion of the school day in remediating basic skills than do teachers in regular classrooms. However, since LD children are being mainstreamed today with increasing frequency, it is a good idea to consider the total set of their academic needs, not merely the remedial aspect. Moreover, the principle of normalization dictates a similar thrust even for the LD child in the self-contained classroom.

Although special education teachers and some elementary school teachers (namely, those who teach the lower functioning regular classes) deemphasize the "nonbasic" subjects, teachers of special curricular areas (particularly, but by no means exclusively, in the secondary schools), by virtue of their training, are subject-oriented and cannot readily deal with the pupil who is deficient in reading, spelling, penmanship, and/or arithmetic. What is needed, of course, is a blend of the two: the ability to teach the subject area(s), but with sufficient flexibility to accommodate the LD child's remedial needs.

The following format will be used in discussing these subject areas: we list the positive implications each area holds for the the LD child. Then we enumerate the pitfalls—in view of the overall perceptual, motoric, behavioral, and cognitive impairment generally attributed to this population. Finally, we suggest modifications which can offset the pitfalls. We list the pitfalls and modifications in table form.

259

SCIENCE

Implications

1. Science can help the LD child understand his world. Because of perceptual deficits, illogical thinking, and/or lack of experience, he may have many misconceptions about his environment. One curriculum bulletin (New York City Board of Education, 1977-78 Series, pp. 70-71) contends that effective teaching of science to brain-injured children can help them to: (1) "look through the trappings of propaganda, dogmatic assumptions, and unreliable sources of information;" (2) develop conceptual skills via classifying objects found in the environment; (3) learn to examine evidence, formulate a hypothesis, then verify its validity; and, (4) diminish fears stemming from misinformation and misconceptions. (For example, one teacher, upon learning that many pupils in her class for brain-injured children were unduly fearful during electrical storms, taught them about lightning and thunder, thereby reducing this specific anxiety.)

2. Science generates many topics that have a high interest level. It therefore can provide motivation to read, write, measure, and the like.

3. Science can provide productive, satisfying leisure-time activities (e.g., gardening, starting rock collections, building telegraph sets). More specifically, caring for pets and plants can be extremely important to LD children because it gives them responsibility. Chandler (1977) found that teaching a class of TMR "babysitting" for houseplants effected a growth in self-esteem since the pupils realize that the plants would live and grow as a direct result of *their* efforts, and that (probably for the first time in their lives) a living thing depended upon them. Moreover, it is well known that horticulture has a therapeutic effect in giving the client a sense of peace and awareness of how life was created, and increased understanding of his relationship to his environment (Washington, D.C., 1977, p. 23).

4. Science can lead to a better understanding of health care (e.g., nutrition and eating habits, exercise, wearing proper clothing, cleanliness). This is especially important for the LD child who may wash, bathe and brush teeth, spasmodically and only partially (owing to disorganization and impulsivity); may consistently eat the wrong foods (perseveratively) or bolt his food (impulsively); and get insufficient exercise since he is rejected from many social groups. Studying science can also lead—not nag—the child toward being more careful, thus preventing accidents. In addition it can give him a good handle on drug, tobacco, and alcohol abuse. (Often knowledge here must be tied in with the child's *feelings*. An excellent resource for adolescents, *The Coping With Series*, by Shirley Schwarzrock & C. Gilbert Wrenn, Circle Pines, Minn., 1971, can augment a science curriculum in a meaningful way. Four of its guidance booklets deal specifically with the concept of food, smoking, alcohol, and drugs as psychological crutches.)

5. Science can create a wedge into socialization by means of projects involving several pupils (e.g., building a weather station, constructing and operating a HAM radio set). A program in marine science for Delaware's exceptional children, entitled *The Sea Beside Us* (an ESEA Title I project) reports of increased opportunity to socialize (jointly preparing meals, setting the table, and planning and participating in campfires), (Watling & Hallard, 1974). A farming project for exceptional children cites gains in spontaneous, informal communication (the students feel freer than

in the classroom), and in social conduct, e.g., sharing one's "harvest" with others (Thach, 1979).

6. The teaching of science can reinforce a sense of structure and of sequence. There are routines for using and storing equipment. An orderly format can be devised for the science experiment itself: For example, first list the topic; then the purpose; next the equipment and material; after that, the procedure; and finally, the findings. Moreover, many natural phenomena appear in regular cycles, hence are consistent and predictable (e.g., seasons, bird migration, the water cycle, night following day). Similarly, scientific principles are consistent: If you rub two objects together, the friction generates heat; if you drop an object from a moving train, it will continue in motion for a while; if you remove oxygen, the fire will extinguish; if you strike a piece of metal with a hammer, sound will travel through it. This factor of predictability can help the LD child get a better grasp of cause-effect relationships.

Siegel and Siegel (1977) list some sequential components in the actual teaching of science. These include: from teacher guidance to independent work; from smaller to larger volumes of work; from simple to more complicated experiments; from the teacher writing up the experiment to the child writing it; from use of models (exaggerated initially) to performing without any prompts or clues.

7. The field of science has many vocational implications for the LD pupil. It relates to various occupations and professions ranging from physicians, engineers, biologists, meteorologists, to medical and laboratory technicians, nurses (and nurses aides), dieticians (and their assistants), horticulturists, and farmers.

8. Through science, the LD student and his classmates can learn about—and come to accept—individual differences. The LD child, particularly on the secondary level, can learn more about himself by studying such topics as the nervous system, perception, and vision. Examples of adaptive behavior in nature can, via analogies, provide positive guidelines and incentives toward developing viable compensatory strategies.

9. Science can motivate the LD child to improve in perception and motor activities. Thach (1979) explains:

> A single garden chore such as planting can help a child in many perceptual areas at the same time. He must space the seeds or plants evenly, placing the seedlings where his eye tells him. Planting in sequence is also difficult for some of our pupils . . . . They must develop body awareness and eye-hand coordination to avoid stepping on the plants.

Similarly, a study of sound can serve as a springboard for learning to differentiate between loud and soft tones, perhaps ultimately leading to improvement in voice modulation.

Pitfalls	*Modifications*
1. The LD child may be uncoordinated: e.g., breaks glass beakers, cuts fingers while stripping wires.	Initially use plastic beakers (if possible); train in the use of wire strippers (at first, use prestripped wire leads).
2. The equipment, material, and ap-	Clear his desk of extraneous material.

Pitfalls	Modifications
paratus may distract the impulsive, motor disinhibited, fidgety child.	Hand him one item at a time. Take out equipment only when it is needed; collect it when the experiment is done.
3. The LD pupil may become impressed with the "magic" aspect and miss the scientific principle.	Emphasize cause-effect relationships. Ask specific questions ("What do you think will happen if . . . ?" "Why will it happen?". Shulene (1975) developed a set of simple pictorial riddles—each picture focuses the child's attention upon a specific piece of scientific information. For example, one cartoon depicts a boy standing in a flooded basement reaching up to turn the switch on an overhead light. Questions such as "Can you tell me about other ways people receive electric shocks?" and "What do you think will make this a safer picture?" are asked.
4. He may "generalize" incorrectly: e.g., the teacher holds bare wires connected to a six-volt battery; later, the child inserts bare wires into electrical wall outlets.	Anticipate this style of thinking. Be one step ahead of the child (i.e., discuss the differences between a six-volt battery and a 110-volt line *before* the mistake occurs).
5. The LD pupil may not understand abstract terms and ideas.	Progress slowly, step by step. Concretize the lesson: use simple terms, models, pictures or real situations. Use many illustrations of the concept being taught.
6. He may encounter difficulty reading the regular science text.	"Rewrite" the text in simple terms. Use pictures combined with small amounts of written material. Utilize high interest-low reading level book.
7a. Some LD children may lack exploratory drive and are overly dependent upon others in selecting areas of interests and activities (Hewett, 1968).	Use the strategies of (1) *forced-choice* (i.e., the child *must* make a choice, but from a small set of alternatives (no more than two or three of them); and/or (2) *first choice* (i.e., the child is invited to choose first, in deference to his tendency of merely falling in line with the others—provided of course that he is sufficiently strong emotionally) (Hewett, 1968, pp. 190–191).
7b. On the other extreme is the LD child who explores too much, but in a random, restless, erratic, purposeless and "driven" fashion.	Structure the lesson. The child needs direction. A brief discussion at the outset can focus upon the *reason* for the experiment, some of the events likely to occur, and effective practices to employ during this exploration. Teacher observations, support, and frequent questioning at strategic intervals help initially. Gradually, the reins can be loosened.

SOCIAL STUDIES

Implications

1. Given a motivated and enthusiastic teacher, one who is capable in child development, pedagogy, and subject-matter, then social studies—because it focuses primarily upon *people*— can be a most interesting subject. Hence, it can effect a more positive attitude toward school and serve as a motivational spur for the LD child to improve in basic skills subjects (particularly, the language arts, i.e., reading, oral and written expression, penmanship, and spelling, but also in arithmetic via charts, graphs, map work) and in study skills (taking notes; using an index, a glossary, the encyclopedia). Moreover, it provides *functional* practice in these areas, thus bypassing, to some extent, the problems of the unmotivated writer and the "blocked" reader.

2. Just as science can help clear up some of the misconceptions regarding the physical world which may accrue to the LD child by virtue of experiential deprivation and/or perceptual deficits, social studies can promote a more thorough understanding of his immediate social environment and community. Since social studies concentrates upon people, the environment, and the interdependence of these, it affords him the opportunity to view things in perspective.

Moreover, social studies has a strong affective component, focusing upon the *feelings* of people, communities, and nations. Ryan (1980) includes an entire section called the "Affective-Evaluative Domain" in his text, *The Social Studies Sourcebook* (Boston: Allyn & Bacon). Some of the classroom activities he suggests are: collecting attitudinal data on controversial topics from class members, selecting a "Celebrity of the Week" from the class (giving reasons), keeping a "Proud Table" (once weekly, each student places an object he feels particularly proud of on the table and is given an opportunity to tell his classmates about it). In the Silver Burdett Social Studies Series (Morristown, N.J., 1976, a series for teaching social studies in elementary and junior high school), pictures as well as the text are highly effective in evoking discussion of feelings and attitudes. This is a vital consideration in the case of LD children, many of whom are socially imperceptive and deficient in "reading" (and expressing) nonverbal communication cues.

3. Social studies can provide the means for helping LD children overcome some of their problems in spatial orientation and directionality. A systematic study of maps, starting with his immediate environment (the classroom) proceeding to maps of the neighborhood, gradually encompassing wider areas and further distances, can be helpful. Initially, maps should be simplified; that is, the streets should be few and well spaced, most of them progressing in north-south, east-west directions rather than diagonally or twisting. Weiss and Weiss (1974) found that providing a child with a set of compass points drawn on a small index card improved his orientation for direction (Figure 14-1).

Sequence is the key: neighborhood walks should precede lengthier trips; walks and outings should precede formal map study. Trips through and around the school building could lead to more distant ones. Initially, the teacher will provide considerable support, assistance and cues, gradually diminishing these. Some children may even require specific instruction in the translation of the concept of top–bottom

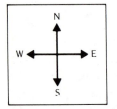

Figure 14-1.   Compass points drawn on a card.

vertically to the horizontal plane so that they then can do seat work involving flat maps.

4. Since at any given grade the *content* of social studies (as in science), regardless of reading level, can be identical to that of the nonhandicapped child, it can serve to enhance the self-concept of the LD child. This is particularly true in the case of mainstreaming: Not only is the LD child in the same classroom as normal children, but he is being taught the same material. Also, it can promote a sense of self-worth since history teaches us that *people* shape events. Hence he learns to cherish his own efforts and becomes aware of his capacity for effecting positive changes—helping others, obeying rules, making charitable donations, working and producing, voting, paying taxes. Finally, it can get him interested in other people(s) and hence less self-preoccupied.

5. Social studies can nourish appreciation of individual differences. Just as one learns tolerance, understanding, and appreciation of people from other regions and cultures, and develops a realization that all human beings have feelings and rights and the potential for achievement, one gains increased respect for the handicapped, viewing them as, first and foremost, human beings. Thus, social studies can be the vehicle by which the LD child's stock rises in his own mind as well as in the eyes of his classmates.

6. Social studies can foster socialization skills. Studying the customs of diverse cultures can make the LD child more cognizant of his own. The message about proper dress, manners, and social conduct can be delivered painlessly instead of via the normal routes of scolding and nagging. In addition, committee work, joint projects, and field trips provide further opportunity to master socializing skills and to increase one's circle of friends.

7. It can help the LD child learn to obey the laws. Many authors have pointed out that LD children are prone to juvenile delinquency when they get older owing to such factors as impulsivity, poor self-concept, gullibility, school failure, and so forth. The likelihood of the LD child emerging as a law-abiding citizen is enhanced by the systematic study of how laws are made and changed; for whose benefits they exist; one's legal rights, responsibilities, and restrictions: the relationship between legality and morality; and the like. There are available to the teacher pertinent training films, audio-visual aids, and teaching materials. For example, *The Coping With Series* mentioned previously contains one booklet entitled "Understanding the Law of Our Land." It encompasses such topics as "Normal Clash With Authority," "Civil Disobedience," "Justice," and emphasizes certain key concepts such as (1) laws—perfect or not—are for everyone, (2) ignorance of the law is no excuse, (3) every act is the result of making a choice. It also shows how proper attitude toward the law can be nurtured through student-body governments.

8. Social studies can effect the emergence of initiative, resourcefulness, decision making, and long-range planning abilities, as well as provide opportunities for sharing and collaborating. This is so since it lends itself so handily to the unit method of instruction which integrates the various subject matter under a unit of interest based on some topic from the social studies or science curriculum. A topic is selected, say *transportation*. The unit is launched. Long- and short-range goals are established. Committees are formed. Each is charged with a specific aspect of the overall topic: for example, letter writing; interviewing transportation workers; computing distances between cities and the cost of running subways; identifying and listing the pertinent raw materials and their geographic sources. The committee works independently over a designated period of time. They pool the fruits of their efforts in a culminative project—assembly program, scrap book, a major trip, a homemade movie incorporating their findings. By judiciously steering the LD child toward a specific committee that can capitalize upon his strengths (while, unobtrusively, affording him some opportunity to shore up his weak areas), the teacher nourishes within the child feelings of belonging and self-pride, and thus sparks motivation.

Pitfalls	*Modifications*
1. The LD child may have difficulty with many of the abstract concepts and terms.	Emphasize those aspects of history and geography that deal with the child's immediate environment. Relate how people lived in the past or how they live in other countries to the child's life. Go a step further and personalize the lesson, alluding to some specifics regarding a particular pupil (e.g., refer to a child's after-school newspaper route, another child's recent trip to New Hampshire). Concretize by using simpler terms, many examples, representative materials (e.g., a timeline to clarify temporal concepts), illustrations and analogies. Stress current events, current mores and topics of interest (sports, music, TV shows, dances). Utilize field trips, audio-visual aids, and guest speakers.
2. The LD pupil may be deficient in reading.	The same content can be found in books of different reading levels. An excellent example is the *The Silver Burdett Series* (already mentioned): The grade level is deliberately not specified, verbiage is sparse, there are many failure-free and success-assured activities. It contains many meaningful photographs. Use simple rexograph sheets instead of texts. Weiss & Weiss (1974) advise that the text of these sheets be simplified with some modification of the vocabulary. The print should be large type, all capital

Pitfalls	*Modifications*
	letters, and well spaced. (They suggest the Orator type from an IBM Selectric Typewriter ball (pp. 73–78).)
3. He may have deficits in writing (spelling and written composition as well as in penmanship).	Reduce the number of written assignments. Accept written outlines initially in lieu of entire essays. Utilize the experience chart (wherein the pupil dictates his words and the teacher does the writing), oral reports, and the tape-recorder. Some LD children, despite incoordination, can benefit by learning to type. There are some educators who have developed special methods for teaching typewriting to LD children: for example, Jack Heller's *How to Master Touch Typing* (Wantagh, N.Y.: Special Education, Step-By Step, 1978).
4a. He may have poor listening skills. This may stem from such factors as distractibility, auditory imperception, restlessness.	Avoid lengthy lectures. Try to cut down on teacher verbiage and encourage more pupil–pupil interaction. Provide for physical movement: changing seats for committee purposes; going from one "center" to another— e.g., the "map corner" to the "graphs and charts table"; seat work interspersed with chalkboard activities. Also utilize manipulative activities— e.g., sorting, matching, collating.
4b. Many LD children find it difficult to take notes. This hinders them in secondary schools and can prove disastrous later in college. Very likely, taking notes constitutes a formidable task for LD children, particularly those prone to neurological overloading, for two reasons: (1) They must do two things at once—listen and write, and (2) there is a continuous lack of synchrony—they listen to the lecturer's *present* words, simultaneously writing about his *past* ones.	The most important way in which the teacher can help here is to be aware of the difficulty, thereby setting the stage for empathy rather than rejection to occur. The teacher should speak slower, not as much, and utilize hand-outs of the lecture in the beginning of the class. There can be actual training in note-taking skills. Hints such as use of abbreviations, underlining, and writing on every other line (thus allowing room for insertions) should be provided. The pupil should get systematic training in outlining initially. (Outlining is, in effect, a simpler form of note taking: in the former, one is asked to outline from visual stimuli—that is, the written text—whereas note taking is tantamount to outlining from auditory stimuli.) An excellent teaching aid in note taking is *Thirty Lessons In Note Taking* by Jenifer Pirie and Alex Pirie (Woburn, Mass.: Curriculum Associates, 1976).

Pitfalls	Modifications
4c. LD children may find instruction limited to visual and auditory modalities insufficient. It may be too unvaried, hence promoting boredom. Then, too, some LD children may be impaired in both of these areas.	Kelly (1979), in a book which devotes an entire chapter to the teaching of social studies in special education, suggests that teachers of LD children incorporate tactile and kinesthetic approaches when instructing them in social studies: e.g., flat maps with roadways having sandpaper surfaces; 3-dimensional maps that have been deliberately distorted, thus facilitating the tactile examination of terrains, objects which can be handled, rubbed, and explored tactually.
5. The LD child may have problems in memory. This will hinder him in remembering historical facts: dates, people's names, the sequence of events. True, the sheer memorization of isolated facts should never be stressed. Of far greater importance are *concepts* such as motivations (of people and of governments) and inter-relationships (of one event to another, of the individual to his country, of people to their environment). Nevertheless, inability to remember essential facts often detracts from mastery of the broader concepts.	Avoid emphasizing memorization. Let the pupil feel free to look up data when needed; provide systematic instruction in the use of reference material. A time-line can help one visualize dates and to avoid gross errors. Visual prompts can help. Songs (e.g., "The Erie Canal") and poems (e.g., "In Flanders Field"), although they do require memorization themselves, can promote the retaining of historical facts. Mnemonic devices can be useful: *Mary Wants Cold Noodles* can cue the child to the relative spatial positions of *M*ontana, *W*yoming, *C*olorado, *N*ew *M*exico. Sometimes games and puzzles (e.g., simple map jigsaw puzzles) can facilitate tactile and kinesthetic memory.
6. Social studies deals with broad outcomes (e.g., "to develop an awareness of our American Heritage," "to understand how the weather affects where and how people live") and hence does not lend itself handily to observable behavioral objectives. Because, with few exceptions (e.g., some discrete tasks in map skills, use of reference work, vocabulary building), social studies does not succumb to task analysis, it is difficult to teach (the teacher may wander, may try to cover too much, may not have any clear goals), difficult to learn, and difficult to measure the results of instruction.	Use discrete, circumscribed topics. The fact that a topic which is broad in scope does not yield to task analysis need not prevent the teacher from subdividing it into a well-organized series of simpler concepts. The instructor should be systematic. Although one cannot often specify a definitive behavioral objective in social studies, it is possible— and necessary—to *plan* "an agenda," that is, an outline of exactly what ideas and facts will be covered in the lesson. The parts of the lesson should be cohesive and unified. The pupil should be required to participate actively (i.e., to *do* something). Appropriate materials should be selected. The pupil's past knowledge—that is, his *entering behavior*—should be taken into account.

CONCLUSION

There are two basic problems (and respective set of recommendations) common to science and social studies. The first involves a self-contained classroom in which the teacher attempts to accommodate disparate reading levels. (It is not unusual for such a class to show a reading-level range from Primer through fifth grade.) Grouping, peer tutoring, and individualized instruction are some recommendations. Use of texts on varied grade levels, fiction and non-fiction books relating to the subject matter, and additional sources of brief reading selections (e.g., some stories in the Readers Digest Educational Series, My Weekly Reader) can help. Texts may have to be broken down, abstracted, and simplified by the teacher. The child who is beginning to read may require individual word cards, phrase cards, and a rebus (combination of words and pictures) approach. Materials with high-independent index are needed to enable the teacher to proffer individual instruction to specific class members. These include programmed instruction material, self-correcting materials, mechanical aids such as Language Master and Systems 80 (which enable the pupil to hear the word at the same time that he sees it—or a picture of it). On the other side of the coin, the teacher must endeavor to circumvent reading at times, so that the child can make more rapid progress with the content area. Taped lessons, oral instruction, and films can be useful. Just as the blind have readers for them, the LD student may also benefit by this service. Field trips, guest lecturers, and various games are additional alternatives.

The second problem is testing. Since the pupil must be graded in these areas, his teachers typically resort to written tests. These should be modified: that is, simplified, kept brief, and accompanied by illustrative material. Of course, oral tests can be employed. Other means of measuring the child's achievement would include some manipulative performance: for example, in science, performing an experiment, handling the apparatus, sorting or matching rocks or metals, might suffice; in social studies, mastery could be assessed through witnessing the child's performance with maps and globe, charts and graph, and by watching him make sortings and matchings of various kinds (natural resources with specific regions, photographs of historical events). Informal observation of the pupil throughout the term should have significant input into the grading system. He should be observed as he answers questions (formally and informally); during his participation in committee work; and at play during subject-related games: for example, impromptu skits dealing with space travel, panning for gold, traveling in a covered wagon; "Geography" (each player must name a place whose initial is the same as the last letter of that place named by the preceeding player); "twenty questions" (related to science and social studies); "What's My Line."

This chapter dealt with the content area subjects only. Clearly, other school subjects could have received similar treatment here, but in the interest of avoiding repetition, suffice it to say that the same kinds of implications, pitfalls, and modifications exist across the total syllabus. For example, home economics improves the LD child's ability to care for himself, thereby shortening his dependency period, which, in turn, increases self-concept. Industrial arts teaches the child to make repairs and to build things, hence it likewise adds to self-esteem. Self-image is further heightened in both cases since the LD child views the activities in which he engages as adult pursuits. These subjects also have vocational and avocational implications, can provide much needed experience in the basic skills subjects, and create opportunities to socialize. Other subject areas—for example, the commercial course subjects such as typing, stenography, clerical practice—hold similar benefits for the LD child.

There are areas of commonality among the pitfalls (and modifications designed to overcome them) as well. Visual-motor coordination may require using thicker file cards initially (clerical practice), needles with larger holes (home economics), and pregrooved pieces of wood for sawing (industrial arts). Memory difficulties may require labeling of the cooking utensils, various shop tools, parts of the typewriter. Initial safety precautions might include using glue instead of nails, cooking lessons involving practicing on unlit stoves and making sure thimbles are available and used. Step-by-step instruction and close supervision throughout are crucial. Conceptual deficits can be accommodated by the teacher preparing in advance a series of the project's end-product (a platter of spaghetti and meatballs, a dress, a pair of wooden book ends, a set of alphabetized cards) in various stages of completion. This enables the LD child literally *to see* the instructional sequence.

Two major tenets exist: First, the LD child's failure in the basic school subjects should not become the teacher's rationale for his failure in the other areas. Teachers should realize that a child who cannot copy from the chalkboard readily may still be able to succeed in social studies, a poor reader may be able to pass science, a deficient speller need not automatically fail home economics. Secondly, these other subjects serve as a vehicle for motivating the child and providing opportunity to use the basic skills in *functional*, *relevant* ways.

REFERENCES

Chandler, C. R. 'Babysitting' for Houseplants. *Teaching Exceptional Children*, Spring, 1977, *9*(3), 61–63.

Hewett, F. *The emotionally-disturbed child in the classroom*. Boston: Allyn & Bacon, 1968.

Kelly, E. L. *Elementary school social studies instruction: A basic approach*. Denver: Love Publishing, 1979.

New York City Board of Education. Division of Educational Planning and Support. *Teaching brain-injured children: A handbook for teachers and supervisors K–12*. Curricular Bulletin #7. 1977–78 Series.

Ryan, F. L. *The social studies sourcebook*. Boston: Allyn & Bacon, 1980.

Shulene, J. A. Question: When is a picture a riddle? Answer: When the riddle is the picture! *Teaching Exceptional Children*, Winter, 1975, 7(2), 68–70.

Siegel, E. and Siegel, R. *Creating instructional sequences*. Novato, Ca.: Academic Therapy Publications, 1977.

Thach, J. M. *New York Times* (article), September 23, 1979, p. 40D.

Washington, D.C.: Department of Health, Education & Welfare. Office for Handicapped Individuals. *Programs for the handicapped*, 77-1, March 25, 1977.

Watling, C. and Hallard, R. E., The sea beside us. *Teaching Exceptional Children*, Fall, 1974, 7(1), 26–27.

Weiss, H. G. and Weiss, M. S., *A survival manual: Case studies and suggestions for the learning-disabled teenager*. Great Barrington, Mass.: Treehouse Associates, 1974.

Physical Education and Recreation*

15

As LD children are mainstreamed, new problems arise for the elementary classroom teacher who generally places the physical education needs of the child in the hands of the physical education teacher. Nondirected, unstructured activities, usually to break up the academic day and to better prepare students for afternoon activities or to serve as the reward for a job well done, negatively show-up the clumsy, motorically-inadequate child in his peer environment. How well prepared the mainstream teacher is to individualize the physical education needs of the LD child is a concern. Blake states (1970, p. 37), "We can no longer afford the mass-oriented approach if physical education is to provide the kinds of learning experiences that are needed to meet individual growth." Vodola supports this statement (1973, p. 6), ". . . the handicapped child can best be prepared for life is he is provided with an individualized physical activity program commensurate with his needs." Cratty contends (1967, p. 10), "To place such a child who is accurately aware of his perceptual-motor difficulties into a group of children whose problems are so obviously different will only compound his emotional problems."

A comprehensive review of the research dealing with the effects of physical education upon physical, cognitive, affective, social, and emotional variables reflects the view that physical education is warranted for the handicapped child (Mann, Burger, & Proger, 1974). However, presently, little research data supports this.

IMPLICATIONS

Physical Fitness

Physical education can foster the LD child's receptiveness to being physically fit. The fact is that many handicapped are out of shape. Lack of exercise and poor nu-

* By Joan Lange Bildman

tritional habits are common problems for learning-disabled children who often are unaware that physical fitness results in personal attractiveness and hence can lead to positive self-image.

A physically fit body can lead to improved general health; a body that is exercised enables that individual to breathe better, demonstrate greater strength, and have more stamina, speed, power, balance, and endurance in place of drowsiness, irritability, tiredness, and breathlessness. Thus there is a significant relationship between physical well-being and receptiveness to classroom learning. In addition, fitness has a direct carryover into daily living, whether the task demands carrying ten school books at once, bringing home a ten-pound sack of potatoes from the supermarket, or bringing in logs for the fire.

Tension Reduction

When LD children perceive themselves as failures, residual neuromuscular tension builds up (Sherrill, 1976). Building in success is the most direct means of maintain-a calm, flexible learner. Some LD children show signs of hypertension with the presence of hyperactivity, facial expressions in which the lines in the face seldom disappear, or through an immobile expression such as a frozen smile or incessant frown, hyperventilation, nervous perspiration, or irregularities in voice patterns.

A number of authors (Vodola, 1973; Sherrill, 1976; Arnheim & Sinclair, 1975) suggest a tension-reduction program so the child may organize in a meaningful way the neural impulses necessary for a task.

Arnheim and Sinclair (1975, pp. 97–100) begin a program of tension release through the use of the child's imagination. The child is instructed to imagine himself floating on a cloud, or lying on a front lawn, for example. At Level II, the child discovers his muscular tension and actively increases or decreases it at will in selected parts of the body. The activities at Level III require the child to be developmentally at least seven years old. Exercises aim at recognition of bilateral body part tension and release. Children with a motor development of nine years of age engage in Level IV to achieve development of unilateral body control through tension-release methods such as tensing the left arm and leg while relaxing the right side. Level V brings the learner into full control of the tension levels of the large muscles; this is usually not achieved until the late teens or adulthood.

The Edmond Jacobson system (1957) involves teaching the child to identify tensions of the various muscle groups. It is recommended that training begin with the child in a supine position with arms at the sides, palms facing downward, and moving to a sitting position at a desk or on a stool. Other techniques (Tai Chi, yoga, deep body awareness) additionally teach effective relaxation through tension reduction.

Socialization Skills

Physical-education activities set the stage for socialization skills; passively, the LD student may identify with sports figures, bowling stars, olympic players, and so on when he achieves understanding, knowledge, and skills in a specific physical activity; active involvement with a peer group comes when the loner (rejected for his inability) is chosen for a team, or is asked to play during free-play time because he possesses adequate motor skills. It is not surprising that "the social success of the growing child with the American culture is partly attributable to his ability to handle balls" (Cratty, 1967, p. 60). Inability to catch and throw balls brings social punishment which in turn brings increased tension, a defeating cycle. The LD child is further insulted by becoming the butt of jokes based on his lack of ability.

Interaction of students with students brings the LD child closer to an understanding of "otherness," acceptance of the rules and procedures in games and sports, and how to manage oneself in group situations. (Impulsivity is reduced—he must wait his turn; perseveration is diminished—he must be sufficiently flexible to accommodate an unexpected play; egocentricity is lessened—he must "out-guess" the other players.)

Accomplishment and Satisfaction

Feelings of productiveness and satisfaction are linked to the use of leisure time. Dancing, bowling, ice skating, swimming, and bicycle riding are "status sports" in today's fitness-oriented culture. By achieving minimal proficiency, the LD child can experience the enjoyment of the skill itself as well as the companionship it brings. Too often the LD child—for various reasons such as diminished self-confidence, and parental overprotection—does not use community recreation facilities where developing simple physical play skills can build self-confidence and bring the student into closer contact with people. Special programs, such as the ANCHOR Program (Answering the Needs of Children with Handicaps through Organized Recreation, sponsored by the Department of Parks and Recreation, Hempstead, Long Island), recognize that summer days and after-school hours are often lonesome ones for the learning disabled, and the need for the continuation of physical activities in a nonthreatening environment is great. With the Atlantic Ocean at their door, students enjoy a program of the creative arts and physical recreation, the latter offering active recreation (swimming, paddleball, handball, tennis, basketball, shuffleboard and horseshoes).

Horseback riding for the learning disabled is a promising physical activity not only for its facilitation of motor skills, but for its promotion of a sense of accomplishment and increased self-confidence (Gaskins, 1976). Project SIRE (Self-Improvement Through Riding Education), a creation of the Connecticut Education Association, focuses on function responsibility, muscle development and coordination, development of a clear self-concept, and the improvement of skills basic to successful learning (Massachusetts SLD Gazette, March, 1979.)

Creativity and Self-Expression

The teaching of physical education can contribute to the child's creativeness and self-expression. With the introduction of movement education in the regular physical education curriculum, LD children are offered a structure emphasizing decision making, spontaneity, imagination, interpretation, and the development of images in bodily form. The demands of precision and literal interpretation found in sports give way to the evocation of personal feelings and ideas as children create a movement. When the student initiates movement, he becomes consciously involved with learning about his environment and develops an awareness of himself, his body, and its capabilities. Movement exploration can aid the development of concepts through integration with a deeper understanding of one's body. Concepts of directions (over-under), size (large-small), intensity (weak-strong), speed (fast-slow), space (far-near), and patterns (squares-circles) are performed in a spatial context in which the learner experiences his body image and physical self (Weisbrod, 1972).

When a child moves, he establishes his separateness from others and also clarifies his body boundaries; these understandings can complement other efforts in positive development of self-concept and the child's body image. This can encourage him to attack new tasks that offer even greater challenges and opportunities which, in turn, stimulate further development of skills and abilities, thereby creating an upward spiral.

Arnheim and Sinclair (1975, p. 23) prefer that movement experiences be used with the clumsy child after confidence has been gained and a possible failure can be tolerated. Hence, a supportive approach to physical education for the uncoordinated child emphasizes failure-free activities—that is, simple movement exploration initially.

Dance movement in both structured and free settings captures the rhythmic elements inherent in all children. Folk and square dancing, ballet and tap dance can provide a sense of organization, group effort, memory training, and perceptual-motor practice. Creative dance brings self-discovery, initiative efforts, and problem-solving skills into focus.

Programs of perceptual-motor development aimed at improving problems of coordination, laterality, left-right orientation, and body image belong in the regular or special-class program as well as in the physical education setting. Purposeful movement takes precedence over movement for movement's sake. Movement in itself is usually accompanied by some thinking (Cratty, 1973, p. 73). As a component of the learning process, it aids pattern recognition, memory ability, and may help in lengthening the attention span (Cratty, p. 73).

Improved Thinking Skills
Through an application of the rules of games and sports, the LD player or spectator can enrich his intellectual powers. For example, having learned the rules and objectives of ice hockey, the focus turns to how best can a goal be made. Discovering that a strategy of making a goal with a rebound tactic calls for higher thinking skills.

Control and Enjoyment of Nature
Control over nature and enjoyment of it are implicit in outdoor education. The vastness of the environment often creates a distraction for some learning-disabled children, thereby reducing the satisfactions normally derived. Through camping experiences, children learn new skills and put social skills into a new perspective (Vannier, 1977; Shea, Phillips, & Campbell, 1972.)

Safety increases for the LD students who use the knowledge of environmental conditions to act in an appropriate manner; for example, observing an approaching thunderhead while fishing demands proper action if one's life is to remain secure. Survival skills can not be left for incidental learning since the learning disabled do not learn by observation and frequently lack the ability to make appropriate generalizations.

This writer observed a class of learning disabled, emotionally-handicapped children in a state park campgrounds setting for an overnight stay. Under the guidance of teacher and aides, the students prepared meals, took part in basic chores, and then proceeded to study and enjoy the forest and ocean. Language skills, counting and measuring skills, social amenities, experiencing a food prepared on an open fire all decidedly affected the students. The outdoors opened up the senses and aesthetic sensitivities of the participants in a natural and personal way.

Pitfalls	*Modifications*
1. The hyperactive child requires a longer period of time and assistance in making a transition from play and sports activities to classroom or vice versa.	Make available a quiet, semidark area where child can lie down before entering the classroom. The area should be free from noise. (Sherrill, 1976, p.234.)
2. The hyperkinetic child often is unable to use the physical education arena effectively, being overwhelmed by excessive space and noise, by numbers of people, by the pressure of timed activities.	In the actual setting, decrease the space. Indoors, use partitions; outdoors, rope off boundaries. Decrease the noise. Use verbal start and stop signals rather than a whistle. Work with small groups. Substitute noise-reducing equipment (yarn balls, nerf-type balls.) Maximize individual involvement at all times. Provide consistency. By designating certain spaces as learning stations, distractions will be minimized. Use a consistent direction of rotation. When accuracy is stressed and speed is deemphasized, the hyperactive child will be more productive. If a speed test must be given, create a nonthreatening environment. Substitute team or individual efforts for finishing the fastest with emphasis on experimenting and discovery with specific concepts (e.g., Who can make the funniest crawling movement?) Success builds bridges to a positive self-concept. Moreover, the very act of offering verbal praise to the hyperactive child results in him stopping and basking in it—hence *listening*. Capitalize on the success in a new motor task. End on a high note where the student feels positive about his efforts. (Sherrill, 1976, pp. 234–35.)
3. Physical-education equipment may distract the impulsive, fidgety player.	Present one piece of equipment only as needed; collect it immediately after use. For children who find it difficult to wait their turn, provide each with his own equipment wherever feasible.

Pitfalls	*Modifications*
4. Many LD children find it difficult to attend to an entire skill or game.	The child should be required to concentrate on only one task at a time. Continual revision of the child's prescription by making the task more demanding as mastery is experienced is recommended for increasing attention span. Shorten the game time or length of time to practice a skill.
5. The child who presents characteristics of dissociation can perform a series of discrete acts while not being able to integrate them into meaningful patterns.	Begin with the isolated skill but move toward elaboration which entails providing a variety of similar but not identical experiences. Finally, promote integration by providing different patterns (e.g., Hop, hop up and down an incline, hop like a bunny, like a kangaroo, hop on both feet, on alternating feet, hop to the tune of "Here Comes Peter Cottontail," hop while verbalizing).
6. Problems of incidental learning can persist since the learning disabled do not readily learn by observation and are often unable to make appropriate generalizations.	Direct training should include such topics as proper attire for different sports, rules of scoring, taking turns, manners considered appropriate for specific games and sports (e.g., shaking hands even when defeated in a game of tennis; being quiet when watching a tennis match).
7. The LD child who perseverates may refuse to test a new strategy or to adopt new rules.	A sequence of activities should be presented, each being distinctly different in starting position, rules, strategies, and skills. Games with concepts of stop-and-go reinforce transition from one activity to another (Sherrill, 1976, p. 301).
8. Many of the abstract concepts and terms in sports and recreation present difficulty for the learning disabled.	Make all learning experiences as concrete as possible. Use a multisensory approach but coordinate all the senses to the same task. Give many examples, use language efficiently by avoiding excessive verbiage, and be prepared to explain idioms (e.g., *shoot* the basketball; catch a *fly*). Relate the concepts to other aspects of the student's life.
9. Figure–ground disturbances may hinder the child from focusing on the task (e.g., the batter who misses the ball might not have	Focus solely on the task to be performed; later introduce background material. Highlight the figure (color the ball, use a large ball).

Pitfalls	*Modifications*
been able to distinguish it from the stands or fields).	
10. The LD child may appear to lack exploratory behavior, or interest in participation in a game or physical-education task.	Many children can stick with a task which is too easy or too difficult, but LD children may be unable to do so. Teacher ingenuity in devising different ways to elicit the same motor response is called for (e.g., asking the student to name two different ways he would like to move across the room, and then have him try each way).
11. Some LD participants can not substitute one sensory modality for another and continue to learn. Receptiveness to physical education is individual, depending on the strengths and weaknesses of the individual's perceptual learning abilities.	Utilization of the senses of hearing, vision, touch and movement for effective instruction in motor therapy depends on individual strength of modalities. The teacher must know when to use or not to use each sense singly or in combination (Arnheim & Sinclair, 1975, p. 46).
12. The child is not always perceptually strong in the visual modality. Physical education instruction relies heavily on both the auditory and visual modalities.	When vision is selected (visual guidance) as a learning avenue, carefully choose learning cues that are appropriate to the task. Teacher demonstration of the skill to be learned demands accuracy of modeling. The learner must mimic the teacher. Visual aids (sequenced photos, slides) can add to understanding the skill accurately. Physical guidance (feeling the action) can serve as a substitute for the visual mode. Initially, the child is taken through correct movements passively, then actively with verbal guidance. Weights or pulling against the resistance can create an awareness of the correct feel of a motor skill (Arnheim & Sinclair, 1975, pp. 46–47).
13. Difficulty in processing information effectively from verbal instruction or cues is often experienced by the perceptually handicapped child.	Use terms and phrases minimally. Initiate directions with concrete words (e.g., Go, Move). Do not talk excessively since it confuses the learner by adding too many possibilities (Arnheim & Sinclair, 1975, p. 47).
14. The learner may have difficulty in motor planning.	Encourage the learner to self-monitor a task by talking to himself describing the stages in executing a motor task. This aids retention, too (Arnheim & Sinclair, 1975, p. 48).

Pitfalls	*Modifications*
15. Complex learning tasks may produce confusion in some learning-disabled students.	With the knowledge of the whole learning task, offer as much of the whole as the learner is capable of grasping; teach the parts separately and sequentially. The child's confidence is built as the parts lead to the whole (Arnheim & Sinclair, 1975, p. 48).
16. The uncoordinated LD child may be afraid to play ball. He may find it difficult to judge the speed of an approaching ball, often perceiving it at a faster speed—hence, he may flinch, close his eyes, or shield his face with his hands as the ball approaches.	Let him play with a balloon first. (It is lighter than a ball; it always approaches the catcher slowly; and, should it strike the child, it doesn't hurt.) A yarnball or a bean bag can be used as an intermediate step. Rolling the ball should precede throwing it; underhand throws should precede overhand ones (Siegel, 1969). (Also see Appendix C.)
17. Having failed so often in the past, the LD child may develop a negative mental set (anxiety, aversion) toward participating in any of the traditional physical-education activities.	Introduce these activities in a non-threatening, novel, pleasurable format. Often, a game approach helps. "Simon Says," "Follow the Leader," and "Charades" can be preludes to calisthenics. Tossing pebbles into a brook can be introductory to throwing.
18. The LD child may be extremely sensitive about his lack of coordination. The movement of one's own body is a highly personal affair. One can, understandably, develop deep feelings of inferiority through inadequate motor performance much more readily perhaps, than in other areas since any criticism of body movement is often taken as criticism of the person himself.	Criticize and remediate sparingly, in private, and matter-of-factly. Avoid value judgments. Praise the child for small signs of growth, for his efforts, for those portions of his performance that are correct. Be on the lookout for ruffled feelings, anxiety, and, especially, in the older child, for facades and subterfuges. Be prepared to allow the child to be a spectator until he feels comfortable participating.

CONCLUSION

A cooperative approach among physical educators, regular classroom teachers, and special-education teachers will help to insure the success of the physical education and recreation program.

The regular classroom and special-education teachers should be made aware of the scope and benefits of such a program. They can assist the physical-education teacher in defining specific goals for each child, provide insight into the child's learning style, strengths and weaknesses, and suggest academic goals which can be developed through game approaches. They can plan follow-up activities and encourage the child to participate in games and recreation during recess and on class outings.

A comprehensive physical education and recreation program not only enhances the child's development during school years, but provides important skills and learning which can be used and built on throughout his life.

REFERENCES

Arnheim, D. D., and Sinclair, W. A. *The clumsy child*. St. Louis: C. V. Mosby, 1975.

Blake, O. Making physical education helpful—not humiliating. In Lauriel E. Anderson (Ed.), *Helping the adolescent with the hidden handicap*, Novato, Ca.: Academic Therapy Publications, 1970.

Cratty, B. J. *Developmental sequences of perceptual-motor tasks*. Freeport, N.Y.: Educational Activities, Inc., 1967.

Gaskins, M. H. Horseback riding and the handicapped. *Science and Child*, March, 1976, *13*, 23.

Jacobson, E. *You must relax, 4th. ed*. New York: McGraw-Hill, 1957.

Mann, L., Burger, R. M., and Proger, B. B. Physical education intervention with the exceptional child. In Lester Mann and David A. Sabatino, (Eds.), *The second review of special education*, Philadelphia: JSE Press, 1974.

Massachusetts SLD Gazette, March 1979.

Shea, T. M., Phillips, T. L., and Campbell, A. Outdoor living and learning complement each other. *Teaching Exceptional Children*, Spring, 1972, *4*, 109–18.

Sherrill, C. *Adapted physical education and recreation*. Dubuque, Iowa: William C. Brown, 1976.

Siegel, E. *Special education in the regular classroom*. New York: John Day, 1969.

Vannier, M. H. *Physical activities for the handicapped*. Englewood Cliffs, N.J.: Prentice-Hall, 1977.

Vodola, T. M. *Individualized physical education program for the handicapped*. Englewood Cliffs, N.J.: Prentice-Hall, 1973.

Weisbrod, J. A. Shaping a body image through movement therapy. *Music Educator Journal*, April, 1972, *58*, 66–69.

Creative Arts*

16

A creative-arts program adds important dimensions to the curriculum. It can be used to bring beauty and pleasure into the lives of learning-disabled children while helping them express themselves artistically and aesthetically. When infused and integrated into the basic academic curriculum, the arts are tools for increasing and enhancing learning and the development of basic skills. The emphasis on process rather than product can encourage a positive attitude toward learning. Creative-arts experiences enable the children to choose fulfilling and meaningful leisure time activities, thus helping them in their total development.

STAGES OF ARTISTIC DEVELOPMENT IN THE CHILD

Learning-disabled children generally resist art experiences that engage them in drawing. Their drawings lack exact representation and play up their poor visual perception skills as well as fine motor control. By developing an awareness of the regular, sequential stages of art all children pass through, coupled with empathy and sensitivity to the LD child's needs, the teacher will be able to make supportive modifications. It makes little sense to rush the child into the next stage if he is more comfortable at a lower level. The statement that the child demonstrates an "immature art form" is specious; the art form indicates the level to which the teacher should address the activities. Lowenfeld and Brittain (1975) identify six stages through which the child develops: scribbling, preschematic, schematic, gang age, pseudonaturalistic, and adolescent art. Not all children will proceed through each developmental stage.

* By Joan Lange Bildman

Between the ages of eighteen months and four years, the child will proceed in ordering *scribbles* starting with random marks and gradually moving to recognizable forms. Scribbles are significant. As the child creates disordered scribbles, controlled scribbles, and named scribbles, the teacher should provide a wide variety of drawing instruments (crayons, chalk, felt pens) and papers which will result in the student's physical and emotional involvement.

The following stage, the *preschematic stage*, generally entered at four years and lasting until seven years, is a natural outgrowth of scribbling, involving a "conscious creation of form." This conscious effort is rooted in the relationship the learner has made to his world. The kinesthetic activity of the previous stage subsides as representation takes over. Forms are recognizable. Color remains highly individualized, reflecting an emotional involvement with few compelling impositions engendered by an understanding of harmony in color. The world of space depicted graphically exists only in relation to the child's concept of himself. Drawing comes naturally for the child during this stage, precluding the need to be taught how to draw. However, since this period is an important one in the area of visual perceptual growth, the LD child exhibiting perceptual difficulties may well need specific instruction.

The *schematic stage* follows for most learners from seven through nine years old. In this stage, the learner's thinking, feelings, perceptions, and interests produce individualized concepts (schema). Objects are now ordered in a space relationship that recognizes the child within the environment. A base line expresses the child's physical orientation; all objects are placed here. The sky line also appears at the top of a page but does not continue to meet the base line. The empty area between the base and sky line is defined as "air space" by many children.

The *gang age* for nine through twelve years reflects a dawning realism steeped in details but displaying rigid action. Colors take on a subtlety of perception while space is dealt with in abstract terms. The base line is replaced with an ability to deal with planes. This stage allows the learner to leave behind the stage of schemata and move into curiosity about himself and others as the next stage is met.

At the high-school level, the *pseudo-naturalistic stage* appears for adolescents aged twelve through fourteen. They consciously create art forms which become items for self-criticism. Naturalism implies attention to increased visual awareness through a focus on shadowing and color changes.

The stage of *Adolescent Art* (14–17 years) gives two directions—one for the specially interested and talented, another for the terminal art participator. At the terminal stage, one would expect to find a great emphasis on encouraging life-long art interest; few programs manage to generate a holistic approach to life in the adult world.

ELEMENTS OF ART

Basic to the self-expressive direction in the visual and plastic arts is an exploration of the elements of art. Within an academic setting, a teacher provides many experiences that focus on balance, sensory awareness, shapes, and colors but for reasons generally outside the arena of art. However, the LD student whose sensitivities to color combinations in dress, appreciation of art works by others, and artistic arrangements of food, flowers, and furniture might be lacking, needs to be taught the elements of art specifically. Line, shape, form, texture and pattern, color, space, and the principles of balance, harmony, rhythm, proportion, and organization—the elements of art—are necessary for self-expression to reach a zenith. Operation of the principles at the subconscious level can result from art experiences that begin with the concrete. When a child brings to class five or six different objects that demonstrate one concept (e.g., objects can hold liquids), the teacher can take the student through manipulative exercises that ask the child to make color dominant, show balance, make the texture strong, and so on, all within self-initiated arrangements.

Several selected sources that deal with the elements of art are:

1. *Art in the Elementary School*, Marlene M. Linderman, Dubuque, Iowa: William C. Brown, Publishers, Inc., 1974.
2. *Creativity, Art and the Young Child*, W. Lambert Brittain, New York: Macmillan Publishing Company, Inc., 1979.
3. *Creative and Mental Growth*, Sixth Edition, V. Lowenfeld and W. Lambert Brittain, New York: Macmillan Publishing Company, Inc., 1975.
4. *Crafts for the Classroom*, Earl W. Linderman and Marlene Linderman, New York: Macmillan Publishing Company, Inc., 1977.

FOCUS ON CRAFTS

For the LD child whose manipulative skills are generally poor, ideas can not be expressed until the hands can execute what the mind dictates. The teacher must directly intervene in skill training. LD students lose interest in a task when they are asked to apply a skill and respond creatively at the same time. By first insisting that the tools and skills be under control, the creative ideas can then be focused on.

Crafts are least preferred as art media when teachers omit individual expression by expecting children to model a step-by-step direction sequence. The direction sequence in itself is not stultifying—LD children need organizing—but the implied statement that the child's outcome should be identical to the model is problematic. Freedom of choice to expand, reduce, to drastically change is needed.

Crafts are excellent modes of expression when children can make the connection between natural earth materials and their crafts. Also, crafts permeate the child's cultural life. Clay, wood, fiber, and paper have been recognized for their functional and decorative application in the learner's daily life. Certainly the LD's experiences with these materials can bring deeper understanding, more accurate perceptual awareness, cultural sensitivity, and a feeling of a place in the world. Specific skills called for through carving, pulling, sanding, folding, modeling, constructing, joining, and squeezing create spatial reality, thereby building a strength in body awareness (Linderman & Linderman, 1977, pp. 1–2).

Teachers commonly misjudge the ability of LD children to handle the tools of crafts (scissors, needle, hammer, saw); instruction and practice with a task-analysis approach is suggested. Sessions outside the art circle will focus on the task alone; bending, pounding, tearing, and cutting without another objective (e.g., torn paper collage) detours the predicted "turned-off" attitude toward the visual and plastic arts. For the student to initiate a torn-paper boat collage, for example, he must have the skill of placement, tearing, pasting, organizing, and a knowledge of shape.

The skill of *cutting* often does not come easily for the learning disabled since it involves eye-hand coordination, a visual discrimination ability (curves, straight lines, diagonals of shapes and forms) and spatial concepts. Lazarus and Carlin (1965, pp. 363–364) suggest a sequence in teaching cutting skills which follows the mastery of fine muscle operations in handling scissors. The steps are:

1. Random fringing. The child discovers for himself the "combined muscle sensations of cutting" when using a six-inch square of construction paper;
2. The one-snip strip. With a three-quarter inch strip of paper sectioned at one-inch intervals by thick lines, the child makes one snip;
3. Practice strip for straight-line cutting. The child is presented with two-inch strips crossed at three-inch intervals with thin lines that require several strokes of the scissors;
4. Half-snip strip. The cutting guide lines extend only half the width leading to control of the length of the line;
5. Long and short lines. The child alternates cutting long lines completely across the strip and short lines half-way across the strip;
6. Cutting curves. Curves are cut in both directions;
7. Zig-zag strips. This entails changing directions.

Following a diagnostic test, the students are engaged in cutting geometric forms.

Pasting and gluing require much control. The LD child might spread the glue too far, miss areas, apply too much glue, put paste on the wrong side, or have poor control when a squeeze tube is used. Direct teaching through a sequencing strategy is imperative. Initially, the amount of glue can be controlled and meted out by the teacher; one egg carton cup (rooted in a no-spill base) can hold designated amounts needed for an entire project. Gradually the student learns to judge the quantities needed. Using a squeeze tube is difficult when both a target and squeeze action are demanded. At first provide graded practice using the squeeze tube alone without a specific target. The use of a squeeze tube begins by learning to pour slow-flowing substances, then moving to rapid-flowing substances. A next step can be pouring with different pressures depending upon the substances used. Small sticks or cotton swabs are serviceable applicators having a built-in control of the amount of adhesive that will be picked up. The teacher should not insist that every child apply glue with his fingers; it is an uncommon practice in everyday life.

Susan Gonick-Barris (1976, pp. 67–73) reported procedures in art that proved successful for LD children who were threatened by a media from a conceptual, tactile, and expressive point. When working with clay, her students had complicated and unrealistic goals without understanding the limits imposed by their skill or the medium. Total, basic exploration of clay began with many sessions of pounding and guided instructions (they were told to, "Make one ball," "make a skinny snake," etc.) followed with an introduction to tools (toothpicks, nails, and objects that made an impression in clay). The clay selected was pliable (wet clay, not plasticine, because its hardness frustrates the child easily) and small (grapefruit size was too overwhelming; tangerine size was just right). The instances of perceived teacher preferential treatment were minimized when each student received an equal amount of clay. Routines established for distribution, collection, and cleanup were consistent. This art activity fostered expressive language skills, e.g., modeling clay foods promoted discussions about such topics as foods liked and disliked, making clay masks stimulated role-playing activities.

Distribution, collection, and clean up in art activities must build in habitual responses if the learning disabled are to internalize responsibility for an activity. Planning and preparation are fundamental; it is important in setting up work-space areas to consider the physical space, seating, lighting, the individual's attention span, degree of distractibility, social compatibility, degree and nature of the project's difficulty, techniques, tools, materials, and time allotted. An atmosphere that is supportive and nonthreatening is essential. Teachers must have first-hand experiences with the materials presented to students (trial run), thereby enhancing the likelihood of anticipating and preventing problems. Teachers who make a match of activity, creator, and materials have a sound beginning.

Pitfalls	*Modifications*
a. The child may have an idea for an art project far above his skill level. Consequently, his attempts result in his frustration, failure, and negative attitude toward "art things."	a. Preparing the child to achieve the idea he is harboring can come about with direct instruction in skills. When the teacher structures projects around the level of skill control, the child will not become frustrated.
b. Materials may have a limitation of which the child is not aware. The incidental learning most children experience often is missed by the special child. Concepts of heaviness, flexibility, and general relationships of various materials, for example, while taught in specific contexts in academic areas, may not have general applicability. This is particularly true in a crafts setting where the child's thinking is not set for analysis, comparisons, and problem-solving tasks.	b. Materials have limitations. Telling the child of guaranteed possibilities and noticeable limitations of materials will conserve time and energy. Use discovery methods wisely. With a knowledge that all glues will not serve as an adhesive for materials such as rocks and shells or that construction paper used in the third dimension can not support pieces of heavy wood, the child can focus on the activity. The former example will provide the child with the information while the latter will ask the child to discover and think through an alternate strategy. Attention to the structure of thinking by providing the student with specific questions to apply in a crafts session will enable the child to make decisions concerning the feasibility of selected materials.
c. The LD pupil may be distracted by the synthesis of several modal-	c. When two or more modalities are brought into close competition,

Pitfalls	*Modifications*
ities. When presented simultaneously, they generally give depth to a learning activity but may create a cancelling-out effect for the special child who tries to attend to all stimuli.	the result may be one acting as a distraction and impeding the effectiveness of the other; e.g., the tactile and the visual may not act in synthesis as the child dips his fingers into glue. Substitute a cotton swab or a stick to put the focus on the visual task.
d. Materials may present a distraction for some LD participators.	d. Some LD children are strongly attracted to various colors, shapes, and textures causing a distraction. Teacher awareness will substitute items. Limiting the quantity of supplies can reduce the stimuli to manageable levels.
e. The child may be overly talkative when in a social group for art purposes. For the LD child who seldom initiates social interaction, the art group can be misinterpreted as a vehicle primarily for verbal discourse since the format is informal and nonthreatening.	e. Social skills are important for the the effectiveness of an art group. Politeness, thoughtfulness of the needs of classmates, sharing of materials, acceptance of the physical closeness of a peer are positives in a group setting. Conversation that detours from the task at hand or is excessive in verbalization can distract some children. Keep verbalization to a minimum, get the nonverbal aspects to emerge. Judicious seating arrangements can help.
f. When the child who exhibits conceptual deficits is presented with the end-product, it stagnates the desire to act creatively.	f. The teacher's desire to foster concept development, on one hand, is achieved when the end-product is displayed. The child's desire for acceptance and need for success are interpreted through the ability to reproduce the model. Withholding a model will promote self-expression. Several variations of a concept, when a model is insisted on, will give freedom to change.
g. Some LD students have difficulty in maintaining attention.	g. By organizing the child's perceptual field, competing stimuli will be eliminated and a limited focus will emerge. Materials needed for the immediate task can be presented; other materials should be introduced when called for; shorter art periods will not lose students as

Pitfalls	*Modifications*
	longer sessions will. Using a variety of activities can prove fruitful.
h. Perserverative behavior in art activities may be displayed by some learning-disabled students.	h. The teacher should impose external controls—build a clay wall around a printing paper, distributing a given number of strips to work into a collage, handing the child a different crayon before he begins to cover the entire page with one color.
i. Impulsiveness may occur when too many stimulating items are present.	i. Impulsivity can have a basis in attentional behaviors. Materials must be singled out and explored from several points so scanning the distinctive features will bring about a more systematic and less cursory approach.
j. Some LD children appear to treat materials destructively.	j. Inadequate motor control of pressure often results in tears, holes and crumpled papers. Practice in handling light, feathery materials (cotton, tissue paper) and heavy materials (plaster, clay) is suggested.
k. The LD pupil may act in a disorganized way.	k. A prearrangement of art materials builds order for the child. Presentation should be logical and sequential. Student selection of materials should be limited initially.
l. The student may not see the transfer value of an art activity to real life.	l. Art activities in themselves do not carry over to grooming and enhancement of one's surroundings unless that context is directly taught. A concept learned in one context (i.e., don't play with your food) may not lead into situations of exceptions (Let's have edible art). The different contexts must be sorted out for the child.
m. Some LD students may be unwilling to explore new situations, reflecting their fear of the unknown.	m. Creating situations that demonstrate trust between student and teacher, where the child is reassured of the outcome, where familiar experiences are provided, or where safety concerns are emphasized, can calm the child's concerns for the unknown.

PHOTOGRAPHY AS CREATIVE ART FOR THE LEARNING DISABLED

Photography has been exalted to a new status among the visual arts in our culture (Kramer, 1978, p. 11). This "photographic explosion" had its own antecedents in the special classroom through the efforts of insightful teachers who put a camera into the hands of children for the making of a "personal vision" and as a mode of creative expression. "Viewing" as well as "doing" has pervaded the special-education scene. Photography, as an active process (the child takes the picture) or as a passive one (the child is the subject of a photograph or examines photographs taken by others), holds many benefits for the LD pupil. It can bring him more sharply in touch with his environment, develop a sense of order, enhance his sense of sequence (e.g., he reviews a series of pictorial events), nurture perception of time and space, and heighten self-esteem.

Getting a camera into the special classroom often created legal restrictions which discouraged teachers from building up the medium. Checking out parental and administrative policies and attitudes is sound advice before getting started. Explaining to parents the values of photography in the learning environment of the LD child will encourage a favorable attitude.

Obtaining cameras and defraying the cost of film and development have been common deterrents to the use of photography in the classroom. It is hoped that the commitment the Polaroid Foundation has made to special-needs children will continue and other companies will follow suit. Applying for Federal grants, watching the photography section of a local newspaper for offers of free use of equipment to special groups, or writing to manufacturers of equipment for donations often produce the desired materials. Still or movie photography are equally preferred; the latter is more expensive. The use of black and white or color depends upon the objective and the child's ability to deal with a color form.

Photography can be used to reinforce body image and body parts. A photo of the child encourages self-identification and the relationship of individual body parts to the whole. Similarities and differences among children promote generalizations as well as fostering acceptance of individual differences. A child's mood that is captured in a photo can become a basis for discussions of feelings and can direct the child to refine his actions to come closer to an appropriate response. Wiig and Semel (1976, pp. 312–313) bring attention to the use of filmstrips and silent movies in training social perception through the presentation of sequential visual stimuli (without written words dubbed in). Films with overstated and unambiguous body language are said to offer better experiences for learners to accurately interpret the true intention of the filmed scenes. Siegel, Siegel, and Siegel (1978, p. 120) recommend the use of a sound movie (with the sound turned down), and/or a videotape of the homemade type where drama majors from a local college volunteer their talents to students lacking in social perceptions.

Photos have an advantage over drawings in depicting more clearly the reality that exists. A child can almost step into the situation depicted and react as a feeling individual. However, some LD students display atypical responses; for example, a nature photo scene depicting serenity, peace, and a sense of beauty may evoke feelings of anxiety and danger; the teacher should accept, not disregard, their feelings.

Literal meaning in photos (what is it?) is but a part of the reasons for including photography in the curriculum. Recognition that feelings are personal and reflect the interplay of a number of variables suggests that teachers must not impose feelings as much as expose children to common expressions.

As an aid to short-term memory, photos can place a child in a time and space arena. Concept development and relationships can be reinforced, visual sequencing memory skills improved, verbal communication skills (as well as nonverbal communication skills) enriched, and the child's interaction with his environment accommodated. By studying sequenced photos, such as a child throwing a ball, LD students can grasp the motor skills involved in a task.

Photos can be useful in more fully developing academic subjects. A science lesson can employ photos of animals, trees, and flowers to establish classifications. A reading lesson can end with a photographic continuation of a theme. Photos in math can show a set of six classmates as the child joins the group, thereby integrating several concepts: self-identification within a social group, orientation in space, and the concept of a "set."

Growing interest in the use of photography as a tool in the educative process has been directed toward helping the learning disabled to modify poor self-concepts. "Self-Directed Photography" is a process (Hedges, 1972, pp. 26-28) embracing the idea that reality is in the individual's *perception* of an event, not in the event itself. The individual is left on his own to react to the field of experiences as he perceives it in a nonthreatening environment. The student selects the perception to record, later verbalizing about the photograph with a discussant.

Meiselas (1974, n.p.) remarks, ". . . making a successful photo fosters a sense of competence in being able to control technology, self-esteem at seeing one's own expression of imagination or beliefs, and self-respect through presenting a statement that communicates with others." For the learning-disabled child, snapping a picture is a visual means by which he learns to structure thinking, engage in decision making by a sorting-out process, select a subject, decide what to leave in view, and judge how close to be to the subject. The child thus sharpens his power of observation.

In the child's hand, a polaroid camera works wonders. It is light-weight, easy to manipulate, inexpensive, and easy to operate: the steps to follow are minimal, placing the emphasis only on the snapping. The instant feedback is invaluable. Given proper guidance and an enthusiasm for the topic, photography can be one of the most rewarding means of expression and learning.

Pitfalls	*Modifications*
a. The LD child may be uncoordinated and demonstrate an inability to synchronize the requirement for steadiness with the pressing of the shutter button; this will result, of course, in blurred pictures.	a. Use one type of camera consistently, particularly one that is light but easy to handle (physically and mechanically, e.g., Polaroid One-Step). Give practice in locating shutter button tactually (blindfolded); practice (without film) holding camera, viewing, pressing shutter button and integration of

Pitfalls	*Modifications*
	steps. Build one task into another to achieve synchronization: hold camera and view, press button. Use tripod to insure steadiness or prop up camera.
b. The LD child may display inappropriate motor energy when asked to to take a picture.	b. Give the child experiences in applying pressure. Provide situations that help the child learn to determine whether heavy or light pressure is needed.
c. The LD child may seem to be perseverating by displaying a prolonged interest in snapping or seeking out one topic.	c. A child's intense interest in taking pictures does not necessarily reflect perseverative behavior. When the activity brings no new cognitive or affective rewards, it will be purposeless. The teacher must make a judgment. Encouraging the child to seek new directions for photographic subjects, and/or building on his interests in one particular area by refining and enriching that topic is suggested.
d. The LD child often has difficulty in coming to attention.	d. The array of subjects to choose from within the environment will result in no choice unless the child is offered a choice within a range. The teacher's sensitivity to the child's preferences is demanded.
e. The child may not be selective.	e. Snapping anything in view is a novice's prerogative. Actively guiding the child's plans will bring forward pre-images.

CREATIVE DRAMATICS

Every learning-disabled child should be given the opportunity for personal and creative growth by participating in creative dramatics. As an art and therapy, dramatics presents an outlet for a whole range of human experiences. When coupled with language, it promotes freedom of expression; it is invaluable as a means of defining and understanding one's feelings. Creative dramatics often creates a sharing experience within the security of a closed group, a feeling of belonging, and a support for one's effort from peer members. It can make inroads for social exchanges. It is nontheatre oriented, facilitating extemporaneous speech and spontaneous movements.

Special self-contained classes of LD children are often requested to follow a regular class format by presenting a class play. Rehearsed lines, a set script, and acting techniques are theatre and drama attributes much different from creative dramatics. There are numerous positives statements of the value of drama, such as memory skills, sequencing, language enhancement, and recognition by the larger social group. A major distinguishing quality is that creative dramatics promotes the individual through "process" while drama results in a product. Both allow personal interpretation but, creative dramatics attends to the *why* and *how* children respond, not to *what* they do. When the activity is directed toward achieving "standard," appropriate responses and behaviors (which LD students need), the freedom of individual expression is contained. Creative dramatics asks the child to be no more than himself, not to live in the shadow of the normal child.

Teachers are concerned that creative dramatics can get out of hand if the child is given too much freedom. Good judgment, on the part of the student, does not always prevail when an activity is selected to dramatize. The teacher's role is not to stand by; she can suggest, direct, and limit the topic; when viewed as a catalyst and synthesizer, the students benefit in self-expression. Carter (1974, pp. 411-417) believes the teacher's function is to provide a stimulus and to initiate a reaction to that stimulus.

Just as students who understand creative dramatics become more effective players, teachers should try it in sessions with colleagues, thus bringing them in closer touch with the art.

The opportunities to communicate through body language and spoken language benefit the learning disabled. By using mime to reinforce the steps of an action (e.g., brushing one's teeth), such processes as memory, motoric expression, integration, and personal interpretation are tapped.

Skill sessions are basic to creative interpretation. Suggesting ways to use specific gestures (e.g., signaling one to speak softly, using one's eye movements to register surprise), add to the student's repertory. This training is critical for some LD children who have difficulty in "reading" other's moods, reactions, true intentions, and who do not express themselves adequately in nonverbal communication.

A sequential approach is necessary throughout. Planning simple activities involving rhythmic movement is suggested for beginners (Carter, 1974, p. 416), leading to pantomime, story dramatizations, and dramatic play with dialogue, real or imaginary. Pantomime is considered basic in the continuum. Common activities (e.g., brushing hair, washing face), when singled out, are easier to perform and interpret than an involved sequence of events (e.g., getting up in the morning) or one action (e.g., driving a car—which has several steps). The observation of a program for LD children in creative dramatics reported by Kaliski (1978) indicates a progression from body movement, pantomime, exploration of shapes, and improvised short plays, to the development of a play based on a theme provided by artists (actors) in residence. Duke (1974) outlines a sequence for creative dramatics that begins with rhythm and movement and leads to mime and pantomime improvisation, role playing, and ultimately to the development of scripted plays. The sequence established by Gillies (1973) begins with pantomime for its value in making play acting fluid and close to real life without the complications of dialogue.

Failure is impossible in creative dramatics. Feelings of independence and competence move in; a positive self-image begins to emerge. The child's alienation from his environment is lessened when creative dramatics is integrated into the curriculum.

Pitfalls	*Modifications*
a. Because the LD child is often self-conscious, he may be reluctant to participate in creative dramatics experiences.	a. By giving the child opportunities to observe other children and classes at creative dramatic sessions, the self-conscious child can overcome feelings of awkwardness. Allow the child to participate when he indicates readiness. By having a child participate with two or three peers, the focus of attention will be shared and the self-conscious child will not feel singled-out. Begin with simple, rhythmic activities using gross muscles and simple concepts (e.g., pretend you are a swan enjoying the afternoon).
b. The LD student who has been programmed into responding in a "normalized" fashion, will find it difficult to let go, to "be himself," and to use his ideas in a free way.	b. Creative dramatics experiences should be used as a discovery and expressive vehicle. When students understand, unlike so many academic areas where the *product* is what counts, that the *process* (the participant's experience) is more important for its playing out of thoughts and feelings, self-expression will emerge.
c. Over-reaction to the proposed creative dramatics activity can produce giddiness and result in behaviors out of control.	c. When the teacher presents the activity in a "matter-of-fact" manner, the students will calm their excessive responses to a dramatic expression. The newness of an activity, in itself, creates many more inappropriate behaviors (on the part of the audience as well as the players) which will be put into a context of being less novel as they become more familiar with the dramatic experience.
d. Creative dramatics often ask children to "think on their feet." LD children who are disinhibited may act spontaneously but out of sequence for a segment of playmaking.	d. Skill sessions are basic to creative interpretation. By suggesting ways to use gestures, to speak softly for example, the student will be guided in conveying an idea or concept. Siegel, Siegel, and Siegel (1978, Chapter 9) consider the importance of using body language effectively for both *sender* and *receiver*. Rather

Pitfalls	*Modifications*
	than acting impulsively, the sender must be able to show an appropriate gesture for a thought. The receiver, likewise, must be able to attend, organize, and think in a logical fashion. Training to bring about adeptness in expressing and receiving designated messages may be in such forms as "Charades," "Skits in Pantomime," and "Facial Expression Activities."
	When stories are to be acted out, the students should discuss the plot and sequence, not to plan out the entire action, but to provide opportunity to clarify the students' ideas and feelings. By recording the audio portions in a story, distinct sequences can be listened to and then reacted to, thereby aiding the learners' organizational skills.

MUSIC

Among the creative arts, music has been accepted more readily as a complement to the academic curriculum. It has been recognized as one of the most flexible, inviting, and rewarding activities for special children. Yet, when one considers the creative components in relation to other creative arts, music experiences rank low. It is said that singing, playing an instrument, or selecting music for listening are creative activities; when "creative" is qualified by "to do" rather than to make one's own unique sounds or responses, it has less of an impact on the child's creative drives. Recognition that music is more often a vehicle and supporting medium toward mastery of basic learning skills, improvement of attention span, reinforcement of laterality, facilitation of self-awareness, improvement of reading, and practice in auditory awareness is commonly displayed. Rejto (1973, pp. 15-24) demonstrated changes in visual skills, recognition of figure-ground, improvement in spatial relationships and auditory skills when piano lessons were initiated with a student diagnosed as learning disabled. The relaxing or stimulating qualities of music and the reduction of anger, hostility, and anxiety have been implied throughout.

A technique for teaching the piano to LD students by recognizing their need to release energies prior to settling down to a formal piano lesson has been developed by May (1979, p. 34.) Her innovative technique called Psychological Musical Musings (PMM) allows the student to get in touch with his feelings and the keyboard as he relates to it by playing anything and anywhere on the keyboard.

That music is good for handicapped children, or that they respond well to music is a vague agreement among educators (Alvin, 1968, p. 3). Rappaport (1966, pp. R-38) reported that music that was not stimulating to most children increased LD students' hyperactivity. He noted that absolute quiet was much more effective.

LD children can not tolerate all music (Cruickshank 1967, p. 114). The musical activity of rhythm games permits too much movement, too much awareness of visual stimuli, and an excessive amount of motor and auditory stimuli. Less music is recommended.

Giacobbe (1972, pp. 40-43) would limit the use of music as the child's ability to handle it dictates. He adds (1972, p. 43), "The tempo of social and musical growth" should be reflected in musical activity that is presented in an orderly sequence and will bring about creative self-expression.

Klein (1980, pp. 1-15) investigated the effects of variations in the tempo of background music on hyperactive and normal subjects. The results indicate that variations in the tempo of background music have a different effect on hyperactive as compared to normal subjects. In a structured task requiring repetitive motor responses, both hyperactive and normal subjects increased the number of errors as the tempo of the music increased; the hyperactive subjects made more errors than other groups under a fast tempo. A condition of slow tempo background music produced performance of the hyperactive children that was closest to that of the normal subjects. Hyperactive children performed best with a "no music" condition when an unstructured task of free drawing was assigned.

Nordoff and Robbins (1971, p. 103) have developed a program of music for handicapped learners which considers learning characteristics of the learning disabled. Words are set to music so that "naturally accented syllables fall on musically oriented beats"; a vocal range within a song is restricted; and, interestingly, dissonant music has been deliberately created to heighten auditory attention and to support rhythm and tempo that capitalize on the stimulation of body rhythm as an organizer.

Music improvisation for the LD child lacks direction today; instead, organization and need for auditory competence are generally stressed. Vernazza (1978, p. 5) thinks that young, special-needs children profit from the security of structured music situations without too many distractions.

Music can be a superb organizer for the learning disabled who present patterns of disorganization. As they listen to sound, they must organize to hear. Music in itself is organized sound. Strong, definable rhythms and clear logical melodies which either repeat or return are elements, according to Vernazza, most children can relate to. Simple, rhythmical songs that emphasize basic musical concepts (slow and fast, loud and soft) that give directions in space and require body actions or an oral response best help the LD child learn organization.

Pitfalls	*Modifications* (Nocera, 1979, pp. 238, 278–281)
a. The child may be somewhat rigid and "on edge," owing to unreliable perceptual feedback.	a. Use routine procedures; introduce new routines gradually. Avoid musical idioms (e.g., "from the top"). Use the child's strongest sensory mode first.
b. The learner may be disorganized in a music setting. Work materials	b. Use consistent procedures. Structure activities. Limit choices. Re-

Pitfalls	*Modifications* (Nocera, 1979, pp. 238, 278–281)
may be in disarray; his responses may be random and meaningless.	duce distractions. Give step-by-step directions.
c. The LD child is often distractible. He may want to touch and play all the musical instruments.	c. Limit the amount and kind of sensory materials in one activity. Position the child so you can easily gain his attention. Simplify the music setting.
d. The child who perseverates may continue to sing or play after the activity has ended.	d. Physically change positions with a new activity. Contrast the activities in a lesson. Keep materials out of sight until needed.
e. The child may demonstrate a short attention span by wandering off in the middle of a music session, appearing bored or fatigued.	e. Try to make the lessons flow smoothly. Provide short, varied, high-interest activities. Repeat successful performances.
f. The LD child may be unable to perform two perceptual motor tasks simultaneously (clap and sing, clap and walk, play and sing).	f. Keep the activity simple in quantity and in degree of sensory requirements. Add another modality only when responses are automatic.

Special education demands exactness in remediation within a framework of interesting and novel modes for learning. For the special child to make optimal gains, educational programs must be comprehensive and should include a strong creative arts component.

REFERENCES

Alvin, J. *Music for the handicapped child.* New York: Oxford University Press, 1968.

Brittain, W. *Creativity, art, and the young child.* New York: Macmillan, 1979.

Carter, T. Creative dramatics for LD children. *Academic Therapy*, Summer, 1974, *9*(6), 411–17.

Cruickshank, W. M. *The brain-injured child in home, school, and community.* Syracuse, N.Y.: Syracuse University Press, 1967.

Duke, C. R. *Creative dramatics and English teaching.* Urbana, Ill.: National Council of Teachers of English, 1974.

Giacobbe, G. A. Rhythm builds order in brain-injured children. *Music Educators Journal*, April, 1972, *59*, 40–43.

Gillies, E. *Creative dramatics for all children.* Washington, D.C.: Association for Childhood Education International, 1973.

Gonick-Barris, S. E. Art for children with minimal brain dysfunction. *American Journal of Art Therapy*, April, 1976, *15*, 67–73.

Hedges, R. Photography and self-concept. *Audiovisual Instruction*, May 1972, *17*, 26–28.

Kaliski, L. A theatre workshop for children with learning disabilities. Paper presented at the World Congress on Future Special Education, Stirling, Scotland, June 25–July 1, 1978.

Klein, P. S. Responses of hyperactive and normal children to variations in tempo of background music. Bar-Ilan University, Ramat-Gan, Israel, 1980. (Unpublished.)

Kramer, H. The new American photography. *New York Times Magazine*, July 23, 1978, 8–13, 24–26.

Lazarus, P. W., and Carlin, H. Cutting: A kinesthetic tool for learning. *Exceptional Children*, March, 1965, *31*, 361–64.

Linderman, E. W., and Linderman, M. *Crafts for the classroom*. New York: Macmillan, 1977.

Linderman, M. *Art in the elementary school*. Dubuque, Iowa: William C. Brown, 1974.

Lowenfeld, V., and Brittain, W. *Creative and mental growth, 6th ed*. New York: Macmillan, 1975.

May, A. A piano teaching innovation—*PMM. *The American Music Teacher*, June–July, 1979, *28*, 34.

Meiselas, S. *Learn to see*. Cambridge, Mass.: Polaroid Foundation, 1974.

Nocera, S. D. *Reaching the special learner through music*. Morristown, N.J.: Silver Burdett Company, 1979.

Nordoff, P., and Robbins, C. *Music therapy in special education*. New York: John Day, 1971.

Rappaport, S. *Perceptual problems*. Proceedings of the Connecticut Association of School Psychological Personnel, Fall Institute, 1966.

Rejto, A. Music as an aid in the remediation of learning disabilities. *Journal of Learning Disabilities*, May, 1973, *6*(5), 15–24.

Siegel, E., Siegel, R., and Siegel, P. *Help for the lonely child*. New York: E. P. Dutton, 1978.

Vernazza, M. *Music plus for the young child in special education*. Boulder, Colorado: Pruett Publishing Company, 1978.

Wiig. E., and Semel, E. M. *Language disabilities in children and adolescents*. Columbus, Ohio: Charles E. Merrill, 1976.

Expanding the Curriculum

17

Special education is currently experiencing an expansion of the curriculum along two avenues. The first is the widened age range now being accommodated via the development of preschool and postschool programs. These are comprehensive in nature: In addition to focusing upon meeting the client's educational needs, the emphasis is also upon such components as outreach and identification; evaluation and follow up; and advocacy along all fronts.

The second aspect of curriculum expansion can be seen in the growth of specific "subject areas" and services.

CAREER EDUCATION

Unlike vocational education, career education should commence in kindergarten and the elementary grades. Instead of emphasizing a particular field of employment, career education is more general and, in fact, goes beyond vocation to include adjustment within the family unit and the community (Gillet, 1978; Klinkhamer, 1973, p. 125). Gillet (1978) believes that "for the learning-disabled child, career education refers to the career of LIVING; not [merely] earning a living" (p. 13). It does not center around a specific course, such as Home Economics, Industrial Arts, Shop; rather it should permeate all courses. For example, Ryan (1980) suggests specific activities relating to career education that can be part of a Social Studies course (e.g., conducting a worker interview; pretending that a famous person from the past is alive and deciding what job he would be likely to hold today). English classes can include writing letters to apply for jobs, completing job applications, participation in simulated interviews, answering and composing classified advertisements, and so on. All subjects—science, math, art, health education—have vocational implications and can lend themselves to some facet of career education. Many authors prefer this infusion philosophy (Brolin & D'Alonzo, 1979; Phelps & Lutz, 1977, p. 29; Gillet, 1978, p. 9) since "Career education should not be conceived of as a time segment of education . . . nor as a separate area . . ." (Klinkhamer, 1973, p. 125). Hickey (1980), however, believes that separate courses should be created; this assures the child of his career education rather than relying on the array of individual teachers to infuse as they see fit.

Reflecting its comprehensive philosophy, career education includes the concepts of *career clusters* (a broad occupational category, such as business and office, construction, food preparation and services, etc., generates a variety of jobs, each requiring different levels and kinds of aptitude) and *career ladders* (i.e., an entering level can ultimately lead to a more advanced one) (Phelps & Lutz, 1977). These concepts make it much more feasible to cater to each pupil as an individual (Phelps & Lutz, 1977, pp. 28-29).

Despite some gains in the career education movement, (e. g., legislative support and funding by the Bureau of Education for the Handicapped (BEH), the creation of the Division on Career Development (DCD) by the Council for Exceptional Children in 1976, and the availability of Career Education material at Special Education Instructional Material Center (SEIMC) and elsewhere, many LD adults continue to be unemployed, underemployed, and misemployed. A three-pronged attack is needed to make career education an integral and effective component of special education:

1. We must convince employers that many handicapped individuals can become capable employees. In fact, the flip side of career education is public relations as it applies to employers and employment agencies.

2. We must enlarge and refine the LD student's skills as a worker while bolstering his self-confidence.

3. Teachers, guidance counselors, and other school personnel themselves must have special aptitudes—i.e., in-depth knowledge of LD children's strengths and weaknesses, understanding of the psychodynamics of their behavior, and an acceptance of the philosophy of career education matched by expertise with respect to appropriate materials and instructional activities.

SEX EDUCATION

All adolescents face the same kinds of problems—that is, doubts, anxieties, possible misconceptions—regarding their sexuality, their self-worth, and their future roles (marriage, family living, etc.). In the case of the LD adolescent (and young adult), the problems are heightened and complicated by such factors as poor self-concept, anxiety, and a paucity of social options. Adolescence is the stage where identity is being established and the school settings provide opportunities to meet new people and try new activities. Yet, for the LD adolescent, the lack of friends, same or opposite sex, appears to peak in mid-adolescence (Kronick, 1978). Peers, who feel more vulnerable at this age, may reject the LD person who has few of the qualities which are valued. This isolation from the peer group may result in a greater dependence upon parents and reduces the opportunities to learn how to interact with peers in a variety of social situations, thereby segregating the adolescent even more.

To date, little training has been provided the LD adolescents in matters regarding their sexuality or social relationships which may lead to marriage. Many authors of texts devoted to teaching the learning disabled *mention* sex education either alone or as part of the curriculum of needed life skills. However, they rarely discuss ways to implement such a curriculum. Often society, including parents, assumes the disabled either have no need for sexual gratification or, if they do, they should sublimate it (Blumberg, 1975).

Although there are problems in implementing sex education programs for all children—for example, lack of adequately-trained teachers and the existence of pressure groups opposed to sex education programs in the schools—Gordon (1971) stated that "Special Education has a special responsibility to include sex in its curriculum" (p. 353). In a book written for youth and young adults with handicapping conditions, Gordon (1975) contends that all ". . . are entitled to full responsible sexual expression" (p. 41).

A report of a sex education workshop for two groups of LD young adults by Rothenberg, Franzblau, and Geer (1979) indicates that knowledge of anatomy, reproductive processes, birth control devices, and veneral disease was either incomplete, confused or nonexistent. The authors could not determine if the misconceptions and confusions were caused by learning problems, per se, or by other factors, such as lack of experience and over-protection. Blom (1971) believes that the greater concerns children with handicaps have than normal children about their bodies, body parts, and body functioning may influence their learning. While LD persons have the same sexual feelings, interests, and desires as their peers, they often require a different way of learning and comprehending the various aspects and nuances of sexuality, sexual behavior, and family planning. However, unless special provisions are made for the LD student, sex education will be provided within the mainstream curriculum.

Schiller (1973) suggests that the general objectives for a sex education program include: factual information; sexual self-understanding; understanding of the opposite sex and of the sexual lifestyles of people of different ages and from different cultures; recognition that sex is a part of life; and encouragement of family planning. These objectives should be developed within a curriculum that is multidimensional and involves teachers, counselors, nurses, social workers, and so forth, and can be incorporated into many courses and subject areas. Rap sessions and role playing can be useful techniques.

Sex-related problems among all adolescents include venereal disease and pregnancy, which have reached epidemic proportions (Public Health Service, 1975; National Center for Health Statistics, 1976). These problems become the concerns of special education within the schools since they ". . . may be the principal institution for servicing the handicapped adolescent" (Cullinan & Epstein, 1979, p. 16).

Sex education, as other areas of the curriculum, must be individualized (Reich & Harshman, 1971). All children should not have the same sex education curriculum.

It should be coordinated with the development stages. The program in the schools should be sequential, beginnning in the early grades so that the children are less likely to learn inaccurate information.

Opportunities for question and further discussion must be provided at every level so that distortions can be minimized. Individual and group instruction should be used. A sex-education program should not only teach the "facts" of sex, but also attitudes. This raises more differences of opinion; that is, What attitudes? Who shall teach them? Under whose auspices?

Gordon includes attitudes within the content of a series of educational comic books published by Ed-U-Press of the Institute for Family Research and Education; for example, sex is not to be used as a weapon or to prove oneself, sex should not be used to exploit others, sex requires responsibility, "males and females have a right to be virgins."

Some parents believe that LD girls, because of their guilelessness are easy prey for men, and, rather than encouraging participation in social groups—even those sponsored by local chapers of ACLD or SEPTA (Special Education Parent Teacher Association)—keep them at home. Instead of such isolation, these girls need an educational program designed to help them learn to adjust to such social encounters. Rap sessions in the schools or in after-school socialization programs often help these young men and women understand and learn to use socialization skills. For example, most teenagers, not just the LD, are concerned about what to say and how to act when they date (Brown, 1980). Schools are the labs for learning social skills. Instruction in planning parties, party behavior, and dancing is needed. Gordon (1975) suggests that mixed-group activities and double dates make talking easier and thus reduce tensions.

The LD teacher can take an active role in helping the student develop an awareness of his social behavior and the consequences. She should provide a climate of trust, making sure to state the limits of confidentiality, give feedback to the student by reflecting what was said in a nonjudgmental manner, and encourage expressions of feelings.

The increase in programs for the LD adolescent and young adult are also leading to an expansion of curricula for sex education and family living. Information can be obtained from the American Association of Sex Educators and Counselors and the Sex Education and Information Council of the United States (SEICUS). A SEICUS report on the Handicapped was published in 1976 and includes a selective bibliography on sex and the handicapped (pp. 8-10).

The concern of professionals for improving sex education for *all* children is underscored by the publication of a double issue of the Journal of School Health in April, 1981 which is devoted to articles on how to implement programs, the training of teachers, and ways to gain community support. An annotated resource list is included. Parent training for their roles in these programs should also be provided. The school and home should cooperate in planning and improving programs: ". . . the goal should be the preparation of people to cope with their internal sex pressures and with their own self-image, and to deal with the social and environmental impact of sexuality that impinges on them day after day" (Schiller, 1973, p. 103).

SOCIAL SKILLS

Develop Social Repertoire

The more skill the LD individual has in social activities (e.g., playing checkers or chess, table tennis, Monopoly, bridge; bowling; square dancing, or social dancing), the more he will be ready to take advantage of opportunities for socializing when they arrive. Thompson (1970) believes: "As many areas of achievement outside of academic as possible should be developed—mountaineering, animal care, mechanical achievement, art, music. Success in any of these areas will be a wedge to participation in the adult world and will make success in other areas more likely" (p. 127).

Increase Social Savoire-Faire

Many LD children (because of poor feedback mechanisms and/or lack of opportunity to socialize) fail to develop the social graces. These can be taught in everyday classroom activities: math lessons can develop knowledge about tipping, language arts can nourish proper conversational—including telephone—behavior, literature —particularly drama— can often lead directly to a study (and practice) of social conduct. These can be augmented with class trips and playground activities.

The teacher need not be the sole instructor of these skills. Many ACLD chapters have established social-recreational groups for all ages including adolescents and young adults. The older groups, led by a trained professional, go on trips, hold dances and parties, conduct weekend excursions, and so on. They plan the trips, discuss appropriate behavior during traveling, and they get considerable experience in informal conversational skills and in playing party games. Role playing and weekly "rap sessions" offer increased opportunity to improve in social savoire-faire.

Strengthening Social Perception

Many LD children are socially imperceptive. Not only are they inept at interpreting nonverbal communication signals, but they often have difficulty in expressing these as well: They stand too close; stare too long; can't tell if a person is bored or enthusiastic, happy or sad, afraid or relaxed, disgusted or proud. They need help in learning to differentiate various tones of voices, facial expressions, eye movements, and postures. If they fail repeatedly to interpret others' moods, intentions, and reactions to them, they will continue to behave inappropriately. Rejection will ensue and they will lose out on opportunities to socialize which they so desperately need.

Fortunately, the LD pupil can be instructed in these skills. A Polaroid camera, a tape recorder, silent films, instructional sets of photographs depicting people expressing various emotions are excellent training aids. Nonverbal communication skills can be developed in conjunction with other subjects: poetry, drama, reading, social studies (e.g., interpreting facial expressions of historical figures' photographs, practice in reciting famous speeches), and so forth. The study of social perceptions can become a separate course in itself. Still another alternative is to make it part of career-education courses (social conduct on the job, deportment during an interview, role playing for jobs that require large amounts of interaction with the public. *Help for the Lonely Child: Strengthening Social Perception* (by Rita, Ernest and Paul Siegel, New York: E.P. Dutton, 1978) discusses a number of activities for the classroom (and home) and contains an annotated bibliography listing texts, juvenile texts, workbooks, commercial games, recordings, instructional card sets, photograph sets, films and film strips, and total programs (published) all designed to facilitate the improvement of social perception, particularly in LD children.

REMEDIATION

Since all LD children, by definition, are deficient in some of the academic skills, they will have problems in mastering other subjects for which proficiency in basic academic skills are prerequisite. This is particularly true in mainstreamed classes. The first hurdle occurs after the primary elementary grades: in grade four, science and social studies—both require considerable language-arts skills—begin receiving more attention. This problem continues and broadens as the child progresses from grade to grade. It reaches its height when he enters secondary school. There, each teacher has a subject specialty, has been trained to teach that subject, and has little time (and often no preparation) for remediating basic skills efficiency. There are several approaches for providing remediation in these areas:

1. Through individualized instruction, the teacher—or paraprofessional, peer tutor, volunteer, etc.—can devote more time to remediation.

2. Modifications can be made in the approach to the subject matter: e.g., a chapter in a science text can be reworded in a more simplified, briefer form. In this way, the pupil engages in the content area but simultaneously receives the remedial practice he needs.

3. The LD student can receive the remediation outside of the classroom: e.g., the resource room, after-school reading programs, a reading clinic, private tutoring.

The LD child may also need remediation in work habits and study skills. This can be done via a direct approach (i.e., showing him specifically what many youngsters learn incidentally), modeling (letting him observe others who have mastered appropriate work habits and study skills—frequently, a buddy system or committee work can be helpful), parent training (this promotes continuity and provides additional opportunity to practice the appropriate skills), and modifications (e.g., using a simplified dictionary at first). Structure is necessary throughout, motivational considerations are crucial, and behavior-modification techniques can be helpful.

Note taking is an important skill—especially for the college bound LD student—which should be taught specifically. Guided practice should be given and a sequential approach employed. Some recommended sequential components are: from outlining written material to outlining oral selections (the written material is easier since it can be referred to as often as necessary); from shorter passages to lengthier ones; from having the selection on tape (so that it can be replayed for verification) to a single presentation. (See appendix C for an entire instructional sequence devoted to note taking.)

Two points of caution should be made: (1) we should not become so intent upon remediation that we ignore the overall curriculum, and (2) since remediation necessarily illuminates the child's deficits, we should approach this in a supportive manner—matter-of-factly, unobtrusively, patiently, sensitively, and with a great deal of empathy.

CONSUMERISM AND INDEPENDENT LIVING SKILLS

The LD child needs school-directed experience and course work in consumerism. Because of gullibility, poor self-concept, lack of assertiveness, and some conceptualization difficulties, he easily becomes "a patsy" in the marketplace. He must be given specific instruction in comparison shopping, in helping to decide whether or not to buy in quantity (How much will it save? Is there a storage problem? Am I likely to need all of it in a reasonable period of time?), in planning to wait for sales (e.g., the annual post-holiday sales), and so on. He must learn to count his change. He must be taught to avoid buying from door-to-door salespeople, to get receipts, to rely on *Consumer's Guide* rather than upon the automobile salesperson's persuasions. Consumerism—like career education—should be included from kindergarten to high school. Elementary-school children can be taught to shop wisely for their school supplies and lunches, whereas pupils in secondary school can learn about buying clothing, furniture, insurance, and vacation "packages." In addition to teaching pupils to spend (and save) money wisely, the subject of consumerism can also entail use of leisure time; health and safety habits (eating nutritiously, wearing proper clothing—this often involves planning ahead in accordance with the weather forecast, cleanliness and good grooming, maintaining a schedule for medical and dental checkups, removing ice and snow from in front of the house, having frayed electrical wires repaired, storing paints and other inflammables appropriately); budgeting of time and money; paying bills on time; care and maintenance of clothing, other belongings, and of the home.

Independent living requires considerable organization. Food, medicines, cleaning materials, even such seemingly mundane items as light bulbs, tooth picks, and toilet paper must be stockpiled, inventoried, and stored conveniently. The individual who no longer lives with his parents must remember a myriad of things: set the alarm clock, bring clothes to the cleaners, change the linen, have eyeglasses fixed, turn off the TV, turn on the light before taking medicine, and so on. It also requires the ability to make decisions regarding socializing in the home—whom to invite (assuming that the LD individual in question has enlarged his circle of acquaintances),what to serve, what time to terminate the gathering, how to deal with "guests" who may abuse the hospitality (and this is not too unlikely in view of many LD individuals' gullibility and poor self-concepts).

These vital areas of consumerism and independent living skills should not be left to chance. They can be incorporated into the curriculum via specific courses in the secondary schools, infusion at all levels and in various subject matter (literature, arithmetic, social studies, health education, science, civics, economics.) Modeling, role playing, behavior-modification techniques, guidance and/or informal discussion groups, field trips and bibliotherapy are some of the vehicles for fostering the necessary skills, knowledge, and attitudes.

DRIVER EDUCATION

A frequently-raised question is whether or not LD individuals should be encouraged to drive in view of their many neurological, perceptual, and behavioral deficits. Impairment in visual perception, auditory perception, spatial orientation, and visual-motor coordination may effect one's ability to master the mechanics of driving adequately. An analogy might be for us to consider how it is necessary to get used to driving a car other than one's own. There is a strange "feeling" to it. We are unfamiliar with the exact locations of the gas pedal, the brake pedal, the bright-light switch, and the door handle. We do not have the "feel" of the steering wheel. We do not automatically extend our hands the proper distance when opening the passenger's door. Being nonhandicapped, we learn these in short order, given sufficient practice. LD children, however, lacking sufficient kinesthetic feedback, may continually have to literally *grope* their way through the driving process and may *never* get the smooth, adequate, and reliable "feel" of the car. Furthermore, impulsivity may hinder judgment, perseveration may render one inflexible in dealing with instantaneous and changing driving conditions, and irritability may result in impatience with other drivers, unfavorable road conditions and with traffic. A poor temporal sense may make it difficult to gauge the car's speed without looking at the speedometer. Distractibility may manifest itself at crucial times. The fact is, however, that many LD adults do drive and drive successfully. They have learned to compensate for their basic deficits. One LD adult passed his driver's test by using masking tape cutouts of the letters *L* and *R* (to assist his instant response to the examiner's command to turn *left* or *right*). These were mounted on the dashboard. Being well coordinated and motivated, he passed with flying colors. At the completion of the test, the examiner noticed the letters and asked about them, whereupon the LD driver explained, "They're my girl friend's initials" (Weiss & Weiss, 1980). The LD driver who is prone to neurological overload must learn to say to his passengers, "It would be better if you didn't talk to me while I drive, so that I can concentrate more on the road." Other examples of compensations include compromises such as driving in the daytime and avoiding night driving, taking shorter trips as opposed to longer ones, and avoiding heavily trafficked areas.

Since each case is individual, no generalization should be made with respect to all learning-disabled individuals. In questionable cases, the neurologist's opinions should be sought.

GUIDANCE AND COUNSELING

One of the most supportive means of helping the LD child adjust and achieve his potential is to establish a definitive school guidance program. All too often in the past, even when guidance counselors were employed in the school, the child with mild learning and/or behavioral problems was overlooked. Since school guidance programs are invariably understaffed, there is a tendency to focus upon only the "emergency" problems—that is, the acting-out and disruptive children (Krugman, 1954, p. 115).

The responsibility for guiding and counseling need not be restricted to counselors and school psychologists. For example, attendance officers seek not only to prevent unnecessary absences, but also to identify the factors that precipitate these, and to develop wholesome relationships with maladjusted children, thereby motivating them toward improved school attendance habits. Similarly, with proper administrative support and orientation, the school nurse, the librarian, even the school secretary and bus driver will, in their interaction with LD students, sustain more positive and supportive relationships.

In addition to fostering good mental hygiene practices throughout the class day, there are specific avenues and techniques for promoting guidance and counseling which are being brought to the attention of teachers: role playing, use of puppetry, creative drama and sociodrama, language arts (e.g., writing an autobiography). Activities geared primarily toward fostering skills in social perception and in non-verbal communication—and there has been increased interest in these areas recently—can frequently serve as springboards into guidance lessons: for example, learning how to recognize an angry face is but a step away from discussing what makes one angry, how to deal with feelings of anger, how to neutralize anger directed toward oneself, whether or not anger can ever be used productively, and so on. Many excellent films, games, and other materials which can be used in conjunction with a well planned guidance program are available to classroom teachers. Several examples of these are:

1. *The Effect of Affect* (by Anthony Cedoline, Novato, Ca.: Academic Therapy Publications, 1977). This text contains over 100 classroom activities designed to develop better relationships, self-esteem, and decision making.

2. *The Coping with Series* (by Shirley Schwarzrock and C. Gilbert Wrenn, Circle Pines, Minnesota, American Guidance Service, 1973). This is a series of twenty-three short books and is geared to the junior-high and high-school pupil. Some of the titles are "My Life—What Should I Do with It?" "Do I Know the 'Me' Others See?" "Parents Can Be a Problem." They can be used in group instruction or individually (as "free" reading material or as supplementary reading to a guidance or counseling session). A teacher's manual containing procedures, and bibliographies for the teacher as well as for pupils is included.

3. *Got to Be Me* (by Merrill Harmin, Niles, Ill.: Argus Communications, 1976). This kit, recommended for students in elementary grades, includes forty-eight colored, humorously illustrated cards. Each contains an unfinished sentence designed to make the child more aware of himself: e.g., "I laugh when—." "I am afraid to—." "I wish people would stop—."

Counseling is not for the child alone. Parent counseling is an important adjunct to a comprehensive guidance program for LD pupils. By getting in touch with their own feelings, parents will be in a better position to understand, cope with, accept, and nurture the needs of their child. Because teacher–child relationships are crucial elements in the LD child's emotional growth, more and more authors are suggesting that the teachers themselves receive guidance and counseling (Larsen & Poplin, 1980, p. 323; Johnson & Morasky, 1980). A number of factors can heighten teachers' feelings of anxiety, anger, and/or fear: the emotional overlays (and subsequent behavioral problems) of the LD child; perceived cause-and-effect relationships (Am I doing something wrong which contributed to the learning disabilities?); special demands (in terms of time and methodology); problems stemming from the requirement of having to interact with a variety of individuals—parents, other professionals, community groups, and so on (Johnson & Morasky, 1980). The school psychologist is assuming an increasingly important role in teacher counseling.

CONCLUSION

Superimposed on all of the preceding areas of curriculum is one crucial consideration. Teachers as well as the LD child's peers in the regular classroom must be educated regarding their roles with respect to the LD individual. Mainstreaming is becoming a potent sensitizing took, providing "hands on" experience for the nonhandicapped to observe, work with, grow to understand, and help the LD child. Counseling, role playing, modeling, and other behavior-modification techniques all have a vital function in this regard. Recently published teaching materials (literature, films, a special puppet set of handicapped characters) can augment instruction. Consultative services, itinerant services, and inservice training can be instrumental in effecting positive teacher attitude. This advocacy for the LD child, this thrust toward consciousness raising, this growing awareness of human rights and the principle of normalization need not end at the classroom walls. It should permeate the neighborhood, the community, and the world. School curriculum will always reflect a given society's mores, culture, and values. The school curriculum of a democracy will differ from those of totalitarian nations. The LD individual's very survival rests upon the degree of acceptance, respect, and appreciation as a human being he receives from others. It was not accidental that when New York Association for Brain-Injured Children first formed in 1958, its official stationery contained this message: "There is no truer test of genuine, as distinct from counterfeit, civilization than the attitude of its society to the handicapped."*

REFERENCES

Blom, G. E. Some considerations about the neglect of sex education in special education. *Journal of Special Education*, Winter, 1971, *5*(4), 359–361.

Blumberg, M. L. Psychodynamics of the young handicapped person. *American Journal of Psychotherapy*, October, 1975, *29*(4), 466– 476.

Brolin, D. E. and D'Alonzo, B. J. Critical issues in career education for handicapped students. *Exceptional Children,* January, 1979, *45*(4), 246–253.

Brown, D. Learning disability: Unsure social behavior means insecure relationships. *LD Observer*, August-September, 1980, *1* (1), 8–9.

Cullinan, D. and Epstein, M. H. *Special education for adolescents: Issues and perspectives*. Columbus, Ohio: Charles E. Merrill, 1979.

Gillet, P. *Career education*. Novato, Ca.: Academic Therapy Publications, 1978.

Gordon, S. Missing in special education: Sex. *Journal of Special Education*, Winter, 1971, *5*(4), 351–354.

————. *Living fully: A guide for young people with a handicap, their parents, their teachers, and professionals*. New York: John Day, 1975.

Hickey, J. Job and training opportunity for special education students. An address given at a workshop held at the Graduate School and University Center of the City University of New York, January 29, 1980.

Johnson, S. W. and Morasky, R. L. *Learning disabilities, 2nd ed*. Boston: Allyn & Bacon, 1980.

* These words appeared in the article "Re: The Other Child" by Father James Rohan, St. Ignatius Loyola Bulletin, June 1958.

Klinkhamer, G. Career education as a philosophy and a practice: An interview with George Klinkhamer. *Teaching Exceptional Children*, Spring, 1973, *5* (3), 124–128.

Kronick, D. An examination of psychosocial aspects of learning disabled adolescents. *Learning Disability Quarterly*, Fall, 1978, *1*(4), 86–93.

Krugman, M. Appraisal and treatment of personality problems in a guidance program. *Education in a free world*. Washington, D.C.: American Council on Education, 1954.

Larsen, S. C. and Poplin, M. S. *Methods for educating the handicapped*. Boston: Allyn & Bacon, 1980.

Phelps, L. A. and Lutz, R. J. *Career exploration and preparation for the special needs learner*. Boston: Allyn & Bacon, 1977.

Reich, M. L. and Harshman, H. W. Sex education for handicapped children: Reality or repression. *Journal of Special Education*, Winter, 1971, *5*(4), 373–377.

Rothenberg, G. S., Franzblau, S. H., and Geer, J. H. Educating the learning-disabled adolescent about sexuality. *Journal of Learning Disabilities*, November, 1979, *12*(9), 576–580.

Ryan, F. L. *The social studies sourcebook*. Boston: Allyn & Bacon, 1980.

Schiller, P. *Creative approach to sex education and counselling*. New York: Association Press, 1973.

Thompson, A. Moving toward adulthood. In Lauriel E. Anderson (Ed.), *Helping the adolescent with the hidden handicap*. Novato, Ca.: Academic Therapy Publications, 1970.

Weiss, H. G. and Weiss, M. *Personal communication*, March, 1980.

Organization and Administration of Learning-Disabilities Programs

18

Because of the variability of the LD group in degree, as well as types, a continuum of services is needed in order to meet their needs. The services required range from a regular class placement with some modifications in methods and materials for the mildly handicapped, to full-time placement in a special school for the severely learning disabled (see Figure 18-1).

Although some have interpreted the concept of least restricted environment to mean the elimination of some special-education alternatives for the LD, such as the self-contained special class and special school, "... effective implementation of least restrictive policies and regulations should actually result in the creation of new alternatives within school systems" (Turnbull & Turnbull, 1978, p. 151). Ideally the child is placed within the least restrictive environment with the goal of moving up to Step One as quickly as possible. The development of alternative models makes this feasible. In the past, once a child was assigned to a special class, it was difficult to return to the mainstream (Hanson, et al., 1973). Each type of setting has its benefits and drawbacks.

Regular class placement, Step One, allows the students to remain fully integrated with their peers, providing an opportunity to learn and interact with non-handicapped classmates. The classroom teacher provides assistance to the LD student by adjusting the curriculum and using special techniques. The consultant is available as a resource person and can aid in procuring materials and scheduling follow-up services from other specialists. The size of many regular classes make it difficult for the regular classroom teacher to individualize instruction for the LD children and for the other children in the class whose special needs must be met. Though modifications in instruction and materials are made, most of the classroom instruction, activities, and curriculum may not be appropriate to meet the needs of

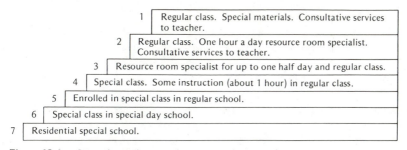

1	Regular class. Special materials. Consultative services to teacher.
2	Regular class. One hour a day resource room specialist. Consultative services to teacher.
3	Resource room specialist for up to one half day and regular class.
4	Special class. Some instruction (about 1 hour) in regular class.
5	Enrolled in special class in regular school.
6	Special class in special day school.
7	Residential special school.

Figure 18-1. Steps in mainstreaming: a continuum of services for the learning disabled.

the LD. In addition, it has been reported that the LD may be rejected socially by their nonhandicapped peers (See mainstreaming issues, p. 329).

At Steps Two and Three, regular class placement with the addition of resource and/or other support services is provided for students who need more assistance than can be given by the regular classroom teacher. The resource teacher and support personnel can provide direct, intense intervention for specific areas of deficit on a regular basis. The LD student can be given special help without being segregated from peers for long periods of time. Special materials and equipment, not available in the regular classroom, can be used in the resource or specialist's classroom.

Many problems can arise at placement in either Step Two or Three. The resource teacher may be pressured to tutor academics rather than remediate underlying problems. Such tutoring tends to develop a few skills rather than in-depth understanding. The students also miss much of the regular classroom program. In addition, conflicts may arise between the resource-room teacher and the regular classroom teacher regarding scheduling, grading, and reporting of student progress.

Students at Step Four are assigned to special classes but spend up to an hour a day in a regular classroom for a subject in which they show particular strength. More severely handicapped LD students spend their entire day in a special class, Step Five, and receive all their instruction from specially-trained teachers within a structured environment. Children assigned to these steps are generally segregated from their agemates and have limited opportunities to have nonhandicapped role models.

At Step Six, special day schools are usually found in large school districts, where school districts unite to offer cooperative services, or when private agencies may provide such programs. The children who attend these schools have severe learning problems which are frequently complicated by other handicapping conditions. Comprehensive services are provided by a team of specialists, e.g., special educators, speech and language therapists, psychologists, remedial reading teachers, physical educators, and so on.

The students in the special school are isolated from nonhandicapped peers in school and at home. They frequently must travel for excessive amounts of time to and from school. The teachers are also isolated and may lose sight of what is appropriate behavior and academic performance for different age and grade levels. Presently only in relatively rare situations is a severely learning disabled child placed in a residential school (Step Seven). Such a placement usually is made when the family situation cannot supply the supports necessary for the child or when an appropriate school placement within commuting distance is not available.*

The choice of program depends on the age of the student and the severity of the disability, the services available, the training of the staff, and the attitude of the school administrator. Most LD children spend part of the school day in the resource room. This permits the child to spend a maximum amount of time with peers in the regular classroom while still receiving help. Children are seen for individual and group instruction in the resource room. In the primary grades, the resource teacher (RT) attempts to remediate deficits and works in ways that utilize areas of strength as well. In the intermediate grades, besides attempting to remediate areas of basic deficits and teaching the child how to learn in new ways, the RT may also function as a tutor of the academic subjects the child will encounter back in the regular classroom. At the high-school levels, the stress is generally on coping skills and tutoring. Vocational training may also be included.

RESOURCE-ROOM MODELS

Since the inception of the resource-room concept for special education in the late 60s, when the effectiveness of self-contained special education classes was questioned, the function of the resource room has been evolving. Wiederholt, Hammill, and Brown (1978) identify five types:

1. categorical—In each resource room, the children who attend are from one area of exceptionality, either LD, MR, ED, etc.
2. cross-categorical—Children are assigned according to instructional level rather than diagnostic category.
3. noncategorical—Children with mild or moderate learning and/or behavior problems are enrolled. They may be from both regular and special education and may not be labelled handicapped. Wiederholt, Hammill, and Brown suggest that 70% to 80% are not handicapped. They believe such a model serves as a bridge between regular and special education.
4. specific skill resource program—Arranged around a skill area, the teachers in this program usually only work with the nonhandicapped who require services beyond what is available in the regular classroom.
5. itinerant resource program—Service is provided to more than one school in in a district when there is no need for a full-time program in each school. Any of the first four formats noted above may be used.

Depending upon the needs of a particular district, any of the five models may be used to provide educational interventions for LD children.

Teacher Skills
Resource-room teachers need many skills in order to perform. They must be able to:
1. Assess strengths, weaknesses and learning styles through the use of formal and informal assessment techniques.

* At times, even high functioning students may attend a residential setting because of factors within the family.

2. Develop and interpret the individual educational program in cooperation with the regular classroom teacher.

3. Use appropriate activities, methods, and materials within the resource room.

4. Structure the environment for maximum learning.

5. Demonstrate activities, methods, and materials for the regular classroom teacher.

6. Act as a consultant to the regular classroom teacher and assist in the selection of appropriate activities, methods, and materials to be used in the regular classrooms.

7. Hold conferences with the classroom teacher and parents.

8. Arrange workshops for regular education staff, parents, and administrators to explain the resource program. Also arrange workshops to explain specific methods and materials, and the ways to identify and evaluate pupils.

9. Schedule students for the resource room and maintain flexibility of schedule to meet changing needs.

10. Analyze curriculum in a variety of subject areas and for a variety of grade levels.

The LD teacher needs additional skills. She must be well organized and able to maintain structure, yet flexible in order to meet the individual needs of the LD child. The skilled teacher uses old materials in new ways and can develop her own materials and procedures for specific lessons or objectives. The teacher of LD children must be able to delay the gratification of seeing an immediate result to her efforts since it may take a long time to see improved performance in either academic or social areas.

Most LD programs have children working with several teachers or other staff members for varying periods of time. The teacher must be able to share the child, as well as the work, with others. Some children attempt to play one adult against the others. The teacher must be able to understand the nature of what is happening to avoid falling into the trap. Time and help should be provided to teachers so they can talk about their feelings concerning personal interactions with the children and other staff members and the feelings of frustration which may arise. Such feelings, when not aired, may give rise to what has been called "burnout." Burnout is a loss of interest in and concern for the children, other members of the staff, or the job. By becoming aware of the sources of stress (both external and internal) related to the teaching situation, burnout can be averted. Faculty "rap" sessions can help staff air their feelings, reactions, and grievances and can give rise to alternative ways to handle problems.

Junior and Senior High School Programs

There is an apparent paucity of LD programs for the adolescent population; approximately 45% are unserved (Miller, Sabatino, & Larson, 1980). Of the programs offered at the junior and senior high school levels, Deschler, Lowrey, and Alley (1979) report that there are five types of programs which differ according to primary emphasis (though most programs contain some elements of each of the others): 1) basic skills, 2) functional curriculum, 3) tutorial, 4) work-study, and 5) learning strategies. The *basic skills* programs reported by 45% of those questioned, emphasize remedial instruction in reading and mathematics; the *functional curriculum* stresses job and daily living survival skills, including consumer education and was found in 17% of the programs; *tutorial* programs stress instruction in the content areas and was noted by 24% of the respondents; *work-study* approaches, which are represented by 5% of the programs in the study, provide career and job-related skills as well as on-the-job experiences. The LD teacher functions as a work coordinator. The last and least common approach (4%), *learning strategies*, teaches the student how to learn by stressing specific strategies and techniques that can be applied in many settings. This approach assumes the strategies can be generalized but does not stress basic skills and adult needs as do some of the other programs. Deschler, et al. noted that teachers felt that LD adolescents with severe disabilities require the functional and work-study approaches, while the mildly handicapped benefitted most from programs that stressed cooperative instruction by the LD teacher and the regular classroom teacher to develop coping skills for use in the regular classroom.

In most settings, the secondary level RT is expected to provide remediation in areas of deficits and, at the same time, help the student keep up in the academic subjects. This makes the role of the secondary level RT an extremely difficult one, since the students will be taking a variety of subjects (social studies, the sciences, mathematics, English, the industrial arts, etc.) on many grade levels. The RT must deal with the requirements of, perhaps, forty regular education teachers. Direct communications with other staff members, which is difficult to arrange at any level, is even more difficult in the junior and senior high schools. A system of communication must be set up in which the teachers of academic subjects can provide the RT with the assignments and schedules for a specified period so that the students' needs can be met in the resource room. Many secondary level RTs have developed forms they use for this purpose.

The RT can help the secondary school teachers meet the instructional objectives in each course by suggesting and demonstrating different instructional methods, activities, and materials. For example, texts that cover the same basic material but have lower reading levels can be used. Students can tape classroom lectures for later review.* Audio visual aids (films, filmstrips, audiotapes, slides, photos, etc.) can be made available to the child who is unable to read so that the concepts covered in the courses can be presented. Tests may be modified by varying the time, presenting them orally, and having answers dictated. Answers and reports can be taped. Many of these activities may be performed in the resource room under the direction of the RT.

Scheduling

Scheduling students into the resource room is a problem at all school levels. The RT must schedule around lunch, physical education, art, music, and so on. If other services are being provided—speech and reading, in particular—this programming must be integrated as well. At the junior and senior high school levels where the depart-

---

* Taping lessons is not always the panacea some believe it to be (Young, 1980). Many problems can occur: 1) The student may tend to ignore what is happening in class since "I'll have it on tape." 2) Listening to a tape can be boring since there is no visual input. 3) Transcribing can be difficult. 4) It may be difficult to locate a particular part of the lesson for future reference.

mentalized structure operates, additional difficulties can arise. To reduce some of the problems, a special education program representative should be included when school scheduling decisions are made.

Classroom Organization

The resource room itself should be located within easy access of the children so that a minimum of time will be lost going back and forth to classrooms. Both the resource room and the self-contained LD classroom must be well organized and large enough for easy movement of students from one activity to another; the creation of various academic and interest centers; and areas for individual and group work. Materials should be easily accessible and storage space should be ample. Cabinets, shelves, and display areas are needed for different subjects and/or activities such as math, science, art, and children's work. The room should not, however, appear cluttered. Though routines are important, it is necessary to eventually include disruptions in order to help the child learn to live in the "real" world where change is not always anticipated.

Staffing

The resource-room concept requires differentiated staffing patterns. Many programs will need the use of aides, paraprofessionals, or support personnel to free either the regular classroom teacher or resource-room teacher for conference time, preparing materials, and/or to provide direct teaching or review activities under supervision.

In addition to providing direct intervention to the LD child, the RT also may supply consultative support to the regular classroom teacher. Though the consultative role is considered important, school organization and policy may limit its use. Even if the RT schedules conference time, unless the classroom teacher is relieved of responsibilities at the same time, the conference cannot occur. Many RTs say the only time they get to speak to the regular classroom teacher is at lunch (if their schedules coincide) and during chance encounters in the halls or when they check in or out of school.

A variation of the RT model is the teacher consultant model, which focuses on serving the mildly handicapped through improvement of the skills of the regular classroom teacher. The student is not required to leave his regular classroom and the stigma of labeling is reduced (see Figure 18-1, Step One). Miller and Sabatino (1978) compared the effectiveness of the resource-room model, where interaction with the regular classroom teacher was at a minimum and direct resource teaching occurred, varying from one 45-minute session daily to two or three sessions per week, and the teacher consultant model. As measured by the WRAT, the academic performance of the students under both conditions showed improvements. That is, both groups of special education students showed significant gains in the word recognition and arithmetic subtests. No significant gains in reading comprehension, as measured by PIAT, were noted in either group. Positive changes in the performance of classroom teachers who worked with the consultants was reported. These researchers caution that although the number of special children a consultant can impact on is greater than the number the RT can serve, the consultant model is time consuming and positive results cannot be assured unless adequate time is allowed for contact between the regular classroom teacher and the RT.

The Individualized Education Program (IEP)

The IEP was mandated by PL 94-142 and is developed by the IEP planning team. This team, which has the responsibility for making specific educational decisions for each handicapped child, must be comprised of a special education teacher, the child's teacher, the child's parents, and, whenever possible, the child. In some states the school psychologist, a language-development specialist, and a physician may also be included. Other specialists may be included in the committee or attend conferences when their expertise will be needed. The team evaluates diagnostic data provided by specialists, and based on the data, decides if the child requires special education, what the placement should be, the ancillary and support services required, when they will begin and end, and the extent to which the child will participate in the regular classroom. A member of the team prepares the IEP, which includes the aforementioned information and also specifies long- and short-range goals. Objective criteria and evaluation procedures and schedules must also be stated. The mandated yearly revisions of the IEP are monitored by the IEP team.

Though the regulations specify that the IEP is *not* legally binding, nor will agencies, teachers or other persons be held accountable if the objectives are not achieved, the IEP can be used to monitor performance and identify areas of weakness. In addition, parents have the right to initiate a hearing if they believe the school is not providing the services needed for implementation of the IEP. In states where competency tests must be passed for high school graduation or in order to be promoted from grade to grade,* the IEP must stipulate any special instructional modifications, that is, untimed tests, taped presentation of written material, taped responses, and use of a calculator in math. When these coping techniques are included in the IEP, they can frequently be used in taking the required exams and in meeting the minimum competencies. It has been proposed that students with handicapping conditions be issued a different diploma. Safer (1980) suggests that if this is done, the skills and competencies that the diploma represents should also be delineated. She cautions that those with special diplomas may be discriminated against when they join the job market.

Grading

Grading, whether in the resource room or the self-contained LD classroom, has always been a difficult issue. Grading procedures will differ from district to district. In some districts, the RT has input into the report-card grade but does not determine it. In other districts, the RT may be responsible for grading basic skill subjects. At the secondary level, some special education programs are given for credit so that the student can use satisfactory attendance and performance in the program to meet requirements for graduation. In other districts, no official credit is given.

The grades themselves are subject to question. Should the grade reflect the child's improvement in performance or should he be measured against the grade norm? Many special education teachers prefer to use a descriptive report or have individual conferences with the student and his parents rather than provide grades. Wiederholt, Hammill, and Brown (1978) believe that good grades motivate a stu-

---

* As of 1980, 31 states had instituted competency standards either for promotion or for high school graduation (Safer, 1980).

dent while poor marks may undermine his confidence. They also suggest that poor grades may reflect inadequacies in the instructional program.

A contract system, used in the regular classroom, resource room, or LD classroom, can help the grading process. The contract is a written agreement between the teacher and the student which stipulates the expected academic or social behavior, the schedule to be met, and the method of feedback, that is, grade. Because the LD student often does not understand what is expected of him in the regular classroom and/or the special education setting. Lott, Hudak, and Scheetz (1975) suggest that a contract be developed that indicates the amount of work to be completed satisfactorily in order to receive a specific grade. The type of grading system and the method to be used should be stated in the IEP so that all those concerned will be informed at the beginning of the program (Kinnison, Hayes, and Acord, 1981).

Record Keeping

Record keeping is of vital importance in any special education program. Daily, ongoing records are needed to ascertain pupil progress, plan appropriate lessons, report to parents and faculty members, and to evaluate individual and program performance. Each teacher determines the type of records to keep. In general, whatever forms or procedures are used, data collection should not be complex or time-consuming. The data should be easy to obtain, record, and retrieve. The records should contain the information the teacher needs in order to make instructional decisions.

ADMINISTRATIVE SUPPORT

For any special education program to succeed, administrative support is vital. If the administration does not believe in the importance of the program, whether self-contained or resource, the available facilities may be inadequate. In a survey of general education administrators in Vermont, the greatest identified training need related to knowledge of trends, research, and programs for the handicapped in order to provide effective education (Nevin, 1979).

The school administrator's commitment to the LD program can be seen in many areas. Support for the regular classroom teacher is shown by providing in-service training in the form of workshops and demonstration courses, developing a professional library for the staff which includes books and periodicals about special education, mainstreaming techniques, ways to modify curriculum and materials, and so on, allocating staff resources to provide time for conferences with LD team members, and keeping an "open-door" policy so that all teachers can share their concerns about the program.

The administrator can support the LD child by helping to set up lines of communication between the school and the home. The administrator can arrange funding so that the disorganized child can have one set of texts at home and one in school, thus eliminating the need to carry books back and forth. Some children can be permitted to arrive a few minutes later and leave school a few minutes earlier if they become disoriented among crowds of children.

The administrator can serve as a liason with community groups for the development of after-school social and recreational programs for LD children, and can also help shape positive community attitudes and acceptance of the special-education child and the special-education programs. Many parents of children in regular education classes look with distrust and misunderstanding at the changes in special education and the impact they will have on the education of their own children. (Interestingly, many parents of children in regular education are asking that IEPs be developed for their children.) Meetings, educational programs, and discussion groups can be planned to help these parents understand the goals and philosophy of the special education program. Positive feelings among these parents, hopefully, will spread to their children in the regular classes.

When program needs are not understood by administrators, scheduling will be even more difficult than what usually can be expected since the needs of special education will be secondary to other programs in the school. At the secondary level, it is advisable to have a special-education person at the meetings of department heads. (Indeed, many districts give special education department status). In this way, the special education program needs can be made known as decisions are being made rather than after the fact. Describing the success of the Special Integration High School Program at Edward R. Murrow High School in New York City, a program administrator said:

> ". . . one final word regarding the coordination of a large unit in a school. The cooperation of the administration and staff is essential. Here at Murrow we have been fortunate in being part of the school from the day it opened. The entire staff is committed to our program. This enables the entire school to have a uniform philosophy, one that accepts individual differences and helps each person achieve the highest level of potential possible." (DEPS, 1978)*

Individualizing Instruction

For several decades, all teachers have been concerned with providing individualized instruction in their classrooms. This is in deference to the recognition that each child is an individual having his own learning style, likes and dislikes, strength-weakness profile, and so on. With the advent of mainstreaming, the search for means of implementing individualization has received increased impetus.

There are two major aspects of individualization. The first involves discerning the individual pupil's needs. Here, the teacher must rely on her own ongoing observation and assessment of the child coupled with reports from the school psychologist, the resource-room teacher, the speech teacher, and other specialists. Consultative and itinerant services can also be utilized.

The second ingredient of individualization centers around logistics. That is, even after the teacher learns what it is that various pupils require with respect to an individualized instructional approach, she will frequently lack the means for implementation unless she receives appropriate and adequate administrative support. The administrator who is able to keep class size at a manageable number, to effect suitable screening and placement procedures assuring that all pupils assigned to the

---

* Reprinted from *Creating Least Restrictive Learning Environments: A Guide for Mainstreaming* by permission of the Board of Education of the City of New York.

class "belong there," and to secure the services of paraprofessionals, teacher aides, volunteers, classroom tutors from upper grades (peer tutoring is another possibility), goes a long way toward promoting individualization. The administrator can also cooperate with and assist school supervisors, special-education supervisors, department chairperson—and in some smaller school systems, assume supervisory duties. He can help make materials with a high "independent" work index available. Some examples of these are programmed materials, high interest/low reading level books, machines that can be utilized by one or several pupils (e.g., taped lessons and ear phones, Languagemaster, Spellbinder, Systems 80), classroom libraries, and math laboratories. Duplicating services must be accessible to facilitate the preparation of individualized worksheets. The development and use of self-correcting materials fosters individualization. Mercer and Mercer (1978) believe that these have significant implication in the education of exceptional children since (1) they provide immediate feedback, (2) should the child make an error, he does so in privacy, and (3) they can help promote attention—that is, some children may approach this device as a game format, rising to the challenge of trying to "get it right." Mercer and Mercer give numerous examples of inexpensive, teacher-made, self-correcting material (e.g., the jigsaw puzzle type in which feedback of the correct match is provided by the fit; a flap made of some flexible material which can be bent to reveal the answer; balance scales; etc.), and advise that the materials should be simple to operate, used optimally for practice or drill purposes (as opposed to teaching new skills), and to change the materials as well as the content frequently. (See Chapter 13 of Tannenbaum's, "How of Instruction".)

The administrator can support the teacher in her efforts to individualize instruction. Some children need to walk around at times rather than sit still. Some classes may work noisily but productively. Not all children benefit by taking some physical object home each day (e.g., their drawing, a clay ashtray they made in arts and crafts); an LD child may "take home" a new spelling word that he learned or a new arithmetical concept. Administration and teacher flexibility is the key to an individualized program.

Evaluation

All aspects of the LD program in a school should be evaluated periodically, that is, student performance, communication with parents, teachers, and other professionals, record keeping, physical environment (including organization and utilization of space), reporting procedures, scheduling, and organization of time. Periodic evaluation serves to assess program effectiveness and thus implement change when data indicates change is needed. Input should be solicited from students, teachers, administrators, parents, paraprofessionals, via forms, questionnaires, and/or interviews. The data derived should highlight program strengths as well as weaknesses. The forms and questionnaires should provide space for respondents to include suggestions for program modifications. Some data will be obtained as the program progresses, while others will be collected near the end of the school year. Data collection should be planned so that it is not a burden for the respondents or the evaluator. When more than one resource program exists in a school, the principal may require a more standardized evaluation procedure in order to compare the effectiveness of each.

"At the end of the school year, RTs (Resource Teacher) should also collect and organize at least the following information about their individual programs:

1. total number of students serviced directly (tutoring or remediating)
2. average number of hours per week spent in direct service
3. total number of students serviced indirectly (not personally worked with)
4. total number of RCTs (Reg Classroom Teachers) serviced
5. total number of educational plans prepared
6. total number of formal consultations with RCTs (Regular Classroom Teacher)
7. total number of In-Service presentations made
8. average time spent with students (weekly)
9. average time used in materials preparation or curriculum modification (weekly)." (Lott, Hudak, & Scheetz, 1975, p. 220)

The objectives included in the IEP that relate to the activities of the resource room should be evaluated.

By comparing the number of objectives reached by the number established, for individual children and for the entire group, a quantitative relationship between the resource program and the stated goals can be determined. For example, if 20 short-term goals were to be met and 16 were reached, the program could be considered 80% effective for that child. Such data can indicate which children benefit most from the program and the effect of the program as a whole.

All the data collected should be included in an annual report. The information in such a report can serve as the basis for renewed or additional funding, improvement in procedures, and better pupil–teacher ratio, among other things.

REFERENCES

Deschler, D. D., Lowrey, N., and Alley, G. R. Programming alternatives for LD adolescents: A nationwide survey. *Academic Therapy*, March, 1979, *14*(4), 389–397.

Division of Educational Planning & Support (DEPS). *Creating least restrictive learning environments: A guide for mainstreaming.* Curriculum Bulletin, 1977–1978 Series, No. 10.

Hanson, R. M., Jacobson, B., Crenson, W., and Rios, N. J. Developing educational models to serve the learning-disabled child in the mainstream of general education. Presentation at symposium, 1973, Rutgers University, New Brunswick, N.J.

Kinnison, L. R., Hayes, C. and Acord, J. Evaluating student progress in mainstream classes. *Teaching Exceptional Children*, Spring, 1981, *13*(3): 97–99.

Lott, L. A., Hudak, B. J., and Scheetz, J. A. *Strategies and techniques for mainstreaming: A resource room handbook.* Monroe, Michigan: Monroe County Intermediate School District, 1975.

Mercer, C. D. and Mercer, A. R. The development and use of self correcting materials with exceptional children. *Teaching Exceptional Children*, Fall, 1978, *11*(1): 6–11.

Miller, S. R., Sabatino, D. A., and Larsen, R. P. Issues in the professional preparation of secondary school special education. *Exceptional Children*, February, 1980, *46*(5): 344–350.

Miller, T. L., and Sabatino, D. A. An evaluation of the teacher consultant model as an approach to mainstreaming. *Exceptional Children*, October, 1978, *45*(2), 86–93.

Nevin, A. Special education administration competencies of the general education administrator. *Exceptional Children*, February, 1979, *45*(5), 363–365.

Safer, N. D. Implications of minimum competency standards and testing for handicapped students. *Exceptional Children*, January, 1980, *46*(4), 288–289.

Turnbull, H. R., and Turnbull, A. *Free appropriate public education: Law and implementation*. Denver: Love Publishing, 1978.

Wiederholt, J. L., Hammill, D. D., and Brown, V. *The resource teacher: A guide to effective practices*. Boston: Allyn & Bacon, 1978.

Young, M. Learning line. *Newsday*, Sunday, March 9, 1980, p. II/133.

Perspectives

part Four

Issues, Trends and Prognosis

19

ISSUES

The overall field of learning disabilities is riddled with issues. These permeate such basic concepts as definition, characteristics of the population, prevalence, diagnostic instruments, and prognosis. From these emanate a host of questions regarding appropriate intervention—particularly instructional methods, but also including the relative merit of psychotherapy, process training, drug therapy, and the like. Notwithstanding the fact that many questions are yet unresolved, the field moves on and professionals, parents, and the clients themselves (many LD children of the past have now matured into adults and have emerged as valuable spokespeople) give testimony to genuine advances made in the field. One point of concensus in the otherwise unsettled community of special education is that the LD child of today is infinitely more fortunate than his counterpart of yesterday because of the growth in the field—and not just the *numbers* of people involved in delivery services, the mushrooming of facilities, programs, materials, and resources, but in the *quality* of these as well. To put it differently, despite the fact that controversial (often diametric) opinions exist on almost every fundamental topic dealing with the education of learning-disabled children, we are still able to help many of them learn, grow, and adjust. Plainly, there is still room for improvement.

Many issues have already been dealt with in varying degrees throughout this book. The issues incorporated in this chapter will be composed of those not yet discussed and, in many cases, an extension of those previously mentioned.

Labeling
The literature suggests that the overall harm done by special-education labels consists of permanent stigmas, humiliation, diminished achievement, lessening of

opportunity, and the emergence of a sequence of events, beginning with attention to the designation, changes in teacher–child interactions, lowering of self-image, and finally resulting in decreased performance (Reschly & Lamprecht, 1979). Morsink (1981) voices concern that (1) labels fail to define discrete groups, (2) do not point the way to any particular treatment, and (3) biased testing often leads to mislabeling. Probably the most frequently cited objection to labeling is that it will affect others' expectations and will become a self-fulfilling prophecy of doom (Rosenthal & Jacobson, 1966; Smith & Neisworth, 1975; Ohlson, 1978; Vance & Wallbrown, 1979).

On the other hand, the practice of labeling (or classifying) special-education children is frequently useful for funding and legislative purposes. It also serves as the framework for establishing special-education programs in the schools. These seldom exist by virtue of behavioral descriptors (classes for aggressive children, resource-room programs for children who manifest written reversals, etc.); rather, placement is made in accordance with the traditional nomenclature—LD classes, MR classes, or ED classes (Lieberman, 1979). Kronick (1977) contends that labeling the child LD provides a name—that is, an *explanation*—for the child's difficulties, simultaneously reassuring his parents that he is *not* mentally retarded or emotionally disturbed. She further believes that "a label is a concise method whereby the short form conveys a body of literature" (p. 103).

There have been recent administrative and legislative movements toward de-labeling in special education. As expected, this trend has not gone unchallenged. *New York Teacher* (1980, p. 7) voiced the following concerns:

· Abuses that may occur as a result of removing the current staffing, class-size and age-span safeguards through de-labeling;
· The lack of specific regulation in the project to preclude the unwarranted movement of special education teachers from one handicapped area to another;
· The confusion about proper teacher certification that will result from the classification standards project's implementation;
· The adverse effects in some classes of mixing children with different handicapping conditions.

Sparks and Richardson (1981), reporting on the results of a questionnaire sent by National ACLD to each state relating to multicategorical/cross-categorical classrooms for LD students, concluded that public schools, by overemphasizing mainstreaming, are failing to meet the needs of all handicapped children for an appropriate education in the least restrictive environment, and, indeed, "may be adopting programs that will eliminate the . . . [special educational] services now available" (p. 60).

There is a tendency toward oversimplifying the controversies between labeling (in the traditional terms, LD, MR, ED) and de-labeling by viewing the former as merely pragmatic and the latter as consistent with lofty ideologies and humanitarian principles (*New York Teacher*, 1980). Easy answers do not exist. In fact, LD adults, themselves, in retrospect, frequently cite advantages of labeling. For example, Haseltine (1978) reports that her peers labeled her (they called her "retard," "dummy," "klutzy"), even if the teachers did not! She writes "I think it would have been much better to have been labeled 'neurologically handicapped' ('learning disabled') by my teachers; but also to have been told that it was okay to be this way: 'We'll work around it and focus on your strengths.'"

A crucial question emerges: If categorizing exceptional children is central to providing optimal services for them, is there any way to neutralize the negative effects of the label? The key may be to avoid supplying labels to the teacher in a vacuum, but to always provide, concomitantly, background information regarding the particular classification: readings, in-service course, training film, consultative services, intervisitations, and so on. This suggestion fits in with the research of Reschly and Lamprecht (1979) who found that "labels may exert a significant effect on a teacher's expectancies *only if other information is unavailable*" [emphasis added] (p. 57). This would include increased exposure time to the handicapped child; the same authors found that "teachers do not retain the expectancy from the label if sufficient opportunity is provided to observe behaviors that are inconsistent with the label" (p. 57).

Juvenile Delinquency and Learning Disabilities

Much of the recent literature has attempted to link juvenile delinquency with learning disabilities (Poremba, 1975; Kratoville, 1974; Ramos, 1978). Poremba (1975, p. 126) has written that more than 50% of the adolescents appearing in juvenile courts present evidence of minimal brain damage. Berman (1978), comparing 45 delinquents with a control group in measures of neurological impairment, found 70.1% of the delinquents scored in the impaired range in at least one of the subtests of the Halstead-Reitan Diagnostic Neuropsychology Battery, whereas in the control group this occurred in only 23% of the cases.

There are, of course, compelling clues that do indeed tend to tie learning disabilities to delinquent and criminal behavior: Poor self-concept, impulsivity, emotional lability, social imperception, and gullibility are some of the factors. Especially significant is the fact that the tolerance level of frustration is frequently reached during adolescence—since the environment tends to buffet the LD adolescent rather than permit smooth entry and assimilation. Being highly suggestible, he can easily be manipulated and exploited by others: if a "friend" tells him to throw a rock through a plate glass window, he may comply unquestioningly. This propensity to become a follower—rather than a leader—would not be so deleterious if he surrounded himself with positive models, but being "marginal" himself, he attracts—or gravitates toward—other marginal, troubled, and troublesome individuals. His learning problems may result in ignorance of the law.

Probably the single most significant clue is that of school failure (Keilitz, Zaremba, and Broder, 1979, p. 8). Authorities are virtually unanimous in reporting poor performance in the skills subjects among the juvenile delinquent population (Poremba, 1975; Duane, 1978; Mulligan, 1970). Certainly, if an LD adolescent drops out of school, he then has the economic incentive as well as the opportunity (more time on his hands) to commit delinquent acts.

Despite the proliferation of authors who espouse the learning disabilities/juvenile delinquency link, no definitive causal relationship has been found to date. In April, 1976, Charles A. Murray, of the American Institute for Research, wrote "The Link Between Learning Disabilities and Juvenile Delinquency: Current Theory and

Knowledge," having been commissioned to do so by the National Institute for Juvenile Justice and Delinquency Prevention, Law Enforcement Assistance Administration (Washington, D.C.). Murray found the case for such a link to be only suggestive, and not strongly documented. This work stated, "the rationales for the link between LD and delinquency comprise one very small segment of a very large causal map . . . LD is only one of many causes of school failure; school failure is only one of the many ways in which the school experience might cause delinquency; and the school is only one of the many settings in which delinquency is thought to be nurtured . . . " (p. 33). (See Figure 19-1).

Murray's concluding statements (pp. 65–66) were:

—the evidence for a causal link is feeble
—with few exceptions, the quantitative link to date has been so poorly designed and presented that it cannot be used even for rough estimates of the strength of the link
—no study has even been started which will compare the development of a set of learning disabled children to a comparable set of nonlearning disabled children (the classic "longitudinal" study)
—no study has yet been conducted which even claims to demonstrate that the average delinquent is more likely to suffer from learning disabilities than is his nondelinquent counterpart.

Further research would have to take into account many additional factors. To begin with, those classified as juvenile delinquents are a select group taken from the total pool of individuals who commit criminal acts: They are the ones who are caught! It has recently been pointed out (Boys Town Quarterly, 1979) that although LD adolescents have approximately the same degree of delinquent behavior as the rest of adolescents, they are twice as prone to wind up in the juvenile courts. The same article suggested that some of the characteristics of LD youth may render them more likely to be treated as "trouble-makers."

A more recent research effort jointly undertaken by ACLD and National State Courts supports this conclusion: ". . . learning disabled and non-learning

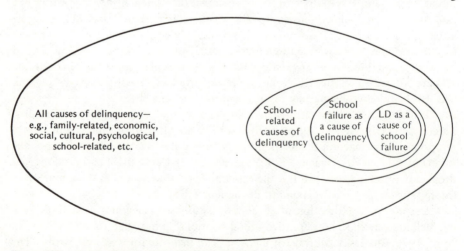

Figure 19-1. A causal map of juvenile delinquency.

disabled children engaged in essentially the same behavior, but that, somewhere in the juvenile justice system, learning disabled children are treated differently. . ." (Keilitz, Zaremba, and Broder, 1979, p. 9).

Lewis and her colleagues (Lewis, Shanok, & Balla, 1979; Lewis, Shanok, Pincus, & Glaser, 1979) compared the medical and social histories of violent delinquence with less violent or nonviolent ones (all of them male). The more violent ones evidenced (1) a disproportionately large incidence of neurological impairment, and (2) a history of having witnessed and/or experienced extreme brutality by parents or parent substitutes with far greater frequency than the less violent or nonviolent delinquents.

The authors concluded that if a LD child has a history of having been physically abused or having witnessed extreme violence repeatedly, it is highly possible that he will become a juvenile delinquent—and a violent one at that. Vulnerability alone (that is, the existence of minimal neurological disorders) is insufficient to cause violence and brutality. "It is important," cautions Lewis (1979), "to make that distinction because there are millions of people who have children with minor neurological disorders who are not violent. It is when you couple the two things that the problem occurs" (p. 12).

Another variable is that of definition. What is legal in one state may be illegal in another. Also, the minimum age for an adjudication of juvenile delinquency varies from region to region.

One must also recognize that the same learning-disabled individual often has strengths as well as weaknesses (Siegel, 1974; Smith, 1979). Just as there are negative factors that push the organism in negative directions, enhancing the susceptibility to delinquency, there are other positive forces—for example, the child's inner strength, his resilience, courage, fruitful compensatory behaviors, overall desire to conform, awareness of reality, some intact modalities—that counteract these and exert pressure in the direction of positive, productive, socially acceptable, and healthy behavior.

Even though a clear-cut causality has not yet been demonstrated, those pioneers who have worked to explore the relationship of learning disabilities to juvenile delinquency have rendered a service to both populations. Poremba (1975, pp. 137-141), a leading proponent of the learning disabilities/juvenile delinquency link, strongly urges intervention in the form of early identification programs, restructuring of the school program, involvement of community agencies, and appropriate legislation. In the opinion of Berman (1974), "instead of sending delinquents to euphemistically named prisons, [we] should realize that these kids are pathetic, disabled people who have never been successful at anything, who hate themselves for their inadequacies and who need disability remediation, encouragement and compassion . . . " (p. 43). He recommends establishing diagnostic and remedial programs not only within the public schools, but also in reformatory and training schools. Though their platforms rest upon the supposition that learning disabilities is a major causal factor of juvenile delinquency—and this is yet to be proven—the action-oriented, comprehensive programs they set forth can go a long way in the prevention and amelioration of the many problems besetting *all* LD children whether juvenile delinquent prone or not, and *all* juvenile delinquents, whether learning disabled or not.

Who Shall Teach the LD Child?

The advent of PL 94-142 has brought to the fore an issue that had been smoldering for several years: Which specialist should teach the learning-disabled child? The American Speech and Hearing Association (ASHA) and the International Reading Association (IRA) are particularly concerned with this question. Both ASHA and IRA believe that there are children labeled LD who would benefit from the services of speech pathologists and remedial reading teachers respectively, both in evaluation and remediation. The controversy has been sparked by limitation of funds (McCarthy, 1978; IRA Resolution on Learning Disabilities, 1976; Wallace, 1976). We will address ourselves to three aspects of the controversy: the LD child who is in need of remediation, the role possibilities, and the continuum of services model.

The definition of learning disabilities is vague, lacking clearly-defined bound-aries. While some adhere to the inclusion of neurological dysfunction (thus limiting the numbers), others include within the group any children who exhibit problems in listening, thinking, reading, writing, spelling, and/or arithmetic, vastly increasing the number to be served within a learning-disabilities framework (Hammill, 1978). In addition, the degrees and types of disability vary. That is, some children have mild to severe deficits in only one academic area, while others exhibit deficits across many areas in varying degrees and/or in nonacademic areas. Thus, while some LD have severe deficits with probable underlying pathology, most are merely underachieving (Larsen, 1976). This view differs somewhat with that of Lerner (1975) who contrasts the population served by LD specialists and remedial reading (RR) specialists in terms of etiology: the LD specialist focuses on the brain-injured child, while the RR specialist works with those whose reading deficits are based in socioeconomic, educational, psychological, or physical factors. Newcomer (1975) suggests that while this may have been true in the early history of LD, it no longer holds today. Marge (1972) recommends that the training program for children with language disabilities should be based on linguistic strengths and deficits rather than the etiology of the disability.

Since many LD children manifest disorders of language and/or reading, it is not easy to determine which specialist (remedial reading, language, learning dis-abilities) should provide the educational interventions. Recent surveys of profes-sional training programs indicate that relatively few RR specialists and speech pathologists are knowledgeable about the learning disabled (Stick, 1976, Jakup-cak, 1975, McCarthy, 1978). Conversely many LD specialists are not specifically trained to work in the area of language development or reading (IRA, 1976; Le-wandowski, 1977; Jakupcak, 1975). Though Lerner (1975) considers that differ-ences in the methods and materials used by LD specialists do exist (for example, LD specialists stress process and RR teachers stress skill development), others question such dichotomies (Lewandowski, 1977; Newcomer, 1975). Even Lerner (1975b) points out that the differences she highlighted are probably a question of degree or emphasis and do not reflect dichotomies. Newcomer notes that there is little improvement to be gained in process training and that it is not an important part of LD programs today. Several specialists in both fields also point out that the methods used by reading and LD specialists are the same, such as multisensory ap-proaches, and diagnostic teaching.

The International Reading Association (IRA) suggests a need for four types of reading specialists,* based on the roles they will assume:

1. The special teacher of reading is responsible for direct remedial, corrective, and/or developmental reading instruction.

2. The reading clinician should have the skills of the special teacher of reading, but because of additional training and experience, should be responsible for the diagnoses, remediation, or plans of remediation for the more severely reading disabled students.

3. The reading consultant works with teacher, administrators, and other school personnel to develop and improve reading programs within the school.

4. The reading supervisor provides leadership for all aspects of the reading programs in the school district and should be able to evaluate district-wide needs and program implementation. Ekwall (1976) notes that sometimes a reading teacher may perform in more than one role.

Stick (1976) believes that speech pathologists are not classroom teachers but are trained to provide clinical services to small groups or to individuals who have communication disorders or who have auditory processing problems. The American Speech and Hearing Association (ASHA) adopted a policy statement in November, 1975, pronouncing that many children labeled LD have impairments in auditory and language processes ASHA members are trained to remediate (Lynn, 1979).

The continuum of services model lends itself to the utilization of many specialists. Who delivers the direct service should reflect the nature of the child's problem and the training of the specialist (Lieberman, 1980). Newcomer (1975) recommends that the division of responsibility be flexible within the mainstreaming model. Larsen (1976) sees the LD specialist's role as one of planning, initiating, and maintaining the educational program. The LD specialist should be able to ascertain which diagnostic and educational strategies to use, the type of placement, and when specially-trained personnel should be used and in what capacity.

Care must be taken not to fragment the child (or his school day) by sending him to a reading teacher and an LD specialist and a speech pathologist and a physical educator, and so on. This type of program can have a negative effect on the LD child, who may very well have difficulty keeping schedules and adjusting to new adults and new groups of children. Many LD specialists do have extensive training in reading or speech (though this is not the norm) and can offer appropriate interventions. Indeed, some teacher training programs offer dual majors in reading and LD or speech pathology and LD. Certainly, training programs in all fields should develop knowledge, skills, and attitudes for working with the LD population.

However, where the LD specialist's knowledge is not adequate or if the deficit is limited to a severe disorder in one area, the services of another specialist should be used, either on a direct teaching basis or as a consultant. In the latter case, diagnostic findings and specific suggestions for remediation can be shared with the LD specialist who will carry out the plan.

* Adapted from *Roles, Responsibilities, and Qualifications—Reading Specialists.* Professional Standards and Ethics Committee of the International Reading Association, Newark, Delaware.

Early Identification

Many concerns have been expressed regarding early identification programs. These include questions about the validity of assessment procedures and measures, the implications of diagnostic data for specific intervention, and the benefits accrued in comparison to possible negative effects (e.g. the stigma of labeling, parental anxiety (Keogh & Becker, 1973).

Positive identification of learning disabilities is usually difficult to make in the young child. Many of the characteristics associated with learning disabilities are exhibited by all young children and it is difficult to predict which ones will continue to manifest these behaviors in ways that will affect their ability to learn (Safford, 1978). Not all children mature at the same rate. Because of developmental lags, many of the behaviors found in the young child may disappear before he reaches first grade.

The predictive ability of screening programs has been questioned by Satz and Fletcher (1979). There is a danger at both ends of the scale; False-positives (indicating a deficit when there is none) can result in the inclusion and labeling of children who are not at risk, whereas false-negatives (failure to identify the child at risk) lead to the exclusion of children who require a prevention program. Using a study by Feshbach, Adelman, and Fuller (1974) as a case in point (over 70% of the high risk children were overlooked), Satz and Fletcher caution that the predictive value of early screening instruments may be minimal and a source of unnecessary risk and cost.

Another issue can also be raised, one Lerner (1976, p. 29) calls a paradox. When identification is made before a learning disability has appeared and if, after treatment, a child does not develop a learning problem, it cannot be ascertained if successful performance was the result of the intervention or if the child never had a learning disability.

Given the inadequacy of most assessment tools, it is best to use the information gathered from them in conjunction with other data. Educationally at-risk children should be identified not only by a preschool assessment battery, but by the birth and medical history, since causes of learning disabilities have also been linked to prenatal, perinatal, and early postnatal factors (see Chapter 4). In addition, teacher assessment in kindergarten and first grade have been found to be good predictors (Keogh, Tchir, & Windeguth-Behn, 1974; Feshbach, Adelman, & Fuller, 1974, Mercer, Algozzine, & Trifiletti, 1979).

After reviewing the literature, Mercer, Algozzine, & Trifiletti (1979) report that teacher perceptions are more efficacious than other predictors. They recommend that the assessment be conducted during the month of December since it affords the children an opportunity to take part in a school program for three months, gives the teacher more time to observe, and still allows for special programming for the spring semester. Keogh (1977), an advocate of early identification of high-risk children, recommends that data derived be used only to make short-term predictions (will the child be successful in kindergarten?) rather than long term. She believes that since children change greatly during the kindergarten year, screening should be conducted in both the fall and spring terms if the assessment is not ongoing. Assessments should be carried out in the child's classroom so that situational behaviors can also be viewed. Strengths, as well as weaknesses, should be identified. The information should be viewed as tentative to allow for changes in performance.

Mainstreaming

The Education for All Handicapped Children Act, PL 94-142, specified that handicapped children should be taught within the least restricted environment and lead to the placement of handicapped children within the educational mainstream. Mainstreaming does not mean that all exceptional children, regardless of handicapping condition, shall be returned to general education classes and that self-contained special education classes will be eliminated. As Hauck and Sherman (1979) point out, children will not benefit from a mainstreaming placement if they remain "in a failure producing environment most of the day" (p. 135). It does mean that after careful screening, children who will be able to profit from assignment to regular classes will be integrated with the nonhandicapped for varying amounts of time (see Chapter 18, continuum of services).

The thrust toward mainstreaming began in the 1960s when the effectiveness of the self-contained special class was questioned by many experts in the field. Dunn (1968) reported that placement in the special class did not improve academic performance, while Meyerowitz (1965) and Borg (1966) found it had a poor effect on the child's self-image. It should be noted, however, that other researchers found that special class placement improved the child's self-concept (Schurr, 1967; Mooney, 1969).

Throughout the nation, regular class sizes have been increasing because of tight budgets. Teachers have voiced their concern that they will have to meet the needs of children with handicapping conditions in addition to meeting the special needs of their other students in classes that are too large. They also contend that unfavorable attitudes of regular education teachers have been reported. They did not have the time for planning, instruction, or construction of materials (Hudson, Graham, & Warner, 1979).

Stephens and Braun (1980) found that teachers who had taken courses in special education and who felt confident in their abilities to teach them were more willing to take handicapped children into their classes. Comparing the attitudes of regular education teachers involved in mainstreaming programs which included inservice workshops with regular classroom teachers who did not have children with handicapping conditions in their classrooms, Harasymiw and Horne (1976) found that the first group felt more favorable toward integration and had more positive feelings about their ability to manage children with varying disabilities than the second group.

Fostering positive teacher attitudes toward mainstreaming appears to be dependent upon providing modifications within the schools; for example, class time, availability of support services, accessibility of material, and so on (Chalfant, Pysh & Moultrie, 1979; Hannah & Parker, 1980).

Both special educators and regular classroom teachers need to develop new skills for their new roles (McIntosh, 1979). Regular teachers must become familiar with the characteristics of the exceptional child, develop screening and observation skills, and learn remedial techniques. The special-education teacher must learn how to adapt regular classroom materials, how to work with regular classroom teachers, how to translate diagnostic data into educational programs, and how to schedule and program to meet each student's needs. If mainstreaming is to work, inservice training must be made available to and accepted by the teachers who are already in the field. Preservice and inservice teacher education must include training in the skills needed by the regular classroom and resource-room teachers to fulfill their new roles. Cooperation between regular and special teachers increases as each becomes aware of the other's areas of expertise.

Newcomer (1977) recommends that the special-education teacher's role expands from providing direct service to children to serving as consultant to the classroom teacher. In general, the special-education teacher does not have enough time to observe in the regular classroom, and the problems of the child in the large group may not be apparent in the small group or one-to-one setting. In addition, work in the resource room may be undone if there is no follow-up in the regular classroom. Special education alone cannot cure all learning problems.

Haring (1977) agrees with Newcomer that the special educator should be a consultant and suggests that the behavioral-techniques training included in the education of the resource teacher can be effective in modifying the regular education teacher's behaviors by using environments that are reinforcing to them. Pryzwansky (1977), reacting to Newcomer's suggestions, says that the goal of the special education resource teacher should be to collaborate rather than to consult.

According to Oldridge (1977), special education will be attempting too much if Newcomer's ideas are followed. The special-education consultant would overlap with others who are available in the schools and would add to an already unwieldy number. Oldridge considers that the problems Newcomer notes are instructional and belong to the realm of the classroom teacher and instruction specialists.

The issue of mainstreaming has become a concern of many teachers' organizations. Several have requested either a moratorium or a weighting of handicapped children; that is, one handicapped child equals five nonhandicapped within a regular education class (Reynolds & Birch, 1977).

The ability of mainstreaming programs for the learning disabled to provide more positive social and educational environments has interested several researchers. In general, the data to date are equivocal: success is reported in some districts and for some age groups and not in others.

Ribner (1978) found that the self-concept of school adequacy was higher among the boys in special classes, while their feelings of general competence were the same as those of the boys in the regular classes. Macy and Carter (1978) report that studies of the effectiveness of mainstreaming programs for LD children in the Dallas school system found improved academic performance.

The LD child's assessment of his own status within a regular education class was studied by Bruininks (1978). The results of questionnaires found that the LD were less socially acceptable than their peers and were less able to assess their own status within the group. Bruininks suggested that if the LD do not recognize their poor status in the classroom, they may not see a need to change their interactions in order to achieve more positive relationships.

Lynn (1979) reports that Orenstein, a researcher, surveying the appeals system in Massachusetts, found that parents complained there was no coordination between the RR and the regular classroom. Some also noted that their children were scapegoated and rejected by their peers (which appeared to be more common for the older children).

Thurman and Lewis (1979) suggest that children with handicapping conditions may be rejected by their nonhandicapped peers on the basis of perceived differences. They recommend that in lieu of focusing upon the commonalities among peers, it may be better to confront the differences and use interventions that "stress the importance of diversity and individual difference" (p. 469).

Maintaining the LD child in regular classes from the beginning of his educational career is beneficial (Denhoff, Hainsworth, & Hainsworth, 1971). Such placement affords the child the opportunity to learn how to adjust and learn along with other children. In addition, Stephens and Braun (1980) found that primary and middle-grade teachers were more accepting of children with handicapping conditions than teachers in grades seven and eight. Rather than using a resource room model in the early grades, Denhoff, Hainsworth, and Hainsworth (1971) recommend modifying the regular curriculum to meet the child's needs.

The issue of mainstreaming will be debated for many years. It will be determined in part by financial considerations and, as Kirk and Gallagher (1979) wrote, "by the values in vogue at the time" (p. 487).

TRENDS

Since learning disabilities is such a new field, almost all of the topics mentioned thus far in this book might be considered as trends. Future ones will not only be influenced by these but also by a host of additional variables—advances in science and medicine, research findings,* socioeconomic conditions, the national political scene

* The concern for comprehensive research in the field of Learning Disabilities is reflected in the establishment of five research institutes by the Bureau for the Education of the Handicapped, U.S.O.E. in 1978.

1. Information processing deficits in the curriculum areas of basic reading, reading comprehension, spelling and arithmetic.

     Teachers College, Columbia University
        Frances P. Connor, Director
        Research Institute for the Study of Learning Disabilities
        Box 118
        Teachers College, Columbia University
        New York, N.Y. 10027

2. Language, reading problems and social behaviors.

     University of Illinois—Chicago Circle
        Tanis Bryan, Director
        Chicago Institute for Learning Disabilities
        University of Chicago at Chicago Circle
        Box 4348
        Chicago, Illinois 60680

3. Learning disabled adolescents.

     University of Kansas
        Donald Deshler, Director
        Research Institute in Learning Disabilities
        University of Kansas
        Room 313 Carrut-O'Leary
        Lawrence, Kansas 66045

as well as politics within and between the professions, demographic conditions (especially whether the numbers of school-aged children declines or expands), and many others.

Five trends will be treated here: (1) the emerging role of parents; (2) the increase and the number of professional disciplines concerned with the LD population; (3) the increasing concern for LD adults; (4) concern with the mildly handicapped; and (5) prevention. In a field characterized by controversy, considerable overlap between issues and trends is expected. Many of the issues discussed in the preceeding portion of this chapter—mainstreaming, early identification—could justifiably have been treated as trends. Conversely, many of those trends that follow could easily have been recorded as an issue (Should parents tutor their children? Are we giving parents too much voice in making educational decisions?). The trends that follow, although significant, should not be regarded as exhaustive, but only representative.

The Emerging Role of Parents

Parents of LD children are assuming an ever-widening role in the overall planning, monitoring, evaluating, and, in many cases, actual implementing of educational programs and a range of comprehensive services for their children. This can be seen by examining the recent trend of "the parent movement" along 3 avenues: (1) the growing number of parent groups (i.e., ACLD chapters), (2) the role of parents in tutoring their children, and (3) parents' specific involvement in the IEP team as mandated by P.L. 94-142.

Parent groups. By becoming increasingly involved in their local ACLD chapters, the parents benefit *themselves* psychologically (they see that they are not alone in their problem, learn to translate some of their anxieties and fears into concrete actions, and become more sophisticated regarding the nature and needs of LD children, thereby removing hitherto uncertainties and doubts). They help their *children* by developing various programs for them. Finally, they contribute to the welfare of *all learning-disabled individuals* to the extent that they function as effective members of a well organized pressure group (i.e., their ACLD chapter).

In 1978, New York Association for the Learning Disabled listed some of its services and programs (Siegel, 1978):

---

4. Identification, assessment, placement and program evaluation.

> University of Minnesota
> James Ysseldyke, Director
> Institute for Research on Learning Disabilities
> 350 Elliot Hall
> 75 East River Road
> University of Minnesota
> Minneapolis, Minnesota 55455

5. Attention problems and Cognitive Behavior Modification.

> University of Virginia
> Daniel Hallahan, Director
> The Learning Disabilities Research Institute
> 164 Rugby Road
> University of Virginia
> Charlottesville, Virginia 22903

- Parent training and support at the local level,
- Information and referral regarding the availability of services and programs throughout the state,
- Publications—books, pamphlets, state and local newsletters, position papers on current issues,
- State and local conferences and workshops for the educator, administrator and parent,
- Representation at the State Legislature,
- Representation with key local and state governmental regulatory agencies,
- Pre-school education and developmental services,
- Specialized elementary schooling for the severely impaired.
- Community residences and programs to develop independent living skills,
- Pre-vocational and vocational training programs,
- Evening and weekend social and recreational programming,
- Summer Camping. (pp. 146, 147)

Perhaps the overriding lesson that parents of learning-disabled children have learned is this: If you want something done, do it yourself.

Parents as teachers of their children. In the past, parents were advised *not* to tutor their own children. For example, Worden and Snyder (1969) found that parental tutoring in dyslexia was unsuccessful and produced ". . . anger, frustration, friction, negativism, loss of motivation and considerable family disorganization . . ." (p. 52). The overall philosophy in the past seemed to be that teaching should be left to the professionally-trained teacher.

The pendulum seems to be moving the other way: a number of authorities now contend that parents have a stake in the education of their children and should be involved directly in the instructional process. The President's Committee on Mental Retardation (1969) made specific recommendations supporting the concept of parental tutoring. Various authors have stated that, in general, parents of LD children can—and should—tutor them and, in fact, have recommended specific instructional techniques to them (Wagner, 1971; Stott, 1972; Thornton, 1979; Thomas, Phelps and Hopping, 1980). Regan (1979) has formulated some comprehensive guidelines for parents of LD adolescents for furthering their vocational education.

> "This is not to say that all parents are equipped to work with their children. Some, being too emotionally involved, become nervous, tense and hostile when supervising and correcting their child; the child, in turn, becomes more anxious and fearful. Through counseling, such parents can gain insight into their own feelings and learn to accept their child's limitations. The skillful teacher may be able to select a minimum of responsibility for these parents—responsibilities that are sufficient to make them feel positively involved with their children, yet are neutral, nominal, and psychologically safe. Many parents, however, are well-adjusted, able and willing to work with their child. The classroom teacher should utilize these parents' cooperation, energies, and attitudes." (Siegel, 1972, p. 25).

The Parent's Role in the IEP Process. With the advent of PL 94-142, parent participation on the school team is mandated. Because of the novelty of this concept—

hitherto very few, if any, education agencies required the inclusion of parents on the interdisciplinary team—the regulations pertaining to this provision were spelled out in considerable detail (Larsen & Poplin, 1980). However, legal mandates, without proper funding and in the absence of adequate monitoring, are insufficient. A recent survey by the National Committee for Citizens in Education (1979) showed that most parents are participating in the IEP meetings—83% of parents of handicapped children reported attending the meetings. However, it was recommended that the *quality* of that participation be improved—for example, 52% of the parents said that the plan was completed prior to their arrival, and about 30% contended that the IEP's did not include ways for parents to check the progress of their children. "Parents can serve as more effective advocates for their children if they're aware of their rights as guaranteed by federal, state and local laws" (Mopsik, 1980, p. 39).

The Increase in the Number of Professional Disciplines Concerned with the LD Population

Recent years have witnessed a surge in the numbers—and kinds—of professionals involved with the LD movement. Many of them serve on the professional advisory boards of ACLD chapters; conduct research; disseminate their findings via conferences, workshops, and publications; and offer direct professional services to LD children. The original disciplines of education, psychology, psychiatry, and medicine have been augmented with a host of others. Optometrists specializing in visual training for the neurologically handicapped have had significant impact upon educational programs, curriculum, teacher-training programs, and so on. Some dentists even focus specifically upon the treatment of LD children. A specialized approach is warranted in deference to (1) this population's explosive behavior and overall anxiety, and (2) the likelihood that many of them receive chemotherapy and/or might have an unsuspected reaction to any medication used by the dentist. Occupational therapists render invaluable input to educators and parents regarding strategies for improving the LD child's faulty body image, spatial orientation problems, tactile and kinesthetic feedback inaccuracies. Lawyers who have become involved in the LD movement have made tremendous contributions. They recommend legal courses of action regarding the rights of parents and/or their LD children, advise parents regarding the preparation of wills, counsel school administrators regarding compliance, and identify legislative targets for the parent groups. Social workers are becoming more and more immersed in the LD field. Case work is necessary in deference to the impact that the LD child generally has upon his family. Social workers who specialize with this population can offer effective guidance and make referrals to appropriate agencies and services. Because of their comprehensive approach, they have contributions to make along a continuum of services, ranging from preschool through vocational and even geriatric programs. Juvenile court judges, probation officers, police officers, and others have come into the movement in the hopes of lowering the incidence of juvenile delinquency among the learning disabled.

Besides these disciplines, others who have equally important contributions to make are often brought into the fold by being invited to address conferences, to receive testimonials, to dedicate the opening of some new facility. Thus politicians, state education department officials, entertainers (they can help with fund raising and with publicity), businesspeople and philanthropists, even the clergy have become more and more sophisticated regarding the nature and needs of LD individuals. The spin-off effect here is that each, in his or her own way, is then better equipped to help (e.g., clergymen can counsel parents, set up social-recreational groups; businesswomen can be helpful in employing the learning disabled).

Since learning disabilities cuts across socioeconomic boundaries, many of these professionals enter the learning-disabled movement, not solely for professional interests nor because they are invited, but as concerned parents. More and more, we are witnessing the emergence of the "parent-professional." Because of their unique perspective, they are often able to make major contributions furthering the understanding and servicing of the learning disabled.

The Increasing Concern for LD Adults

Currently, post high-school programs for the learning disabled are receiving increased attention.* This is to be expected inasmuch as the "LD movement" began about two decades ago; at that time, the clients were principally of elementary school (primary classes) age or younger, but yesterday's LD child is today's LD young adult. His visibility forces the issue.

For the lower functioning LD young adults (i.e., for those who are not destined for college, and who, in some instances, will require a more sheltered type of employment), community residences are being developed. These enable the LD adult to live away from home. The clients travel to jobs and/or job training while residing in a house or an apartment located in a residential section of the community, thus reflecting the tenet of normalization. The LD adults plan meals, share household chores, learn to budget, and assume more responsibilities in caring for themselves. The typical program has social-recreational activities as well as a psychological component (usually in the form of professionally led "rap session"). Trained professional counselors are in residence and supervise all phases of the program. On-site supervision decreases as the ability to live independently increases.

Adult education and literacy training programs are becoming more available to the LD adult. They are held largely during evening hours and are community-based. Many colleges offer Continuing Education programs (non-credit courses in a variety of fields) which LD adults are able to attend. Still another source of post high school education are the English and Citizenship courses designed chiefly for foreign-speaking adults. Because Teaching English as a Second Language (TESL) relies on a highly structured and systematic methodology, contains sufficient repetition, utilizes a functional (i.e., a conversational) approach, and uses high interest-low reading level texts and workbooks, it may prove highly beneficial to native born LD adults. All of these programs, in addition to their educational value, foster social as well as vocational (and avocational) gains.

The number of college programs available to the LD student has increased. The Education for All Handicapped Children Act of 1975, PL 94-142, has many key features, one of which is of particular concern to the older learning disabled person: By September 1, 1980, a free appropriate education must be available for all handicapped individuals between the ages of three and *twenty-one*. Thus, while the law

* Several directories of services have been published. An example is *Listing of Services for the Postsecondary LD Adult* (First Edition-1980) Academic Therapy Publications, Novato, California 94947.

does not stipulate post-secondary education, per se, if the educational concern of the older learning disabled individual is guaranteed under the law, the extension to post-secondary programs appears appropriate.

In addition, Section 504 of the Rehabilitation Act of 1973, effective June 1, 1977, does apply to universities and post-secondary schools. This law states that such institutions "... shall make accommodations for handicapped students by constructing or altering facilities, providing flexibility in requirements for degree programs, and in the manner in which students are instructed and evaluated in the program" (Marsh, Gearheart, & Gearheart, 1978, p. 229).

These programs include regular colleges that make no direct provision for LD students but have supportive features such as: a flexible system of course selection; pass-fail or even pass-no credit grades (only passed courses are listed on the students official transcript); relatively low admission requirements (or, in some instances, open enrollment); and so on. Some colleges have a set of remedial writing courses pegged at different ability levels which all students must take (Paul, 1980).

In addition, some colleges have special programs designed exclusively for the learning disabled. Among these are Curry College in Milton, Massachusetts; College of the Ozarks, Clarksville, Arkansas; Annhurst College in Woodstock, Connecticut; Westminister College in Fulton, Missouri; Adelphi University in Garden City, New York; University of Plano in Plano, Texas (this college includes training in neurological organization based upon the theories of Doman and Delacato).*

Some of the colleges, while open to LD students, are restricted to the more able. On the other hand, some (for example, the Para-Educator Center for Young Adults at New York University, New York City) deal specifically with those individuals evidencing pronounced disabilities in learning and who fall in the 75–100 IQ range.

If colleges continue to admit LD students, they must incorporate into their curriculum supportive features that will enhance the likelihood for college success. Marsh, Gearheart, and Gearheart (1978) suggest six components that should be included in post-secondary programs:

1. The use of tape recorders for recording notes, class assignments, and tests.
2. Peer tutoring for communicating course content and concepts (not for remediation).
3. Special counseling for program planning (including vocational concern) and behavioral counseling.
4. Instruction in study techniques.
5. Instructors willing and able to work with these students by incorporating modifications in presentation of materials, types of exams, types of assignments, etc.
6. A person and an office or department responsible for the program.

Additional alternatives to accommodate LD college students center purely along logistic lines. These include starting college later, perhaps after working several years; attending evening college part-time while working (either full- or part-

---

* The citing of specific colleges is done for informational purposes only and should not be construed as an endorsement of them.

time); initiation into college via private tutoring, television college courses, or even correspondence courses; enrolling in a college that is small, well staffed and supervised rather than a large university (which might prove to be overwhelming and devoid of any personalized support); and attending a two-year college (at least initially).

The LD college student has his counterpart in the LD employee. Many adults who had or continue to exhibit learning disabilities have achieved success in a variety of occupations (Alley & Deshler, 1979; Rogan & Hartman, 1980). Here, too, one sees increased awareness of and concern for this population. Many agencies—Civil Service, Office of Vocational Rehabilitation, Department of Human Resources—are providing pertinent services and/or jobs for the learning disabled.

Undoubtedly, a crucial factor in the expanding facilities for the LD adult is the fact that many LD adults themselves are emerging as highly visible and effective spokespeople for their group. They are active in local and regional ACLD chapters as advisory board (and/or executive board) members. They address conferences, workshops, PTA's; serve on various task forces; and some have testified before legislative committees. Their writings have appeared in newsletters—in some cases, they are the actual publishers—and in professional journals. They have founded organizations specifically for LD adults; for example, *The Puzzle People* (122 Belvedere Drive, Mill Valley, Calif. 94941; contact person: Jo Ann Haseltine); *Time Out To Enjoy, Inc.* (113 Garfield St., Oakpark, Illinois 60304; contact person: Dian Ridenour, Marge Wilson). In addition, National ACLD, 4156 Library Road, Pittsburgh, Pa. 15234 has formed a LD Adult Committee.

Concern with the Mildly Handicapped

One of the characteristics of the contemporary phase of the learning-disabilities field is a growing concern for the mildly handicapped (Lerner, 1980). In a sense, this tendency was ushered in simultaneously with the founding of the National A.C.L.D. in 1963. By zooming in on the segment of the exceptional population who evidenced learning disorders despite the absence of mental retardation, significant emotional disturbance, physical handicap, sensorial impairment, and so on, we were, by definition, beginning to service the mildly handicapped. As the numbers of identified LD children grew, and as the number of parent groups mushroomed, more and more services were created.

This movement leaped ahead with the advent of mainstreaming and its emphasis upon placing handicapped children—wherever possible—in regular classrooms. This policy highlights the mildly handicapped since, generally speaking this population is mainstreamed, the more severe learning disabilities cases being assigned to self-contained classrooms, segregated schools, and the like. The mandate for IEP's, the establishment of resource rooms, and the refinement of diagnostic instruments further enhanced the likelihood that the mildly handicapped would no longer be overlooked. At times, however, well-intentioned legislation can have a paradoxical, deleterious effect. For example, some regular classroom teachers opt *not* to refer a possible undiagnosed case of learning disabilities for a diagnostic work-up since, even if their suspicions are confirmed, the student will remain in their class—only now they will have to participate in conferences, write IEP's, and be burdened with additional recordkeeping. Often, they are willing to assume the instructional responsibility and endeavor to help the child overcome his learning problem, but without making a referral (Meyen & Moran, 1979).*

This population, despite the mildness of their handicap, need our continued support in that they are so easily misunderstood, so often frustrated because they generally compete with nonhandicapped, and because they do not readily elicit acceptance and compassion. Although we are beginning to make in-roads, the goal is far from reached. Meyen and Moran (1979) contend that many of the mildly handicapped are not currently being served owing to such factors as fear of labeling, the priority given to the more severely handicapped, the lack of this group's visibility, and the mistaken, overly simplistic belief that a remedial program of subject matter is all that is needed.

Helping the mildly handicapped is intimately linked with the overall topic of prevention. That is, the mildly handicapped child who goes unrecognized and un- served today often grows up to be a more severely handicapped adult.

Growing Interest in Prevention

The last decade has seen a growing interest in the prevention of learning disabilities. Whereas most "cascade" models depicting the total range of alternative placements for the learning disabled list regular class placement as the zenith, Lerner (1980) places *prevention* at the top.

Any thrust toward the prevention of birth defects frequently resulting in pro- found handicapping conditions and even in stillborn delivery would be pertinent to the mildly handicapped (that is, the learning disabled) as well. Clearly, if a pregnant woman is a drug abuser, and hence, stands a risk of giving birth to a seriously defec- tive baby, then there may also be the likelihood for a more mildly handicapped one. Therefore, educational programs regarding the risks involved in the use of marijuana and other drugs, in alcohol abuse, and dangers from tobacco and caffein will also be instrumental in reducing the incidence of learning disabilities.

Similarly, anti-poverty programs generate a quest for better nutrition and ob- stetrical care, pollutant-free environment, sufficient and appropriate pediatric clin- ics and daycare centers, more outreach and early identification programs, passage of legislation—coupled with parent orientation—aimed at eliminating child abuse, in- gested lead poisoning and other such dangers. Hence, our current concern with im- proving the quality of life for the poor is, in effect, a direct assault upon the inci- dence and the severity of symptomatology of learning disabilities. This is not to suggest that we are meeting the needs of all—or even most—of the poverty stricken, but complacency has lessened, as more and more concerned citizens begin to devote their effort toward promoting pertinent legislation, funding, research, and public- health education.

There has also been increased activity with respect to supplying information to, questioning, even monitoring, the medical profession. For example, the American Foundation for Maternal and Child Health, Inc., A Nonprofit Foundation for Inter- disciplinary Research in Maternal and Child Health (30 Beekman Place, New York, N.Y. 10022), conducts frequent conferences and workshops relating to the pre-

* Perhaps, these children are being served to some extent through services provided for those who have been judged to be pupils with special educational needs (PSEN) but have not been identified as having handicapping conditions.

vention of birth defects. These have great relevance to the medical profession—especially obstetrics, gynecology, anesthesiology, and pharmacology. The reports of these proceedings are printed and disseminated, frequently being brought to the attention of ACLD advisory boards, the department of Health, Education and Welfare and other government agencies, and, of course, are fed back to the medical profession itself. Recently, an active member of New York Association for the Learning Disabled persevered successfully in her efforts to convince officials of the necessity of publicizing the possible serious dangers involved in induction of labor. Consequently, Public Health Law 2503-A was passed mandating that pertinent information be furnished to an expectant mother regarding the methods and procedures the physician is planning to use and the effects upon the child and mother that might reasonably be expected. In addition, the Food and Drug Administration (FDA) announced (1) the requirement of labeling all oxytocin products, (2) the recommendation that these drugs no longer be used for elective induction of labor and (3) in those cases where medical reasons necessitate their use, the expectant mother must be under the continuous observation of personnel qualified to recognize complications (*The News*, New York Association for Learning Disabled, 1979).

We are finally getting away from our old habit of fixating upon the LD child's deficits in learning to the virtual exclusion of other—often more significant—problems. We are beginning to concentrate once more upon the "whole child." Though this concept—once in vogue—is a crucial one, it was frequently used as a cliché and hence lost considerable ground. More recently, it was dealt the death blow as some short-sighted parents continue to oversimplify the scope of their LD child's problems. Educators, urged on by these parents who mistakenly espoused lack of academic proficiency as the sole culprit, began to aim all of their spotlights upon the diagnostic-prescriptive model. Fortunately, we are returning to our concerns for the child's ability to develop and maintain interpersonal relationships, to cope with adversity and stress, to build a positive self-concept, and to grow affectively. In short we realize that his emotional health is paramount. More and more, this renewed interest in the "whole child" is gaining ground (but just as categorical labels change, so do philosophical terminologies, so we now call it "holistic education," "humanism," "the affective domain," etc.). Parents in increasing numbers are seeking (and, in many instances, helping to establish) appropriate counseling services for their LD children as well as for themselves. LD young adults are beginning to offer retrospective testimony asserting the need for more supportive relationships (Haseltine, 1978, Wilson & Ridenour 1979; Weaver, 1980). Researchers, in reviewing the literature, report "a growing awareness of the importance of affective and motivational factors in the instruction of learning disabled children" (Bendell, Tollefson, & Fine, 1980). The 1980 International Conference for the Association with Learning Disabilities included a significant number of workshops specifically dealing with the LD child's emotional adjustment: for example, "Developing Self-esteem in the LD Child," "Helping the Learning Disabled Student Gain Social Acceptance and a Positive Self-Concept," "Self-Esteem: A Classroom Affair, 101 Ways to Help Children Like Themselves," "Loneliness, Social Imperception and Learning Disabilities," "Emotional World of the Learning Disabled Adolescent," and "Stress and the Learning Disabled Child."

We are learning to place academic achievement in perspective and to view it as one—but by no means the only, and perhaps not even the best—means of fostering emotional adjustment. At the bottom line, if we could wave a magic wand and be granted only one wish it would be that the LD child learn to like himself more. As we begin to examine longitudinal studies and individual narratives of LD young adults, we see over and over again that success—perhaps adjustment is a better word since there are varying definitions of success—is dependent more upon the emergence of a positive self-concept than upon an increased reading or arithmetic performance level. The embodiment of this belief can be seen in the LD adult who still has significant or even profound learning problems, but has made productive compensation and adjustment. Our ultimate goal, then, is one of *prevention*—the prevention of emotional disturbance.

PROGNOSIS

The Range of Prognoses

In general, the prognosis for LD children is considered a favorable one (Doll, n.d.; Laufer, Denhoff, & Solomons, 1957, p. 48; Thelander, Phelps, & Kirk, 1958, p. 409; MacIlvaine & Cooper, 1970; Golick, 1979). Just as there is extreme intragroup variability with respect to the behavioral and learning characteristics of the LD population, one finds a wide span of prognoses for them as well—ranging from total failure to total success. Because few longitudinal studies have been conducted to date and there is therefore a paucity of correlated data, what one finds, instead, are descriptive studies (that is, some random examples), overall impressions, and viewpoints. Perhaps a lot depends upon the outlook of the writer. At any rate, one finds pessimistic reports: "... The problem doesn't go away ... I would say that 50 to 75 per cent of our (LD) clients ... are not making it (Trout, 1979)*; "The underlying disabilities do not appear to have gone away. Many of these [college] graduates are still in trouble" (Lynn, 1979, p. 163)*; "Brain-injured individuals suffer from a permanent condition ..." (Gordon, 1970, p. 254). Specific examples of failure are suicide; juvenile delinquency (Berman, 1974; Poremba, 1975; Ramos, 1978) including murder (Silver, 1979): psychosis (Aranov, 1969, reports that paranoid reactions are common); disastrous marriages (Anderson, 1963); drop outs from high school as well as from college (Lynn, 1979, p. 128); unemployment, "underemployment" (being employed well below one's capacity), or "misemployment" (finding employment in fields for which one has no aptitude); and so on.

On the other hand, favorable reports include completion of college and graduate schools (MacIlvaine & Cooper, 1971; Lehtinen-Rogan, 1971; Golick, 1979; Rogan & Hartman, 1980); successful employment as professionals, technicians, business people (MacIlvaine & Cooper, 1970; Wilson & Ridenour, 1979; Rogan & Hartman, 1980); successful marriages (Golick, 1979). In certain respects, the fact that we live in an age of specialization makes it possible for many LD individuals to circumvent failure. "To have certain brain inefficiencies may be of no great problem

---

* These sources refer to failure in the circumscribed area of academics, and do not necessarily imply total failure in day-to-day functioning.

in our society. One can avoid [the fields of] singing or drawing [and can], if lost, depend on others to find one's way . . ." (Calanchini & Trout, 1971, pp. 213-214).

Despite the significant number of LD adolescents and adults who meet with dire consequences, the fact that so many can—and do—"make it," demonstrates that, on the whole, the prognosis for LD is a favorable one. After all, stating that a prognosis is favorable in no way guarantees its eventuation; it merely stipulates a *potential.* The mentally retarded, the psychotic, the deaf, the blind, the speech impaired, the motor handicapped, *regardless of the quality of intervention*, have definite, significant limitations placed upon their future accomplishments and status. In the case of the LD child, because of the *minimal* quality of the handicap, because the undamaged portions of the brain can often "take over" for some of the damaged ones provided that the total damaged area is not too extensive, because of the existence of so many strengths, no such limits exist. Although there will be no "smooth sailing," and there will be many "danger zones" to avoid (or overcome), the possibility for success—*in many cases, total success*—stands. Bender (1949) believes that brain-injured children, like all children, have a "miraculous capacity" for growing, maturing, and developing normally. She is optimistic, pointing our that this push toward normality far exceeds "the damaging tendency resulting from . . . structural pathology or destructive and depriving influences in the environment" (p. 413).

The LD Adolescent and Adult:
Problems and Strengths

When the LD child was younger, some of his shortcomings—gullibility, openness, complete trust in others—endeared him to all. In adolescence, this is no longer the case: in fact, his "different-ness," excitability, egocentricity, unmodulated movements and voice tend to "rub us the wrong way." He does not have many outlets, so he is constantly "under foot" at home, prolonging his dependency period and aggravating parent-child relationships which, in many cases, are tenuous to begin with. The normal turmoils of adolescence are heightened in his case since he brings along a host of additional psychological problems. By the time he reaches this period, he has experienced *cumulative* failure; hence, self-esteem and motivation dwindle. He is more lonely, depressed, and isolated now; the opportunities to "go places and do things" are there *but he must opt for them and take the initiative.* Instead, he tends to withdraw.

Fortunately, growing up presents not only hurdles for the LD child, but distinct gains as well. He becomes stronger physically; neurological maturation occurs so that he is now, though neither graceful nor agile, able to perform many of those tasks requiring coordination he formerly could not; his mental age has increased (this can be seen in the difference in intellectual functioning between a six-year-old and a nineteen-year-old, each having an IQ of 100). In addition, he may have learned to compensate productively for some deficit area. For example, a LD adolescent or adult who has learned over the years that he cannot succeed in tasks requiring athletic or mechanical aptitude, may have discovered that he has verbal strengths. Gradually he goes "the verbal route," growing in his ability to "play on" words, develops a sense of humor, and hence advances in the social arena. Closely allied to this phenomenon of compensation is the process of gaining cognitive control over neurological and/or behavioral deficits. That is, persistence and motivation coupled with superior problem-solving potential and effective survival strategies, which a significant number of LD individuals seem able to create—after all, this is more a function of intellect than of neurological status—help them overcome many of their weaknesses (Lynn, 1978, p. 7).

Finally, the LD individual, upon reaching adulthood, faces a more benign environment than at any time in his past. Children are often cruel to one another; adolescents, beset with self-doubt and identity crises of their own, seek to bolster their ego by belittling their LD counterpart. Adults, on the other hand, being more secure, can afford to be more accepting and tolerant of individual differences (Siegel, 1974, pp. 12-13).

Factors Effecting the Fulfillment of Favorable Prognoses

Whether any individual—handicapped or not—meets with success or failure depends upon a multitude of factors. Some examples are: genetic determinants such as reaction to stress, ability to cope with hardship; attitude and value system; personality; degree of acceptance by family, neighbors, friends; political, social and economic conditions; and just plain luck! Beyond these, additional variables can influence the fruition of the favorable prognosis that so many authors ascribe to the LD population:

1. *The Individual in questions must indeed be LD as opposed to MR, emotionally disturbed, or some other category.* A certain percentage of parents whose children are actually MR or emotionally disturbed, deny or disavow (often at the subconscious level) the true classification, and instead proclaim that their child is LD. There is less stigma to the LD label: the term "mentally retarded" conjures up an image of incurability and of genetic causation (untrue, in many instances) and parents of emotionally-disturbed children have frequently been told that they are to blame for their child's plight (again an unwarranted assumption, in most cases). There is no such accusatory finger pointed at parents of LD children given that the causes, by and large, are considered accidental. Also, some parents of MR and ED may desire to have their children mingle with high-functioning children—that is, the LD ones. They become active in the local ACLD chapter and their child enrolls in its social-recreational groups. In addition, it is not uncommon for MR and ED children to be misdiagnosed as LD. (This probably accounts for the relatively low rate of return over the years of children from classes for LD to the regular class.) At any rate, the prognosis is not the same for all categories of exceptionality.

2. *The degree of attendant strengths is significant.* General health, stamina, intelligence, social strengths, emotional adjustment all play a significant role. Clearly, levels of professional and vocational attainment and the development of coping strategies, productive compensatory behavior and problem-solving abilities relate to intelligence; and while some authors, for example, Bakwin (n.d.), regard IQ as a salient factor in the LD child's ultimate success, there probably is not a simple linear relation. Kranes (1980, pp. 173, 174), reporting on LD adolescents with IQs ranging between 75 and 95 enrolled in New York University's Para-Educator Center for Young Adults, writes, "the students who have the greatest personal and social problems are often the most able in the cognitive areas." Favorable self-concept

(Gordon, 1970, p. 51) and overall psychological adjustment (Gordon, 1975, p. 105) are frequently cited as the cornerstones to attainment of the LD child's potential. Stated differently, *the single greatest pitfall to avoid with respect to the LD child's success in functioning optimally as he emerges into adulthood is emotional disturbance and emotional illness.* All of us, therefore, must relate to him in ways consistent with a good mental hygiene approach. Counseling and therapy services must be available for the LD child, his parents, and even for his teachers.

3. *Appropriate education and effective management at home are essential.* The former helps to bring the child's performance in line with his actual mental ability (i.e., diminishes underachievement), whereas the latter is necessary for reducing anxiety. Both further the emergence of a positive self-concept since (1) they maximize the likelihood for the LD child to grow, to learn, to succeed along all fronts and (2) a genuinely appropriate education and effective home management reflects acceptance, a supportive and nonpunitive attitude and affective nurturing.

4. *A positive and optimistic attitude by the significant people in the LD child's life—as well as by the child himself—is paramount.* There is a knack of looking at things in perspective. The existence of the LD child in the family can be traumatic. Yet LD children can make *positive* contributions to the family in terms of family solidarity, a shift toward more meaningful values, more effective home management for all, and parent education (Scagliotta, 1969). Smith (1978, p. 108) adds "most of us enjoy the child for much of the time and share laughter, joy, and wonder with him as well as tears." MacIlvaine and Cooper (1970, p. 141), after presenting several case studies depicting successful LD adults, conclude:

> Perhaps the thread that holds these stories together is not just the neurological problems, *but the fact that failure was not accepted by the parents, the professionals, or the handicapped person himself.* [emphasis added] Specific help, wedded to drive and a positive faith, seems to have made it possible for these people to lead successful lives in the adult world.

5. *Society's attitude toward individuals who are handicapped or who appear "different" must be one of acceptance, tolerance, and understanding.* Even the highest functioning LD, the one who has made optimal adjustments, will still have some vestigial areas of deficit (Siegel, 1974, pp. 49-52; Kronick, 1969, pp. 182-183). Fortunately, the trend seems to be in a direction that is favorable to the disabled population. Witness the ongoing gains and civil rights legislation, the worldwide concerns with human rights, the periodic drives to employ the handicapped, legislation mandating college enrollment of individuals who are handicapped but otherwise qualified, and by the virtual (though by no means complete) demise of stigma attached to receiving psychotherapy. (Years ago, the knowledge that a worker had formerly undergone treatment by a therapist would be grounds for dismissal; today, psychiatric service is one of the fringe benefits that many labor unions actively seek.)

This accepting attitude and increased public awareness must be coupled with a commitment to action: funding and appropriate legislation for continued research and for a broad range of educational and vocational alternatives, and support services. All of these considerations are linked to the economic health of our country. In a tight economy, public funds earmarked for special education and rehabilitation will dwindle. Also, if unemployment increases, the LD—like other minority groups—will be the "last hired, and first fired."

What is Success?

Varying degrees of success exist. For some LD individuals, limited, rather than complete, success is possible. Some of the lower functioning LD adults will be able to function only in protective environments such as hostels or sheltered workshops. Some can adjust to adult independent living, but cannot deal with the pressures of marriage. Others can marry successfully, but will find parenting stressful. Some may be able to adjust to part-time rather than full-time employment, and may require parental subsidizing of their marriage (Gordon, 1970, p. 254). Civil Service may be a haven for some, permitting them to avert the pressures, prejudices, and lack of security which often exist in private industry. Some will be able to drive cars, but may be advised to limit their driving to brief neighborhood trips. Colleges are beginning to accommodate LD students: for example, some who are deficient in reading can still pass their courses with the aid of readers, taped lessons, and special lecture note "hand outs." Similar modifications can enable LD adults to succeed vocationally and professionally despite considerable academic shortcomings (e.g., availability of a calculator for the dyscalculic, a stenographer for the dysgraphic). Many will be underemployed—and, in some cases, this may be well advised if it serves to reduce anxiety.

Richards (1981) believes that there will always be some LD individuals who will never learn to read, but that they still can be successful. He suggests that we (1) encourage them to get their information from television and radio instead of from newspapers and books*; (2) emphasize vocations in which reading is not essential (for example, mechanics and construction); (3) provide them with *nonreading specialists* who will teach them to use secretarial help, the tape recorder, the Talking Book program (educational recordings made specifically for the blind), and, in some cases, the typewriter; and (4), above all, to focus their attention upon ". . . nonreading heroes to show them that success was not necessarily tied to the technical skill of reading. They need to identify themselves in a positive way as a poor reader." (p. 63).

Most LD cases on record come from middle-class, high-achieving parents. Those professionals who evaluate them and plan programs for them are, likewise, middle-class high achievers. Hence, there may be a tendency to view the LD adolescent or adult as a failure or as a marginal achiever, when, in fact, he may be successful—*but on his own terms*. Maybe he is content to be underemployed, avoiding the "rat race," while deriving satisfaction from avocations, service to the community or to political parties. He may have dropped out of college or even high school and yet continued to self-educate himself. Parents may be disappointed in that their LD young adults have only one or two friends rather than a wide circle of them. Yet, the individual in questions may be vary content with this status. In fact, an abundance of social contacts brings with it an abundance of obligations which can heighten disorganization and anxiety.

We can help the LD person best by regarding him as an individual, separating

---

* Research (Sawyer and Kosoff, 1981) suggests that it is not uncommon for dyslexics to manifest intact listening comprehension skills.

our values, needs and problems from his. Whether one regards an LD adult as a success or as a failure is often a matter of relativity.

> In a large sense, the problems encountered by minimally brain-dysfunctioned adolescents and young adults are similar to, if not identical with, those faced by the nonhandicapped. Parent-adolescent conflicts abound in many families, completely independent of the cast's neurological status. All adolescents experience a basic, *common* turmoil, with its roots in hormonal and physiological changes, psychological tugs, and societal demands. Many individuals with no known medical/psychological etiology are socially inept, unskilled mechanically, and have difficulty learning to drive a car. Failure in school, at work, or in marriage is by no means the exclusive province of the brain-injured. Many otherwise "normal" adults are hopelessly disorganized, unable to use their leisure time productively, exercise poor judgment, and do not function completely independently. It is safe to say that most people— including the minimally brain-dysfunctioned— do not live up to their potential.

> The essential "differentness" of the minimally brain-dysfunctioned population does not lie, then, in the kinds of problems they face, in the occasion of failure, or even in their potential for achievement. Rather, it can be seen in the greater *likelihood* that these difficulties will occur and, once they do, in the minimally brain-dysfunctioned adult's relatively meager resources for dealing with them. (Siegel, 1974, pp. 125–126)

REFERENCES

Alley, G. and Deshler, D. *Teaching the learning disabled adolescent: Strategies and methods.* Denver: Love Publishing, 1979.

Anderson, C. *Jan: My brain-damaged daughter.* Portland, Oregon: Durham Press, 1963.

Aranov, B. M. Reactions of child, family & teacher to handicap in the child. In Doreen Kronick (Ed.), *Learning disabilities: Its implications to a responsible society.* Niles, Ill.: Developmental Learning Materials, 1969.

Bakwin, R. M. *The brain-injured child: Cerebral damage* (pamphlet). Albany: New York Association for the Learning Disabled, n.d. (n.p.).

Bendell, D., Tollefson, N., and Fine, M. Interaction of locus-of-control orientation and the performance of learning disabled adolescents. *Journal of Learning Disabilities,* February, 1980, *13*(2), 83–86.

Bender, L. Psychological problems of children with organic brain disease. *American Journal of Orthopsychiatry,* July, 1949, *19*(3), 404–414.

Berman, A. Delinquents are disabled. In Betty Lou Kratoville (Ed.), *Youth in trouble.* Novato, Ca.: Academic Therapy Publications, 1974.

————. From the perspective of Allan Berman. In Nancy P. Ramos (Ed.), *Delinquent youth and learning disabilities.* Novato, Ca.: Academic Therapy Publications, 1978.

Borg, W. *Ability grouping in the public schools.* Madison, Wis. Dunbar Educational Research Sciences, 1966.

Boys Town Quarterly. Boys Town, Nebraska, October 31, 1979.

Brown, D. Learning disability: Unsure social behavior means insecure relationships. *LD Observer,* August–September, 1980, *1*(1): 8–9.

Bruininks, V. L. Actual and perceived peer status of learning-disabled students. *Journal of Special Education,* Spring, 1978, *12*(1), 51–58.

Calanchini, P. R., and Trout, S. S. The neurology of learning disabilities. In Lester Tarnopol (Ed.), *Learning disorders in children: Diagnosis, medication, and education.* Boston: Little, Brown, 1971.

Chalfant, J. C., Pysh, M. V. D., and Moultrie, R. Teacher assistance teams: A model for within-building problem solving. *Learning Disabilities Quarterly,* Summer, 1979, *2*(3), 85–96.

Denhoff, E., Hainsworth, P., and Hainsworth, M. Learning disabilities and early childhood education: An information-processing approach. In H. R. Myklebust (Ed.), *Progress in learning disabilities, vol. II.* New York, Grune & Stratton, 1971.

Doll, E. A. *Behavior syndromes of CNS impairment.* A Devereaux Reprint (pamphlet). Devon, Pa.: Devereaux Schools. n.d.

Duane, D. D. From the perspective of Drake D. Duane. In Nancy P. Ramos (Ed.), *Delinquent youth and learning disabilities.* Novato, Ca.: Academic Therapy Publications, 1978.

Dunn, L. M. Special education for the mildly retarded: Is much of it justified? *Exceptional Children,* Sept. 1968, *35*(1): 5–22.

Ekwall, E. E. *Diagnosis and remediation of the disabled reader.* Boston: Allyn & Bacon, 1976.

Feshbach, S., Adelman, H., and Fuller, W. W. Early identification of children with high risk of reading failure. *Journal of Learning Disabilities,* December, 1974, *7*(10), 639–644.

Golick, M. Learning disabilities—an optimistic outlook. *Perceptions: The newsletter for parents of children with learning disabilities,* March, 1979, *1*(7), 1, 6, 8.

Gordon, S. Sense and nonsense about brain injury and learning disabilities. *Academic Therapy,* Summer, 1970, *5*(4), 249–254.

———. *Living fully.* New York: John Day, 1975.

Hammill, D. D. Adolescents with specific learning disabilities: Definition, identification, and incidence. In L. Mann, L. Goodman, and L. J. Wiederholt (Eds.), *Teaching the learning disabled adolescent.* Boston: Houghton Mifflin, 1978.

Hannah, E. P., and Parker, R. M. Mainstreaming vs. the special setting. *Academic Therapy,* January, 1980, *15*(3), 271–278.

Harasymiw, S. J. and Horne, M. D. Teacher attitude toward handicapped children and regular class integration. *Journal of Special Education,* 1976, *10*(4): 393–396.

Haring, N. G. Special education services for the mildly handicapped. *Journal of Special Education,* Summer, 1977, *11*(2), 188–195.

Haseltine, J. To be labeled or not. *Academic Therapy (Letters),* November, 1978, *14*(2), 233–235.

Hauck, C., and Sherman, A. The mainstreaming current flows two ways. *Academic Therapy,* November, 1979, *15*(2), 133–140.

Hudson, F., Graham, S., and Warner, M. Mainstreaming: An examination of the attitudes and needs of regular classroom teachers. *Learning Disabilities Quarterly,* Summer, 1979, *2*(3), 58–62.

International Reading Association. State reading requirements for learning disabilities certification in the U.S. *The Reading Teacher,* December, 1976, *30*(3), 306–309.

Jakupcak, M. J. Areas of congruence in remedial reading and learning disabilities. *The Journal of Special Education,* Summer, 1975, *9*(2), 155–158.

Keogh, B. K. Early ID: selective perception or perceptive selection. *Academic Therapy*, Spring, 1977, *12*(3), 267–274.

Keogh, B. and Becker, L. D. Early detection of learning problems: Questions, cautions, and guidelines. *Exceptional Children*, September, 1973, *40*, 5–13.

Keogh, B. K., Tchir, C., and Windeguth-Behn, A. Teachers' perceptions of educationally high risk children. *Journal of Learning Disabilities*, June/July, 1974, *7*(6), 367–374.

Keilitz, I. Zaremba, B. A., and Broder, B. K. The link between learning disabilities and juvenile delinquency. Some issues and answers. *Learning Disabilities Quarterly*, *2*(2), 2–11, Spring 1979.

Kirk, S. A., and Gallagher, J. A. *Educating exceptional children, 3rd ed.* Boston: Houghton Mifflin, 1979.

Kranes, J. E. *The hidden handicap: Helping the marginally learning disabled from infancy to young adulthood.* New York: Simon & Schuster, 1980.

Kratoville, B. L. *Youth in trouble.* Novato, Ca.: Academic Therapy Publications, 1974.

Kronick, D. What is success? In Doreen Kronick (Ed.), *Learning disabilities: Its implications to a responsible society.* Niles, Ill.: Developmental Learning Materials, 1969.

————. The pros and cons of labeling. *Academic Therapy*, September, 1977, *13*(1), 101–104.

Larsen, S. C. The learning disabilities specialist: Roles and responsibilities. *Journal of Learning Disabilities.* October, 1976, *9*(8), 498–508.

Larsen, S. C., and Poplin, M. S. *Methods for educating the handicapped.* Boston: Allyn & Bacon, 1980.

Laufer, M. W., Denhoff, E., and Solomons, G. Hyperkinetic impulse disorder in children's behavior problem. *Psychosomatic Medicine*, January, 1957, *19*, 38–49.

Lehtinen-Rogan, L. E. How do we teach him? In Ellen Schloss (Ed.), *The educators' enigma: The adolescent with learning disabilities.* Novato, Ca.: Academic Therapy Publications, 1971.

Lerner, J. W. Remedial reading and learning disabilities: Are they the same or different? *The Journal of Special Education*, Summer, 1975, *9*(2), 119–133.

————. Response to Critics. *The Journal of Special Education*, *9*(2): 179–181. Summer, 1975B.

————. *Children with learning disabilities, 2nd ed.* Boston: Houghton Mifflin, 1976.

————. Sorting out the confusion (an address). In-service professional development program sponsored by the Commission des Ecoles Catholiques de Montreal and the Federation of English Speaking Catholic Teachers Inc., Montreal, March 28, 1980.

Lewandowski, G. Learning disabilities certification: A needed revision. *The Reading Teacher*, November, 1977, *31*(2), 132–133.

Lewis, D. O., as quoted in article in *SLD Gazette*, August–September, 1979, *9*(10), 12.

Lewis, D. O., Shanok, S. S., and Balla, D. A. Perinatal difficulties, head and face trauma, and child abuse in the medical histories of seriously delinquent children. *American Journal of Psychiatry*, April, 1979, *136*(4a), 419–423.

Lewis, D. O., Shanok, S. S., Pincus, J. H., and Glaser, G. H. Violent juvenile delinquents: Psychiatric, neurological, psychological, and abuse factors. *Journal of the American Academy of Child Psychiatry*, 1979, *18*(2), 307–319.

Lieberman, L. Are special needs killing the education system? In *SLD Gazette*, November–December, 1979, *10*(2 & 3), 11, 12.

———— Territoriality—who does what to whom? *Journal of Learning Disabilities*, March, 1980, *13*(3), 124–128.

Lynn, R. *Learning disabilities: The state of the field 1978*. New York: Social Science Research Council, 1978.

———— *Learning disabilities: An overview of theories, approaches, and politics.* New York: The Free Press, 1979.

MacIlvaine, M., and Cooper, D. Some stories of real people. In Lauriel E. Anderson (Ed.), *Helping the adolescent with the hidden handicap*. Novato, Ca.: Academic Therapy Publications, 1970.

Macy, D. J., and Carter, J. L. Comparison of a mainstream and self-contained special education program. *Journal of Special Education*, Fall, 1978, *12*(3), 303–313.

Marge, M. The problem of management and corrective education. In J. V. Irwin and M. Marge (Eds.), *Principles of childhood language disabilities*. Englewood Cliffs, N.J.: Prentice-Hall, 1972.

Marsh, G. E., Gearheart, C. K., and Gearheart, B. R. *The learning disabled adolescent*. St. Louis: C. V. Mosby, 1978.

Massachussetts SLD Gazette, August–September, 1979, *9*(10), Wellesley, Mass.

McCarthy, F. E. Remedial reading and learning disabilities in battle. *The Reading Teacher*, February, 1978, *31*(5), 484–486.

McIntosh, D. K. Mainstreaming: Too often a myth, too rarely a reality. *Academic Therapy*, September, 1979, *15*(1), 53–59.

Mercer, C. D., Algozzine, B., and Trifiletti, J. Early identification—an analysis of the research. *Learning Disability Quarterly*, Spring, 1979, *2*(2), 12–24.

Meyen, E. L. and Moran, M. R. A perspective on the unserved mildly handicapped. *Exceptional Children*, April, 1979, *45*(7), 526–530.

Meyerowitz, J. Family background of educable mentally retarded children. In H. Goldstein, J. W. Moss, and L. J. Jordan (Eds.), *The efficacy of special education training in the development of the mentally retarded*. Urbana: University of Illinois Institute for Research in Exceptional Children, 1965.

Mooney, T. J. A study of the efficacy of the administrative placement of educable mentally retarded children in various educational settings when compared in a self-concept scale. Unpublished doctoral dissertation, Syracuse University, 1969.

Mopsik, S. J. Legislation, litigation and rights. In Stanley J. Mopsik and Judith A. Agerd (Eds.), *An educational handbook for parents of handicapped children*. Cambridge, Mass.: Abt Books, 1980, pp. 39–62.

Morsink, C. V. Learning disabilities. In A. Edward Blackhurst and William H. Berdine (Eds.), *An introduction to special education*. Boston: Little, Brown 1981.

Mulligan, W. The NH adolescent and juvenile law. In Lauriel E. Anderson (Ed.), *Helping the adolescent with the hidden handicap*. Novato, Ca.: Academic Therapy Publications, 1970.

Murray, C. A. *The link between learning disabilities and juvenile delinquency: Current theory and knowledge*. Washington, D.C.: National Institute for Juvenile Justice and Delinquency Prevention, Law Enforcement Assistance Administration, April, 1976.

National Committee for Citizens in Education. Columbia, Md., 1979.

Newcomer, P. L. Learning disabilities: An educator's perspective. *The Journal of Special Education*, Summer, 1975, *9*(2), 145–150.

————. Special education services for the mildly handicapped: Beyond a diagnostic and remedial model. *Journal of Special Education*, Summer, 1977, *11*(2): 153–165.

New York Association for the Learning Disabled, Albany, New York, *The News*, July–August, 1979, *18*(4).

New York State United Teachers, Albany, New York. *New York Teacher*, January 27, 1980, *21*(20).

Ohlson, E. L. *Identification of specific learning disabilities*. Champaign, Ill.: Research Press, 1978.

Oldridge, O. A. Response. Future directions for special education: Beyond a diagnostic remedial model. *Journal of Special Education*, Summer, 1977, *11*(2), 167–169.

Paul, J. Learning basic writing skills in college. *American Educator* (American Federation of Teachers), Spring, 1980, *4*(1), 14–16.

Poremba, C. D. Learning disabilities, youth and delinquency: Programs for intervention. In Helmer R. Myklebust (Ed.), *Progress in learning disabilities*, *volume III*. New York: Grune & Stratton, 1975.

President's Committee on Mental Retardation. *The six-hour retarded child*. A report on a conference on problems of education of children in the inner city, August 10–12, 1969, Office of Education, U.S. Department of Health, Education, and Welfare.

Pryzwansky, W. B. Collaboration or consultation: Is there a difference? *Journal of Special Education*, Summer, 1977, *11*(2), 178–187.

Ramos, Nancy P. (Ed). *Delinquent youth and learning disabilities*. Novato, Ca.: Academic Therapy Publications, 1978.

Regan, M. The parent's role in vocational education starts early. *Perceptions: The Newsletter for Parents of Children with Learning Disabilities*, March, 1979, *1*(7), 4.

Reschly, D. J. and Lamprecht, M. J. Expectancy effects of labels: Fact or artifact? *Exceptional Children*, September, 1979, *46*(1), 55–58.

Reynolds, M. C., and Birch, J. W. *Teaching exceptional children in all America's schools*. Reston, Va.: Council for Exceptional Children, 1977.

Ribner, S. The effects of special class placement on the self-concept of exceptional children. *Journal of Learning Disabilities*, May, 1978, *11*(5), 319–324.

Richards, J. It's all right if kids can't read (an interview). *Journal of Learning Disabilities*, February, 1981, *14*(2): 62–67.

Rogan, L. L. and Hartman, L. D. *A follow-up study of learning disabled students*. Address at the International Conference of the Association for Children with Learning Disabilities, Milwaukee, February 29, 1980.

Rosenthal, R., and Jacobson, L. Teachers expectancies: Determinants of pupils' IQ gains. *Psychological Reports*, August, 1966, *19*(1), 115–118.

Safford, P. L. *Teaching young children with special needs*. St. Louis: C. V. Mosby, 1978.

Satz, P. and Fletcher, J. M. Early screening tests: Uses and abuses. *Journal of Learning Disabilities*, January, 1979, *12*(1), 56–59.

Sawyer, D. J., and Kossoff, T. O. Accommodating the learning needs of reading disabled adolescents: A language-processing issue. *Learning Disability Quarterly*, Winter, 1981, *4*(1):61–68.

Scagliotta, E. G. Contributions of the learning disabled child to family life. In Doreen Kronick (Ed.), *Learning disabilities: Its implications to a responsible society*. Niles, Ill.: Developmental Learning Materials, 1969.

Schurr, K. T. The effect of special class placement on the self-concept of ability of the educable mentally retarded child: Part II. Doctoral dissertation, Michigan State University, 1967.

Siegel, E. *Special education in the regular classroom.* New York: John Day, 1969.

_____. *Teaching one child.* Freeport, N.Y.: Educational Activities, 1972.

_____. *The exceptional child grows up.* New York: E. P. Dutton, 1974.

_____. *Helping the brain injured child,* 5th printing (minor revision). Albany: New York Association for Learning Disabled, 1978.

Silver, Larry B. The minimal brain dysfunction syndrome. In J. Noshpitz (Ed.), *Basic handbook of child psychiatry, vol. 2,* New York: Basic Books, 1979.

Smith, R. M., and Neisworth, J. T. *The exceptional child.* New York: McGraw-Hill, 1975.

Smith, S. L. *No easy answers: The learning disabled child:* Wash, D.C.: Dept of Health, Education & Welfare, 1978.

_____. *No easy answers, teaching the learning disabled child.* Cambridge, Mass.: Winthrop Publishers, 1979.

Sparks, R., and Richardson, S. O. Multicategorical/cross-categorical classrooms for learning disabled students. *Journal of Learning Disabilities,* February, 1981, *14*(2): 60–61.

Stephens, T. M., and Braun, B. L. Measures of regular classroom teachers' attitudes toward handicapped children. *Exceptional Children,* January, 1980, *46*(4): 292–294.

Stick, S. The speech pathologist and handicapped learners. *Journal of Learning Disabilities,* October, 1976, *9*(8), 509–519.

Stott, D. H. *The parent as teacher: A guide for parents of children with learning disabilities.* Belmont, Ca.: Lear Siegler/Fearon, 1972.

Thelander, H. E., Pheips, J. K., and Kirk, E. W. Learning disabilities associated with lesser brain damage. *Journal of Pediatrics,* October, 1958, *53*, 405–409.

Thomas, D., Phelps, D., and Hopping, R. Parents as integral members of the treatment team. *Perceptions: The Newsletter for Parents of Children with Learning Disabilities,* February, 1980, *2*(6), 6.

Thornton, C. Parents can help: Success strategies. *Perceptions: A Newsletter for Parents of Children with Learning Disabilities,* September, 1979, *2*(3), 1, 8.

Thurman, S. K., and Lewis, M. Children's response to differences: Some possible implications for mainstreaming. *Exceptional Children,* March, 1979, *45*(6), 468–470.

Trout, S. As quoted in Roa Lynn, *Learning disabilities: An overview of theories, approaches, and politics.* New York: Free Press, 1979.

Vance, H. R., and Wallbrown, F. Labeling of LD children and teacher perception. *Academic Therapy,* March, 1979, *14*(4), 407–415.

Wagner, R. *Dyslexia and your child.* New York: Harper & Row, 1971.

Wallace, G. Interdisciplinary efforts in learning disabilities: Issues and recommendations. *Journal of Learning Disabilities,* October, 1976, *9*(8), 59–65.

Weaver, R. An autobiography of a dyslexic youth. *Massachussetts SLD Gazette,* March, 1980, *10*(6), 9, 10.

Wilson, M., and Ridenour, D. LD, adult and making it. *Perceptions: The Newsletter for Parents of Children with Learning Disabilities,* February, 1979, *1*(6), 4–5.

Worden, D. K., and Snyder, R. D. Parental tutoring in childhood dyslexia. *Journal of Learning Disabilities: Viewpoints,* September, 1969, *2*(9), 482.

Afterword

In retrospect, one thing is clear: Even the most effective educational intervention and the most appropriate and supportive home management will not, in themselves, suffice. Negative attitudes and hostility directed toward those suffering from learning and behavioral disorders drastically diminish the effectiveness of any educational program and can significantly counteract the emotional comfort proffered by even the most accepting of families.

Professionals—and parents, too—must become increasingly aware that education, psychiatry, and rehabilitation are only partial means of bringing fulfillment to the LD child. We must discern and become a vital part of forces in human relations, civil rights, public relations, morality, consciousness raising, and spiritual guidance. Value systems and attitude formation are crucial. Teachers must advocate for the LD child in the classroom as well as outside. Administrators, in addition to supporting the child, the teacher, and the program, must relentlessly seek to educate the community regarding his problems, his needs, his strengths, his potential. Government agencies, foundations, the media, civic organizations, church groups and employers are vital links in the chain as we approach our ultimate goal: *to return a more acceptable individual to a more accepting society.*

Diagnostic Assessments

appendix **A**

An alphabetical listing of some of the tests mentioned in the text is provided below. The number(s) following the name indicates the chapter in which it appears. The publishers names are noted after each test. Their addresses are found in Appendix B.

Additional test information and evaluative data can be found in Buros, O.K. (Ed.), *Mental Measurement Yearbook*, Highland Park, New Jersey: Gryphon Press.

Test	*Publisher*	*Grade/Age*	*Description*
Assessment of Children's Language (12)	Psychologists Press	3–7	Assesses levels of receptive difficulty.
Adelphi-Parent Administered Readiness Test (APART) (5)	Mafex Associated	K–1st	Ten subtests which can be administered by nonprofessionals include 4 related to grade tool subjects. Visual perception and memory concept formation, auditory sequential memory and two measures of divergent thinking.
Bender-Gestalt Test for Young Children (5)	Grune & Stratton	Ages 5–10	Determines visual-motor integration by evaluating copying of nine shapes.
Boehm Test of Concepts (5, 13)	Psychological Corporation	K–1st	Assesses understanding of abstract concepts—size, shape, distance, quantity, etc.

Test	Publisher	Grade/Age	Description
Boston Diagnostic Aphasia Examination (12)	Lea & Febiger	Aphasic Patients	Yields many scores, e.g.: severity rating, fluency, auditory comprehension, naming, automatized speech, reading comprehension, writing, music (rhythm), etc.
Botel Reading Inventory (12)	Follet Publishing Company	Elementary grades	Screening device to evaluate mastery in phonics.
Brown-Carlsen Listening Comprehension (12)	Harcourt, Brace, Jovanovich	Grades 9–13	Measures comprehension of receptive language.
Cognitive Skills Assessment Battery (5)	Teachers College Press	Pre-K to K	The test battery includes areas deemed necessary for success in kindergarten and first grade, e.g.: coordination, memory, comprehension, etc.
Detroit Test of Learning Aptitude (4)	Bobbs-Merrill	Pre-K to Adult	Measures 19 aspects of mental processing. Different subtests are chosen for each child.
Developmental Indicators for Assessment of Learning (DIAL) (5)	Dial Incorporated	$2\frac{1}{2}$–$5\frac{1}{2}$	Assesses sensory, motor, and concept language development.
Developmental Test of Visual-Motor Integration (VMI) (5, 10)	Follet	K–age 15	Ability to copy 24 designs of increasing difficulty.
Devereau Behavior Scale (5)	Devereau Foundation	Elementary through High School	Rating scales.
Durrell Analysis of Reading Difficulty (12)	Harcourt, Brace, Jovanovich	Grades 1–6	Oral and silent reading, listening comprehension, phonics, hand writing, and spelling.
Frostig Developmental Test of Visual Perception (5)	Consulting Psychologists Press	Pre-K to Grade 2	Subtests include: position in space, spatial relationship, form constancy, visual-motor coordination, figure-ground.
Gates-McKillop Reading Diagnostic Tests (12)	Teachers College Press	Grades 2–6	Battery of 17 individually administered tests of skill development in reading.
Gilmore Oral Reading Test (12)	Harcourt, Brace, Jovanovich	Grades 1–8	Individual analysis of oral reading skills. Uses paragraphs of graded difficulty.
Goldman-Fristoe Test of Articulation (5)	American Guidance Service	Grade 1–age 16	Individual assessment of articulation in words and sentences. For children who make errors, imitation is used.

Test	Publisher	Grade/Age	Description
Illinois Test of Psycholinguistic Abilities (ITPA) (5, 12)	University of Illinois Press	Ages 2–10	Twelve subtests are used to derive a profile of strengths and weaknesses in communication (receptive, integration, and expression of various modalities).
Key Math Diagnostic Arithmetic Test (13)	American Guidance Service	Grades K–8	Individual test: 14 subtests are divided into 3 areas: content, operation, and application.
Louisville Behavior Checklist (5)	Western Psychological Service	Ages 3–18	Teacher ratings of social and emotional behaviors in school settings.
Lincoln-Oseretsky Motor Development Scale (5)	Western Psychological Service	Ages 6–14	Fine and gross motor skills.
Mathematics Concept Inventory (13)	Educational Development Corporation	K–6	Screening device of mathematics performance including measurement, fractions, numbers, computation, and geometry.
Meeting Street School Screening Test (5)	Crippled Children and Adults of Rhode Island	Ages 4–6	Individual screening.
Memory-for-Designs Test (5)	Psychological Test Specialists	Ages 8.5 and over	Copying designs from memory.
Minnesota Test for Differential Diagnosis of Aphasia (12)	University of Minnesota Press	Adults	Group subjects into 5 major categories and 2 minor categories: 9 auditory, 9 visual and reading, 15 speech and language, 10 visual-motor and writing, 4 numerical relations, and arithmetic.
Northwest Syntax Screening Test (12)	Northwestern University Press	Ages 3–7	Individual test of expressive and receptive language.
Peabody Individual Achievement Test (PIAT) (12, 13)	American Guidance Services	K–grade 12	Screening for achievement in mathematics, reading recognition and comprehension, spelling and general information.
Peabody Picture Vocabulary Test (5)	American Guidance Service	Ages $2\frac{1}{2}$–18	Assesses receptive language.
Picture Story Language Test (12)	Grune & Stratton	Ages 7–17	Evaluates developmental scale of written language. Five scores include: total words per sentence, sentences, syntax, abstract and concrete thinking.

Test	Publisher	Grade/Age	Description
Pupil Rating Scale (5)	Grune & Stratton	Grades 1–6	Scale is completed by the teacher.
Purdue Perceptual-Motor Survey (5)	Charles C. Merrill	Ages 4–10	Assesses motor development and motor skills.
Sequential Tests of Educational Progress (STEP-II) (12)	Educational Testing Service	Grades 4–12	Battery of tests evaluates ability to apply learning in reading, language, science, mathematics, and social studies.
Slingerland Screening Tests for Identifying Children with Specific Language Difficulty (12)	Educator's Publishing Service	Grades K–5	Group test using school related activities to determine perceptual-motor performance.
Southern California Perceptual-Motor Tests (9)	Western Psychological Service	Ages 4–8	Six tests which include: imitation of postures, crossing midline of the body, bilateral motor coordination, right-left discrimination and balancing.
Southern California Sensory-Integration Tests (9)	Western Psychological Services	Ages 4–10	Battery of: figure-ground, visual-perception tests, kinesthetic-tactile tests, copying, and balancing.
Stanford-Binet Intelligence Scale (Revised) (5)	Houghton Mifflin	Ages 2–adult	Individual intelligence test.
System Fore (13)	Foreworks Publications	Preschool through high school	Criterion-referenced assessment in language, reading, and mathematics.
Test of Language Development (TOLD) (12)	Empiric Press	Ages 4–9	Individual test of vocabulary and grammatic usage and understanding.
Vineland Social Maturity Scale (5)	American Guidance Service	Birth to adult	Measures social maturity by interview with parents.
Wechsler Adult Intelligence Scale (WAIS) (5)	Psychological Corporation	Ages 15 and above	Individual intelligence test for adults. Samples similar behaviors to WISC-R.
Wechsler Preschool and Primary Scale of Intelligence (WPPSI) (5)	Psychological Corporation	Ages 4–$6\frac{1}{2}$	Individual intelligence test for preschoolers.

Test	Publisher	Grade/Age	Description
Wechsler Intelligence Scale for Children (Revised) (WISC-R) (5)	Psychological Corporation	Ages 5–15	Individual intelligence test yields verbal, performance, and total IQ scores.
Wepman Test of Auditory Discrimination (5)	Language Research Associates	Ages 5–8	Individual measure of auditory discrimination of pairs of words.
Wide Range Achievement Test (Revised) (WRAT) (12, 13)	Guidance Associates	Ages 5–adult	Individual test of word recognition, computation, and spelling.

Addresses of Test Publishers

appendix B

American Guidance Service, Inc., Publishers' Building, Circle Pines, Minn., 55014
The Bobbs-Merrill Co., 4300 W. 42 St., Indianapolis, Ind., 46206
Consulting Psychologists Press, 577 College Ave., Palo Alto, Ca., 94306
Crippled Children and Adults of Rhode Island, The Meeting Street School, 33 Grotto Ave., Providence, R.I.
Devereau Foundation, Devon, Pa., 19333
Educational Progress, Division of Educational Development Corporation, Tulsa, Oklahoma.
Educational Testing Service, Princeton, N.J., 08540
Educator's Publishing Service, 75 Moulton St., Cambridge, Mass., 02138
Empiric Press, Austin, Texas
Follett Educational Corporation, 1010 W. Washington Blvd., Chicago, IL., 60607
Foreworks Publications, Box 9747, N. Hollywood, Ca., 91609
Grune & Stratton, 111 Fifth Avenue, New York, N.Y., 10003
Guidance Associates, 1526 Gilpin Ave., Wilmington, Del., 19800
Harcourt Brace Jovanovich, Inc., 757 Third Ave., New York, N.Y. 10017
Houghton Mifflin Co., One Beacon St., Boston, Mass., 12107
Language Research Associates, Box 95, 950 E. 59 St., Chicago, Ill., 60637
Mafex Associates, Inc., 90 Cherry St., Johnstown Pa., 15902
Charles E. Merrill, 1300 Alum Creek Dr., Columbus, Ohio, 43216
Northwestern University Press, 1735 Benson Ave., Evanston, Ill., 61301
The Psychological Corp., 757 3rd Ave., New York, N.Y. 10017
Teachers College Press, Teachers College, Columbia University, 1234 Amsterdam Ave., New York, N.Y., 10027
University of Illinois Press, 5801 Ellis Ave., Chicago, Ill., 61801
Western Psychological Services, 12031 Wilshire Blvd., Los Angeles, Ca., 90025

Instructional Sequencing

CATCHING A TENNIS-SIZED RUBBER BALL

Behavioral Objective. When told to catch a tennis-sized rubber ball thrown over-hand for a distance of 40 feet or less, whether directly to the pupil or some distance from him (a radius of 5 feet), with average speed, he will do so without any aids or prompts.

Entering Behavior. The pupil is somewhat clumsy and erratic, but has the necessary fine and gross motor control, and visual perception to master the task.

Sequential Components

√   **1.** from a large ball to small ball

√   **2.** from standing close to pupil to moving further away (Some teachers advocate standing so close to pupil initially that you can actually hand him the ball, thus insuring success.)

√   **3.** from rolling the ball to the pupil to throwing the ball to him (Although catching a rolled ball requires a somewhat different negotiation than catching a thrown ball, it still requires ocular pursuit and grasping. The predictable path, and the fact that the ball can be rolled slower than it can be thrown, both facilitate success.)

√   **4.** from underhand throw to overhand throw

√   **5.** from slow throws to faster throws

√   **6.** from physical reinforcement (a teacher aide stands behind the pupil and guides his hands through the catch) to no reinforcement

√   **7.** from verbal cues to none

    8. from using a baseball glove (even for a large ball thrown slowly) to bare-hand catch

9. from a striped ball to a solid colored ball (This can prevent the ball from becoming "lost" in the background.)

√ 10. from bouncing the ball to the pupil to throwing the ball to him

√ 11. from throwing the ball directly towards the pupil's chest, thus requiring a minimum of movement to throwing the ball some distance from his chest requiring stretching, running, catching with one hand, etc.

√ 12. from a lighter ball (e.g., a nerf ball) to a heavier one (i.e., the traditional rubber ball)

Instructional Procedure

1. Using a large (basketball-sized) nerf ball, stand directly in front of the pupil, hand him the ball, saying "now" to coincide with the moment of contact. A teacher aide stands behind the pupil, guiding his hand through the "catch."

2. Same as step 1, but move three feet away from him, rolling the ball directly toward the pupil, still providing the verbal cue and the physical guidance.

3. Same as step 2, but increase the distance to six feet, substitute a somewhat smaller, rubber ball. Bounce it directly to him still providing the verbal cue and physical guidance.

4. Same as step 3, but throw underhand slowly—directly at the pupil—instead of bouncing.

5. Gradually increase the distance and make slow, overhand throws directly at the pupil.

6. Same as step 5, but increase the distance even more, gradually begin using a tennis-sized ball, and fade out the physical guidance, but still use the verbal cues. Continue throwing slowly.

7. Increase the distance to 40 feet and gradually throw faster, aiming some throws directly at the pupil and some a few feet away.

8. Same as step 7, but fade out the verbal cues.

MULTIPLYING A TWO-PLACE NUMBER BY A ONE-PLACE NUMBER

Behavioral Objective. When given 10 multiplication examples (written) of a two-place multiplicand by a one-place multiplier, five of which require "carrying," in vertical position e.g., $\frac{75}{\times\ 3}$, $\frac{24}{\times\ 2}$, the pupil will be able to do them.

Entering Behavior. Knowledge of the multiplication tables (not perfectly), place value, how to multiply such examples without "carrying" and the concept of multiplication; familiarity with the process of "carrying" (from prior experience in addition).

Sequential Components

√ 1. from use of special "multiplication-addition" cards to no cards. (Although the pupil has prior knowledge of the concept that multiplication is really a special case of addition, this visual prompt may assist him in multiplication.)

```
    32      32
  X  4      32
  ─────     32
          + 32
```

```
    75      75
  X  3      75
  ─────   + 75
```

✓ 2. from easier numbers to harder numbers:
   a) from no "carrying" to "carrying"
   b) from easy tables (e.g., 2, 3, 4, 5) to harder ones (e.g., 6, 7, 8)
   c) from examples necessitating adding within decades to those requiring closing the tens (e.g., 24 + 4 to 28 + 5)
   d) from the easier form of commutation to the harder form (e.g., 35 + 2 to 32 + 5)
   3. from illustrative examples on display to none
✓ 4. from multiplication matrix chart available to none
   5. from graph paper (large spaced) to unlined paper

$$\frac{\square}{48}$$

✓ 6. from memory box $\underline{\text{X}\quad 3}$ to memory
   7. from color coding tens and ones to none
   8. from verbal cues (e.g., "start with the ones") to none
   9. from regrouping e.g., $\underline{\text{X}\quad 4}^{76} = \underline{\text{X}\quad 4}^{70} + \underline{\text{X} 4}^{6}$ to traditional format
   10. from materials (e.g., dimes and pennies, squared materials) to numbers
   11. from placing an X marking the beginning space of the product to none
✓ 12. from the teacher and pupil verbalizing the entire example (in unison) to working from memory
✓ 13. from drill in determining whether or not a given example requires "carrying" to none
✓ 14. from computing the addition portion in writing to doing it mentally

Instructional Procedure

1. Give the pupil several "easy tables" multiplication examples involving no "carrying" e.g., $\underline{\text{X}\quad 3}^{32}, \underline{\text{X}\quad 2}^{43}, \underline{\text{X}\quad 4}^{22}$, providing appropriate multiplication/ addition cards for reference; a multiplication matrix chart is available throughout; the pupil recites the procedural steps in unison with the teacher (following the demonstration and explanation).
2. Give the pupil several cards involving "carrying," gradually proceeding from easier to harder numbers. Provide a memory box. Matrix chart is still available and continue with unison recitation.
3. As the examples get more difficult, allow the pupil to use written computation for the addition portion.

e.g., $\begin{array}{r} {}^{6}79 \\ \underline{\text{X}\quad 7} \\ 3 \end{array}$ $\left(\begin{array}{r} 49 \\ + \ 6 \end{array}\right)$ ← pupil writes

Continue as in step 2.

4. Provide special drill in determining, by inspection, whether or not given examples require "carrying."
5. Same as 3, but fade out the use of the multiplication/addition cards.
6. Same as 5, but fade out the memory box.
7. Same as 6, but fade out the matrix chart.
8. Same as 7, but pupil now computes the addition portion mentally.
9. Same as 8, but fade out the unison recitation.

TAKING NOTES FROM AN ORAL PRESENTATION

Behavioral Objective. When given an oral presentation of 30-minute duration, on any topic within the pupil's vocabulary knowledge, reasonably well organized, and delivered at a normal pace, the pupil will be able to write appropriate notes in out-lined form without any cues or prompts.

Entering Behavior. The pupil has adequate hearing, vision, and motor coordination. His "strategy" for note taking is to try to transcribe verbatim; he encounters difficulty trying to write and listen simultaneously.

Sequential Components
√ 1. from outlining reading selection (and/or thoughts) to taking notes from speaker
√ 2. from *brief* lecture (speaker stops) to longer one
√ 3. from having tape recorder (going back to verify) to no tape (*one* presentation only)
√ 4. from supplying the pupil with an outline hand-out prior to the lecture (requiring filling in) to no outline
√ 5. from easier material to harder material
  6. from personalized material to more general
√ 7. from exaggeratedly *slow* presentation to faster
√ 8. from perfectly organized talk to one including some tangentials
  9. from having important (and difficult words) printed on the chalkboard to no such aid
√ 10. from providing cues (e.g., "abbreviate," "write the numeral, not the word," "think of one summary word") to no cues
 11. from an oral abstract of the talk with discussion (pencils down) to taking notes
√ 12. from a tutor (teacher, teacher aide, volunteer) taking notes part-time (alternating with pupil) to the pupil functioning independently
√ 13. from a subject with which the pupil is familiar to new ones

Instructional Procedure
1. Begin with a brief reading selection (two paragraphs), below grade level, on a subject of personal interest. The pupil is handed an outline (requiring fill-ins). Provide verbal cues—"abbreviate," etc. A tutor alternates with the pupil in completing the fill-ins.

2. Same as step 1, but gradually increased to a selection on grade level, of three to four pages in length.
3. Same as step 2, but introduce more general subjects.
4. Same as step 3, but eliminate the outline handout.
5. Same as step 4, but fade out the assistance of the tutor.
6. Same as step 5, but fade out the verbal cues.
7. Repeat steps 1-6 while taking notes on a brief oral lecture (instead of from a reading selection). The presentation is perfectly organized, spoken exaggeratedly slowly, and the pupil is provided a tape recorder for verification.
8. Same as step 7, but speak in normal tempo.
9. Same as step 8, but gradually increase the length of the presentation to the full 30 minutes.
10. Same as 9, but start interjecting some portions containing tangential points.
11. Same as 10, but gradually eliminate the use of the tape recorder.

Author Index

Subject Index